African American
Christian Ethics

African American Christian Ethics

Samuel K. Roberts

THE
PILGRIM
PRESS
Cleveland

For Judith

For life...for good

The Pilgrim Press, Cleveland, Ohio 44115
www.pilgrimpress.com

© 2001 by Samuel K. Roberts

Scripture quotations unless otherwise noted are from the New Revised Standard Version Bible, copyright © 1989 by the Division of Christian Education of the National Council of the Churches of Christ in the United States, and are used by permission.

All rights reserved. Published 2001

Printed in the United States of America on acid-free paper

06   05   04   03   02   01   5   4   3   2   1

Library of Congress Cataloging-in-Publication Data

Roberts, Samuel K.
   African American Christian ethics / Samuel K. Roberts.
     p.   cm.
   Includes bibliographical references and index.
   ISBN 0-8298-1424-8 (pbk. : alk. paper)
   1. Christian ethics. 2. African Americans – Religion.   I. Title.

BJ1231 .R6 2001
241'.089'96073 – dc21

                          2001021115

Contents

Preface

Toward the end of the now elapsed twentieth century, the study of African American religion grew to an astounding level of maturity and fullness. Serious volumes of considerable weight and depth were produced by scholars who delighted in sharing with the world the fruits of labor in a field that had been shamelessly overlooked or ignored by researchers in the early part of that century. The range of offerings has been prodigious—from ecclesiastical histories to personal biographies, from cultural anthropology to literary criticism. The richness of African American religious consciousness and the attendant scholarship that has mined the depths of that consciousness are marvels to behold. This volume relies on the wealth of that scholarship as it seeks to present a comprehensive Christian ethic by addressing theological problems inherent in such a task, reflecting on ways in which the classical foundations and sources for a Christian ethic are refracted through the African American experience, and finally applying that ethic to particular contexts of concern for African Americans.

The black theological renaissance known as black theology that erupted on the American scene just past the midpoint of the century inspired many persons to reconfigure the religious consciousness of African Americans from the perspective of liberation. This movement rightly encouraged a generation of scholars to shift the fulcrum for research and scholarship in favor of the cultural and psychological yearnings of a people who now dared to look within themselves for normative standards of beauty and ethical behavior. Expectedly, an attempt was made to articulate a Christian ethic for African Americans in the light of the black theology message.

Major R. Jones's book *Christian Ethics for Black Theology: The Politics of Liberation* appeared in 1974 in the wake of James H. Cone's groundbreaking book of 1970 entitled *A Black Theology of Liberation*. If Cone was right that a new theological paradigm for envisioning the task of theology in the light of the political ideology known as black power was needed, then it followed that a new way of conceiving Christian ethics for black people had to be fashioned as well. Joining Cone and Jones in this endeavor in these early years of black theology was J. Deotis Roberts, whose book *Liberation and Reconciliation: A Black Theology* was conceived as a rejoinder to Cone's landmark work. Roberts's subsequent book, *A Black Political Theology*, was conceived as a statement that sought to couch theological reflection within the context of an ethical concern for the political dynamics that were coming forth with almost volcanic intensity in the decade of the 1970s. Since that time another generation of scholars has been inspired to explore virtually all aspects of African American life from the perspective of Christian ethics. These works range from an ethical assessment of political and economic aspirations to the critique of modern life from an African American womanist perspective.[1]

This present work proceeds from the assumption that no credible Christian ethic for African Americans will be complete until a systematic appropriation of four sources for a Christian ethic is offered. These sources are Holy Scripture, ecclesial tradition, human knowledge, and human nature. Moreover, all four of these sources must be appropriated through a faith orientation that is informed by Christian notions of the nature of God, Jesus Christ as God incarnated, and the continuing work of the Holy Spirit. For the purposes of crafting an African American Christian ethic, these affirmations of faith must be shown to have meaning within the organic soil of the black experience.

This book was begun in the summer of 1998, about the same time when an earlier work, *In the Path of Virtue: The African American Moral Tradition*, was in the copyediting phase. As I awaited the appearance of that book, it dawned upon me that much more had to be said about the moral

---

1. Many works produced by African American Christian ethicists during the past quarter century come to mind. The problem of methodology was addressed by Enoch Oglesby in *Ethics and Theology from the Other Side: Sounds of Moral Struggle* (Washington, D.C.: University Press of America, 1979). A related methodological problem of understanding the normative ethical consciousness of slave religion was the focus of Riggins R. Earl Jr. in *Dark Symbols, Obscure Signs: God, Self, and Community in the Slave Mind* (Maryknoll, N.Y.: Orbis Books, 1993). A thoughtful treatment of the ethical implications of black denominationalism was Peter Paris's *The Social Teachings of the Black Churches* (Philadelphia: Fortress Press, 1985). For significant assessments of the ethical implications in the quest for political and economic power, see Theodore Walker Jr., *Empower the People: Social Ethics for the African-American Church* (Maryknoll, N.Y.: Orbis Books, 1991); Darryl Trimiew, *Voices of the Silenced: The Responsible Self in a Marginalized Community* (Cleveland: The Pilgrim Press, 1993); Cheryl J. Sanders, *Empowerment Ethics for a Liberated People: A Path to African American Social Transformation* (Minneapolis: Fortress Press, 1995); and Robert M. Franklin, *Another Day's Journey: Black Churches Confronting the American Crisis* (Minneapolis: Fortress Press, 1997). The critical value of the womanist perspective in African American Christian ethics has been evidenced in Cheryl A. Kirk-Duggan, *Exorcising Evil: A Womanist Perspective on the Spirituals* (Maryknoll, N.Y.: Orbis Books, 1997); Cheryl J. Sanders, ed., *Living the Intersection: Womanism and Afrocentrism in Theology* (Minneapolis: Fortress Press, 1995); Emilie M. Townes, *In a Blaze of Glory: Womanist Spirituality as Social Witness* (Nashville: Abingdon Press, 1995); and Katie G. Cannon, *Black Womanist Ethics* (Atlanta: Scholars Press, 1988). An intercultural and African diasporic approach to Christian ethics has been provided in Peter Paris, *The Spirituality of African Peoples: The Search for a Common Moral Discourse* (Minneapolis: Fortress Press, 1995); and Enoch Oglesby, *Born in the Fire: Case Studies in Christian Ethics and Globalization* (New York: The Pilgrim Press, 1990).

tradition of African Americans, particularly that aspect of the tradition that sought to meld the *content* of Christian faith with the oftentimes harsh *contexts* of life. It was precisely at this interstice between *content* and *contexts* that Christian African Americans had lived out their notions of the faith in perpetually inhospitable circumstances. Yet it was precisely in the living out of that faith in such circumstances that one could discern the basis for a theological ethic of profound dimensions. I was determined to explore those dimensions, not so much to seek an account for the historical development of a Christian ethic for African Americans, as had been partially the case in the *Virtue* book, but to seek to explicate the theological affirmations that were foundational to such an ethic, including the roles of Holy Scripture, tradition, human nature, and the need for human beings to know with some degree of certainty the veracity of the ethical claims they make in the course of initiating ethical actions.

When I was in the course of plotting the basic outline for this book, Mark A. Wainwright, one of my students at the School of Theology of Virginia Union University, providentially showed me an outline of a college course (Introduction to Ethics from a Black Christian Perspective) that had been taught by the late Herbert O. Edwards at Morgan State University. Holding pages of this manual, many worn and dog-eared, I was transported back to a time when I heard Professor Edwards offer a public lecture on Christian ethics at Union Theological Seminary in New York City when I was a student there in 1968. This book is dedicated in part to the memory of Professor Edwards and that entire generation of African American ethicists and theologians who pointed the way to those of us who attempt, albeit inadequately, to follow in their footsteps. Also among any pantheon of lights who led our way in those years would surely be the eminent sociologist of religion C. Eric Lincoln, who passed from our midst in May 2000, as I was finishing the last pages of this book. It was Professor Lincoln who sat on my dissertation committee over twenty-five years ago and whose prowess as a teacher I have valued throughout my subsequent professional career. I was fortunate to see him at his home in Durham in the late summer of 1999 and to share with him my ideas for this book. I say this even as I recall squirming fitfully on a couch in his study as my old teacher interrogated me on the cogency of my arguments. The apprentice will never equal the master; the offering is made nevertheless.

I have been encouraged by many persons during the course of my work on this book. I wish to thank Ronald Stone of Pittsburgh Theological Seminary and Miles Jones of the School of Theology of Virginia Union University, both of whom share with me a passion for the theological vision of Paul Tillich. Boykin Sanders, another colleague at the School of Theology of Virginia Union, deserves thanks for occasional help with Greek to English transliterations. I wish to also thank Professors Charles Swezey and Douglas Ottati of Union Theological Seminary in Richmond for their steadfast friendship and delightful dialogue. Edward Leroy Long, J. Deotis Roberts, James Cone, and Delores Williams must be thanked for their counsel and for words of encouragement as well. I wish to thank Timothy G. Staveteig, the publisher of the Pilgrim Press, and George R. Graham, Editorial Director of Professional and Academic Books, for their enthusiastic support. I owe as well an immeasurable debt of gratitude to John Eagleson and Ruthann Dwyer for their exemplary professionalism and keen editorial judgment. Adam Bond very graciously consented to help me with the indexing; I am grateful to this young scholar. I am, of course, solely responsible for the viewpoints expressed in this work, and while I would covet immensely the full approbation of my friends, they should not be implicated if associated with me, nor indicted if questioned.

Finally, no words can adequately express the debt of gratitude I owe to my wife, Judith Mayes Roberts. I must thank her for her amazing patience with my foibles, affirmation of my dreams, and celebration of my gifts, such as they are. For all of her prayers and faith expressed during the divine gift of my spiritual transformation, this book is offered in love and gratitude.

PART I: FOUNDATIONS

1

A Framework for an African American Christian Ethic

Does he not see my ways,
and number all my steps?
—Job 31:4

I mean to lift up a standard for my King,
All over this world I mean to sing.
—American Negro spiritual

The present study assumes that an African American Christian ethic exists and that the exploration of the warrants and sources for normative behavior and reflection on the practical implications of such an ethic are worthwhile pursuits. The general thesis of the book is that African American Christians have developed by virtue of their history and culture a unique ethical consciousness. I will argue in part that such a consciousness has emerged from the fundamental attempt on the part of African Americans to make sense of their sojourn within the context of American history. Their appropriation of Christian symbols and worldview within this experience has been foundational to the development of this unique African American Christian ethic.

This chapter will seek to establish the theoretical framework for the entire book. In order to do this, I will set forth what I take to be the essential paradox in the historical African American embrace of Christianity. The bulk of the chapter will be my attempt to resolve this paradox, and in so doing, I will suggest the essential foundational elements for a framework for contemplating the very notion of an African American Christian ethic.

THE ESSENTIAL PARADOX OF AFRICAN AMERICAN CHRISTIANITY

Except for the indigenous Indian peoples in North America, all persons in what is now the United States must acknowledge that the religious heri-

3

tage of their ancestors was grounded in other times and other places. I am referring specifically to the pre-Christian histories of the Europeans and Africans in ancestral homelands before destiny brought them together in a tortured relationship on the North American continent. That relationship began with the age of European expansionism in the middle fifteenth century, and at least one strand of it has culminated in a chronicle of events that we now call American history. Well before the Puritans of Massachusetts could invoke the wrath of a fearsome God, their ancient forebears in the British Isles invoked Druid spirits. Well before German Lutherans could affirm their Reformed faith in America, their ancient forebears had sought out the divine presence of spirits in the dark forests of Saxony. And well before captured Africans learned to address the divine by a Christian name, their ancient forebears had worshiped quite contentedly at the shrines of Yoruba deities such as Shango and Ogun and sought to be obedient to the pervasive force in the universe known among the Ashanti as *nyama*. Thus, well in the background of virtually all people within the American social landscape is a heritage that could properly, although uncharitably, be called a pagan past.

Yet in this day and time, many Americans—black and white, descendants of worshipers of Nyame and Norse gods and other deities—affirm the primacy of Christian faith. These Americans, from devout believers to nominal members of mainline denominations, have imbibed a consciousness of Christianity. The reality is that at the present time many Americans have nurtured a unique social and religious consciousness that has been shaped for the most part by Christian faith. While white and black Christians share the same faith, the relationship between them has been anything but harmonious. Historically, the relationship between the European practitioners of Christian faith and captured Africans has not always been felicitous, nor has it always been free of hypocrisy. But Christian faith *has* had an undeniable effect upon the evolution of African American religious consciousness and the development of ethical consciousness as well.

But therein lies the first hint of a paradox that has haunted African American Christianity since the first enslaved Africans on American shores came to profess belief in the Christian faith. Fundamental to any assessment of the full nature of an African American Christian ethic is the recognition that Europeans introduced the Christian faith to captured Africans under the brutal conditions of chattel slavery. The fact is inescapable that slavery facilitated and supported European expansionism in the New World. It is also equally true that in the course of enslavement, the Christian religion was introduced to the enslaved Africans, first by Catholic countries, primarily Portugal and Spain. Portugal led the European countries in developing the transatlantic slave trade as early as the 1450s. Protestant nations, principally England and

Holland, joined in the trade in the sixteenth century and would introduce the Christian faith to those persons they enslaved as well.

Both Catholic and Protestant sensibilities regarded the enslaved African as an inferior.[1] But beyond this shared commonality, some significant differences existed between the motives for indoctrination and the historical contexts in which these two major branches of Christianity would bring Africans in bondage into the faith. While Catholic sensibility tended to regard the African as inferior, it nevertheless affirmed that the enslaved could be brought into the fellowship of the faithful and baptized legitimately into the faith. Baptism would in no way alter the African's inferior status, but it would confirm a place for the African—a subordinate place to be sure—within the divinely ordained social order. There was, therefore, no hesitation in baptizing Africans and bringing them into the fold of the faithful. In fact, Catholics considered it a holy duty to do so, thus saving the Africans from an infidel and pagan existence. Catholic priests, we are told, even baptized captured slaves at the very point of embarkation, prior to the Middle Passage, that perilous journey across the Atlantic into bondage.[2] Thus we may see, even through the sad glimpse of retrospect, the ironic picture of priests celebrating the liberation of African souls as their captured bodies were stuffed into the fetid holds of slave ships.

In contrast, Protestant sensibility was initially rather indifferent to the spiritual welfare of enslaved Africans. A popular notion among the English was that Africans had no souls at all; therefore, attempts to Christianize them initially seemed the height of folly. However, toward the end of the first century of English colonization in America, the Church of England became alarmed at the low state of religious affairs in the colonies. Slaveholder and slave had to be rescued from the presumed moral decay of colonial frontier society. Thus, in 1701 the Society for the Propagation of the Gospel in For-

---

1. In 1452, Pope Nicholas V granted the Portuguese king the authority to attack and enslave "the Moors, heathens and other enemies of Christ" who lived south of Cape Bajador, thus giving the approval of the church to the institution of slavery and paved the way for Portuguese conquest and occupation of societies that were not Christian. See Colin A. Palmer, "The First Passage, 1502–1619," in *To Make Our World Anew: A History of African Americans*, ed. Robin D. G. Kelley and Earl Lewis (New York: Oxford University Press, 2000), 9. Protestant sensibilities made way for the assumption of the natural inferiority of Africans and their presumed natural role as slaves in the enterprise of European expansionism into the New World. John Hawkins's voyage to Guinea in 1562 during which he acquired by force three hundred blacks for sale in Hispaniola signaled Protestant England's entry in the slave trade. Hawkins's subsequent voyages had the support of a notable shareholder in his enterprise, Queen Elizabeth I, the titular head of the Church of England. See Daniel P. Mannix and Malcolm Cowley, *Black Cargoes: A History of the Atlantic Slave Trade, 1518–1865* (New York: Viking, 1962), 21–22.

2. Colin A. Palmer, "The First Passage, 1502–1619," in *To Make Our World Anew: A History of African Americans*, ed. Robin D. G. Kelley and Earl Lewis (New York: Oxford University Press, 2000), 34. See also Frank Tannenbaum, *Slave and Citizen: The Negro in the Americas* (New York: Vintage Books, 1946), 64.

eign Parts was organized with the expressed purpose of taking the gospel to the American colonies, especially those in the hinterland. The initiative was only partially successful, due in part to the rather indifferent attitude many priests took with regard to their religious charges. Planters were reluctant to let their slaves attend religious indoctrination sessions. Moreover, many English Protestants in the colonies felt that baptizing a slave would undermine the slave system since under English common law no Christian could hold another Christian as a slave. Only after the bishop of London clarified matters in 1725 by ruling that the religious status of a slave would in no way affect the slave's civil status were planters in the English colonies in America free to proselytize their slaves. Nevertheless during the eighteenth century Protestant planters in the South were for the most part indifferent to the religious condition of their slaves.

Eventually, in the first half of the nineteenth century, Protestant slaveholders would come to value indoctrinating their slaves in the Christian faith. Such proselytizing proceeded out of a sense of guilt or because of an attenuated sense of Christian duty or even out of a utilitarian motive like the one advanced by Charles C. Jones. A Presbyterian minister and self-styled "apostle to the slaves,"[3] Jones believed that indoctrination in the Christian faith would make slaves more docile and obedient to their holders. While at the end of his "ministry" Jones believed that he had failed in his mission, since slaves seemed to resist his peculiar interpretation of the Bible, he nevertheless believed in the efficacy of his method and the rationale for bringing enslaved Africans into the Christian household of faith.[4]

In retrospect, a real paradox lies at the heart of the African American embrace of Christianity. A faith that African Americans historically affirmed as one that couched theologically their hopes for liberation was itself introduced to them by persons whose aim was to enslave them and keep them in bondage. In a very real sense, the Christian faith was introduced to black people by white people whose ethical behavior was ultimately repugnant to the very ideals of that faith, as black people would come to understand it. Such is the essential paradox inherent in the appropriation of the Christian faith by black people.

Among the vexatious and nettlesome problems inherent in this paradox is the relationship between the universal and the particular. Are there "universal" tenets of truth inherent in the Christian faith that are available to all believers in the faith without regard to the particular vantage points from which they approach the faith? Or must the truths of the Christian faith

---

3. Erskine Clarke, *Wrestlin' Jacob: A Portrait of Religion in the Old South* (Atlanta: John Knox Press, 1979). See also Charles C. Jones, *The Religious Instruction of the Negroes in the United States* (Savannah: T. Purse, 1842; reprint, New York: Books for Libraries Press, 1971).
4. Clarke, *Wrestlin' Jacob*, 40–41.

always and only be perceived through the particular perspectives of those vantage points of culture? If the perception of these truths is relative to particular cultures, what does this say about the legitimacy of any presumed universals within the faith?

A RESOLUTION OF THE PARADOX

In order to explicate an ethic within African American consciousness this paradox must be resolved, and the resolution must be worked out in such a fashion as to affirm what we know about Christian faith and what we know about human groups as they behave in religious ways. Either through intuition, natural theology (theological perception unaided by revelation), or revelation, we may presume with some degree of confidence that if God is to be God, then God must be conceived apart from and independent of the limited perspectives of finite human beings. At the same time, we must presume that no vision of God is contemplated apart from human consciousness, a consciousness that inevitably is evidenced through the unique phenomenon of human culture. Moreover, we may also presume that no religious or theological system is essential or innate within human beings. We are not born genetically disposed toward any faith system. We have already seen how theological and religious sensibilities may in fact shift according to historical exigencies. The descendant of a Druid becomes an Anglican rector. The descendant of a Yoruba *oba* becomes a Baptist deacon. All we may presume to say is that human groups will invariably evidence a propensity to conceive of and articulate a relationship with the ineffable Other. And human beings will do this within the medium of human interaction known as culture.

The resolution of the paradox thus proceeds with two affirmations: that God is beyond the limited perspective of human beings and that all human perspectives of God, *including one's own,* are indeed limited and perspectival. In order to work out this paradox, we must begin to lay the foundation for a vision of God that is resistant to the human tendency to shape the divine according to human ideals and standards. And we must also begin to lay the foundation for a view of religion in society that recognizes the pliability of human culture, that acknowledges how the divine is always perceived through the phenomenon of human cultures. Such is the foundation for a framework for our approach to determining the contours and outlines of an African American Christian ethic.

The remainder of this chapter will address the following issues and concerns. A vision of God is best served when it is not limited by the perspectives of the cultures out of which the vision emerges. At the same time, no vision of God cannot help but be articulated according to the cultural material at hand. Thus, a tension exists between our desire to fashion a vision of God that is beyond our culture and a vision limited nevertheless by our inability to envision God *except by* the cultural apparatus of our culture—language, symbols, ideas, and so on. Any theology based on cultural centrism is doomed to fashion a vision of God not entirely worthy of the God it affirms. Such has been the tragic fate of Eurocentric theologies and to an equal extent, for slightly different reasons, theologies based on Afrocentrism. Let me now work through a historical analysis to support this assertion.

THE CULTURAL IDOLATRY OF EUROCENTRIC THEOLOGY IN AMERICA

European expansionist claims on the North American continent were accompanied by the imposition of European religious institutions on the emerging American cultures. Catholic missionaries and priests not only blessed the work of the conquistadors but also joined them in the imposition of Spanish culture, first in Florida and then in the American Southwest and the Far West. French expansionist claims followed the same pattern as well in the lower Mississippi Valley, notably Louisiana, and much farther north in Canada. Most prominent, however, in terms of pervasiveness of cultural imprint was the presence of the imperialist claims and accompanying religious hegemony of the English in America, that tradition begun by the English Puritans who became the American Pilgrims in what would come to be known as New England.

English Puritanism was one of the three emergent strands of the Protestant Reformation of the early years of the sixteenth century, the other two being the movement in Germany led by Martin Luther and the one in Switzerland, including France, led by John Calvin. While all three strands of the Reformation severed relations with the Church in Rome, the English Reformation came about initially for political, rather than theological, reasons. When the church refused to annul King Henry's marriage to Catherine of Aragon, he insisted that the Convocation of Canterbury do so in 1533. In the next year Henry forced the English Parliament to declare him the supreme head of the Church in England, thus severing all ties with Rome.

Thus in England a national church preceded any real attempts to institute a theological and spiritual reformation. However, attempts to purify the national Church of England and to infuse it with theological and spiritual reformation led inexorably to the development of Puritanism in that country. Such attempts were tried and repulsed, first under the reign of Henry's Catholic daughter, Mary Tudor ("Bloody Mary") from 1553 to 1558, and later under his Protestant daughter, Elizabeth, who, like Henry, reigned as the head of the national church and was alternately either hostile or indifferent to the reform impulse. During her reign from 1558 to 1603 the Puritan movement was born in the prison cells into which many ministers were thrown for their beliefs.

Perhaps the one book that began the Puritan movement was by a Protestant minister who had escaped England under the persecution of Mary. John Foxe fled to Frankfurt and there wrote the classic *The Book of Martyrs*. In that book he asked the one question on which would turn the future of England's religious—and political—future. Would the people of England, he asked, insist that their church *and* their state be purified according to biblical principles? Elizabeth, ever politically cautious and adverse to religious extremism, held out the view that England should be religiously inclusive and should base its life on reason as well as religious tradition. By 1570, two points of view were in irreconcilable conflict. One view—held by the queen and the Anglican Church—advanced a more rationalistic understanding of church and state, and another group—increasingly referred to as the Puritans—affirmed that purification of both church and state should proceed according to biblical principles.

The full flowering of the Puritan dream would take place, not in England, but an ocean away in the New World of North America. The transition from English Puritan to American Pilgrim came about as Puritans gave up their hope that England could be transformed into a religious and political entity according to the dream of John Foxe. Such persons effectively "separated" themselves from the Church of England and struck out on their own—leaving England initially for Holland and then later for America, landing at Plymouth Rock in 1620. The popular and uncritical view of the colonial Pilgrims is that they left England to seek refuge from religious persecution; it is completely erroneous.[5] While indifferent to the demands of the Separatist Puritans, Elizabeth was not as persecutory as her extremist Catholic sister. While Elizabeth certainly was no friend of the Puritan party or their vision of reformation, neither was she given to the zealous campaign of religious persecution as had characterized Mary. Elizabeth desired a more rationally based state, a precursor to the modern liberal secular state. There might have been a place for the would-be Separatists in such a state, along with other religious persuasions, but the Separatists wanted much more—a state governed according to their narrow vision of what they believed the Bible demanded.

The English Puritans who came to Massachusetts in 1620 were determined to forge an ordered life devoted to purity of doctrine and practice, a dream that had eluded them in England and continental Europe. In the New

---

5. I am joined in this assessment by Thomas Jefferson Wertenbaker, *The Puritan Oligarchy: The Founding of American Civilization* (New York: Scribner's, 1947), 344.

World, on the North American continent, they would be able to establish a world to their liking and religious requirements. But sadly, in the charting of the contours of this new order, the Puritans would employ their own cultural standards without regard for other peoples and other cultures.

Among the English Separatists who came to America was William Bradford, who was elected the second governor of the Plymouth Colony in 1621. Bradford wrote his memoirs some thirty years later in a work entitled *Of Plymouth Plantation*. As he chronicled the early hardships of the English Puritans, their persecution in England, and their aborted efforts to secure religious freedom in Holland, he described the American frontier in this way: "The place they had thoughts on was some of those vast and unpeopled countries of America, which are fruitful and fit for habitation, being devoid of all civil inhabitants, where there are only savage and brutish men which range up and down, little otherwise than the wild beasts of the same."[6] Aside from the obvious racism inherent in Bradford's designation of the inhabitants of America is the problem of his view of them as essentially invisible persons. While the inhabitants of the land are considered "savage and brutish men," he, with some risk of outright contradiction, still considered the places in which they roamed as "unpeopled" countries.

Perhaps unconscious of his own motives and assumptions, Bradford began a mind-set that would be typical of American theological cultural imperialists in their total contempt and disregard for any culture but their own as they forged a theological vision of their sojourn in America. Their mission to this New World in North America was assured the help of God, for "their condition was not ordinary, their ends were good and honorable, their calling lawful and urgent; and therefore they might expect the blessing of God in their proceeding."[7] Bradford's vision was unabashedly an *English* vision for *English* people in the New World as they sought to build a new covenantal community in America. In this vision, he could invoke the biblical assurance God gave the people of Israel, which according to his vision was directed pointedly to English people. Asked Bradford toward the conclusion of his essay, "What could now sustain them but the spirit of God and His grace?" In his answer he invoked God's care over them: "May not and ought not the children of these fathers rightly say: 'Our fathers were Englishmen which came over this great ocean, and were ready to perish in this wilderness; but they cried unto the Lord, and He heard their voice and looked on their adversity' (Deut. 26:5–7)."[8]

---

6. William Bradford, excerpt from *Of Plymouth Plantation*, in *The American Puritans: Their Prose and Poetry*, ed. Perry Miller (Garden City, N.Y.: Doubleday Anchor, 1956), 12.
7. Ibid., 14.
8. Ibid., 18.

The tie with England and all things English, including those who remained in the country, continued for the English descendants living in America. Edward Johnson (1598–1672) wrote a treatise entitled *Wonder-Working Providence of Sion's Savior* in which he envisioned a permanent spiritual link between the Pilgrims in the New World and their forebears in the Old. Wrote Johnson, "For England's sake they are going from England, to pray without ceasing for England. O England! Thou shalt find New England prayers prevailing with their God for thee; but now, woe alas! What great hardship must these our endeared pastors endure for a long season!"[9]

In their sojourn in this strange New World, the chroniclers of the Pilgrim experience in America were always conscious of the special regard God, they presumed, had for them. John Winthrop would come to articulate very forcefully this special favor that God had upon the people now assembled in New England. Winthrop saw the hand of God dealing favorably with the people of English extraction during the crisis-filled years of the settlement in Massachusetts. In his journal entry of June 4, 1647, Winthrop noted the epidemic that had swept through the area taking a considerable toll among the Patuxet, the Wamponoag, the French, and the Dutch. But insofar as it affected the English, he saw the hand of God at work, for "such was the mercy of God to his people, as few died, not above forty or fifty in the Massachusetts, and near as many at Connecticut."[10]

In New England the Pilgrims were free to establish a Christian commonwealth, a dream that the great English Puritan thinker Richard Baxter hoped would have come to pass in his homeland. In fact, even as Baxter was formulating his vision in England, the Rev. John Eliot of Roxbury, Massachusetts, was writing in 1660 a treatise entitled *The Christian Commonwealth*. Eliot advocated a "system of unified administration, modeled on the scriptural system of the ancient Israelites, under God, the supreme king."[11]

Imbued with this sense of a holy commonwealth, organized under the supreme governance of God and self-consciously identified as the covenantal people of God, the Puritans not surprisingly developed a religious consciousness with a fierce xenophobia with respect to those who were not in such a commonwealth, which would include not only unregenerate whites but also indigenous Indians and, to be sure, alien Africans, who by the midyears of the seventeenth century were being imported into the colony as slaves. The Puritan hope for a theocracy in America was accorded some degree of fulfillment in the Massachusetts Bay Colony, a religious refuge

---

9. Edward Johnson, excerpt from *Wonder-Working Providence of Sion's Savior*, in *The American Puritans*, ed. Miller, 35.

10. John Winthrop, excerpt from his *Journal*, in *The American Puritans*, ed. Miller, 47.

11. Herbert W. Schneider, *The Puritan Mind* (Ann Arbor: University of Michigan Press, Ann Arbor Paperback, 1958), 25.

for faithful Puritans but an unforgiving and hostile redoubt for outsiders, freethinkers, and nonconformists. The fervor of Puritan radicalism was ultimately countered by the ideology of the new republic's founders that forbade the establishment of religion. Yet within American religious consciousness would forever remain a strand of sentiment and thinking that would tend to join the destiny of the religious and cultural establishment with the favor of Almighty God. Even as the Puritan establishment decreased, in its place emerged an Anglo-American cultural and political establishment that presumed to wield power over the American scene.

The correlation of cultural hegemony and the presumption of divine favor would be seen a century after the founding of the nation when the Protestant establishment sought to counter the challenges presented to the American nation at the end of the nineteenth century. Among the issues before the country were immigration of unassimilated ethnic groups from Europe, the rising demands of the working class, the question of how the second generation of post-Emancipation blacks would fit into the American scheme of things, and the rising specter of urbanization. One emerging speaker for the Protestant establishment in the 1880s was the Congregational pastor of a church in Topeka, Kansas, named Josiah Strong. Strong believed in liberal theology, even defending the theory of evolution against theological conservatives, but his social Darwinism supported a racist Anglo-Saxonism inherent in his thought.

In his most famous book, *Our Country*, written in 1885, Strong affirmed that Anglo-Saxons were God's chosen race. Moreover, he dourly predicted, "If I do not read amiss, this powerful race will move down upon Mexico, down upon Central and South America, out upon the islands of the sea, over upon Africa and beyond. And can anyone doubt that the result of this competition will be the survival of the fittest?"[12] Strong was suspicious of any lack of conformity to the values his class had sought to impose upon those who, in his estimation, constituted an unruly and undifferentiated American populace. He was fearful of the way cities were teeming with immigrants from Europe, whose languages and customs he found strange and alien. He yearned for a nation in which newcomers to the American scene would defer to the established leadership class and its values, values undergirded by a firm belief that God had ordained the American nation to rule the world and white Anglo-Saxon Christians to in turn rule the nation.

An implicit Eurocentrism within American culture produced a religious hegemony in which it was presumed that Anglo-American perspectives

---

12. Josiah Strong, *Our Country: Its Possible Future and Its Present Crisis* (New York: American Home Missionary Society, 1885), 174–75; see also Thomas F. Gossell, *Race: The History of an Idea in America* (New York: Schocken Books, 1965), chap. 8, "The Social Gospel and Race," 176–97.

ought to determine the normative values in American society. It was, however, the rejection of Euro-American Christian hegemony and its glib presumptions that God had ordained a social order in which black people were inferior that elicited the singular theological movement of the latter half of this century known as *black theology*. The genius of this emergent phenomenon in the decade of the 1960s was its uncovering of the hidden assumptions of a "white theology" and its opposition to the pretensions of such a theological system. Thus was black theology offered to the American public as a viable option. We now turn to an analysis of that theological vision, its hopes and its limitations.

PRECURSORS TO A BLACK THEOLOGY

The suggestion that the underlying assumptions of the Protestant religious establishment within American history is free from some particular reference to the cultural hegemony of Europe, specifically English-oriented history, is without foundation. Indeed, it was primarily the presence of the hidden assumptions in such an establishment that warranted the challenge of black power and black theology. Were it not for the arrogance of Eurocentric theology within American religious consciousness, the peculiar reasons for the emergence of a black theology might never have taken shape in quite the way it did.

I will argue that the grounds for a uniquely African American Christian ethic can be asserted in such a way that does not entail the narrow xenophobic contours that much of the black theology movement assumed in the first decades of its existence. Nevertheless, a unique African American Christian ethic will critique the pretensions of a Eurocentric heritage that presumed that it was coterminous with what could be called a "universal" ideal. In order to get to this point, we will review the basic outlines of black theology and the theological ethic that this movement suggested.

Prior to the civil rights movement the reality within much of American society was that black people had no full assurances of being welcomed into all aspects of American life. Black people could not always live where they desired; they could not always use public modes of transportation as they desired. When black people traveled, they could not always secure lodgings for the night. In many southern states, owing either to outright hostility or legal contrivances such as poll taxes and intimidation, black people could not vote as they desired. With the advent of the civil rights movement, generally dated with the Montgomery bus boycott from December 1955 to November 1956, a series of confrontations with white America was unleashed that challenged the popular and legally enforced restrictions that denied blacks full access to the amenities of American life. The eradication of these restrictions constituted in essence the relatively modest demands of the civil rights movement: merely to be treated like other Americans.

The nature of the demands of the civil rights movement determined in good measure the nature of the strategies used to secure them. If the initial demand was merely for blacks to be treated like other Americans, it is not surprising that the strategies employed to secure it would be consistent with what was deemed the best in the American tradition. The movement's essential strategy was to appeal to what were deemed universal legal values embedded in sacred documents of the American republic: the Declaration of Independence and the Constitution. On many occasions, Martin Luther King Jr., the undeniable prophet of the movement, asserted that the movement itself was anchored in "those great wells of democracy which were dug deep by the Founding Fathers in the formulation of the Constitution and the Declaration of Independence."[13] Hoping to change white Americans through moral suasion, the specific tactics used by the movement were nonviolent resistance, peaceful protests, and the adroit use of news media, particularly print and television. The objective was to change the hearts of white Americans.

Very close to this agenda for social change was a theology of the civil rights movement, as articulated chiefly by Martin Luther King Jr. King affirmed a God that made no distinction between persons or races and championed the "brotherhood of man" as the ideal relation between human beings. God's ultimate will for the moral universe, King believed, was to bring about justice, perhaps painfully, perhaps slowly, but inexorably to bring it about. King was fond of quoting the words of James Russell Lowell in the hymn "Once to Every Man and Nation": "Truth forever on the scaffold; wrong forever on the throne; yet behind that scaffold sways the future, and behind the dim unknown, standeth God keeping watch above his own." In other words, the destiny of the moral universe was in God's sure hands, not the unsteady and quirky hands of a flawed humanity.

However, God's justice could not be brought about through violence. King insisted that nonviolent resistance was "the only morally and practically sound method open to oppressed people in their struggle for freedom" and that it was the key to lasting and profound change. Its "transforming power," he declared, "can lift a whole community to new horizons of fair play, goodwill and justice."[14] Given the movement's affirmation of

---

13. Martin Luther King Jr., "An Address before the National Press Club," July 19, 1962, in *A Testament of Hope: The Essential Writings of Martin Luther King, Jr.,* ed. James M. Washington (San Francisco: Harper & Row, 1986), 103.

14. Quoted in Jo Ann Robinson, "Nonviolent Resistance," in *Encyclopedia of African-American Civil Rights,* ed. Charles D. Lowery and John F. Marszalek (New York: Greenwood Press, 1992), 406.

the ideological and theological framework of interracial pluralism, it really had no choice but to appeal to the goodness of human hearts within the context of interracialism to get its demands met. There was simply no other way; separatism was not an option both theologically and given King's reading of American history and his faith in the ultimate triumph of constitutionalism.[15]

The early victories of the movement tended to vindicate King's faith in his theological vision and the power of the Constitution to rectify social injustices. The Montgomery Improvement Association (MIA), the organization formed by Montgomery blacks that led and organized the bus boycott, trained people in nonviolent tactics, appealed to national public sympathy but ultimately appealed to the courts in their struggle. After failing to get the city to agree to limited desegregation of the buses, the MIA filed suit in federal court on February 1, 1956, challenging the constitutionality of the bus segregation ordinances. On November 13, 1956, the U.S. Supreme Court upheld the lower court's ruling that the segregation of Montgomery's buses was unconstitutional. Other victories ensued.

In 1957 King was able to fashion a group of black ministers across denominational lines, named the Southern Christian Leadership Conference (SCLC), whose aim was "to coordinate local, nonviolent direct action protest movements." The group's first action, in 1957, was a prayer pilgrimage to Washington, led by King, which attracted twenty-five thousand people. Two years later in 1959, by which time King had moved SCLC to Atlanta in order give it a more powerful regional and national platform from which to launch its activities, another march—this time a youth march on Washington—drew forty thousand persons. Mass marches were followed by dramatic, televised "sit-ins," which were used to publicize the wrongs of segregation. The first sit-in took place in Greensboro, North Carolina, in 1960.

Throughout the next few years, the SCLC brilliantly mobilized blacks, organizing the marches, filling up the jails, and displaying to an international television audience the mindless violence of southern whites. It sponsored and helped sit-in movements and demonstrations across the entire South

---

15. For sources on the ideology of the civil rights movement, see Joan V. Bondurant, *Conquest of Violence: The Gandhian Philosophy of Conflict* (Berkeley: University of California Press, 1965); Severyn T. L. Bruyn and Paula M. Rayman, eds., *Nonviolent Action and Social Change* (New York: Irvington Publishers, 1979); Robert Cooney and Helen Michalowski, *The Power of the People: Active Non-Violence in the United States* (Culver City, Calif.: Peace Press, 1977); Gene Sharp, *The Politics of Nonviolent Action* (Boston: P. Sargent, 1973); Mulford Q. Sibley, ed., *The Quiet Battle: Writings on the Theory and Practice of Non-Violent Resistance* (Garden City, N.Y.: Doubleday, 1963); August Meier, Elliott Rudwick, and Francis L. Broderick, eds., *Black Protest Thought in the Twentieth Century*, 2d ed. (New York: Macmillan, 1980).

during those early years of the 1960s.[16] King himself, and the movement by extension, received international affirmation with the awarding of the Nobel Peace Prize in 1963.

Within the context of rising expectations as well as impatience with the tactic of nonviolent resistance, the seeds for dissension within the civil rights movement began to sprout. The enfranchisement of so many black people at one fell swoop occasioned by the Voting Rights Act of 1965 led many to ask the next logical question: How shall we exercise the political power that the vote offers? In other words, what are we going to vote for? Moreover, many younger people in the movement, particularly those young black college students who were members of SNCC, the Student Nonviolent Coordinating Committee, began to ask pointed questions about the ideology of the movement: How does the affirmation of a universal notion of "brotherhood," or shared human kinship, square with the fact that black people have particular needs and interests? Does not the obligation to appeal through moral suasion to the presumed goodness of whites suggest an inferior status of the one making the appeal? The answers to such questions were provided by the emerging voices in the movement that would ultimately come to be known as the "black power" advocates.

Sensing the unrecognized depth of white racism and the intransigence with which many whites would greet black attempts to move into the American power structure, the younger members of the civil rights movement became more and more alienated from their elders. In the summer of 1966, in the midst of particularly frustrating attempts to secure voting privileges for blacks in Lowndes County, Alabama, the young people of SNCC yelled out the cry, "Black Power." This cry heard throughout America and around the world was an affirmation that the only true way to achieve black integrity within the American social system was through securing power, rather than pleading for justice. Moreover, the quest for power had to be pursued separately from interracial coalition politics; the doctrine of universal human kinship had become impoverished as a means for attending to the particular interests and concerns of black people.

---

16. For excellent treatments of the strategies and campaigns during the civil rights movement, see Adam Fairclough, *To Redeem the Soul of America: The Southern Christian Leadership Conference and Martin Luther King, Jr.* (Athens: University of Georgia Press, 1987); David J. Garrow, *Bearing the Cross: Martin Luther King, Jr. and the Southern Christian Leadership Conference* (New York: W. Morrow, 1986); David J. Garrow, ed., *We Shall Overcome: The Civil Rights Movement in the United States in the 1950's and 1960's* (Brooklyn, N.Y.: Carlson, 1989);

Stephen B. Oates, *Let the Trumpet Sound: The Life of Martin Luther King, Jr.* (New York: Harper & Row, 1982).

THE EMERGENCE OF A BLACK THEOLOGY
AND ITS PROBLEMATIC ASPECTS

The awakening of a radical black political consciousness in the middle years of the 1960s culminated in a radicalization of the theological vision as well. The basic assertion of the black power movement was the affirmation that the political norms and expectations of the white-controlled power structure need no longer be deferred to as black people charted a political course in this country. Such a radicalization resulted in the birth of black theology in the last years of that explosive decade. James H. Cone, a young assistant professor at Union Theological Seminary in New York City, came on the theological scene with an explosion, the publication of his first book, *Black Power and Black Theology* (1969), which was followed closely by *A Black Theology of Liberation* (1970). In these books and countless lectures and articles, Cone quickly became the eloquent and forceful proponent of "black theology."

The influence of the ideology of black power on Cone was palpable in his book *Black Power and Black Theology*. Cone understood and defined black power to be "complete emancipation of black people from white oppression by whatever means black people deem necessary."[17] Moreover, it meant black freedom, black self-determination, wherein black people no longer had to view themselves as people without human dignity but as men and women with the ability to carve out their own destiny. It meant black people "taking care of black folks' business, not on the terms of the oppressor, but on those of the oppressed."[18] Cone absorbed all of the passion of the exploding black ghettos of the decade called the "turbulent sixties" and used his pen as a weapon poised for battle. He reflected the existential absurdity articulated by the sullen black masses of men and women who were still convinced that white people viewed them as nonpersons. As such, there was a biting edge of defiance in his posture and work: "In an absurd world that defines some men and women as non-persons, the black person is obliged to reject the very reasonable option of suicide or despair and to seize the option to *fight back with the whole of his being*."[19]

The advent of black power and the first stirrings of a black theology were like liberating and refreshing breezes to many black people who were beginning to detect a vacuousness in Martin Luther King's appeal to universal brotherhood while the needs and interests of oppressed black people lay unattended. Moreover, many were growing weary of the glacial-like pace

---

17. James H. Cone, *Black Theology and Black Power* (New York: Seabury Press, 1969), 6.
18. Ibid.
19. Ibid., 12; emphasis in original. Cone notes the options outlined by Albert Camus in his existentialist philosophy, namely, those of despair and suicide when confronted with the absurdity of reality.

of real changes in the lives of black people that nonviolent resistance hoped to achieve. James Cone's book served the very valuable function of galvanizing the attention of a new generation of theological thinkers who desired to construct a theological system that was truly freed of white hegemony and norms.

But how free was Cone's vision from the normative system against which he so vigorously rebelled? Unfortunately, an element of reactionism in his work ironically reified the very worldview that he sought to dismantle. For example, as a preliminary step toward constructing a theology of liberation that would emanate from oppressed black people themselves, Cone wrote, "There is, then, a need for a theology whose sole purpose is to emancipate the gospel from its 'whiteness' so that blacks may be capable of making an honest self-affirmation through Jesus Christ."[20]

The problem with this position, of course, is that in a curious fashion it presumes as fact the specious assumption that white culture had always made about Christian faith, that is, that whiteness was somehow identical with the essence of that faith and tradition. Cone, even in his anger against white culture, presumed as much. If this is not true, why else would he feel obliged to "emancipate the gospel from *its* 'whiteness' "?[21] Further on, Cone asks, "Must black people be forced to deny their identity in order to embrace the Christian faith?"[22] The very fact that these two realities are posed in a mutually exclusive fashion, as if one precluded the other, means again that Cone has implicitly relinquished Christian faith to the exclusive domain of whiteness.

But there are other problematic areas. All varieties of black theology presumed that a personal God had voluntarily made a choice to affirm the oppressed, particularly the black oppressed. Sensing a historic affinity with the oppressed Hebrews of the Old Testament, black theology as well affirmed the role of God in granting black people divine favor and leading them out of slavery. In *Black Power and Black Theology*, Cone affirms this tradition by noting that in the Old Testament God's righteousness is understood, not in some abstract way, as was the case in Greek thought, but rather within the historical context of living human communities. God acts in such a way that divine righteousness is made evident. Writes Cone: "If God is to be true to himself, his righteousness must be directed to the helpless and the poor, those who can expect no security from this world."[23] Thus God in accord with divine righteousness must choose the poor and disinherited.

---

20. Ibid., 32.
21. Ibid.; emphasis added.
22. Ibid., 33.
23. Ibid., 45.

By the time Cone wrote his second book, *A Black Theology of Libera-tion,* he would go even further and declare that divine righteousness is made evident by God's favoring the *black poor and disinherited.*[24] Black theology would affirm, at least in the thought of James Cone, that indeed black people and their particular existence should be considered normative for Christian consciousness as well. Moreover, ways of interpreting scripture, views about who and what was the will of God, how the saving power of Christ should be interpreted—everything suddenly had to be interpreted through the her-meneutic of what God was now doing in, through, and for black people. Indeed, God became black. Declared Cone:

> God himself must be known only as he reveals himself in his blackness. The blackness of God, and everything implied by it in a racist society, is the heart of black theology's doctrine of God. There is no place in black theology for a colorless God in a society when people suffer precisely because of their color. The black theologian must reject any conception of God which stifles black self-determination by picturing God as a God of all peoples.[25]

Others joined Cone in articulating a black theology. Prominent among them was the United Church of Christ pastor and black nationalist Albert Cleage Jr., whose church, the Shrine of the Black Madonna in Detroit, had become an unabashed center for radical black Christianity. In 1968 Cleage published *The Black Messiah,* a book of sermons in which he asserted that Jesus was a black revolutionary whose primary ministry was to lead a revolt against the Roman Empire.[26]

Without question, black theology proposed a radical and different way of understanding who and what God is. But how different was it actually? Some observers articulated a suspicion that in Cone's hands the tribal god of Eurocentric exclusivism had merely been exchanged for the tribal god of Afrocentric exclusivism. Critical reactions to black theology from white and black scholars followed. While virtually all black scholars hailed the initiative of conceiving a theological agenda from the perspective of radical black consciousness, many believed that some claims could not be justified. Leon Wright, a black Howard University Divinity School professor, wrote an article in that institution's *Journal of Religious Thought* in which he said:

> Further, the proposition should be sternly questioned as to that mys-terious alchemy of revelation or selection whereby Blacks become a

24. James H. Cone, *A Black Theology of Liberation* (Philadelphia: J. B. Lippincott, 1970).
25. Ibid., 120.
26. Albert Cleage Jr., *The Black Messiah* (New York: Sheed and Ward, 1968). See also his *Black Christian Nationalism: New Directions for the Black Church* (New York: William Morrow, 1972).

"Chosen People" as opposed to a "chosen" status for any other suffering or depressed minority. In other words, it should not be supposed that one advances the cause of a "black theology" merely by painting faces black or partisanly juggling spiritual preferences before God, respecting persons or groups. Whatever the case for black theology may turn out to be, let us not cavalierly create a set of mythological assumptions whose credibility deserves only to "de-mythologized" at the same instant. If racism is bad, it cannot achieve respectability by masquerading within any preferred ethnic or racial stock.[27]

The critical reactions of black scholars were particularly important since they had to overcome what surely might have been hesitancies to betray the young black David who had just stood up against the white Philistine theological establishment. To be sure, among the early critical comments from other scholars were those directed at the nature of the enterprise of black theology itself, one of which came from Cone's own brother, Cecil, in a very thoughtful appraisal entitled *The Identity Crisis in Black Theology*.[28] It was soon clear, however, that as the decade wore on the critiques of James Cone would be forthcoming from at least three perspectives on the theological spectrum.

Far to the right of Cone would be the response from conservative evangelically oriented black thinkers. Anthony Evans, leader of a prominent Dallas congregation, charged that Cone's racial parochialism and nationalist hermeneutic was a violation of a biblically based universalism. Evans could appreciate the uniqueness of black experience but allowed that it must be seen as "real but not revelatory, important but not inspired."[29]

Taking a more centrist viewpoint was the critique of J. Deotis Roberts. Roberts felt that black theology violated the reconciling power of the gospel since its moral trajectory led inexorably to racial separatism. For Roberts, such a focus was at variance with the hope of Christian faith: the reconciliation of people of different races. In fact, for Roberts it was within such reconciliation that true freedom lay. Said he: "It is my belief that true freedom overcomes estrangement and heals brokenness between peoples."[30]

27. Leon Wright, "Black Theology or Black Experience?" *Journal of Religious Thought* 26, no. 2 (summer 1969): 54.

28. Cecil Wayne Cone, "The Identity Crisis in Black Theology: An Investigation of the Tensions Created by Efforts to Provide a Theological Interpretation of Black Religion in the Works of Joseph Washington, James Cone, and J. Deotis Roberts" (Ph.D. diss., Emory University, 1974).

29. Anthony Evans, *Biblical Theology and the Black Experience* (Dallas: Black Evangelistic Enterprise, 1977), 52.

30. J. Deotis Roberts, "Black Theology in the Making," *Review and Expositor* 70 (summer 1973): 328. Roberts's initial response to Cone's position was issued in *Liberation and Reconciliation: A Black Theology* (Philadelphia: Westminster Press, 1971).

Joining Roberts in this centrist position was Major R. Jones, who felt that Cone's vision of an exclusivistic God was untenable. "If God is not the God of all of the people," said Jones, "then he is the God of no people."[31]

Well to the left of all these theologians, including Cone, was William R. Jones, then an assistant professor of theology at Yale Divinity School. Jones weighed into the debate with the unfortunately titled but brilliant work *Is God a White Racist? A Preamble to Black Theology.* Jones charged that despite its attack on white racism, black theology still had not adequately dealt with the question of theodicy: how can black suffering be squared with the historic and continued suffering of black people? Jones declared that unless black theology was prepared to jettison the entire idea of theism and adopt a "humanistic"-oriented stance, then the project did not go far enough.[32]

Central to all three of these critiques and perspectives on the theological spectrum was a concern in black theology about God's nature and how that nature manifested itself to humankind. Was God really black, and was God disposed to favor black people? Or should God necessarily be considered a universal, impartial God? Could God be legitimately viewed as universal and impartial and still be responsive to the urgent concerns of suffering black people? On this question turned the intellectual and moral integrity of the entire project. Perhaps anticipating the attacks accusing him of racial exclusivism because of his identification of God with blackness, Cone had laid the foundation for an alternative interpretation of this assertion in *A Black Theology of Liberation.* Espousing a tack that reflected Paul Tillich's view of the symbolic nature of all theological discourse, Cone explained:

> The focus on blackness does not mean that *only* blacks suffer as victims in a racist society, but that blackness is an ontological symbol and a visible reality which best describes what oppression means in America.... Blackness, then, stands for all victims of oppression who realize that their humanity is inseparable from man's liberation from whiteness.[33]

But, as Gayraud S. Wilmore shrewdly observed in his book *Black Religion and Black Radicalism,* Cone's explanation really does not solve the problem. All Cone has done in the name of universalizing black theology is to eviscerate it. All it could do now was to offer a bland symbolic potpourri for all the world's suffering people. The project would therefore fail

---

31. Major R. Jones, *Christian Ethics for Black Theology: The Politics of Liberation* (Nashville: Abingdon Press, 1974), 69.

32. William R. Jones, *Is God a White Racist? A Preamble to Black Theology* (Boston: Beacon Press, 1973).

33. James H. Cone, *A Black Theology of Liberation,* 27–28.

to understand that black suffering has been real and cannot be adequately addressed as long as it is thrown in with all the other woes of the world. Nevertheless, if Cone continues in justifying black theology by virtue of God's special relationship with black people, then he is still beset with all the problems that such an exclusive theology is bound to suffer. Sympathizing with Cone's dilemma and seeking to provide a way out, Wilmore argued that a distinction could be made between the "particular" and the "singular." He drew upon the thinking of philosopher J. V. Langmead Casserley, who offered this distinction between the two terms:

> The advent of Christianity forced a new problem upon the attention of the ancient world—the problem of the singular.... There is a profound distinction between the term "particular" and the term "singular." The "particular" is the individual as seen by the man who is looking for the universal, and who will feel baffled intellectually until he finds it; the "singular," on the other hand, is the individual seen from the point of view of the man who is out to capture and enjoy the full flavor of its individuality."[34]

Wilmore infers from Casserley's distinction between the singular and the particular that black theology's valuable contribution might be its assertion that black religion and the black experience are unique in the world's history. On this basis one can come to appreciate black theology's true worth. In this light then, the legitimacy of black theology would hinge on this question: "does it [black theology] find in the experiences of the oppression of blacks in the Western world, *as black*, a singular religious meaning?"[35] In this sense, then, skin color is not completely irrelevant in theological discourse as long as white domination continues and justifies its existence in a world where race matters. It is not simply being oppressed that enables other peoples of the world to share in blackness, even symbolic existential blackness, any more than, as in Wilmore's trenchant terms, "putting on a blindfold delivers one into the experience of being blind."[36]

Wilmore's attempt to rescue black theology from provincialism and narrow exclusivism is laudable. Yet even the notion of the presumed singularity of the black experience of which Wilmore speaks cannot spare black theology, so conceived, from still assuming a *reactionary* posture with respect to white existence and culture. Wilmore writes:

34. Gayraud S. Wilmore, *Black Religion and Black Radicalism*, 2d ed. (Maryknoll, N.Y.: Orbis Books, 1983), 217, quoting J. V. Langmead Casserley, *The Christian in Philosophy* (New York: Scribner's, 1951), 31.

35. Wilmore, *Black Religion and Black Radicalism*, 218.

36. Ibid.

> There is no intention in this position to shut out white persons from the black religious experience or to devalue the revelatory significance of the experience of other oppressed peoples. It is simply to affirm that black theology authenticates itself in the unique experience of being black in the particular circumstances of white, Western civilization.[37]

Wilmore's last sentence in the above statement is troubling, for it suggests that the integrity of a black perspective is seen *relative to* white, Western civilization. In such a position, white civilization still could retain the power to regard blackness as alien, negative, and different. Wilmore's attempt suggests again the reactionary posture that we found so disturbing in James Cone. It is as if the moon can only secure its identity by virtue of the sun.

TOWARD AN ALTERNATIVE PARADIGM

In reviewing the black theology project, we have seen some of the real problems that were—and still are—inherent in it. I point these problems out with no sense of glee or smug intellectual self-righteousness. That scholars are now able to discuss and debate issues within black theology is a testimony to the richness of the thought of the first authors, particularly James Cone, who dared put their vision to paper so that the world could take notice. Therefore, what follows is only my attempt to move beyond some lingering problems in order to build upon the worthy edifice of black theology.

The challenge is this: Can we contemplate a theological (and subsequent ethical) vision that takes seriously the experience of black people without incurring the narrow exclusivism that was indicative of so much of black theology in its classic stage? Is there a way of constructing a theology that is able to account for the singularity of the black religious experience without presuming that it has legitimate claims to exclusive normative status among other viable theologies? How can we account for the universality of God and the peculiar favor God bestows on human beings in the midst of their peculiar experiences? I believe that a way awaits us provided we reconcile these warring claims in a unified vision of a universal God and God's purpose and plan for African Americans as they seek a theological vision that can undergird their ethical consciousness.

Just as we encountered a paradox in the African American embrace of Christianity, another paradox emerges as we attempt to reconcile a notion of a God we seek. It appears that we can only come to understand God through the cultural structures we ourselves erect as long as we live as social beings. Yet we must always acknowledge that a vision of God we profess to

---

37. Ibid.

worship requires that we acknowledge the cultural perspectives as limited and finite. The very cultural structures through which we secure a vision of an unlimited God are themselves limited. Basically, the argument that I want to put forward is this: A fruitful way of conceiving of an African American theology and an attendant Christian ethic would be to always hold in tension the affirmation of a God *beyond* culture by persons inextricably grounded *in* culture.

Inevitably, we shall propose—to be worked more in detail in the next chapter—that an African American Christian ethic that aspires to intellectual integrity and moral consistency is one that posits a God conceived as the *ground of being* rather than a God of *personal being*. The latter notion of God tends to inevitably take on the idealized formulations of the believers in such a God, their prejudices as well as their values. Such a God becomes in fact the servant of the worshipers. At the same time, an African American Christian ethic would have to affirm that all human conceptions of God are culturally grounded for the fundamental reason that to be human is to be culturally grounded and anchored. Since this is true, no culture can presume to be superior or inferior to another.

For human beings, nothing can be more profound than to muse on the meaning of that without which no human striving is possible—the very notion of being itself. Fundamental to all enjoyment of life, all hope for attaining desirable goals in life, is a basic affirmation that the substance of life, the very being that undergirds life, has purpose and meaning. To attach meaning and purpose to the very fiber of being in one's life and to be fascinated by and enthralled with such being are fundamentally *religious* feelings. They are religious because only religion proposes and answers ultimate questions. Religion is whatever humans do when they seek to find meaning and purpose to their being. Religion is whatever human beings do when they seize the opportunity to muse upon the meaning of their being. Whatever means we devise to affirm the meaning of our being becomes the substance of our religion. All human life is oriented toward seeking fulfillment and the satisfaction of aims in accordance with a perceived ultimate meaning. Such ultimate meaning is necessarily lodged within a focus on being itself. On what else would the ultimate rest? (I am aware that the ultimate goal of Buddhism is to transmigrate away from being, but even there a means is devised to offer meaning within being, that is, the Fourfold Path). Thus to be human is ultimately to be concerned about the meaning of one's being. Since we have already defined religion as concern with meaning about being, and since all humans are oriented toward seeking meaning in their being, then it follows that to be human is to be religious in the basic sense of that term.

The devising of that by which we consider the meaning of our being has always been, and forever will be, hammered out in the crucible of culture.

Therefore, all cultures will be expected to devise different ways for affirming the meaning of being. This is not surprising. Since all cultures do this, and necessarily so, then no one culture can be considered normative for all and another deemed aberrant. In a real sense, all are *singular* since all will propose legitimate and slightly different means for considering the ultimate dimensions of being. These means may be different from all others, but all share the same *formal* tendency; that is, all share the same morphology of mechanisms by which meaning can be attached to being; only the content and specific details of each render each culture different.

All things human take place within the medium of human interaction known as culture. No idea is formulated, no ideal contemplated or aspired to, no norm established, except that it be formulated, contemplated, or established within that complex web of interactions. All human life takes place within the medium of human culture. There are no *culture-less* human beings. Human beings develop and exercise their being within the context of culture. In a very real sense this is not a profound observation, for we share it even with other animals, especially higher order primates.[38] Animals, human and otherwise, develop and exercise consciousness consistently and without cessation within the context of culture. All notions of custom and morality and all perceptions of the good are mediated through a matrix of human interactions. No ethic comes into being and prominence unless it comes out of a culture; it emerges from a culture and can never be seen apart from that culture out of which it springs.

Since all religions must evidence cultural mechanisms by which they affirm the meaning and purpose of being, it follows that all religions are mediated through the medium of culture. Where else would religion find an organic home except in the context of culture? (Even the solitary mystic is considered solitary *only* because she has spurned the culture of community. And to be sure, even the desert ascetics in early Christianity formed inevitably a "community" of solitary seekers.) Therefore, it would follow that religion must necessarily be a cultural phenomenon. Moreover, insofar as human beings live out their lives within their culture, they cannot help but be religious in Paul Tillich's understanding of this term. The essence of religion is acknowledging something of ultimate concern. Tillich asserts that "religion is not a special function of man's spiritual life, but it is the dimension of depth in *all* of its functions."[39] Thus, any separation of the

---

38. In a report issued in June 1999, a research team of nine prominent primatologists, including Jane Goodall and Frans B. M. de Waal, identified thirty-nine behaviors that vary in prevalence and style among seven chimpanzee communities in parts of West and East Africa. See *New York Times*, June 17, 1999.

39. Paul Tillich, *Theology of Culture* (London and New York: Oxford University Press, 1959), 5–6, emphasis added.

sacred from the secular is tragic and has no real foundation, for "both of them are rooted in religion in the larger sense of the word, in the experience of ultimate concern."[40]

So, to recapitulate, to be human is to be religious, and to be religious is to be cultural. No human being can remain a human being unless she successfully manages to find meaning and purpose in being itself. No human can remain human unless he participates in the cultural mechanisms that facilitate articulating the meaning in being itself; such mechanisms are necessarily provided through the medium of human culture. In other words, nothing can be more prior or primal for us as human beings, no matter our ethnic or racial identifications, than the issue of being itself and the issue of culture itself. We cannot conceive of what it means to be human apart from profound meditations of the meaning of being, always mediated through the vast array of human cultures.

Therefore, I am suggesting that we shift the groundwork for an African American Christian ethic away from notions that tend to yield distortions of God and justifications for racial and cultural exclusivism to ones that can truly support the absolute transcendence of God. I will suggest that we move from a notion of God as *personal being* to a God as *ground of being,* that without which being itself cannot be. Moreover, I will propose that we shift the focus from the *accidents* of cultural orientation (the peculiar aspects of particular cultures) to the *formal structure* of the cultural medium through which religious attempts to find meaning in being take place, which will enable us to perceive the singularity of any culture, without presuming that that culture should be considered normative for all human beings. Such an approach is indicative and representative without presuming to be absolutely normative and, therefore, exclusive.

In this book, I strive for a discussion that takes note of race but understands that race is a modern fiction, for the older and more secure way of looking at the world's peoples is to look at them through the prism of culture, not race. My thesis affirms that cultures are *singular* but never exclusively *normative.* Therefore, my treatment of African American culture and history as evidential of an African American Christian ethic will purport to be nothing short of an exposition of a singular cultural phenomenon. While this culture and ethic may be *exemplary* in terms of providing compelling examples to people of other cultures, I will never presume it to be a normative view for all the world's people. To this extent I face head-on the viability of the methodology of "Afrocentrism," and it is now to a critique of this method that we turn.

---

40. Ibid., 9.

Perhaps the scholar most associated with "Afrocentrism" is Molefi Kete Asante, chairman of the department of African American studies at Temple University. In three books, *Afrocentricity* (1980), *The Afrocentric Idea* (1987), and *Kete, Afrocentricity, and Knowledge* (1990), he has articulated the shape and contours of this idea. Quite rightly, Afrocentrism challenges the arrogance of Eurocentrism and Eurocentric views of knowledge and normative behavior and orientation. If the regnant way of looking at the world, of organizing and interpreting data through a Eurocentric orientation, is rejected, what should replace it? Asante's answer is Afrocentrism, which he defines as "primarily an orientation to data."[41] Such an orientation points to "a position, a location" from which one interprets and organizes the data around oneself in the world at large. To this extent, Asante and the Afrocentrists are in agreement with the commonsensical observation of the proponents of the sociology of knowledge when they assert that for human beings all perspectives on knowledge of the world reflect one's social location.[42] As Asante says, "The Afrocentric study of phenomenon asks pointed questions about location, place, orientation and perspective relative to any piece of human knowledge. This means that the data could come from any field or place and be examined Afrocentrically."[43]

All would agree that we organize and interpret data *according to* the position we occupy in a society or the social location in which we live in a culture. Knowledge is always perspectival in nature. But Asante seems to be rightfully aware of the precarious nature of such an epistemological enterprise: "Like scholars in other disciplines, Afrocentrists are exposed to the hazards of place and position. We can never be sure that our place is as secure as we want it to be, but we do the best we can with the resources of mind at our disposal. Moreover, this perspective is not excluded to those who might not share the same skin color or race as African peoples."[44] Does Asante believe that shared perspectives can transcend racial categories and ethnic identity as perspectives for organizing data? Surprisingly so, it would appear. He says at one point, "Afrocentricity is not a matter of color but of perspective, that is, orientation to facts."[45] But the problem is this: how can orientation to data be separated from color, or at least the shared history and culture that shared color has produced? Isn't this like presuming that a person can really share the existential condition of blindness by simply

---

41. Molefi Kete Asante, "Afrocentric Systematics," *Black Issues in Higher Education,* August 13, 1992, 16.

42. See Peter Berger and Thomas Luckmann, *The Social Construction of Reality: A Treatise in the Sociology of Knowledge* (Garden City, N.Y.: Anchor Books, 1966). See also Werner Stark, *The Sociology of Knowledge* (London: Routledge & Kegan Paul, 1958).

43. Asante, "Afrocentric Systematics," 17.

44. Ibid.

45. Ibid.

putting on a blindfold? Does Asante really believe that Eurocentrists or persons from any other cultural perspective can suddenly and miraculously become Afrocentrists and share the same "orientation to facts"? He *must* believe this, or he would not have declared that "Afrocentricity is not a matter of color." Rather than affirming forthrightly that indeed Afrocentrism is exclusive, even as the term implies, Asante feigns a universalism, which upon closer inspection simply does not hold up to scrutiny.

That problem aside, Asante admits that the view of the world that emerges from the Afrocentric perspective is qualitatively better than the perspective of someone who looks at data from another perspective. Quoting him:

> The historian, sociologist, psychologist and political scientist may examine the Battle of Gettysburg and see different elements and aspects because of the different emphases of the disciplines. In a similar manner, the Afrocentrist would look at the Civil War or any phenomenon involving African people and raise different questions than the Eurocentrist. These questions are not more or less correct but *better* in an interpretive sense if the person doing the asking wants to understand African phenomena in context.[46]

But if the Afrocentric perspective is better, then it must be more correct; if not, what then would "better" mean? Unless "better" connotes that one perspective is epistemologically more reliable than another, then the notion of it is rendered useless. Asante has also said, "Afrocentrists have always said that our perspective on data is only one among many and, consequently, the viewpoint, if you will, seeks no advantage, no self-aggrandizement and no hegemony."[47] But how can these two assertions be correct at the same time? That is to say, how can one assert that the perspective of Afrocentricity is *better* than other perspectives and at the same assert that it is merely *only one among many*? A more modest claim might simply assert that the Afrocentrist view is a *singular* claim among all of the other singular claims from other cultures and perspectives, as our own present methodology is suggesting.

Another issue arises from the thought of Asante that goes to the viability of the method he uses. His theory tells us what Afrocentrism does, but it does not tell us exactly *how* it does it: "Everything must be run through the sieve of doubt until one hits the bedrock of truth. Our methods, based on the idea of African centeredness, are meant to establish a clear pattern of

---

46. Ibid.
47. Ibid., 21.

discourse that may be followed by others."[48] How does this method work? If the "bedrock of truth" is encountered, how can this be known conclusively if it has already been admitted that one is confronting data from only *one* of the perspectives available to humans? Is Asante therefore an epistemological absolutist, whose method if pursued in the context of a particular cultural orientation would necessarily make him a cultural chauvinist? Has he not merely traded the arrogance of Eurocentrism for the arrogance of Afrocentrism? I fear that Afrocentrism has inherently the same fatal flaw as Eurocentrism: the tendency to regard one's own limited perspective as absolute and normative for all human beings. The one thing for which we should be grateful to the Afrocentrism school of thought is that it has freed us from the hegemony of Eurocentrism. Asante should be hailed as a thinker who helped us in championing a perspective that allows Africans and persons in the African diaspora "to be subjects of historical experiences rather than the objects of racist Eurocentric perspectives."[49]

As the reader might discern from the foregoing discussion, the framework for this book seeks to affirm the absoluteness of God while at the same time acknowledging the limitations of the cultural lenses through which we have a vision of God, a theme that we explore in depth in chapter 2. Thus a theological absolutism must be joined to a cultural relativism. Moreover, as a Christian, I must also affirm the doctrines that uphold the work of Christ and the Holy Spirit in the life of the Christian and, as will be discussed, within the historical journey of African Americans. Thus chapters 3 and 4 respectively will seek to discover who and what Christ is for African American ethical consciousness and how the Holy Spirit functions in ethical discernment.

Part 2 examines how the four classic sources for a Christian ethic might be viewed within the African American historical and cultural framework. These classic sources for a Christian ethic are Holy Scripture, tradition, human nature, and reason. Each will demand a careful analysis of the ways in which African Americans have appropriated scripture, wrestled with the demands of their ecclesiastical traditions, pondered the perplexities of human experience, and sought clarity of thought in their affirmations about the reality of God in their lives. Such musings have been and continue to be a source of great fascination and wonder for the believer.

Finally, Part 3 offers reflections on ways in which the foundations and sources give shape to ethical responses to particular contexts within the African American community. Chapter 9 looks at sexuality, commitment, and family life. Chapter 10 focuses on the topics of medicine and bioethics. Chapter 11 explores the pursuit of justice in the court system, the work-

---

48. Ibid., 17.
49. Ibid., 16.

place, and the voting booth. Besides addressing issues of critical concern to the African American community, these chapters offer examples of how individuals within the context of community may draw on the foundations and sources of the Christian faith to decide on courses of responsible action in the world. Faithfully responding to such issues is at the core of our calling as Christians and gives impetus to this work, which attempts to establish a framework for ethical response from the African American perspective.

2

God as the Ground of Being

In the LORD GOD
you have an everlasting rock.
—Isaiah 26:4

My God is a rock in a weary land.
—American Negro spiritual

A theological foundation for a Christian ethic must at the very minimum answer satisfactorily two major concerns. First, it must profess that which must necessarily be God, that which is prior and fundamental to all reality. That is, the theological foundation must answer a fundamental question about *being* by exploring the nature and ground of reality and how God is understood in relation to reality. Second, the foundation must address in a satisfactory manner the problem of *moral evil* insofar as such evil impinges upon the lives of human beings and all of creation. It is not so much an issue of seeking to avoid evil as it is to understand its nature, origins, and ways by which its power might be mitigated. This chapter will seek to propose a notion of God that can serve as the theological foundation for an African American Christian ethic. In so doing, I will necessarily have to address the questions of the nature of God and the nature of moral evil. Both issues are joined in the consideration of the notion of *theodicy,* the attempt to reconcile the goodness of God with the persistence of moral evil. All of this we must do as we attempt to formulate a Christian ethic for African Americans.

Long before we were, God was, and long after we shall have gone, God will be. We encounter God when we come into existence, but God remains after we return to dust. Such are the sentiments of the religious person as he or she might reflect on the nature of God. Indeed, such have been the sentiments of human beings from prehistory, through ancient times, until even today, as men and women seek to articulate whom they are talking about and what they mean when they speak of God. But for the reflective person, there are problems when one seeks to really understand what is meant when persons speak of God. To what are people referring when they speak of God? On what basis, rational or otherwise, can human beings affirm the existence of the Divine? What constitutes "evidence" for the existence of God? Need evidence, in the conventional sense, be necessary to plausibly affirm the existence of God? All of these, and more, are among the dazzling and perplexing questions that come to mind when we begin to ponder the question of God.

From the dawn of human civilizations, human beings have displayed a strong fascination with the world around them that was unseen, mysterious, and transcendent. That world was infused with spirits, or certainly infused with a quality of existence that could be regarded as spiritual. The world of the spiritual was qualitatively different from the world of the mundane. Moreover, it was in such a world that deities and gods lived and had their being. Thus spiritual beings shared in the same existential reality as deities and gods. Ancient peoples have always maintained a close relationship with either one deity or many gods that have helped explain order in the cosmos and the purpose and meaning of human life and existence. The many peoples of the African continent are to be counted among the world's ancient peoples. A rich mosaic of cultures and peoples, steeped deeply in time, comprise the African continent. Persons of African descent have named that divine mystery that undergirds yet transcends life by many names: *nyama,* Allah, God. The various names by which people of color have identified this mysterious wholly Other Presence is a testimony not only to the utter pervasiveness of God but also to the spiritually rich cultures among people of color that have affirmed the power and presence of the Divine.

The present task is to propose a theological orientation for a uniquely African American Christian ethic. In chapter 1, I set forth the broad outlines of such an orientation and proposed that an African American Christian ethic could avoid the cultural exclusivism inherent in cultural centrism if it focused on a God of *ground of being* rather than a God of *personal being.* But any exploration into the nature of God must be done so within the context of the mediating power of culture and the singularity of a people's history. All products of human consciousness, including religion and theology, must be considered within the context of human culture. Theological musings always take place at the intersection of a perception of mystery and the values and intellectual framework available in one's culture.

Theology is literally "a word about God." It is that and it is more. Theology, as practiced within the academy and the church, is a rigorous intellectual and spiritual inquiry into the nature of God. How can we account for the existence of God and prove it? As we seek to develop a thesis that an African American theology would do well to focus on a notion of God as ground of being rather than a notion of God as personal being, we start exactly where the ancients started, that is, with an inquiry into the origin and nature of the cosmos. After all it was probably speculation about how the cosmos, or the heavens, came to be that sparked the first speculation about the nature and existence of God anyway.

COSMOLOGY AND THE SEARCH FOR GOD: TWO WARRING TRADITIONS

There are currently two warring theories about the origin of the universe or cosmos: the steady state theory and the big bang theory. The former holds that the universe has always existed and always will exist. According to the latter, somewhere between 15 and 20 billion years ago the cosmos began with a gigantic explosion, the effects of which we are still observing, as cosmic bodies travel away from each other at faster and faster rates. If the universe is expanding, the reasoning goes, it is proof of an initial explosion that sent all elements of the cosmos reeling outward.

In a similar way, Christian theology has inherited and attempted to in-corporate into its vision and methodologies at various times and levels two warring thought systems: the Greek, or Hellenistic, and the Hebraic-Judaic. The desire among Christian thinkers to insure a suitable measure of rational-ity in theological discourse has been satisfied to some extent by appeals to the Greek inheritance. The affirmation that any credible notion of God must affirm God's will and action made evident in human history has always been indebted to the Hebraic-Judaic tradition.

Both streams of thought and religious consciousness have fed and nour-ished Christian thinking and theology, but the admixture has not always been an easy or harmonious one. Fissures and fault lines are apparent to this day. In an effort to secure the absoluteness of God, the Hellenistic as-pect of Christian heritage affirmed the utter perfection and immutability of God. The Platonic ideal was the vehicle used to put God on a lofty plane of contemplation. God's utter transcendence was also assured, with God's now having been raised to a level of existence quite beyond the changing imper-fections of the material world. The major difficulty, however, with such a God was virtual inaccessibility to human affairs and human history. As if anticipating this critical flaw in a conception of God, the Hebrews of the an-cient Near East were determined to conceive of their God as one that would be able to engage them in the oftentimes messy terrain of human history. Moreover, the Hebraic-Judaic religious consciousness affirmed a personal aspect of the divine being. Conceived in virtually humanlike terms, particu-larly the Yahwist conception of God in the Old Testament, this consciousness has the Creator walking in the garden in the book of Genesis, even displaying anger and compassion as human beings do; this God seems to have feelings, including love and hatred, as humans have.[1]

In a very real sense, the two major traditions that have informed Christian theological discourse, the Hellenistic and the Hebraic, can be paired with the two warring traditional explanations for the nature of the cosmos. On the one hand, classical Greek philosophy, beginning specifically with the pre-Socratics, particularly Anaximander, affirmed an explanatory principle of all things, the *apeiron*, as "indefinite and without beginning," which would account for all things in the world that come to be.[2] Once having come into being, matter would be eternal. On the other hand, the Judeo-Christian tradition categorically rejected the earlier view and affirmed that time and matter had a specific beginning and would have a specific end. The two are juxtaposed, ever in conflict, and therein lies a tension that continues to manifest itself in various theological problems that persist to this day.

Traditional personal-being theism, the belief that God is a being and has personal attributes not unlike those of human characters, has staked its life, if you will, on the credibility of the big bang theory. Despite our protestations that faith has no need of science to justify the claims of faith, the scientific suggestion that the universe "started" gives reassuring comfort to those who have pressed their belief that there was a beginning at which time God started the universe. The Christian doctrine that has traditionally articulated this hallmark of faith is the notion of *creatio ex nihilo*—creation out of nothing—but it is not without problems.

First of all is the issue of the actual biblical text upon which the doctrine of creation ex nihilo was based. The first two verses of the creation story recorded in Genesis 1 from the pen of the so-called Priestly writer (actually the later of the two versions, the other appearing in Genesis 2:4ff. from the so-called Yahwist writer) reads:

> In the beginning when God created the heavens and the earth, the earth was a formless void and darkness covered the face of the deep, while a wind from God swept over the face of the waters. (Gen. 1:1–2)

Now clearly within the imagination of the writer are two important elements that bespeak preexisting matter: (1) the earth is without form but is still a distinguishable entity, perhaps amorphous, unshaped, but nevertheless existing; and (2) the Spirit of God moves over the face of the waters.

Did waters exist prior to creation? Defenders of the ex nihilo thesis will protest that this is merely a reference to the Hebraic tendency to associate

---

1. See Genesis 3:8.
2. Richard H. Popkin, ed., *The Columbia History of Western Philosophy* (New York: Columbia University Press, 1999), 7.

water with formlessness and chaos. But if this is the case, then why not consider the whole story as a symbolic rendering of God's power to act in creation and nothing more? Are the claims inherent in the doctrine of creation ex nihilo much more ambitious than either the language or the author intended? At best the language is ambivalent, clearly poetic, in an attempt to account for the creation of an ordered and orderly universe, as opposed to the formless void that the Creator God confronted.

Christian theology puts forth a great deal of effort in carefully analyzing the symbols and words and concepts that the faithful use as they attempt to come to terms with the reality known as God. It is no surprise that Christian theologies would come to use special words and assign special meanings to some words that nonbelievers use as well. The word "nothing" is such a word. What does the foregoing say about the veracity of the assertion *creatio ex nihilo*? Can God actually be an exnihilator,[3] or one who is able to create out of nothing? Or are we obliged to understand "nothing" in a special sense, as Christian theologies have perforce been obliged to do?

Many Christian theologians seem to have understood the word "nothing" in a special sense. Take, for example, Daniel L. Migliore's explication of creation ex nihilo: "According to classical Christian doctrine, God creates *ex nihilo*, 'out of nothing.' 'Nothing' is not primordial stuff out of which the world was created. Created 'out of nothing' means that God alone is the source of all that exists. The creation of the world is an act of sovereign freedom."[4] Now clearly, this is a specialized way of talking about "nothing" and "creation." What is being conveyed is the unshakable Christian affirmation that God is the source of all that exists and the one whose creative power defies human imagination and logic. Behind this intentional use of a specialized notion of creation, behind the assertion that God creates out of nothing, behind all of these assertions, is an unabashed rejection of pagan Greek thought.

Classical Greek thought affirmed the notion of the permanence of matter. If Christian thought was to be successful in declaring emancipation from such thinking, then a radically different way of understanding how God relates to created matter was required. The notion of creation ex nihilo meets this requirement and should be understood as such within this context. The doctrine itself, therefore, is an attempt, not to describe processes within the physical world, but to make affirmations pertinent to the metaphysical realm, the realm that undergirds being itself. The doctrine is an attempt to describe the awesome creative power of God and thus is best articulated

---

3. This is a term coined by Mortimer J. Adler, *How to Think about God* (New York: Collier Books, 1980), 34.

4. Daniel L. Migliore, *Faith Seeking Understanding: An Introduction to Christian Theology* (Grand Rapids: Eerdmans, 1991), 84.

through the use of metaphor, poetry, or some specialized kind of language that Christian theology employs. I believe this is exactly what has happened, thus the mystery and ambiguity with which God is seen in the biblical account of creation. The biblical account was not meant to offer a matter of fact or scientific account of how time and cosmos began. It was meant to affirm the ineffable mystery and power of a transcendent God.

Second is the issue of the development of the doctrine itself. The first Christian writer to conceive of the idea of creation ex nihilo was Clement of Alexandria, and he did so as a definitive rebuke of pagan cosmogony reflected in Plato's *Timaeus* (although according to Jaroslav Pelikan, Clement himself was indebted to the *Timaeus* for much of his thinking on the cosmos). Clement accused the pagan philosophers of "deifying the universe." Instead of "seeking the Creator of the universe," these philosophers needed to be told that "the sheer volition [of God] is the making of the universe. For God alone made it, because he alone is God in his being. By his sheer act of will he creates; and after he has merely willed, it follows that things come into being."[5]

Clement's contemporary Tertullian went even further in elaborating this notion of creation ex nihilo in his *Against Hermogenes*. Conceding that creation out of nothing was not explicitly stated in the Bible but only implied, Tertullian argued—from silence— that "if God could make all things out of nothing, Scripture could well omit to add that he had made them out of nothing, but it should have said by all means that he had made them out of matter, if he had done so; for the first possibility would be completely understandable, even if it was not expressly stated, but the second would be doubtful unless it was stated."[6] Such a suggestion would have been doubtful for Tertullian because in his mind a God coequal with matter was unthinkable; moreover, there would always be the problem of evil. How could a God conquer evil or keep it in check if such a God was only equal to the matter from which evil emanated? Tertullian's God had to be transcendent to nature and reality, and if transcendent, then there was every possibility, even if unstated explicitly in the biblical text, that God had created the universe out of nothing. This bold affirmation had to be made if Christian faith was to declare any independence from Greek pagan thought.

The doctrine of creation ex nihilo appears therefore to be quite problematic. It does not enjoy a sound biblical foundation. Neither can it be said to rest on sound reasoning about the nature of the universe and reality.

---

5. Clement of Alexandria *Protrepticus*, or *Exhortation to the Greeks*, 4.63.3; quoted in Jaroslav Pelikan, *The Christian Tradition: A History of the Development of Doctrine*, vol. 1, *The Emergence of the Catholic Tradition (100–600)* (Chicago: University of Chicago Press, 1971), 36.

6. Pelikan, *The Christian Tradition*, 1:36.

The doctrine appears to be a statement of faith, a faith that was born in the midst of an intense struggle with pagan philosophical thought. While therefore the doctrine of creation ex nihilo may not enjoy a sound biblical foundation, and seems to be repugnant to reason, for the believer it conveys a statement of faith that God's freedom and love are so great that God *could* create the cosmos out of nothing. Thus, of the two warring versions of the origin of the cosmos, the Hebraic-oriented version would secure affirmation for the Christian, but only by virtue of the prerogative of faith. But before conceding this point entirely, let us shift the perspective slightly.

A POSSIBLE SYNTHESIS OF COSMOLOGIES?

Perhaps the two cosmologies are not antithetical in nature at all. Indeed, upon further thought I would argue that the two theories may not be mutually exclusive—one precluding the other. The steady state theory assumes that matter and time are eternal and that they have always existed and always will. The big bang theory affirms that time and matter, or at least the time-space continuum, began at a cataclysmic moment, after which the universe came into being. In a real sense, the big bang theory may not have the power to suggest conclusively that time or space did not exist prior to the cosmic explosion that set the universe into motion, that there was *nothing* prior to the big bang. What may be more safely asserted is that the human ability *to know* the state of things prior to the big bang is finite, not that time and space are finite and limited to the moment when the big bang occurred.

Even assuming that we could one day know conclusively what the state of matter and time was at the occurrence of the big bang, we would still be left with the inescapable conclusion that *something* happened at the big bang. If something happened or exploded, then how can we still say that *nothing* existed prior to it? Thus it might well have been that the big bang occurred within the context of a universe that is, cosmically speaking, always in a steady state. But even with this attempt to reconcile the two cosmologies, we are left with the perfectly reasonable and rational assertion that if something exploded, then we can never credibly argue that creation occurred out of nothing, as the doctrine of *creatio ex nihilo* asserts. The conclusion therefore is that *some thing* has always existed.[7]

The notion of a personal-being God cannot enjoy much credibility if it relies on the coherence of the doctrine of creation ex nihilo. If the idea of a finite universe is dispelled, as the incoherence of creation ex nihilo would imply, then another classic argument for the existence of God, the

---

7. For a fuller discussion of the problems of the doctrine of creation, see Colin E. Gunton, *The Triune Creator: A Historical and Systematic Study* (Grand Rapids: Eerdmans, 1998).

ontological argument, becomes tenuous as well. This argument, first articulated by Anselm with subsequent similar arguments for the existence of
God expounded by Thomas Aquinas, was based in large measure on the
presumption of such a finite universe, a universe that is alien to the steady
state theory. Foundational to Anselm's philosophical work was a posture
grounded on a deep faith in what he perceived to be the indisputable reality
of God. Belief in God was prior to rational knowledge about God. Anselm
intensely believed *in order that* he would one day understand the dynamics
of faith. He did not seek to understand that he would believe; rather he
believed in order that he would understand.

A great irony of course is that Anselm developed an argument for the existence of God that depended, not upon the certainties derived from human
experience, but upon the certainty of preexistential reason, or a priori logic.
Anselm pushes us to contemplate a being "than which none greater can be
conceived." Anselm conceded that it is of course possible to entertain a notion of God in our minds that does not comport with reality in the actual
world around us. Thus a person can hold in her mind the notion of such
a being, the *idea* of God in her mind, but still not believe in God as that
supreme being. Thus an object might exist in one's mind but still not have a
reality independent of one's mind. But Anselm insists that such a God that
exists only in the mind or that could *possibly* exist cannot be greater than
God as God *actually* exists.[8] God must be incapable of *not* existing. Thus we
are back to Anselm's original assertion: the God of mere idea or possibility
proving no match for the God of actuality.

One soon suspects that the suppleness of Anselm's argument just might
be the source of a possible flaw. Aside from our deep faith, how can we be
certain that what we *think* to be this God *is* this actual being "than which
none greater can be conceived"? It would appear that all that Anselm has
done is simply juxtapose two conceptions of God, one as idea and the other
as actual, and simply presume that the latter has greater ontological weight
than the former. Anselm is forced into this problematic if he is intent on
proving that God exists as a being within the cosmos of other beings.

Thomas Aquinas's Five Arguments for the existence of God likewise are
grounded in an attempt to prove God's existence as a being. Taking his inspiration from the thought of Aristotle, especially the latter's notion of the
Unmoved Mover, as spelled out in the *Metaphysics* (bk. 8), Aquinas attempts
to prove the existence of God through appeals to motion, causation of existence, the ideas of contingent and necessary objects, degrees and perfection,
and the argument from intelligent design. The argument from motion presumes that the natural state of all bodies is rest; that is, all bodies except one

---

8. Anselm *Proslogion*, chap. 2.

need another body to move them in order for them to in fact move. That one body that needs none other to move it is the Unmoved Mover, or God. The argument from causation is similar in that it presumes that no object creates itself. The one thing that is uncaused but still *is,* is God. The third argument, contingent and necessary objects, builds on the first two in that a distinction is made between a being that cannot exist without a necessary being causing its existence (contingent beings) and a necessary being, or one that must exist for all of the other contingent beings to exist. The argument from degrees and perfection gets its inspiration from the human propensity to make distinctions between a notion of absolute perfection of any quality and the discernment of the lack of perfection, or degrees toward perfection. God becomes the notion of absolute perfection. Finally, the argument from intelligent design presumes that the cosmos has an inherent order and that some intelligent designer or architect must have put shape and order to it.

Aquinas's arguments from motion, causation of existence, and contingent and necessary beings make sense only if a fixed and limited cosmos is presumed. The arguments presume a philosophical system and ontology consistent with a cosmos begun by creation ex nihilo; the cosmos was limited, fixed, and finite. After the infinite retrogression presumed in all three arguments, the cosmos will inevitably reach an end. Within such a finite cosmos, we are perfectly justified in seeking the causes for effects, for in such a framework there can be no uncaused effects. Every effect must have a cause behind it. We are even justified in tracing, through ultimate retrogression, all of the causes of all the effects until we get to the Ultimate Cause of everything that is. The notion of an uncaused cause, or an Unmoved Mover in Aristotle's and Aquinas's argument, makes sense only in the context of a finite universe. Moreover, the argument from motion makes sense only if we presume that rest is the natural state of bodies, but it should be clear that this presumption reflected the scientific certainty of earlier ages and cannot enjoy credibility today. We now understand that all of matter is constantly in flux, characterized by a dizzying whirl of atoms, electrons, and other subatomic particles.

THE PROBLEM OF PERSONAL-BEING THEISM AND MORAL EVIL

The notion of personal-being theism suffers as well when we assess the issue of moral evil and attempt to address that problem within the context of personal-being theism. The issue will ultimately come down to whether we can adequately square the notion of a personal, loving God with the existence of moral evil in the world. Does personal-being theism afford us adequate moral consistency and integrity of God as God deals with humankind in the midst of suffering when evil is present? Does the divine command theory of human morality, which is itself based on personal-being theism, suffer from moral inconsistency? These and other related questions we now seek to address.

Behind the questions we have just raised is the age-old question of the relationship between religion and morality, indeed between theology and ethics in some sense. Do we need God to be good? Can we be good without God? Plato raises the question of the relationship between morality and religion in an intriguing way in his dialogue called *Euthyphro*. After Euthyphro seems intent on prosecuting the alleged killers of his father on manslaughter charges, Socrates senses an opportunity to examine the very foundation for moral judgments. At one point, he asks a seemingly innocuous question, "Is the pious being loved by the gods because it is pious, or is it pious because it is being loved by the gods?"[9] In the particular confines of the dialogue, the question posed is whether God commands what is good *because it is good* or whether the good is good *because God commands it*. Or to put it another way, which is prior, the good or God? Behind the question is whether religion is necessarily the foundation for ethics or whether ethics is autonomous from religion.

Either way we answer these questions involves problems. If we presume that a thing is good *because* it is good, we run the risk of affirming that a thing's goodness can be established apart from God, in other words, that the good is prior to God. If we presume that a thing is good because God *commands* it, the essence of the divine command theory, we run the risk of admitting that God is arbitrary in designating those things deemed to be good. Why is this thing so deemed as opposed to that? The first problem suggests that God is not omnipotent; the second suggests that God is arbitrary, possibly inconsistent, and thus subject to moral imperfection.

Plato took the position that religion must serve morality, rather than the opposite. If a thing is good because the gods say so, then the gods are vulnerable to attacks of being arbitrary and hence less than beings that could legitimately be regarded as divine and perfect. In fact, there is a civil war going on among the gods; they cannot even agree as to what is good. The suggestion is quite clear with Plato that the gods ought to be subsumed under the good. But even among Christian thinkers some have insisted that God must be subsumed under the notion of the good; that is to say, the good is prior to God's divinity. Aquinas, for example, maintained that certain kinds of action are divinely prohibited *because* they are wrong, rather than because God prohibits them. William of Ockham, on the other hand, has been interpreted to say that rightness simply means, or is equivalent to, "com-

---

9. Plato *Euthyphro*, in *Plato: Complete Works*, edited with introduction and notes by John M. Cooper (Indianapolis: Hackett, 1997), 10a.

manded by God."[10] Continuing in that tradition, Franklin I. Gamwell, in *The Divine Good: Modern Moral Theory and the Necessity of God*, argues that moral theory must affirm the reality of a transcendent being, which is the bedrock of our notions of morality despite the modern consensus that has affirmed the autonomy of morality from religion in the aftermath of the Enlightenment, particularly in the work of Immanuel Kant.[11]

Clearly, a way must be found that preserves the moral consistency and integrity inherent in the autonomy of ethics from religion as well as acknowledges the necessity of God in theological and ethical discourse. I believe there is a way for theists to affirm the priority of goodness as opposed to the arbitrariness of God inherent in the divine command theory. This way is to affirm that God is simply the ground of being and will be consistently good since God's goodness conforms to that which can never change, that is, the good. It is the very nature of God to conform to this standard, this norm. The good is obviously inherent in being (surely not in not-being!). Since God is the ground of being and since the good is inherent in being, the question of who creates good is either moot, unanswerable, or irrelevant. The good simply is an inherent and necessary aspect of being. As long as the good is inherently grounded in being and as long as God is the ground of being, then the good cannot be considered apart from God, and neither can God be considered apart from the good. God's power is limited therefore to being and acting within the limits of the good. There are some things that God simply cannot do: examples being making squares circular, not being, or lying. God is therefore limited in that God cannot violate rules of logic or violate the moral constraints of goodness. The theist could therefore limit God's so-called omnipotence but would grant what might be called an epistemological advantage to God by affirming God's omniscience.[12] God always knows what is right since the ground of being is foundational to the right or the good. Furthermore, it would be perfectly reasonable to grant omniscience to God since all humans can safely assume that for God to be God, God must know more than our finite minds know.

Perhaps the only reason for discussing the nature of God along the lines I have raised is because the issue of God's relationship to human beings lies in the balance. (It should be stated quite quickly that God is in relationship to the whole created order, not only to human beings.) But the relationship with humanity is a special one since human beings alone within the created

---

10. Gene Outka and John P. Reeder Jr., eds., *Religion and Morality: A Collection of Essays* (Garden City, N.Y.: Anchor Books, 1973), 1.

11. Franklin I. Gamwell, *The Divine Good: Modern Moral Theory and the Necessity of God* (Dallas: Southern Methodist University Press, 1990).

12. Louis P. Pojman, *Ethics: Discovering Right and Wrong*, 3d ed. (Belmont, Calif.: Wadsworth, 1999), 195.

order show evidence of having a consciousness that enables them to be in relationship with each other and also with a transcendent reality, namely, God. Christian theology affirms the gift of consciousness and the gift of free will, even if these gifts are shrouded in a profound and tragic ambiguity about life, as intimated in the story of the expulsion from the garden. Only after disobeying God were the prototypical first humans' eyes opened, and they became aware of themselves as creatures that should be ashamed. This is consciousness—consciousness of being other than God and juxtaposed to God and consciousness of ourselves in juxtaposition to each other. Ironically in this primordial and paradigmatic instance, this misuse of freedom brought about our consciousness of ourselves as beings separated from God, and therefore as beings in need of restored relationship with God.

The critical issue of this discussion is the existence and persistence of moral evil in the world. What are we to make of the problem of evil in the face of our attempts to affirm not only that God exists but that we may believe *in* God? And how do such attempts square with the beliefs in a personal-being God? Aside from natural disasters, which should never be considered *moral* evils, humankind is subject to a variety of frailties, ills, imperfections, and unforeseen mishaps. Then too, there are the unspeakable evils that humans visit upon each other, particularly during times of war—the atrocities, the planned genocide. There is also the evil that appears amongst us in daily life—the rapes, the wanton taking of human life by enraged and hate-filled persons. As David Hume somberly observed, "Man is the greatest enemy of man. Oppression, injustice, contempt, contumely, violence, sedition, war, calumny, treachery, fraud; by these they mutually torment each other."[13]

Any moral evil that exists in the world, I am suggesting, is a result of the misuse of human freedom, not anything that God has done. God cannot do evil; it is impossible for the One who is the ground of being, the One that conforms to the very essence of the good, to do anything but the good, certainly not evil. Natural disasters are not to be considered moral evils; no choice on the part of God is involved in the occurrence of hurricanes, tornadoes, earthquakes, or the like. Their explanations may be found in a confluence of air currents and geological fault lines. And to be sure these phenomena conform to natural laws inherent in being itself. Even God does not, would not, and indeed cannot repeal the laws of gravity, thermodynamics, and the like.

Only in the moral world, the moral order, where wills are called into play may we properly speak of the action of God. Since God can only be good

---

13. David Hume, *Dialogues concerning Natural Religion* (New York: Oxford University Press, 1993), 97.

and has no alternative upon which to be and act, it follows that God's will cannot be other than in conformity to the good. In this sense, God is not free to be other than wholly good. We, on the other hand, have the burden of choice, the burden of responsibility to act. And it is precisely in the misuse of the freedom that we have been given by virtue of our creation that evil in the world is to be explained. To understand the presence of evil, look for no angry God, no devil or antichrist running amok. No, evil may be placed at our doorsteps because of the misuse of our freedom. In fact, I would argue that the problem of theodicy will forever remain insoluble as long as the issue of human culpability in the creation of moral evil is not adequately addressed.

BEYOND PERSONAL-BEING THEISM

Contemporary theology seems to be offering many interesting options with regard to the cogency of personal-being theism. Paul Tillich, of course, argued that God should be considered, not as another being within being, but rather as the ground of being.[14] Gordan Kaufman, in his summation of his life's work as a theologian, *In the Face of Mystery*, seems to affirm that the personal-being notion of God cannot be squared with our views of the cosmos. Kaufman urges us to conceive of a cosmic evolutionary-historical process that characterizes or pervades all reality. In this cosmos is a significant amount of creativity, a manifestation of which is the creation of human historical existence and human consciousness. The latter phenomena have not eventuated due to some absurdity in the evolution of the cosmos; the evolution of humanity and human consciousness has somehow been embedded in the very nature of how things are. The mystery that accounts for this creative process in the cosmos is that which Kaufman chooses to call God. Thus for Kaufman, God is not some personal being outside of the cosmos creating it but is the mystery of all that comes into being in that cosmos. God can therefore be seen, not as some being over and against the cosmos, but as critical to the mystery of creation within the cosmos.[15]

James Gustafson challenges the notion that a God of personal agency alone can claim support in scripture.[16] After reflecting on the age-old issues of cosmology and their import on theological consciousness, Paul Brockelman has come to conclude that God can be experienced in astonishment and

---

14. Paul Tillich, *Systematic Theology*, 3 vols. (New York: Harper & Row, 1967).

15. Gordon Kaufman, *In the Face of Mystery* (Cambridge: Harvard University Press, 1993), 60–61.

16. James Gustafson, "Alternative Conceptions of God," in *The God Who Acts: Philosophical and Theological Explorations*, ed. Thomas F. Tracy (University Park: Pennsylvania State University Press, 1994), 63–74.

wonder precisely as the "sheer actuality or existence of things, a mysterious, creative force throughout the universe that is apprehended in and through the manifold of everything that is."[17]

Thus human beings experience a sense of awe and wonder whenever we intuit that being itself has a transcendence about it—that the essence of being is more than is-ness of particular beings, like cats, antelopes, our selves, even gods. God is quite transcendent to *beings* but quite immanent in *being* itself. Personal-being theism always runs the risk of regarding God as another being within being; ground-of-being theism rightly regards God as beyond beings but wholly the ground of all that exists. I am not proposing simply a reassertion of classical pantheism, that is, the belief that God is simply all that we behold in the world. I am rather proposing that God is the ground of being, that which undergirds with being itself and that without which being cannot be or continue to be. Such is God.

TOWARD AN AFRICAN AMERICAN CONCEPT OF GOD FOR CHRISTIAN ETHICS

The conception of God that we need in African American Christian ethics is one that can provide assurance of a God that is unambiguously good but also one that can affirm divine intent in human history to vindicate the oppressed in the singularity of their experience. In a sense, we are seeking to steer clear of the distortions to which theology is prone when it accentuates one of the two heritages—the Greek or the Hebraic—to the exclusion of the other. Just as no credible theodicy can emerge as long as an exclusive notion of personal-being theism prevails, the inheritance from Hebraic consciousness; so no credible God of history can emerge as long as God is held captive to the abstract forms of Platonic idealism. On the one hand, God must be available to human historical consciousness, even to the singularity of particular historical moments and to the cultural manifestations of human beings. On the other hand, God must be rescued from the fate of arbitrariness, of which the God of personal-being theism and the divine command theory is so prone.

A theological vision for an African American Christian ethic would do well to affirm a notion of God as the ground of being in order to avoid the moral inconsistency inherent in the divine command theory and the

---

17. Paul Brockelman, *Cosmology and Creation: The Spiritual Significance of Contemporary Cosmology* (New York: Oxford University Press, 1999), 82. For some penetrating essays on cosmology and theological argumentation, see William Lane Craig and Quentin Smith, *Theism, Atheism, and Big Bang Cosmology* (Oxford: Clarendon Press, 1993); and Christopher Southgate et al., eds., *God, Humanity, and the Cosmos* (Harrisburg, Pa.: Trinity Press International, 1999).

conceptual poverty of personal-being theism. Personal-being theism, it has been shown, can easily be appropriated by cultural and racial exclusionists, thereby legitimizing the very racism of which black people have for too long been victims. There is little to be gained, morally and intellectually, by incorporating such a view of God into an African American Christian ethic. Further, any credible solution to the problem of theodicy must come to terms with the presumption of the misuse of human freedom, rather than the impotence or indifference of God. The ultimate goal in this chapter is to document this thesis within the rich body of oral literature including Negro spirituals and sermons. But getting there requires us to consider the religious consciousness of West African cultures, the cultural moorings from whence came the forebears of African Americans.

From African to African American Religious Consciousness

African societies had developed highly sophisticated cosmologies and theologies well before contact with the Europeans who would seek to destabilize these societies and enslave their members, and then go on to justify such enslavement on theological and religious grounds. Virtually all societies from which the enslaved came conceived of the Divine as pervasive throughout the entire realm of reality. In Ashanti religion *nyama* is that force that is basic to all reality; it, and it alone, undergirds all reality; it is the ground of all being. That a close relationship exists between *nyama*, the ground of all being, and the High God is seen in the name for the latter, Nyame, which is clearly a cognate derivative. The High God, Nyame, superintends the divine reign over creation through lesser deities who actually attend to the affairs of human beings. Only in dire circumstances and seemingly hopeless situations would appeals to the High God be encouraged. Day-to-day affairs are pretty much, theologically speaking, in the hands of special deities. In the Yoruba faith, Olodumare—the "owner of all destinies," the Almighty, the ground of life, from whom all comes and to whom all life returns—is the High God.[18] Thus, both *nyama* and the High Gods, whether among the Ashanti or the Yoruba, have grounding functions. *Nyama,* the pervasive force throughout the universe, is the ground of all being, and the High Gods, constituent parts of that pervasive force, function as the ground of all life. All this must be kept in mind as we proceed toward an understanding of the African American concept of God for the ethic we seek.

18. Joseph M. Murphy, *Santeria* (Boston: Beacon Press, 1993), 8; see as well Murphy's other important work on African diasporan religion, *Working the Spirit: Ceremonies of the African Diaspora* (Boston: Beacon Press, 1994). Among the Akan people of Ghana, Onayamne, the High God, fulfills the same function as does Nyame among the Ashanti. For good accounts of African traditional religion, see E. G. Parrinder, *African Traditional Religion* (Westport, Conn.: Greenwood Press, 1976); Benjamin C. Ray, *African Religions: Symbol, Ritual, and Community* (Englewood Cliffs, N.J.: Prentice-Hall, 1976).

The transatlantic slave trade that began in the middle years of the fifteenth century and that would not abate until some four centuries later in the middle of the nineteenth century constituted a great rupture in the cultural and political affairs of western Africa. Not the least of the cultural systems that suffered a cataclysmic assault were the religious worldviews of the Africans who were captured and forcibly transported to the plantations of the New World. The enslavers took no care to facilitate a smooth transitioning to the New World of the cultures and worldviews of their captives. New names were given upon arrival; old names were cast aside. Religious rituals and customs were forbidden. Certain parts of the European colonies even outlawed drumming. Eventually, for a significant portion of the enslaved, the deity of Christian faith would come to supersede the deities of African cultures.

An interesting question now intrudes itself into our discussion: what would account for the eventual syncretism that occurred as African religious views met the Christian faith of the Europeans? This question is critically related to the central paradox relative to the African American embrace of Christianity, which was suggested in chapter 1. Its resolution will go to the heart of the texture of a conception of God eventually affirmed by African American Christians.

As John Mbiti suggests, a fundamental change in the Africans' "thought patterns, fears, social relationships, attitudes, and philosophical disposition" took place in the process of eventually adopting Christian faith.[19] At this point we must dismiss any sweeping generalizations that suggest that all African American slaves became Christians or totally embraced Christian faith. Historical and anthropological evidence points to the vibrant retention of Africanisms in countries like Brazil and a corresponding resistance to the inculcation of Christian faith. Evidence of African-influenced faiths managed to exist alongside Catholicism, which most planters wanted their slaves to embrace. Prominent examples of such faiths are Condomble in Brazil, Vodou (from the West African *vudu*) in Haiti, and Santeria in Cuba. But even in North America, a significant portion of enslaved Africans held on tenaciously as best they could to the faith of the ancestral homelands. As late as 1849, Henry Bibb, who would escape slavery and become a devout Methodist and active abolitionist, complained about the prevalence of what he termed the "superstitious use of charms" by slaves.[20] He decried the ubiquitous presence of root doctors and herbalists on plantations as well.

---

19. John Mbiti, *African Religions and Philosophies* (New York: Praeger, 1970), 146.

20. *Narrative of the Life and Adventures of Henry Bibb, an American Slave* (New York: published by the author, 1849), 25–32, passim, in *Afro-American Religious History: A Documentary Witness*, ed. Milton C. Sernett (Durham, N.C.: Duke University Press, 1985), 77–78.

His outrage was an ironic testimony to the tenacity of African religion in America, even after over two centuries in bondage and of his equally ardent embrace of Christian faith. A stratum of the religion of the Old Country never died. William D. Pierson has shown how suicide attempts on board slave ships were attempts to return through death back to Africa.[21] John Blassingame and Nathan Huggins have advanced plausible views about the survivability of African religions even in slavery.[22]

The relative success of the First and Second Great Awakenings in attracting blacks to evangelical Christianity must be set beside the relative failure of the Society for the Propagation of the Gospel in Foreign Parts to win significant numbers of slaves to Christian faith. Planters were either indifferent or resistant to evangelization of their slaves. Moreover, the appropriation of Christian religion in the slave insurrections of Denmark Vesey in 1822 and Nat Turner in 1831 probably convinced many slaveholders of the inadvisability of indoctrinating their slaves in the Christian faith. In a classic study of Virginia slavery, Luther P. Jackson asserted that only one out of every nine blacks was on official church rosters by 1860.[23] As late as the Civil War probably no more than one-quarter of the slaves were Christian. Michael G. Gomez, in a provocative and illuminating treatment of acculturation patterns during slavery, deduces that only 22 percent of the black community "may have been Christian by the dawn of the Civil War."[24] Religious beliefs and patterns from the Old Country did not die away quickly; adherents held on to them tenaciously and resisted any facile Christianization.

Even if we acknowledge that not all enslaved Africans and their descendants became practicing Christians, we still have the question before us as to what disposed those who did become Christian to adopt the faith. What dynamics facilitated this process? Further exploration of the dynamics involved in this forced migration to the New World and the dynamics inherent in syncretism might reveal how this transformation took place. I would propose that at least two factors must be considered if we are to arrive at a trustworthy and nuanced account of how captured Africans came to embrace

---

21. William D. Pierson, "White Cannibals, Black Martyrs: Fear, Depression, and Religious Faith as Causes of Suicide among New Slaves," *Journal of Negro History* 62 (1977): 147–59.

22. John W. Blassingame, *The Slave Community: Plantation Life in the Antebellum South* (New York: Oxford University Press, 1972), 20–24; Nathan Irvin Huggins, *Black Odyssey: The Afro-American Ordeal in Slavery* (New York: Pantheon Books, 1977), 62–77; see also William Shuttles, "African Religious Survivals as Factors in American Slave Revolts," *Journal of Negro History* 56, no. 2 (1971): 97–104.

23. Luther P. Jackson, "Religious Development of the Negro in Virginia from 1760 to 1860," *Journal of Negro History* 16 (1931): 232–34.

24. Michael A. Gomez, *Exchanging Our Country Marks: The Transformation of African Identities in the Colonial and Antebellum South* (Chapel Hill: University of North Carolina Press, 1998), 260.

significant aspects of Christian faith. The first factor is a theological issue and has to do with the issue of theodicy; captured Africans had to reconcile the presumed integrity of their deities with the suffering to which they were being subjected. The resolution of this question, begun during the existential moment of the "twilight of the gods,"[25] moved the African to consider the spiritual worth of the Christian God. The second factor is a complex socio-historical issue of creolization, that is to say, the process of intergenerational adaptation from one culture to another, otherwise known as acculturation. Let us look now more closely at both of these factors.

The Issues of Theodicy and Creolization

The question of theodicy and justification of divine goodness in the face of human suffering must have been raised by all of the captive Africans who became caught up in the nefarious trafficking in human flesh that constituted the African slave trade. The issue of theodicy, as evident from its etymology, joins concerns about God (*theos*) and justice (*dike*). The question of God's goodness, *any god's* goodness, was never far from the pained musings on why innocent persons should be caught up in the cruel net of the transatlantic slave trade. The captive African must have at some point after capture and during confinement in the *baracoons*, or slave holding pens that began to dot the western coast of Africa during the seventeenth century, "Why have the gods deserted me? What oblation have I failed to render properly to my *loa*, or pagan deity?" This theological watershed for the captured African constituted "the twilight of the gods" and could be considered the prior theodical moment to the one that would surface in Afro-Christianity during slavery. Even before being placed in the holds of the slave ships, captured Africans had to have pondered why their gods had deserted them. What force in the moral universe had eclipsed their power to protect innocent and obedient devotees of their shrines?

One critical aspect in the discussion of theodicy—monotheistic or polytheistic theodicy—is a crucial aspect of the cultures from which many of the captured Africans came, the belief in the protective power of the gods. These cosmologies helped explain misfortune and evil, particularly a reversal of fortune such as enslavement or capture in war. An implicit assumption was that if misfortune befell someone, the reason lay either with that person (i.e., the person had disobeyed a deity) or with the deity itself (i.e., the deity had become ineffectual, impotent, or powerless to protect the devotee).

---

25. Albert Raboteau uses a similar phrase, "death of the gods," for the title of chapter 2 in his classic work *Slave Religion: The Invisible Institution in the Antebellum South* (New York: Oxford University Press, 1978), as he describes the traumatic religious transition from Africa to the New World.

The devotee had in essence ceased to be a protégé of the deity because of the diminished power of the deity to protect.[26] The twilight of the gods—the first theodical moment for Africans—would presage the eventual second theodical moment for their descendants, for African Americans who would ask of the God of Christian faith, "Why?" Thus one possibility as to why some Africans would be disposed to accept Christianity, when offered, was that Christianity offered a notion of a deity who, it turns out, had proven worthy of the trust of another enslaved people—the ancient Hebrews. Another possibility is that the Christian deity resembled more than any other deity of West Africa the High God, the one whose power is far greater than the lesser deities, the very deities whose power seemed to have been eclipsed in their devotees' tragic reversal of fortune. At any rate, Christianity offered for some the golden opportunity to align themselves with a new deity as they sought a new destiny in a New World.

With respect to the second factor, that of "creolization," many factors were at work along the tortuous path from prior and total avowal of African theological systems to the eventual embrace of the Christian faith. A continuing problem for historians and anthropologists is trying to understand what was going on in the minds of the first two generations of captured Africans in America. Were they straddling two cultures, and if so, how long could this continue with some degree of coherence in their own minds? What happens to *any* displaced group of persons who find themselves in a radically different culture than the one in which they reached maturity or began life?

Colin A. Palmer, in an article entitled "Rethinking American Slavery," muses on such questions. He discusses the complex issues of acculturation of the first generations of enslaved Africans in America during what he calls the "the long first century" (1619–1730). After 1730, a native-born creole culture had emerged, characterized by natural increase, more acculturation in English-dominated patterns of behavior, speech, and the like. Prior to that time, however, the frequent importations from Africa and other dynamics tended to keep the cultural locus focused toward Africa or at least made the cultural context somewhat ambiguous. In such a case there would be a great deal of tension between loyalty to African sensibilities and sensibilities required in a new European-dominated cultural setting. Generally speaking, the greater the frequency of importations directly from Africa, the lesser the degree of acculturation to European-based patterns and the more likelihood

---

26. Colin A. Palmer, "Rethinking American Slavery," in Joseph E. Harris et al., *The African Diaspora* (College Station: Texas A & M University Press, 1996). See also Monica Schuler, *"Alas, Alas, Kongo": A Social History of Indentured African Immigration into Jamaica, 1841–1865* (Baltimore: Johns Hopkins University Press, 1980), for support of this thesis.

for the continuation of Africanisms and African ways of viewing reality and religion.[27]

When the first Africans were introduced into the Chesapeake colonial societies of Virginia and Maryland, little was done on the part of the planters to instill Christian faith initially. However, we cannot presume that all the conditions were ripe for the full retention of African religious practices. The seemingly more viable Christian God had a powerful theological lure over the deities whose power apparently had been eclipsed. In addition, the first Africans had to contend with the problem of not always having the benefit of their "clergy" or priests to preside over religious ceremonies. In terms of access to the sacred lore and the special ways in which the words had to be chanted and intoned, they were in critical need of religious specialists. The absence of such persons could not help but constitute a void in the worshiping community. An analogous situation would be the perpetual absence of enough men among observant Jews to constitute a *minyan*, the required number for communal worship. Over a period of time, the effects of such a deficiency would be catastrophic. For the Africans, such was a dire possibility. As Colin Palmer writes: "For a people whose lives were built around ceremony and ritual and who drew strength from their religious practices conducted in a particular setting, they must have experienced a spiritual death."[28] Although the suggestion that a spiritual death ensued may be an overstatement, Palmer is certainly justified in pointing out the spiritual trauma that enslavement and the paucity of religious specialists, men and women so critical to divining destiny in many West African faiths, could have engendered.

The result of all these social influences, that is, historical and cultural dynamics that surely came into play as the first generations of displaced Africans became acculturated and at the same time resisted acculturation, was a religious consciousness that might be best termed Afro-Christianity. Mechal Sobel has offered this view, although she terms the tradition an "Afro-Baptist" faith. Sobel suggests that Africans brought with them core beliefs in a "sacred Cosmos," to which were added over time white cultural

---

27. For more insights in the fascinating phenomenon of acculturation among Africans in American slavery, see Gerald W. Mullin, *Flight and Rebellion: Slave Resistance in Eighteenth-Century Virginia* (London: Oxford University Press, 1972); Sylvia P. Frey, *Water from the Rock: Black Resistance in a Revolutionary Age* (Princeton: Princeton University Press, 1991); Sidney Mintz and Richard Price, *The Birth of African-American Culture: An Anthropological Approach to the Afro-American Past* (Boston: Beacon Press, 1992); John K. Thornton, *Africa and Africans in the Making of the Atlantic World, 1400–1680* (Cambridge: Cambridge University Press, 1992); Peter Wood, *Black Majority: Negroes in Colonial South Carolina from 1670 through the Stono Rebellion* (New York: Norton, 1974); Alan Kulikoff, *Tobacco and Slavery: The Development of Southern Cultures in the Chesapeake, 1680–1800* (Chapel Hill: University of North Carolina Press, 1986).

28. Palmer, "Rethinking American Slavery," 95.

elements, some of which were Christian. All were "syncretically blended into the Afro-Baptist world view."[29]

Palmer urges us to recognize what emerged from the slave experience as something more than a syncretism of African religious beliefs and Christianity. He argues that

> the African-born slaves who became Christians incorporated Christian theology into their existing belief systems, reinterpreting it and transforming it in the process. This new complex of belief—an emerging Afro-Christianity—met some of their spiritual needs, but it did not generally replace core African beliefs, nor did it always suffice. In fact, Africans continued to express a profound faith in the efficacy of their charms, rituals, and religious principles, even as they sought the comforting ministrations of a Christian clergyman.[30]

Thus in actuality, two systems came to coexist: one was the dynamic, ever evolving blend of African and Christian beliefs that can be called Afro-Christianity, and the other was the African core beliefs that remained beyond the reach of Christian influences.

Images from the Spirituals

Afro-Christianity, the emergent form of religion practiced by Africans in American bondage, was one that infused the Africans' own sensibilities within the formal contours of Christian faith in such a way that it met their emotional and spiritual needs. What concepts of God were prominent in such a Christian faith? Without doubt, the image of God within the consciousness of slaves reflected in large measure the personal-being theism of evangelical Christianity, which was introduced to them first during the Great Awakening of the middle years of the eighteenth century. A second wave of revivalism throughout the nation during the so-called Second Great Awakening, beginning with the end of the eighteenth century and extending into the third decade of the nineteenth, reached even greater numbers of blacks, slave and free. This God of evangelical Christianity intervened in history by freeing Israelite slaves, the implicit hope being that God would do the same thing for them. The rich imagery of the spirituals attests to this personal-being concept of God. At the same time, there are indications that the descendants of enslaved Africans never completely divested themselves of a profound belief in a divine presence that undergirded being itself. Thus the conception of God within the African American Christian

---

29. Mechal Sobel, introduction to *Trabelin' On: The Slave Journey to an Afro-Baptist Faith* (Westport, Conn.: Greenwood Press, 1979).

30. Palmer, "Rethinking American Slavery," 96.

slave consciousness was richly nuanced, incorporating aspects suggestive of personal-being theism, yet infused throughout with an affirmation that God is fundamentally the ground of all being.

Aside from the personal reminiscences of slave narratives, much of the repository for views of the conception of God among African American slaves may be found in the Negro spirituals. Most of the collections of such spirituals were put together in the years immediately after the Civil War, although there are certainly earlier references to religious songs sung by slaves from periods earlier than the Civil War.[31] Among the earliest is perhaps that of Colonel Thomas Wentworth Higginson, whose essay in the *Atlantic Monthly* in June 1867 offered an analysis of thirty-seven songs in which he comments on the creation, texts, and social context of the spirituals. He would later expand upon this essay in a work entitled *Army Life in a Black Regiment* (1869). Perhaps the most extensive collection of spirituals produced immediately after the Civil War was the one by William Francis Allen, Charles Pickard Ware, and Lucy McKim Garrison entitled *Slave Songs of the United States*.[32] Other articles about the spirituals appeared in periodicals such as *Dwight's Journal of Music, Putnam's Monthly, Lippincott's Magazine*, and *The New England Magazine*.

The God that emerges from the corpus of the Negro spirituals appears to be a remarkable conflation of many aspects of the West African High God and the divine force that permeates all of existence. And to be sure, the popular conception of God in evangelical Protestantism, embraced by many slaves who were drawn to the Christian faith during the First and Second Great Awakenings, is evident as well. Though transcendent, this God appears to have a keen interest in the affairs of everyday human beings. In the words of one spiritual, "He sits high and looks low." This God delivers Daniel from the lions' den.

---

31. Some of these may be seen in Rev. Charles C. Jones's dismissive characterization of slave songs in Erskine Clarke, *Wrestlin' Jacob: A Portrait of Religion in the Old South* (Atlanta: John Knox Press, 1979).

32. William Francis Allen, Charles Pickard Ware, and Lucy McKim Garrison, eds., *Slave Songs of the United States* (New York: Peter Smith, 1867). The story of the transcriptions of early Negro spirituals is a rich and fascinating one. Lucy McKim Garrison, one of the editors in the *Slave Songs of the United States* volume, began taking down spirituals in printed form as early as 1862, when she visited the Port Royal "contrabands," those former slaves who had escaped to Union lines in and around Port Royal, South Carolina. Her findings appeared in a letter to the editor of *Dwight's Journal of Music* in 1862 under the title "Songs of the Port Royal Contrabands" (Boston, November 8, 1862). Thomas P. Fenner's *Religious Folk Songs of the Negro as Sung on the Plantations* was first published in 1874 and reissued by Hampton Institute in 1909. William E. Barton published "Hymns of the Slave and Freedman" in the *New England Magazine* (January 1899). Barton's method was to record the musical remembrances of two former slaves. A Liberian musicologist, Nicholas Ballanta spent time in and around the Georgia Sea Islands, seeking to discover structural similarities between West African musical sensibilities and the Negro spirituals; his book *Saint Helena Island Spirituals* (New York: G. Schirmer, 1925) was the result.

Reflecting the thought forms of the evangelical awakenings, slave conceptions of God also were rendered in anthropomorphic terms. God is a father figure, even a "Man of War," as in the following:

> My God He is a Man—a Man of war,
> My God He is a Man—a Man of war,
> My God He is a Man—a Man of war,
> An' de Lawd God is His name.[33]

This spiritual goes on to recount the creative works of God, how God created the celestial bodies, the birds of the air, and beasts of the field and also how God "tole' Noah to build an ark" and "tole' Moses to lead the chillun, from Egypt to the Promised Lan.'" For persons whose limbs were constantly constrained by the dictates of the slave regimen, there appears to have been a palpable exultation in the sheer freedom of motion and action that accrues to divine prerogative. Moreover, this force and power, this ability to get things done, is conceived of in the light of the eventual liberation of black people from the bonds of slavery. Thus, within the spirituals are clear renderings of God in the form of heroic, manlike characters. God becomes a God "like a mighty man," a man of great valor and strength. Perhaps any anthropomorphism in the spirituals is conceived by virtue of the liberation from bondage that this God effects.

Yet, we err if we presume that aspects of God in the African American slave consciousness were limited to the personal-being concept of God, evidenced in the anthropomorphic renderings and the limitations of such imagery. The liberating personal-being God certainly met the needs and hopes for the corporate liberation of the people held in bondage, just as the Israelite slaves, as a people, were delivered by their God. Graphic portrayals of the exploits of such a God certainly stirred the hearts of the oppressed and steeled them against the adversities of bondage. Yet, even given the powerful exertions of this God on behalf of the suffering and the oppressed, certain theological problems remain. From whence did the suffering and the moral evil of slavery come? If the source of the evil does not come from God, is evil's source a being other than God? Does not the persistence of the evil suggest that this being has power equal to that of God? As long as personal-being theism remains *the exclusive* operating image of our view of God in African American theological consciousness, an adequate theodicy in black theology will never be satisfactorily solved. Personal-being theism will forever be met with a stone wall.

---

33. "My God Is a Man of War," in *The Negro Sings a New Heaven: A Collection of Songs,* ed. Mary Ellen Grissom (1930; New York: Dover Publications, 1969), 29.

Responses to Theodicy

At one time or another, most black people have given serious theological thought to the theodicy question and may have come close to questioning the traditional conception of God as a personal, omnipotent, and benevolent being. In his classic study of African American conceptions of God, Benjamin E. Mays discerned a questioning of traditional conceptions of God within the generation that was born just after the turn of the twentieth century. He saw it in writers such as Countee Cullen, Langston Hughes, and W. E. B. Du Bois.[34] But an anguished questioning of God's nature was evident in African American religious consciousness much earlier than more recent times. In fact we have a record of one such instance recorded in the unlikely source of the memories of Bishop Daniel Payne, the venerable divine of the African Methodist Episcopal Church. While born free in 1811 in Charleston, South Carolina, Payne knew firsthand the opprobrium with which the slaveholding society viewed free blacks. He also was keenly aware of the arrogant use of power that the slaveholding society, manifested in his case by the state of South Carolina, could display in order to preserve slavery. When the South Carolina legislature in 1834 passed a law that forbade the teaching of blacks, effectively shutting down a school Payne had started, he confessed:

> Sometimes it seemed as though some wild beast had plunged his fangs into my heart, and was squeezing out its life-blood. Then I began to question the existence of the Almighty, and to say: "If he does exist, is he just? If so, why does he suffer one race to oppress and enslave another, to rob them by unrighteous enactments of rights, which they hold most dear and sacred?"[35]

Modern African American theologians as well have experienced discernible anguish as they seek to reconcile black suffering with the presumed goodness of God. Almost without exception, the work of black theologians has actually been commentaries on suffering and implicit attempts at solving the problem of theodicy. To some degree, God's very nature has been confronted by these thinkers who have mused upon the meaning of black suffering within the context of God's presumed goodness. While the notion of God as personal being is never far from these ruminations, as the issue of suffering is cast upon the backdrop of divine nature, this concept seems to undergo subtle and fascinating modifications, depending upon the thinker under review.

---

34. Benjamin E. Mays, *The Negro's God as Reflected in His Literature* (1938; New York: Atheneum, 1968), 218–44.
35. Daniel A. Payne, *Recollections of Seventy Years* (1888; New York: Arno Press, 1969), 28.

King's Affirmation of an Able God. In his writings and speeches, Martin Luther King Jr. articulated a theodicy, as would be expected since his life's work became a mission of ending black suffering under segregation according to his perception of God's will in history. In his first book of sermons, the classic *Strength to Love,* King regarded evil as "stark, grim, and colossally real" in a sermon entitled "The Death of Evil upon the Seashore."[36] While the history of humanity reveals the struggle between good and evil, Kings understands the Christian faith as clearly affirming that "in the long struggle between good and evil, good eventually will emerge as victor."[37] King understands God to be working actively in the moral universe for the triumph of the good. In "Our God Is Able," another sermon in this volume, King affirmed his unshakable belief that God "is able to subdue all the powers of evil" and indeed desires to do so, for God "is not outside the world looking on with a sort of cold indifference."[38] Then continuing, King allows that the power of this God is actually moderated and complemented by the active participation of human beings in the common struggle to bring about the good:

> Here on all the roads of life, he is striving in our striving. Like an ever-loving Father, he is working through history for the salvation of his children. As we struggle to defeat the forces of evil, the God of the universe struggles with us. Evil dies on the seashore, not merely because of man's endless struggle against it, but because of God's power to defeat it.[39]

King ultimately admitted in this sermon that he was unable to answer the question as to "why God is slow in conquering the forces of evil."[40] But in admitting his inability to answer this question fully, he did in fact offer his insight into the nature of God. In order to preserve human freedom, God necessarily limited divine sovereignty: "By endowing us with freedom, God relinquished a measure of his own sovereignty and imposed certain limitations upon himself."[41] This does not mean, however that God is powerless. King redefines power by always viewing it in tandem with God's purpose for human beings, which is inextricably linked with maintaining human freedom: "God cannot at the same time impose his will upon his children and also maintain his purpose for man. If through sheer omnipotence God were

---

36. Martin Luther King Jr., *Strength to Love* (New York: Harper & Row, 1963), 58.
37. Ibid., 59.
38. Ibid., 103, 64.
39. Ibid., 64.
40. Ibid.
41. Ibid.

to defeat his purpose, he would express weakness rather than power. Power is the ability to fulfill purpose; action which defeats purpose is weakness."[42]

God deals with evil through maintaining at all costs God's purpose for human beings, which is to maintain their freedom, without which they cease to be human beings. King appreciates the fact that as human beings we are not "blind automatons; persons, not puppets."[43] Self-limited by such constraints, God becomes active through the freedom conferred on humanity. Yet we as human beings may rely upon God who "does not forget his children who are the victims of evil forces. He gives us the interior resources to bear the burdens and tribulations of life."[44] The other resource that human beings can rely upon is God's "two lights: a light to guide us in the brightness of the day when hopes are fulfilled and circumstances are favorable, and a light to guide us in the darkness of the midnight when we are thwarted and the slumbering giants of gloom and hopelessness rise in our souls."[45]

As a public theologian, King also sought to call the nation to repentance and lead his own people in the context of radical social change and transformation. King believed that all people were created good by God and are free to weigh options of choice.[46] For King as well the "beloved community" becomes a Christian eschatological ideal that mitigates suffering and transforms the effects of evil into good.[47] King attempts to solve the problem of the presence of evil in part by regarding suffering as a virtue and affirming unearned suffering as redemptive.[48] In fact, it will only be through nonviolent action, the willingness to suffer, rather than the willingness to inflict suffering on others, that will bring about a new world "where men and women can live together, where each has his own job and house and where all children receive as much education as their minds can absorb.[49] In other words, suffering proves its redemptive nature through the bringing about of a truly just society.

---

42. Ibid.

43. Ibid.

44. Ibid., 65.

45. Ibid., 66.

46. Martin Luther King Jr., *Where Do We Go from Here: Chaos or Community?* (Boston: Beacon Press, 1967), 97–98.

47. See Kenneth Smith and Ira Zepp Jr., *Search for the Beloved Community: The Thinking of Martin Luther King, Jr.* (Valley Forge, Pa.: Judson Press, 1974), 119–40; see also Walter Fluker, *They Looked for a City: A Comparative Analysis of the Ideal Community in the Thought of Howard Thurman and Martin Luther King, Jr.* (Lanham, Md.: University Press of America, 1989), 81, 90–91.

48. Martin Luther King Jr., "Suffering and Faith," in *A Testament of Hope: The Essential Writings of Martin Luther King, Jr.*, ed. James M. Washington (San Francisco: Harper & Row, 1986), 41.

49. Martin Luther King Jr., "Nonviolence: The Only Road to Freedom," in *Testament of Hope*, ed. James M. Washington, 61.

Goatley's Concept of Godforsakenness. The enormity of human suffering, remembered historically and observed contemporaneously, has caused David Goatley to reflect on the meaning of African American slave suffering using a concept he calls "Godforsakenness." According to Goatley "one can know Godforsakenness when the positive experiences of life—both actual and conceptual—which are in some measure attributable to the goodness of the immanent God, are radically reversed, transforming life into an abyss of negativity and destruction."[50] Goatley explicitly states that he is not raising the theodicy issue in his work but rather seeks to "reflect on the issue of whether God is present with those who endure the extremities of human suffering"[51] Yet this disclaimer seems rather disingenuous since any affirmation of God's presence in the midst of suffering must necessarily raise the very issue that theodicy seeks to solve, that is, how to reconcile the existence of a just and powerful God with innocent suffering. At any rate, Goatley points us to some interesting areas of thought as we confront the seeming absence of God in the midst of so much black suffering during slavery.

Goatley appropriates the thinking of Eberhard Jungel, who argues that one needs to conceptualize God's omnipotence as the withdrawal of God's omnipresence. Correspondingly, one also needs to think of God's omnipresence in terms of God's withdrawal of God's omnipotence.[52] Goatley goes on to say:

> He [Jungel] argues that one's withdrawn state is essential to one's person. This is especially true with God. While absolute presence is obliterated by one's absence, God's presence is exclusively known simultaneously with God's absence. Consequently, revelation is essential for God to be known. Since God's essence is explicitly known through revelation, revelation is integrally related to the connection between presence and absence. For Jungel, either God must be declared dead, or our thinking of God demands renewal.[53]

Goatley goes on then to marshal an idea in the thinking of Dietrich Bonhoeffer, who in *Letters and Papers from Prison* offers a variation on God's permissive will. According to Bonhoeffer, God allowed "himself to be edged

---

50. David Emmanuel Goatley, *Were You There? Godforsakenness in Slave Religion* (Maryknoll, N.Y.: Orbis Books, 1996), 12.

51. Ibid., 11.

52. Eberhard Jungel, *God as the Mystery of the World: On the Foundation of the Theology of the Crucified One in the Dispute between Theism and Atheism*, trans. Darrell L. Guder (Grand Rapids: Eerdmans, 1983).

53. Goatley, *Were You There?* 72.

out of the world and on to the cross. God is weak and powerless in the world, and that is exactly the way, the only way, in which he can be with us and help us."[54] Thus God "explodes the alternative of presence and absence."[55] In other words, presence and absence are not diametrically opposed; they are taken up into the person of God as being "present as the one who is absent in the world."[56] Goatley goes on to say: "That the person of God absorbs the idea of presence as absence is analogous to the quality of 'removedness' that belongs to the human experience."[57]

Wolfhart Pannenberg agrees with Bonhoeffer's conception of God and elucidates it by referring to concepts of presence, concealment, and personal being. Integral to the personhood of humans is the fact that humans are not totally existent for other humans. The freedom within the personhood of humans means that they can conceal part of their being. They are also free to disclose themselves.[58] Goatley builds on Bonhoeffer and Pannenberg to conclude: "Hence the freedom of God permits God to reveal and conceal Godself. If God could not be concealed, God would not be free. If God were not free, God would not be God."[59] Goatley's argument is certainly evocative of the ambiguity inherent in our attempts to understand what the presence of God connotes, but insofar as it solves the theodicy problem, the results are inconclusive. And to be sure, he never proposed to solve this enigma in the first place.

Other theologians, such as James H. Cone, the first widely acknowledged proponent of a black theology, have sought to bring some clarity to the issue. In fact, one could say that Cone's entire theological project was an attempt to vindicate black suffering in a theologically meaningful way. Ultimately, Christ as Liberator incorporates the values and goals of black power and leads the oppressed to a free and complete way of life.[60] The theodical problem seems to be solved through the quest for communal power effected by the work of the liberating Christ. But one looks in vain in Cone's analysis for the cause or origin of evil, unless the proponents of racism might be blamed for the evil of segregation and oppression.

---

54. Dietrich Bonhoeffer, *Letters and Papers from Prison* (New York: Macmillan, 1953), 219–20.

55. Goatley, *Were You There?* 73.

56. Ibid.

57. Ibid.

58. Wolfhart Pannenberg, "Speaking about God in the Face of Atheist Criticism," in *The Idea of God and Human Freedom*, trans. R. A. Wilson (Philadelphia: Westminster Press, 1973), 112.

59. Goatley, *Were You There?*, 73.

60. James H. Cone, *Black Theology and Black Power* (New York: Seabury Press, 1969), 34–61; idem, *The Spirituals and the Blues: An Interpretation* (New York: Seabury Press, 1972), 16–19.

Major R. Jones affirms that black people are God's chosen people. Yet inherent in this chosen status has been the scourge of slavery: "It may well be that from the inception of American slavery, black people became chosen people simply because of what that has meant to them as a slave. It is quite reasonable to contend also that the black people have been chosen by God because of what they have meant to their masters."[61] Jones sees a positive value in the suffering that black people have endured in their role as God's chosen people. For him the theodicy problem is solved somewhat by acknowledging the ultimate benefits to American society garnered through the unmerited suffering of its former slaves. Yet at no point does Jones ponder what in the nature of God would bring such suffering to pass or for what reason.

J. Deotis Roberts, a thoughtful critic and commentator on the black theology project, is intent on preserving a religious tradition that can adequately attend to the psychological needs of the oppressed, to fortify them against the rigors of oppression.[62] But for Roberts, these needs can only be met if the omnipotence and the omnibenevolence of God are both true,[63] which does not solve the theodicy problem. As Roberts leaves the issue, the only way in which the oppressed can maintain some kind of psychological equilibrium is to simply live with the indissolubility of the problem of God's goodness and the presence of evil.

Thurman's Fellowship of Suffering. While not a systematic theologian, Howard Thurman provides a rich resource for reflecting on the nature of God and the quest for meaning in African American suffering. Thurman acknowledges the presence in the moral universe of a "dramatic principle that is ever alert to choke off, to strangle, the constructively creative,"[64] which for Thurman appears to be the evil force in the moral universe. Human beings can—and do—align themselves with this principle and therefore work for evil: "Those persons who are working on behalf of the avowedly evil in life recognize this fact and seek to utilize it to the full."[65] Juxtaposed to evil and those who work for this force are the good and those who work for it. Thurman asserts that "the good must be worked at, must be concentrated upon, if it is to prevail in any short-time intervals."[66]

---

61. Major R. Jones, *Christian Ethics for Black Theology: The Politics of Liberation* (Nashville: Abingdon Press, 1974), 43.

62. J. Deotis Roberts, "Black Consciousness in Theological Perspective," in *Quest for a Black Theology*, ed. James Gardiner and J. Deotis Roberts (Philadelphia: The Pilgrim Press, 1971), 71.

63. J. Deotis Roberts, "Black Theology and the Theological Revolution," *Journal of Religious Thought* 27 (spring–summer 1971), 14.

64. Howard Thurman, *Deep Is the Hunger* (New York: Harper & Row, 1951; Richmond, Ind.: Friends United Press, 1990), 51.

65. Ibid.

66. Ibid.

For Thurman, racial hatred is one such manifestation of evil and, as such, is "destructive."[67] Yet Thurman calls for putting hatred into a "causal perspective."[68] That is, we must understand that "individuals are the creatures of training, background, culture, of personal frustrations and collective frustrations."[69] Thus, the evil that comes from any human being is a result of formative factors in that person's background and environment. Recognizing the causal factors in any person's disposition to hate prevents even those hated from demonizing the hater and thereby reducing the humanity of even those who participate in evil by hating.

With the publication of *The Luminous Darkness: A Personal Interpretation of the Anatomy of Segregation and the Ground of Hope* in 1965, Thurman spoke directly to the issue of racial segregation in America. As the subtitle suggests, this work offered his personal reflections on the moral sin of racial segregation in America. Thurman had earlier written on the existential condition of being oppressed in his book *Jesus and the Disinherited* (1946), but it was in *Disciplines of the Spirit*, a book that antedated the *Luminous Darkness* by about four years, that Thurman offers a marvelously subtle notion of the meaning of human suffering and a conception of God that seems to push beyond the confines of personal-being theism. According to Thurman, suffering is rooted in pain and actually has no meaning "outside of consciousness."[70] One of the mitigating factors in suffering is that a community of sufferers is created; that is, "there is a fellowship of suffering as well as a community of sufferers."[71]

Regarding the "strange and awful vitality in the suffering of the innocent,"[72] Thurman has some truly arresting thoughts. He is drawn to the author Margaret Kennedy, whose novel *The Feast* advanced the notion that "the entire human race is tolerated for its innocent minority."[73] Thurman writes:

The innocent ones are always present when the payment falls due—
they are not heroes or saints, they are not conscious burden-bearers
of the sins and transgressions of men. They are the innocent—always
there. Their presence in the world is a stabilizing factor, a precious in-

---

67. Howard Thurman, *The Growing Edge* (New York: Harper & Row, 1956; Richmond, Ind.: Friends United Press, 1974), 5.
68. Ibid., 6.
69. Ibid.
70. Howard Thurman, *Disciplines of the Spirit* (New York: Harper & Row, 1963; Richmond, Ind.: Friends United Press, 1977), 66.
71. Ibid., 75.
72. Ibid.
73. Ibid., 78.

gredient maintaining the delicate balance that prevents humanity from plunging into the abyss.[74]

Thurman makes the startling observation that "if there were no suffering there would be no freedom. Freedom cannot be separated from suffering. This, then, may be one of the ways in which suffering pays for its ride."[75] Ultimately for Thurman the logic of all suffering is death; that is, it is within the context of ultimate death that suffering must be placed and understood. In the context of this truth, the subtlety of Thurman's thought yields a notion of God that begins to transcend traditional and orthodox conceptions of God as merely personal being. More than personal being, God is the substance of the life principle itself. In the context of our attempts to wrest some meaning from suffering, we struggle ultimately against death, Thurman suggests. But the God in and of life redeems the pain of human suffering even if suffering eventuates in death: "Life and death are the experience of living things, and here Life in some sense becomes identical with God. To say that man's spirit is driven to deal with the issue of death is equivalent to saying that man is driven to a face-to-face encounter with Life and its Creator, out of whom come life and death as experiences in Life."[76] Thus while Howard Thurman does not offer a theodicy per se, he does offer a conception of God that seems to move beyond the tight confines of personal-being theism and a theory of human agency that explains evil and its persistence.

Jones's Humanocentric Theism. William R. Jones, after assessing the theodicies of major black theologians, including James Cone, Deotis Roberts, and Major Jones (curiously yet understandably overlooking Thurman), has offered what might be considered the most radical solution to the theodicy problem for black theology. In effect, Jones demolishes the entire scaffolding that undergirded all of the other theodicies. He starts anew. Jones opts for what he calls "humanocentric theism" as foundational to what he regards as a more viable theodicy. In Jones's humanocentric theism, God affords humans a greater place in working out the destiny of the moral universe. It is within this plan of God that the critical role of humans has been ordained. Jones quotes Martin Buber, who asked, "Has God need for man for His work? He wills to have need of man."[77] Thus for Jones, "God's endowment of man as a codetermining center of power is the most authentic expression of his sovereignty."[78] Understood in this fashion, God's sovereignty assumes

---

74. Ibid., 79.
75. Ibid., 81.
76. Ibid.
77. Martin Buber, *Hasidism* (New York: Philosophical Library, 1948), 108–9.
78. William R. Jones, *Is God a White Racist? A Preamble to Black Theology* (Boston: Beacon Press, 1973), 188.

a self-imposed limitation of power, a power that is now shared with human beings to effect good within the moral order.

Jones's vision for the solution of the theodicy problem in black theology has much merit. For one thing, it relieves God from the charge of being responsible for moral evil in the world, including black suffering and the evils of racial oppression. Human beings have the power to bring evil into the world and have the power, with God, to bring about good in the world. However, one troubling issue is Jones's name for this vision: humanocentric theism runs the risk of obscuring the distinction between humanity and God. If the method is humanocentrically oriented, how is one ever sure that what purports to be God is not merely human values and concerns idealized and pushed to an ultimate level? Where is God's independence from human beings? Since Jones's system assumes that God's self-limitation and humanity's empowerment are inherent in the structure of reality itself, the basic orientation of the system seems ontologically grounded and oriented. Thus, if anything, the vision should go under the rubric *onto-centric,* as awkward as this term might appear to be. God is the ground of being, and inherent in this structure of being is the opportunity of humans to use their freedom to chart the course of the moral order with God.

God as Rock

We have seen the difficulty many black theologians have experienced in seeking to reconcile a workable theodicy with the personal-being theism that seems to be implicit in their theological visions. And we recognize the promise of William Jones's humanocentric system. There are biblical warrants available to support an African American conception of God with the degree of moral consistency required by the ethic we seek. The images we seek must offer a vision of a God that is unalterably consistent with the good and that sufficiently allows for human freedom. Moreover, these images must have been appropriated by the African American historical consciousness as a result of blacks discerning within certain biblical stories and texts views of God that were consistent with the exigencies of their reality. Our concern, therefore, is not so much to scour the Bible in seeking images for our theological project, but rather it is to discern what black people themselves have affirmed about God, as discerned from biblical lore. Such an image is found in the view of God as the Rock.

The images of God as the Rock are replete in the Old Testament. In Deuteronomy 32:4 is a text that could serve as the locus classicus for a biblical understanding of a vision of God that affirms the immutability of divine existence (a requisite of Greek classical thought) as well as God's intimate involvement with human history (a requirement of the Hebraic tradition). Our thesis requires a theological vision that will not only bridge these two traditions but can serve as a foundation for an African American theological consciousness. In the Deuteronomy text, God is viewed as the Rock, perfect and just. The King James version of the text reads: "He is the Rock, his work is perfect; for all his ways are judgment: a God of truth and without iniquity, just and right is he." The New Revised Standard Version puts it thus, beginning at verse 3:

> For I will proclaim the name of the LORD;
>   ascribe greatness to our God!
> The Rock, his work is perfect,
>   and all his ways are just.
> A faithful God, without deceit,
>   just and upright is he.

As the text continues, we have a glimpse of the exact ways in which God as Rock interacts with humanity. Jeshurun is denounced for growing fat and lethargic, forsaking the God "who made him, and scoffed at the Rock of his salvation" (v. 15). Further on, in verse 30 of the same chapter, the writer asks,

> How could one have routed a thousand,
>   and two put a myriad to flight,
> unless their Rock had sold them [the enemies of Israel],
>   the LORD had given them up?"[79]

The fate of Israel's enemies is sealed, according to the writer, because "their rock is not like our Rock" (v. 31).

What is remarkable about the foregoing passage is that images of two seemingly warring traditions are held together in an amazing creative tension. An impenetrable, immutable object such as a rock actually is viewed as the progenitor of a living human being. Moreover, Jeshurun, a man come to life from the Rock, exercises a modicum of free will, although in his case he exercises it poorly. He scoffs at his Creator and leads a dissolute, undisciplined life, leading to his destruction.

The spiritual and existential power inherent in the image of the Rock was apparent to enslaved African Americans, those so bereft of power and so in need of spiritual replenishment in their sad state of existence. The opportunity to find refuge in such a Rock is powerfully expressed in the spiritual "I Got a Home in-a Dat Rock."

---

79. In the New Testament, the image of the Rock is associated with Christ: "And all drank the same spiritual drink. For they drank from the spiritual rock that followed them, and the rock was Christ" (1 Cor. 10:4).

I got a home in-a dat Rock, Don't you see?
I got a home in-a dat Rock, Don't you see?
Between de earth an' sky,
Thought I heard my Saviour cry,
you got a home in-a dat Rock, Don't you see?

Poor man Lazrus, poor as I, Don't you see?
Poor man Lazrus, poor as I, Don't you see?
Poor man Lazrus, poor as I, When he died he foun' a home on high.
He had a home in-a dat Rock, Don't you see?

Rich man, Dives, He lived so well, Don't you see?
Rich man, Dives, He lived so well, Don't you see?
Rich man, Dives, He lived so well, when he died he foun' a home in
    Hell,
He had no home in-a dat Rock, Don't you see?[80]

Another critical aspect of slave existence that demands our attention is the incredible personal anguish and loneliness of slave life. Within the African American experience profound feelings of loneliness must have been a constant companion for the slave. The ubiquitous auction block, uncertainty, loneliness on the journey—all of this must have occasioned many slaves to wonder where God was during all this misery. A spiritual such as "Sometimes I Feel like a Motherless Chile" bespeaks this loneliness, so endemic to slave life. A God that could meet the exigencies and needs of such profound loneliness had to be a God that was constant, certain, dependable, always present. Such a God is found in the imagery of the spirituals.

Consistent with our thesis that the image of God as ground of being has been endemic to African American religious consciousness is the classic spiritual "My God Is a Rock in a Weary Land." The slaves who could sing, "My God is a rock in a weary land, a weary land, a weary land, My God is a rock in a weary land, A shelter in the time of storm," betokened such a view of God. There was surely a need for something that could anchor the soul that was being ravaged by so many imponderables on so many sides. Not only did this spiritual support and sustain slaves in their arduous sojourn, but it would come to give comfort and courage a century later to their descendants, young civil rights workers, as they met snarling dogs and mean-spirited police officers.

Even in the spirituals that embody notions of personal-being theism are indexes of God's eternality, as if to offset the mercurial nature of personal being. The corporate authors of the spirituals meant to convey the belief that while

---

80. James Weldon Johnson and J. Rosamond Johnson, *The Book of American Negro Spirituals* (New York: Viking Press, 1925), 96–98.

God could be rendered in anthropomorphic terms, so much of God was immutable, timeless, and stable that personality could not obscure the assumption that this God was also close to the ground of all being, if not the ground of being itself. The spiritual "My Lord's A-Writin' All De Time" captures the essence of a timeless God, yet one involved in the mundane affairs of human beings, especially as the righteous are justified and the wicked punished:

> *Lead:*
> Come down, come down, my Lord, come down,
>
> *Response:*
> My Lord's a-writin' all de time,
> An' take me up to wear de crown,
> My Lord's a-writin' all de time.
>
> *Lead:*
> King Jesus rides in de middle of de air,
>
> *Response:*
> My Lord's a-writin' all de time,
> He's callin' sinners from ev'ry where,
> My Lord's a-writin' all de time.
>
> *Chorus:*
> Oh, He sees all you do,
> He hears all you say,
> My Lord's a-writin' all de time.
> Oh, He sees all you do,
> He hears all you say,
> My Lord's a-writin' all de time.[81]

Another spiritual affirms God's timelessness even as God acts in time. The message of "He's Jus' de Same Today" is that time is no boundary; that is, chronological periods cannot constrict God's being.

> When Moses an' his soldiers, fom Egypt's lan' did flee,
> His enemies were in behin' him, An' in front of him de sea.
> God raised de waters like a wall, An' opened up de way,
> An' de God dat lived in Moses' time is jus de same today.
>
> When Daniel faithful to his God, would not bow down to men,
> An' by God's enemy he was hurled into de lion's den,
> God locked de lion's jaw we read, An' robbed him of his prey,
> An' de God dat lived in Daniel's time is jus de same today.

---

81. Ibid., 123–25.

Response:
Is Jus' de same today, Jus' de same today,
An' de God dat lived in Moses' (Daniel's) time is jus' de same today.[82]

Of enormous value for the slaves must have been the comfort derived from the thought that God as ground of being would be there no matter what. Recognizing the power and worth of such a God, even the enslaved could secure power to endure, power to resist, power to prevail, power to join God in bringing about good in the moral universe. Moreover, the will to believe in such a God was quickened all the more as the slave mused upon the constancy of God's spirit.

As human beings seek meaning in life, they seek a certainty of mind and spirit as they gaze out upon the void. As they seek to give utterance to that which seizes mind and spirit, the human mind and spirit begin to witness to a degree of certainty in affirming notions about the cosmos, about life and about destiny, indeed about being itself. William James put it this way: "Of some things we feel that we are certain: we know, and we know that we do know. There is a something that gives a click inside us, a bell that strikes twelve, when the hands of our mental clock have swept the dial and meet over the meridian hour."[83]

The Africans who ultimately became enslaved African Americans were tenacious in holding onto a belief and confidence in a basic aspect of existence that staved off ultimate despair and hopelessness. As long as there was life, and the ground of life within the grasp of their consciousness, then hope could survive. The ultimate option for the slave in his or her loneliness was this: either opt for nonbeing through complete submission to the dehumanizing brutality all around or opt for being and resist, however subtly or overtly, the dehumanizing forces. In other words, the slave could either affirm that One without whom being cannot continue or risk becoming a captive to ultimate despair. It is when the solitary soul is confronted with the enormity of the surrounding moral and existential cosmos that one is most likely to experience a breakthrough to that which transcends the mundane.

The enslaved Africans who learned to call the ineffable One by the name of God the Father discerned in this being a permanence that was unshakable, solid, and true. They regarded such a being as a Rock in a weary land, an anchor in the time of storms. Such a belief, ever so strong, in such a God, ever so eternal, would forever anchor them and their descendants and be for time without end "a shelter in the time of storms."

---

82. Ibid., 80–81.
83. William James, "The Will to Believe," in *The Will to Believe and Other Essays in Popular Philosophy* (1897; New York: Dover Publications, 1956), 13.

3

Christ as Liberator and Reconciler

Jesus Christ is the same yesterday and today and forever.
—Hebrews 13:8

O when I come to die,
O when I come to die,
O when I come to die—
Give me Jesus.
—American Negro spiritual

A Christian ethic for African Americans affirms that Jesus Christ is not only God made incarnate among human beings but also is the exemplar for moral action and ethical reflection. African American Christian faith has appropriated a vision of Christ that has undergirded the quest for full liberation as human beings. Such a quest has been viewed as consistent with God's will that all God's creatures be privileged to actualize themselves to their fullest capacity without constraint by adverse forces. This quest for liberation has manifested itself in civil society, as in the great struggle for freedom from slavery, but also has manifested itself in a spiritual dimension as well, as in the continuing struggle to chart ways of living in the world as free and spiritually vital persons. In both dimensions, Christ has been an exemplar and one worthy of being emulated and followed by disciples. Just as by virtue of God's rocklike and constant nature the African American Christian has exercised the "will to believe," so, in responding to the person of Jesus Christ, the African American Christian is enjoined to exercise the "will to follow."

FROM THE *JESUS OF HISTORY* TO THE *CHRIST OF FAITH*

There would be no Christian faith were it not for the assertion that Jesus Christ is the Son of God made incarnate among human beings. Peter's confession at Caesarea Philippi that Jesus is "the Messiah, the Son of the living

God" (Matt. 16:16) is foundational to Christian faith. But the moment the believer entertains this assertion, a paradox of immense proportion emerges. How can one man among all people who have ever lived in the world, one man who lived and died as did so many others, be considered the Son of God? Is he both human and divine? How could God become a man and share the divine nature with this particular man, born in an insignificant village in Palestine and executed as a religious troublemaker by the Romans two millennia ago? The disciplined reflection on the nature of Jesus Christ and the transformation by which the Jesus of history became the Christ of faith is called "Christology."

The outline of a biography of Jesus of Nazareth is necessarily sparse. In Christendom Jesus' birth has been used to delineate our notion of the passage of time, as in "before Christ" (B.C.) or *anno Domini* (A.D., "in the year of the Lord") or, according to more recent usage, "before the common era" (B.C.E.). Despite these designations, Jesus was probably born closer to the year 4 B.C.E. during the Roman occupation of Palestine, in the little village of Bethlehem. As a young man, he began an itinerant ministry, preaching a message of a coming reign of God. Within this message is the announcement of God's grace freely extended to humankind, with an expected response of repentance. Jesus drew to himself a closely knit band of disciples and an increasing range of admirers, which ultimately sparked the ire of the Jewish religious establishment. He was eventually executed by the Romans, after a trial prompted by the displeasure of the religious authorities. However, Jesus' disciples were convinced of his resurrection three days later, a message that they and subsequent generations of believers would preach as the cornerstone of Christian faith.

The message of the resurrection underscores a residual ambiguity about the nature of Jesus that had probably been in the minds of many followers and persons who were overwhelmed by the force of his person and presence. He must have been considered by many people to be "more than" other human beings. A critical reconstruction of the textual development of the New Testament reveals a gradual development of the notion of the divinity of Christ and the notion of the virginal conception (Luke and Matthew) and ultimately his preexistence with God (John). Paul, the first writer of letters that eventually became a part of the New Testament canon, was not reluctant to affirm the humanity of Jesus. Writing almost thirty years after the crucifixion (58–60), Paul seems to know nothing of the miraculous circumstances of Jesus' birth, which only much later writers (Matthew, ca. 80–85, and Luke, ca. 85–90) would affirm. The most Paul can say about Jesus' birth is recorded in his Galatians letter: "But when the fullness of time had come, God sent his Son, born of a woman, born under the law" (Gal. 4:4). In his most theological epistle, Romans, Paul allows that Jesus is God's Son, yet he "was descended from David according to the flesh and was declared to be Son of God with power according to the spirit of holiness by resurrection from the dead, Jesus Christ our Lord" (Rom. 1:3–4). Likewise Mark, writing some ten to fifteen years after Paul had written his principal letters, emphasizes the humanity of Jesus and does not seem to know anything extraordinary about Jesus' birth.

Only with the Gospels of Matthew and Luke does the conviction take shape that Jesus' birth had to have been shrouded in extraordinary circumstances, much like that of other epoch-making personalities. Matthew recounts a special star that appeared at the time of Jesus' birth. Luke has angels telling the news of his birth to shepherds. Both affirm, *for the first time*, a notion of a virginal conception, although the two accounts differ in some details. Writing even later than Matthew and Luke, sometime on the eve of the second century, John regards Jesus in rather metaphysical dimensions, while not mentioning a virginal conception. He affirms that Jesus was preexistent with God from the very beginning: "In the beginning was the Word, and the Word was with God, and the Word was God" (John 1:1). The critical biblical texts and doctrinal witnesses are not univocal on the notions that would support the unambiguous divinity of Jesus, or even of the virginal conception prior to his birth, though from the beginning there seems to have been a clear recognition of his humanity.

During the first four centuries of its existence, the early church struggled with the issue of determining how it should understand the meaning of the man whose message and life had turned the world upside down. Early Christians were certain that God had done something extraordinary through this Jesus, who preached the coming of the reign of God, healed many of afflictions, was crucified by the Roman authorities, and, they were convinced, had been raised from the dead by God. His miracles, the power of his teaching to transform lives, was evidence for his followers that he was more than a mere mortal. This feeling that Jesus was "more than" other teachers or holy men led inexorably to the tendency among some early Christians to obscure the humanity of Jesus and emphasize the supposed divinity of the Master. The implication, of course, was that he only *appeared* to be human during his earthly sojourn.

In the first century a Gnostic-inspired belief system called "Docetism" (from the Greek *dokein,* "to appear") became an attractive option for many early Christians. Gnosticism taught a kind of cosmic redemption through mastery of knowledge; thus, spirit and mind were more favored entities than flesh and the body. Even as Docetists sought to understand the salvific role of Jesus, they would emphasize his divinity, evidenced through the presumption that he only "appeared" to be human in his earthly sojourn. The major weakness, however, in this view was ironically its strength. If Jesus only appeared to be human but was in reality wholly divine, and if he was held up as a moral exemplar for mortal humans, what hope had they of emulating him if they were limited in their mortality? Such a Christ was clearly beyond the capacity of flawed humans to emulate or follow.

Docetism met its demise in what was for many an unmourned death in the early church. Early Christians knew intuitively, even decades after the crucifixion, that Jesus of Nazareth had walked on the earth. They also knew that he was more than an apparition. As Paul professed, for their sake "he became poor" (2 Cor. 8:9). Yet within the conviction that Jesus was human like other people lay the seeds for another doctrinal strain that would ultimately be rejected as heretical. Various forms of "adoptionism" were inspired by the conviction of Jesus' utter humanity, which was subsequently transformed by God in order to effect his status as God's Son. Adoptionism affirmed that the human Jesus was "adopted" by God or elevated at some point in his life to divinity.

Another form of adoptionism, Ebionism (from the Greek word *ebion,* which means "poor") similarly suggested that Jesus was merely a divinely inspired prophet of God but could not be considered on the same level as God. He was more of a moral exemplar than a Savior. Arianism, perhaps the most prominent of these adoptionist views, constituted the christological views of Arius (256–336), a priest at Alexandria. Arius contended that the Son, while preexistent, was not identical with God but was the first of God's creatures. Jesus was *homoiousios* (Greek for "of like substance") with God, someone on the order of a heroic demigod. Thus adoptionism, ranging from the varieties evidenced in Ebionism and Arianism, overemphasized the humanity of Jesus to the exclusion of his necessary divinity if salvation was to be attained with his aid.

Adoptionism offered the quite understandable affirmation that Jesus was a man, as the biblical record affirmed in so many ways. But the Christian who seeks to understand Jesus as Christ is not entirely satisfied with this assertion that Jesus was a man. To be sure, Jesus was human, but one is certain that there is "something more" within his persona that would warrant his being considered as the Son of the living God. But to assert that Jesus is divine *and* human would require constant diligence in terms of maintaining conceptual clarity and consistency, lest the assertion fall into a distortion. If it fell one way and overemphasized the *humanity* of Jesus, it risked losing the salvific power that only a divine Christ could offer. If it overemphasized the *divinity* of Christ, it risked positing a Christ who was irrelevant to the human condition. If Jesus Christ's humanity is obscured or minimized, and correspondingly his divinity accentuated, then the resulting Christ, a Christ endowed with divine and supernatural capabilities, is less able to have meaning for the human condition. What hope have humans to be as perfect as the God they worship? Raymond Brown, the late Roman Catholic New Testament scholar, put it this way:

A Jesus who walked through the world, knowing exactly what the morrow would bring, knowing with certainty that after three days his Father would raise him up, is a Jesus who can arouse our admiration, but still a Jesus far from us. He is a Jesus far from a mankind that can only hope in the future and believe in God's goodness, far from a mankind that must face the supreme uncertainty of death with faith but without knowledge of what is beyond. On the other hand, a Jesus for whom the future was as much a mystery, a dread and a hope as it is for us, and yet at the same time a Jesus who would say, "Not my will, but yours!"—this is a Jesus who could effectually teach us how to live, for this is a Jesus who would have gone through life's real trials. Then we would know the full truth of the saying, "No man can have greater love than this, to lay down his life for those he loves" (John 15:13), for we would know that he laid down his life with all the agony with which we lay it down.[1]

For Jesus Christ to be the moral and spiritual exemplar for those who profess to be Christians, a delicate balance had to be struck between his humanity and his presumed special link with a divine Father God. In seeking in part to counter the appeal of Arianism, the first systematic Christology was produced by Athanasius. His treatise *On the Incarnation of the Word* ultimately became the foundation for the Nicene Creed of 325. Emerging as the champion of Nicea, Athanasius thus defeated his opponent Arius, who having lost face and favor, experienced intermittent exile for the rest of his life. Arianism was denounced again at the Council of Constantinople in 381.

Nicene affirmed that there is "more" to Jesus than his human dimensions, desires, proclivities, and needs. Jesus is "very God and very man." Eventually, an orthodoxy would develop that would seek to hold two seemingly irreconcilable assertions together: that Jesus was divine *and* human, or as Søren Kierkegaard would later term it, "the absolute paradox of God-man."[2] A kind of conceptual tightrope walking, a feat attempted in the very formulation of the Nicene Creed, was required of Christology. The creed affirmed in part that "for the sake of us men and for the purpose of our salvation," Christ "came down [from heaven] and was made flesh, was made man, suffered, was raised on the third day, ascended into the heavens, and

---

1. Raymond Brown, *Jesus, God, and Man* (Milwaukee: Bruce Publications, 1967), 104–5.
2. Søren Kierkegaard, *Training in Christianity* (Princeton: Princeton University Press, 1941), 37; quoted in John Macquarrie, *Christology Revisited* (Harrisburg, Pa.: Trinity Press International, 1998), 14.

will come to judge the living and the dead." The preexistent Son was declared to be "God from God, Light from Light, true God from true God, begotten not made, of *one* being [Greek *homoousios,* "of the same substance"] with the Father." The creed was elaborated upon and amended in 451 at the Council of Chalcedon, when Jesus was recognized as sharing the same nature with God. Indeed Jesus was very God and very man.

The early Christian church and doctrine of the church developed within the cultural and belief systems of the Greco-Roman world. Most of the intellectual and doctrinal battles that were fought among theologians of the faith involved a reconciliation between the Judeo-Hebraic heritage of the Old Testament with the thought forms of Greek and Roman culture. By the time of the Council of Chalcedon in 451, the church had been able to appropriate and reject ideas and conceptual frameworks from Hellenistic culture as it pleased. It should not be surprising therefore that Christian thinking would avail itself of available conceptual tools and a framework in order to understand the paradox of the God-man in Jesus Christ.

The terminology of the Chalcedonian formula and the debates that led up to it are fascinating, if not maddening, in its arcane complexity. Three major terms framed the debates: *ousia, physis,* and *hypostasis.* At one time *ousia* was translated as "substance," but to modern ears "being" seems to convey what the discussion was about. Critical questions in this regard abounded: Did Jesus Christ and the Father share the same *being?* Is Jesus "of one being or substance" (*homoousios*) with the Father? The second important term in the development of the doctrine was *physis,* meaning "nature." While "being" is quite stable, "nature" implies that aspect of a person that is more fluid and changeable; it is emerging and becoming. Would the two natures of Christ have a fluidity, for example, each flowing into the other and vice versa? What are the characteristics of such a God-man creature? Is there conflict or an easy harmony, and if so, how is this achieved and which aspect is dominant? The third term was *hypostasis,* a concept that might best be connoted by the modern terms "person" or "personal center" or "self." Given the presumption that one person is thought to have only one personal center, not two, this critical concept forces us to protect the unity of Christ's nature *wherever* the analysis might lead us. Eventually two views would emerge using the notion of *hypostasis: anhypostasia* and *enhypostasia.*

Anhypostasia (literally meaning "the state of being without a *hypostasis* or personality") is the notion that although Jesus had two natures, a divine and a human one, as Chalcedon teaches, these two natures "concur," or are united in a single person (*hypostasis*), and this person is the divine Logos. So in this instance the human *hypostasis* is superseded and replaced by the *hypostasis* of the divine Logos. Jesus Christ is therefore without a human *hypostasis.*[3] The divine nature has invaded and effaced the human nature. It seems that all of the human is not only dominated but actually evacuated to make room for the invasive divinity. The direction of critical action appears to move from divinity downward toward humanity.

The later doctrine, *enhypostasia,* arose as a modification of *anhypostasia* and concedes that Jesus did indeed have a human *hypostasis,* which was taken up and absorbed *into* the *hypostasis* of the divine and eternal Logos. The critical action is just the opposite from the process in *anhypostasia.* Here the action appears to be moving from humanity upward toward divinity. For all of their difficulty, these two seemingly opposing doctrines end up reasserting the original paradox of Christology: that Jesus has a divine and human nature. However, the doctrines differ significantly in how they describe the process and the direction of that process. These differences aside, the enigma remains; the paradox endures.

THE CHOICE OF A CHRISTOLOGY

As we seek to understand the import of each of these two Christologies, *anhypostasia* and *enhypostasia,* for Christian ethics, much lies in the balance. We must find a way of affirming that Jesus is "something more" without alienating him from the human condition, the human condition that reveals itself in the circumstances and cultures of all the world's peoples, wherever people confess Jesus as Lord and Christ of faith. Of the two doctrines, I would suggest that *enhypostasia* is less problematic and resolves the paradox better. *Anhypostasia* effaces the human; the divine comes down and evacuates it, canceling it out. If we are to hold out for a theory that recognizes the human as a starting point—oftentimes a messy and morally inadequate starting point to be sure—then we must appropriate a notion that affirms how God *redeems* the human, not how it is canceled and discarded. Clearly, *anhypostasia* does not rise to this challenge and hence is untenable as a Christology for the vision of Christian ethics I embrace. On the other hand, *enhypostasia* recognizes a movement that goes from the human toward the divine. The human is not canceled out or evacuated. In fact, a way is found to transform the human such that it now shares a degree of ontological unity with the divine.

This movement from the human to the divine—this continuing mystery— made so evident in how Jesus became Christ—can be facilitated if, and only if, we reconsider the relationship between the human and the divine. Now, clearly there is a great gulf and difference between the mortal and the im-

---

3. John Macquarrie, *Christology Revisited* (Harrisburg, Pa.: Trinity Press International, 1998), 45.

mortal, between that which is of flesh and that which is of spirit. We need never delude ourselves that we are divinities clothed with the garments of mortality. But surely we are more than flesh. There is spirit as well in our being. If this is so, what if we were to affirm that the difference between the human and the divine is only a matter of *degree* and not *kind?* What if we could affirm that the notion of the divine is not alien in terms of *ousia,* or substance?

H. M. Relton, in an important work published in 1917 called *A Study in Christology,* understood the implication of this line of thinking and constructed his own Christology accordingly. He believed that "the truly human character of the Word made flesh" had been obscured in the development of Christology and also that "there is an essential affinity between the human and the divine," which is a necessary condition for the possibility of incarnation. The heart of his argument is this affinity:

> The presupposition of the doctrine of *enhypostasia* is the existence of such an affinity between the human and the divine as to make the advent of the latter into the former not the advent of some alien element, but the advent of something which by its very constitution and nature could coalesce with the human, and by its union with and subsistence in the human, give to the latter a completeness and perfection which it could receive in no other way.[4]

John Macquarrie seems to follow the same line of reasoning and approach. By choosing *enhypostasia* over *anhypostasia* we are affirming that the Word being made flesh cannot mean that the divine becomes transformed into the finite, thereby obliterating the human and the finite; rather the finite is "assumed" into the infinite, assumed into God. This line of thought begins to seem quite plausible when we begin to reflect deeper on our nature as human beings. Even in our finiteness there is an "unbounded" aspect to human living. Anyone who has ever dreamed, been able to entertain visions about what is *possible* as opposed to what is, knows intuitively that we are not bound by our physical limitations. Anyone who has ever experienced union with the divine, that ineffable Other, has a sense that we are more than flesh. Therefore the Christian understands that a critical aspect of our humanity is our disposition to be open to a mutual embrace with that which transcends us, the divinity that we believe has shaped us. To be fully human is be open to such a possibility. Thus the Christian believes that achieving the fullest extent of our humanity will mean incarnating God's existence in the world. Who among us has evidenced this most acceptably, most faithfully, even to the point of death? That person is Jesus of Nazareth, who by

---

4. H. M. Relton, *A Study in Christology* (London: SPCK, 1917), 147–48.

such obedience to God and the grace of God has become the Christ. This is exactly why he is held up as Savior to anyone who believes in him. Thus in this Christ we have an example of what can happen when "the human *hypostasis* is transfigured by a constant immersion in the divine Spirit."[5]

I believe that we are ultimately able to know this Jesus Christ, this Word of God made flesh, even this God-man incarnate, for the fundamental reason that Jesus and the humanity that has been redeemed by him both participate in being. Neither God nor we nor his Son Jesus Christ is alien from the others to the extent that all of us fail to participate and have our being within being, with God understood to be ground of being, and not limited to a being within being. To this extent the Gospel writer John was really not that far from the mark to be convinced of the preexistence of the Logos: "In the beginning was the Word, and the Word was with God, and the Word was God" (John 1:1). The Logos has always been here and will always be here, much as God the Father has been here and always will be here. Hebrews 13:8 puts it less philosophically and more poetically: "Jesus Christ is the same yesterday and today and for ever." Even now, to a certain extent the stuff out of which humanity comes shares in this aspect of preexistence if one appreciates the preexistence of the basic matter and building blocks of life that are constituent and basic to human life.

CHRIST AND CULTURE

Christ and the Problematic of Cultural Representations

The doctrine of the incarnation affirms that God has manifested Godself in the form of a human being, specifically in the person of Jesus Christ. Divinity and humanity meet on the plane of human existence. Throughout the ages Christians in various cultures have expressed full fidelity to this doctrine, affirming its universal application throughout the world and wherever men and women seek the salvation that Christ offers. Yet these Christians have inevitably seen this Christ through the prisms of their own particular cultures, times, and conditions of existence. As John Macquarrie has stated, "From the very beginning, the church's attempts to express its

---

5. Macquarrie, *Christology Revisited*, 79. In a real sense, *enhypostasia* anticipates several modern approaches to Christology, that is to say, "from below" as opposed to the ancient creeds, including the notion of *anhypostasia*, which fashioned Christology "from above." Rudolf Bultmann, in his demythologizing project, was an inspiration to an approach "from below"; see his *Kerygma and Myth* (New York: Harper & Row, 1961) and *Theology of the New Testament* (New York: Scribner, 1951). A few contemporary Roman Catholic theologians, such as Edward Schillebeeckx, *Jesus: An Experiment in Christology*, trans. Hubert Hoskins (New York: Crossroad, 1980), and Walter Kasper, have chosen to begin their christological inquiry "from below" rather than from above. They start with the fully human Jesus and then go on to discover and confess the saving presence of God in him.

beliefs concerning Jesus Christ have been couched in the language and ideas of whatever the prevailing culture happened to be."[6]

A familiar Christian children's hymn proclaims: "Jesus loves the little children, all the children of the world. Red and yellow, black and white, they are precious in his sight. Jesus loves the little children of the world." When these little children grow up, if they remain or become Christians, they will repay the compliment to Jesus. They will love him, revere him, and *see* him through the peculiar lenses that constitute their cultures and periods of history. Jaroslav Pelikan has shown in a sweeping survey the fascinating ways in which Jesus has been viewed from the vantage points of historical periods.[7] Starting with the image of the Rabbi in the first century, through the Light unto the Gentiles thereafter, through the Monk who rules the world of high medieval monasticism, through the Universal Man of the Renaissance, through the Poet of the spirit of romanticism, to finally the Liberator of modern political consciousness, Jesus has straddled the centuries because each age could see itself in the mirror of his countenance. Not surprisingly, in the graphic arts, Jesus bears an uncanny resemblance to the ethnic groups whose artists have sought to immortalize the divine image. In the hands of an artist like Albrecht Dürer Jesus has the features of a Nordic German; he assumes a Mediterranean cast in the hands of Raphael or Caravaggio; with Rubens he resembles any Dutch or Flemish young man; with El Greco, Jesus knows the Spanish soul.

Christ and African American Religious Consciousness

Not surprisingly, cultural and ethnic portrayals and understandings of the person of Jesus consistent with black culture and condition of existence have appeared within African American religious consciousness. We see the first indications of this phenomenon in the period of slavery itself, particularly as articulated through the Negro spirituals.

The African American historic insistence on seeking a level of freedom consistent with God's will for his people everywhere has required that Jesus Christ occupy a central place in the religious consciousness of Christian black people. The oral testimonies, either through the spoken word or the musical genre of the Negro spiritual, have afforded ample evidence of the place of Jesus Christ in this consciousness. The songs and spirituals that emanated from the African American religious experience reveal a fascinating view of who and what Christ was for blacks held in bondage. These songs become in a very real sense the "texts" by which we are able to discern a christological orientation and faith assertion.

---

6. Macquarrie, *Christology Revisited*, 11.

7. Jaroslav Pelikan, *Jesus through the Centuries: His Place in the History of Culture* (New Haven: Yale University Press, 1985).

Even early spirituals, those that were recognized or compiled prior to the collections that were produced after the Civil War, reveal fascinating views of the nature and role of Christ within the consciousness of African American slaves. One such compilation has been preserved in the writings of Rev. Charles Colcock Jones, the Presbyterian minister, slaveholder, and self-styled "apostle to the slaves." Jones's notations on the spirituals he heard being sung on his plantation come from the years of his "ministry" to them during the 1840s in Liberty County, Georgia. Born there in 1804, Jones went on to take theological training at Andover Seminary and later at Princeton Seminary, after which he returned to Liberty to run the plantation left him by his father. Evidence gleaned from his letters to his future wife reveal that he agonized over the morality of slavery during his seminary years. He considered supporting the aims of the American Colonization Society and even considered the emancipation of his own slaves. But he soon became resigned to the fact that if he was to pursue a ministry in his beloved county, then he would have to put such notions aside.

Jones passionately wanted to preach and minister to his slaves and those of other planters. Still somewhat ambivalent about slavery but wishing to accomplish this goal, he would need the approbation of the neighboring planters. He was able to persuade them on the idea of providing religious instruction for their slaves by arguing that such instruction would in fact make them more receptive of their servile status, which he would accomplish by emphasizing those texts in the Bible that seemed to support slavery and the obedience slaves owed their masters. Jones reasoned that if he could teach the slaves a version of Christian faith based on selected portions of the Bible that seemed to give approval to slavery, then he would have found a powerful justification for their servile status. An added boon would be that to the extent the slaves became faithful Christians according to Jones's criteria, they would have internalized the very justification for their enslavement.

Jones's message to the slaves not only reflected a perspective that was alien to their natural desire for freedom, but it also reflected a conventional theological orthodoxy that enjoyed little consonance with their religious sensibilities. That orthodoxy, as articulated in the Westminster Confession, affirmed Christ as "mediator between God and man, the prophet, priest, and king; the head and saviour of his church."[8] Jones, ever dutiful to his mission, attempted to teach the slaves the conventional hymns and songs so

---

8. "Of Christ the Mediator," in the Westminster Confession, reads: "It pleased God, in his eternal purpose, to choose and ordain the Lord Jesus, his only begotten Son, to be the mediator between God and man, the prophet, priest, and king; the head and saviour of his church, the heir of all things, and judge of the world; unto whom he did, from all eternity, give a people to be his seed, and to be by him in time redeemed, called, justified, sanctified, and glorified." See George S. Hendry, *The Westminster Confession for Today* (Richmond, Va.: John Knox Press, 1960), 94.

familiar to him in his Presbyterian faith and sought to steer them away from their own religious leanings.

But the slaves had radically different ideas about who Jesus as Christ was and the proper way to express worship of such a Christ. One practice that Jones particularly disapproved of, but one that the slaves practiced nevertheless in deference to African religious consciousness, was the ring shout. The ring shout consisted of two concentric circles in which slaves sang and marched, the singers in each circle moving in opposite directions to the singers in the other circle. In singing the song "Down to de Mire," dancers would take turns in the center of the ring on their knees, heads touching the ground, while others would rotate in their circles, passing shouters and pushing the heads of each ritually "down to de mire." The first verse of this spiritual went like this:

> Sister Emma, Oh, you mus' come down to de mire
> Sister Emma, Oh, you mus' come down to de mire.
> Sister Emma, Oh, you mus' come down to de mire
> Sister Emma, Oh, you mus' come down to de mire.[9]

To be sure, Jones was probably indifferent to these particular words in the spiritual, perhaps less so to the dancing that the slaves engaged in while they sang them. While he certainly would have preferred that they learn European forms of worship and liturgy, he could very well have dismissed the ring shout as nothing more than a quaint diversion of a backward people. But it was the second verse that outraged all of the Presbyterian piety in Jones when he heard the slaves sing,

> *Jesus* been down to de mire
> You must bow low to de mire
> Honor *Jesus* to de mire
> Lowrah Lowrah to de mire
> Lowrah Lowrah to de mire
> *Jesus* been down to de mire

In this spiritual the slave has bridged the gulf between the Christ of an exalted state and the condition in which the slave must carry on, in "de mire." In technical terms, the slave has devised a "low" Christology in which to view the relationship that has been forged between the believer and Christ. The slave understands that Jesus is such a friend that he can leave his exalted state and can be with the slave in "de mire," or share misery with the slave. Such imagery would of course have been alien to Jones, whose familiarity

---

9. Erskine Clarke, *Wrestlin' Jacob: A Portrait of Religion in the Old South* (Atlanta: John Knox Press, 1979), 47.

with the Westminster Confession would have made the slaves' concept seem utterly foreign. The slave has in effect adapted the Christology of the slaveholder's religion and made it fit the slave's needs. If the slaveholders had thought about it, and perhaps they did, they would have reasoned that if their high Christology could be manipulated in such a fashion, what was to prevent the slaves from envisioning Jesus as a liberator, that is, one who has determined that they should be free? What was to prevent the slaves from affirming a notion of Christ that spurned the high Christology of orthodoxy in favor of a low Christology that met their particular needs?

A review of other spirituals reveals that this is exactly what happened within the religious consciousness of African American slaves. Liberation and freedom became the focus of much of the religion, although because of its "opaqueness," to use Charles Long's term, one cannot reduce this religion to any one dimension.[10] That notwithstanding, it can be affirmed that liberation was a clear design of Christian slaves, and they believed that such liberation would be effected by Jesus as a conquering messianic hero. Moses, of course, joins Jesus as the other great hero of black slave religion by virtue of his leading the Hebrew people from bondage to liberation. The well-known spiritual "Go Down, Moses," of which there were probably twenty-five stanzas, is a veritable epic poem that recounts the saga of the great Hebrew's leadership in freeing his fellow Hebrews from slavery. The song starts with a dialogue between God and Moses in which God orders Moses to lead the Israelites out of Egypt. It continues with a description of the crossing of the Red Sea and the destruction of Pharaoh's army. The story ends with Joshua's taking the people on to the promised land.[11]

Despite the hero status of Moses, it is Jesus, the Son of God, "de Lawd," who stands as God's chief emissary in leading the people to freedom. The richness of the imagery surrounding the view of Jesus Christ as Liberator is astounding and full. Military as well as naval imagery is evident in the spirituals in putting forth this image of the one who leads his people in the fight for liberation. Many of these spirituals have been preserved in a collection[12] documented during the Civil War by Colonel Thomas Wentworth Higginson (1823–1911), a militant New England abolitionist who became

---

10. See Charles Long's seminal essay, "Structural Similarities and Dissimilarities in Black and African Theologies, *Journal of Religious Thought* 33 (fall–winter 1975); also see "Freedom, Otherness, and Religion: Theologies Opaque," *Chicago Theological Seminary Register* 72 (winter 1983): 13–24.

11. Olli Alho, *The Religion of the Slaves: A Study of the Religious Tradition and Behavior of Plantation Slaves in the United States 1830–1865* (Helsinki: Soumalainen Tiedeakatemia Academia Scientiarum Fennica, 1976), 75–76.

12. Thomas Wentworth Higginson, "Negro Spirituals," *Atlantic Monthly* 19, no. 116 (June 1867): 685–94.

a Union officer and who commanded the first freed-slave regiment to fight against the Confederacy.

Commanding the 1st South Carolina Volunteers, Higginson had ample opportunity to hear the religious stirrings of men who had been slaves but who now fought as free men. When Colonel Higginson heard his men singing spirituals, and no doubt corporately *composing* songs around camp-fires, as soldiers have done for ages, he noted the prominence of martial images that were associated with this heroic figure Jesus. Jesus is referred to as "my soldier" at one point and "my general" at another time. Throughout, Jesus is a liberator, as when the singers expect the coming of the Messiah: "Children we all shall be free, when the Lord shall appear," or "We'll soon be free, when Jesus sets me free." In the spiritual "We'll Soon Be Free," recorded in Higginson's collection, the soldiers anticipated that

> We'll soon be free
> De Lord will call us home;
> We'll fight for liberty
> De Lord call us home.[13]

It was Higginson's good fortune to hear the singers' interpretation of the imagery and personages in these spirituals that have martial images. A drummer boy told him, "Dey tink 'de Lawd' mean for say de Yankees."[14] Coupled with their own efforts to secure their freedom by fighting in the Union army, "de Yankees" embody as well the liberating effects of Jesus' intent that his followers be free.

The role of Messiah-warrior is further illuminated by the cosmic battles in which Jesus is engaged with his archenemy, Satan. The antagonism between the two is in most cases presented as a struggle for the souls of men and women. At stake is the deliverance of a soul:

> Old Satan, come before my face
> To pull my kingdom down,
> Jesus come before my face
> To put my kingdom up.
>
> Satan mount de iron grey
> Ride half way to Pilot-Bar
> Jesus mount de milk-white horse
> Say you cheat my fader's children.[15]

---

13. Thomas Wentworth Higginson, "Negro Spirituals," in *Afro-American Religious History: A Documentary Witness,* ed. Milton C. Sernett (Durham, N.C.: Duke University Press, 1985), 128.

14. Ibid.

15. Alho, *The Religion of the Slaves,* 75.

The great cosmic conflict between Jesus and Satan will be concluded with the victory of the former over the latter. In a spiritual entitled, "Mighty Day," the slaves envisioned the utter destruction of their nemesis, Satan, the one who had sought always to snare the soul during their mortal lives. The spiritual views the ultimate subduing of this mortal enemy:

> And then I see old Satan
> And they bound him with a chain,
> And they put him in the fiar,
> And I seen the smoke arising.
> They bound him in the fiar
> Where he wanted to take my soul,
> Old Satan gnashed his teeth and howled,
> And missed po' sinner man's soul.[16]

The image of Jesus as Liberator fulfilled a communal expectation among slaves for eventual freedom. The people as a group would be able to walk triumphantly away from slavery as the Hebrew slaves had done. Yet a facet of the perception of Jesus healed the wounds of the individual slave. Jesus could meet the spiritual needs and calm the existential pathos of each *individual* as well. Slave life was fundamentally a lonely existence. Each one in bondage had to "walk that lonesome valley" by oneself, and "nobody can walk it for you." With no control over the material aspects of one's life, the disposition of one's own fate, nor that of family members or friends, each person started each day alone, not knowing how it would end. The only constant in such a life was God, the source of all being, and one who had come to fight for the slave's liberation. This One was a dependable friend who would never betray and a sibling who could never be sold away. The slave could sing, "I want Jesus to walk with me," because this Son of the living God was a constant friend and understood more than anyone else the pathos of the slave's life.

Curiously enough, not only was it affirmed that Jesus could identify and empathize with the slave's life; it is clear that the reverse was true as well. The slave could very well empathize with the travails and hardships that Jesus had to endure. The slave realized that before Jesus could ascend into heaven and wield the cosmic power he did over Satan and evil, he had to go through the same pains of anguish and mortality of which they were so familiar. Slaves were particularly drawn to the last week of Jesus' life on earth, the whippings, the humiliation, the scourging, the torture endured during the crucifixion. They could easily identify with the words in this spiritual:

---

16. Ibid., 85.

> They nail my Jesus down,
> They put on him the crown of thorns,
> O see my Jesus hanging high!
> He look so pale an' bleed so free:
> O don't you think it was a shame,
> He hung three hours in dreadful pain?

Slaves could lament with sorrowful, dirgelike chants how "they crucified my Lord, an' He never said a mumbalin' word," even when the "blood came twinklin' down ... He never said a mumbalin' word."[17] Where in all of sacred choral literature will one find words full of such pathos as the following, in describing the torture of the crucifixion?

> They hung him high,
> Stretched him wide
> He bowed his head
> And then he died.

It is particularly in the context of all this suffering that the crucified Christ endured for humanity that the slave singer must have summoned up a particular modicum of gratitude when the refrain of this spiritual was sung:

> That's love,
> That's love,
> That's love.[18]

There is finally the hope that Jesus will usher in a new age of peace, harmony, and ultimate transformation. One might speak of millennialism in the spirituals as well as eschatological hope. In the execution of his messianic duties, Jesus takes on the persona of a conquering warrior leader. He rides on a milk white horse, as portrayed in the book of Revelation 6:2: "I looked, and there was a white horse! Its rider had a bow; a crown was given to him, and he came out conquering and to conquer." Further, in Revelation 19:11: "Then I saw heaven opened, and there was a white horse! Its rider is called Faithful and True, and in righteousness he judges and makes war." Such an appearance leads the slaves to exult in song:

> Ride on, King Jesus
> No man can hinder me.

---

17. "Crucifixion," in James Weldon Johnson and J. Rosamond Johnson, *The Book of American Negro Spirituals* (New York: Viking Press, 1925), 174.

18. I am indebted to Miles Jones, my colleague in the School of Theology of Virginia Union, for his facility in remembering the words to this spiritual.

> O, Jesus is mighty man!
> No man can hinder me.[19]

To be sure, the new age that comes about will involve a stern judgment and rebuke against those who enslaved and brutalized the slaves in this world. The new age that is to come will signify a complete reversal of the social order that pride, greed, and arrogance engendered in this world, where slavery and oppression were known. These spirituals speak of a new day, a breakthrough into newness that the slave could never know in this world— Jesus as Christ does this. Curiously, *he* judges, not God. He judges, for he knows of the pains of mortality and has suffered as the slaves have suffered. Eschatological hope allows us to see, with confidence, that which is sure to come. The key thing here is breakthrough: Jesus facilitates this breakthrough into a new life and a new world.

With freedom from earthly bondage, a newcomer to heaven joins the "number of de band" who are "singing a new song" of praise to God.[20] The "number" is a clear allusion to the number of those saved among the tribes of Israel, "one hundred forty-four thousand" (Rev. 7:4). Marks of this new citizenship in heaven include a crown, white clothes, a white robe, golden shoes, and a harp. Those who are saved are allowed to enjoy all the pleasures of heaven on the very first day of their new life in heaven; the "welcome day" culminates in the heavenly "camp meeting" with all the saved souls sitting at a big "welcome table." Such anticipation could therefore prompt slaves to sing, even while in slavery, "I'm going to sit at the welcome table one 'o these days." Moreover, in this celestial paradise the dejected state endured in life will be blissfully reversed. There will be "no rebukin' " and "nobody there to turn me out" and, of course, no death in "dat land."

Within the Negro spirituals we have therefore the corpus for a Christology affirmed within the religious consciousness of the slaves. On the one hand, Jesus Christ is the leader who effects the physical liberation of the slave. Yet on the other hand, he becomes the one who ensures the liberation of the soul as well, freeing it from the clutches of Satan, just as the liberation of the body rescues the slave from the clutches of the slaveholder.

BLACK CONSCIOUSNESS AND NOTIONS OF CHRIST

By the time of the renaissance in African American theological consciousness in the mid-twentieth century, black people would yearn to conceive

---

19. Theodore F. Seward and George L. White, comps., *Jubilee Songs: As Sung by the Jubilee Singers* (New York: Biglow and Main, 1884), 54.

20. "My Army Cross Over," in Alho, *The Religion of the Slaves*, 97.

of Jesus in their likeness and regard him as one who was familiar with their existential condition and cultural context. Actually, the antecedents of a militant insistence that Christ could be viewed as a black man extend back to a much earlier time. As early as 1829, Robert Alexander Young could refer to Christ as "black" in his "Ethiopian Manifesto." In this work, a blend of abolitionist fervor and black nationalism, Young excoriated the institution of slavery and prophesied the coming of a black messiah who would liberate his people "from the infernal state of bondage, under which [they] have been so long and so unjustly laboring."[21] The irascible bishop of the African Methodist Episcopal Church Henry McNeal Turner, ever one to pique conventional sensibilities, declared in an 1898 speech:

> We have as much right biblically and otherwise to believe that God is a Negro, as you buckra, or white people have to believe that God is a fine looking symmetrical and ornamented white man.... Demented though we be, whenever we reach the conclusion that God or even that Jesus Christ, while in the flesh, was a white man, we shall hang our gospel trumpet upon the willow and cease to preach.[22]

At least two poets of the Harlem Renaissance in the 1920s, Langston Hughes and Countee Cullen, offered poetic renderings of a black Christ. In his poem "Christ in Alabama" Hughes captured the pathos of Christ, viewed through the prism of black suffering. In that context, "Christ is nigger, Beaten and black," and ultimately is killed "on the cross of the South."[23]

Similarly, Countee Cullen published a long elegiac poem in 1928 entitled "The Black Christ."[24] In an earlier book of poems, entitled *Color*, he had expressed a deep confluence between the person of Christ and the existential condition of black people. In a very moving poem, "Heritage," he affirmed that black people and Christ had shared a "kindred woe."[25]

---

21. Robert Alexander Young, "The Ethiopian Manifesto," repr. in *The Ideological Origins of Black Nationalism*, ed. Sterling Stuckey (Boston: Beacon Press, 1972), 33–34. See also Kelly Brown Douglas, *The Black Christ* (Maryknoll, N.Y.: Orbis Books, 1994), especially chapter 1 for historic roots of African American concepts of Christ as a black man. Another helpful critique of black Christology is Theo Witvliet, *The Way of the Black Messiah: The Hermeneutical Challenge of Black Theology as a Theology of Liberation*, trans. John Bowden (London: SCM Press, 1987).

22. *Respect Black: The Writings and Speeches of Henry McNeal Turner*, ed. Edwin Redkey (New York: Arno Press, 1971), 176.

23. Langston Hughes, *The Panther and the Lash: Poems of Our Times* (New York: Alfred A. Knopf, 1969), 37.

24. Countee Cullen, *The Black Christ* (New York: Harper & Brothers, 1928), 77.

25. Countee Cullen, "Heritage," in *Color* (New York: Harper & Brothers, 1925), 36–41.

CHRIST IN THE BLACK THEOLOGY MOVEMENT

The black theology movement that began in the decade of the 1960s not only affirmed a theology that identified God with contextual and onto-logical blackness but identified the Son of God, Jesus Christ, with these attributes of existence as well. The theologians of the black theology move-ment attempted to put into theological and christological terms the spiritual and cultural urgings of black forebears and the logic of the regnant radi-cal black consciousness of the time. In general, three types of Christologies emerged in the context of the black theological consciousness during this period. Two of these views put forth a notion of Christ that could support black revolutionary consciousness; they differed with respect to whether the focus of christological analysis should be on physical attributes or a shared existential condition with black people. A third sought to explore a dialec-tic between a particularism that could nurture black consciousness and a universalism that could affirm the image of Christ and the "desire of all nations."

The Racialist Christology of Albert Cleage Jr.

A Christology based on the physical characteristics of the Jesus of history was the position of Albert Cleage Jr., who published a volume of sermons entitled *The Black Messiah*. The Detroit pastor of a largely black congrega-tion within the United Church of Church, Cleage advanced a notion about Jesus that affirmed his essentialism in terms of his racialism. Within this shared racialism with black believers would black national consciousness find a way to celebrate the life of Jesus Christ and follow him in his revolu-tionary program. For some time during the 1960s, Cleage had preached to his congregation of a Jesus whose mission was consistent with their ideals of black nationalism and liberation. But this pastor went much further than merely affirming that Jesus could identify with the political struggles of black people in America.

Cleage took the bold step of declaring that Jesus was, in fact, a black man. Emphasizing Israel's Semitic background and early links with Africa and noting the inclusion of persons from Africa in the ethnic strains that made up the nation of Israel, Cleage came to the conclusion that Jesus him-self was black and that he was a revolutionary fighting against the Roman authorities. Cleage's viewpoint is well summarized in the Black Christian Nationalist Creed, which is outlined in detail in his second book, *Black Christian Nationalism: New Directions for the Black Church*. The creed urged the believer to affirm: "I believe that Jesus, the Black Messiah, was a revolutionary leader, sent by God to rebuild the Black Nation Israel and to liberate black people from powerlessness and from the oppression, brutality, and the exploitation of the white gentile world."[26]

All of this amounted to an astounding version of Christian faith. Cleage could tell his congregation: "So then, I would say to you, you are Christian, and the things you believe are the teachings of a Black Messiah named Jesus, and the things you do are the will of a black God called Jehovah."[27] A black people set apart from politically liberal sensitivities to radical revolutionary consciousness, led by Jesus of Nazareth, a black zealot, formed the heart of Albert Cleage's Christology. For him, Jesus was without a doubt a black man struggling against the oppressive forces of Roman-occupied Palestine, just as later black men and women would struggle against police-occupied urban ghettos in twentieth-century America.

The Existentialist Christology of James H. Cone

James H. Cone uses an ontological analysis of the shared existential reality of black people and the Oppressed One, who is Jesus, to support his vision of Christ. He begins his christological investigation in *A Black Theology of Liberation* with the question, "What does Christ *mean* for the oppressed blacks of the land?"[28] That he would even pose the question this way meant that Cone approached Christology primarily as a matter of hermeneutics rather than a matter of pure historical investigation into the ethnic heritage of Jesus, as had been the primary reference point for Albert Cleage. Cone affirms that if Christ is to have any meaning for black people, he would have to join black people "in their condition."[29] But at the same time, Cone decries the "chief error of white American religious thought, which allows the white condition to determine the meaning of Christ."[30]

Why should appeal to one condition be lauded and the other denounced? Apparently, the condition of black people can enjoy normative value with respect to Christ's identity because black people share in the condition of the oppressed, the very people with whom Jesus identified and shared his life. In some respect, Cone seems to share the perspective of the theologians of the New Quest[31] in that he seeks an interrelationship between the Jesus of

26. Albert Cleage Jr., *Black Christian Nationalism: New Directions for the Black Church* (New York: William Morrow, 1972), xiii.

27. Albert Cleage Jr., *The Black Messiah* (New York: Sheed and Ward, 1968), 37; see also his *Black Christian Nationalism*.

28. James H. Cone, *A Black Theology of Liberation* (Philadelphia: J. B. Lippincott, 1970), 198, emphasis added.

29. Ibid., 199.

30. Ibid., 202.

31. The "New Quest" biblical scholars are to be distinguished from the "Old Quest" investigators. The latter, working in the last half of the nineteenth century, sought to uncover the historical Jesus apart from the myths and accretions they believed were so present in the Gospels. They therefore made a radical distinction between the Jesus of history and the Christ

history and the Christ of faith: "We want to know who Jesus *was* because we believe that that is the only way to assess who he *is*."[32] Thus Cone has a real confidence in the historical method, believing that such investigations will reveal who this Jesus was. And for him the fact that the black condition can become normative for access to the meaning of Christ is confirmed in history. Yet, perhaps sensing the circularity in this posture, Cone advises, "We are not free to make Christ what we wish him to be at certain moments of existence. He *is* who he *was,* and we know who he was through a critical, historical evaluation of the New Testament Jesus."[33]

Previously in the same work Cone referred to Jesus as "that particular Galilean in the first century."[34] Yet while Cone recognizes Jesus as "that particular Galilean," he is more than merely that for black people: "Black Theology believes that the historical kernel is the manifestation of Jesus as the Oppressed One whose earthly existence was bound up with the oppressed of the land."[35] One need go no further than the contemporary black community to see an oppressed community, sharing the same existential reality as the people to whom Jesus came. Concretely, to speak of the presence of Christ today means focusing on the forces of liberation in the black community. And for Cone, the reason for the oppression is couched squarely in the condition of blackness. As he writes: "Since the black community is an oppressed community because, and only because, of its blackness, the Christological importance of Jesus Christ must be found in his blackness. If he is not black as we are, then the resurrection has little significance for our times."[36]

In Cone's vision, there is a tension, even if unstated, between the Jesus that will emerge through the hermeneutic of black consciousness (Christ of faith) and Jesus as he is in and of himself (Jesus of history). This latter vision is linked with Cone's recognition of the singularity of the "kingdom," or reign, of God. Cone affirms that Jesus is best understood as the Oppressed One who announces the reign of God. Participation within this reign seems not to be confined to racial or ethnic identification, for as he says, "To repent is to affirm the reality of the kingdom by refusing to live on the basis of any

---

of faith but, as it turned out, read into Jesus their own values, presuppositions, and ideals. Thus Albert Schweitzer could call the Old Quest a failure for this reason. The New Quest scholars, students of Rudolf Bultmann, sought a continuity between the Jesus of history and the Christ of faith. The New Quest wisely believed that in the mind of believers both reinforced the other and that to focus on one to the exclusion of the other would produce a distortion of Jesus Christ.

32. James H. Cone, *A Black Theology of Liberation,* 201.
33. Ibid., 212.
34. Ibid., 210.
35. Ibid., 202.
36. Ibid., 213.

definition except according to the kingdom."[37] And the reign is nothing but "the rule of God breaking in like a ray of light, usurping the powers that be that hold humans as captives."[38]

For Cone, Jesus Christ is more than one who came to lead people in a political insurrection. The symbol of the cross underscores that: "The theological significance of the cross and resurrection is what makes the life of Jesus more than just the life of a good man who happened to like the poor."[39] Says Cone: "*The finality of Jesus lies in the totality of his existence in complete freedom as the Oppressed One, who reveals through his death and resurrection that God himself is present in all dimensions of human liberation.*"[40] The free in Christ can now "deny any values that separate him from the reality of his new being."[41] Thus, by virtue of a shared existential condition of oppression, Jesus is black for James Cone: "Indeed, if he cannot be what we are, we cannot be who he is. Our being with him is dependent on his being with us in the oppressed black condition, revealing to us what is necessary for our liberation."[42]

The Dialectical Christology of J. Deotis Roberts

J. Deotis Roberts offers an alternative both to Cleage and Cone by insisting that the universal reconciliation that God holds out to all persons in Christ cannot be squared with either the exclusive racial focus of Cleage or even the narrow existential focus of Cone. Either view for Roberts would lead toward further alienation of human beings. While Roberts was clearly an advocate for black liberation, he was as equally an ardent proponent for human reconciliation across racial and class lines. Roberts believed that "the black man is not to be liberated and separated, but liberated and reconciled. The same applies to whites. The liberating gospel is also a reconciling gospel. It brings us together. In Christ there is no black or white—all are one in him."[43]

Roberts has been accused of betraying the black radical political agenda by advocating a universal Christ who was above particular political or cultural expressions.[44] This is somewhat unfair; Roberts was attempting to delineate a dialectic between the particular and the universal. "Particularism and universalism," he wrote, "both have their place in the context of

---

37. Ibid., 209.
38. Ibid.
39. Ibid., 210.
40. Ibid., 210, emphasis in original.
41. Ibid., 211.
42. Ibid., 213.
43. J. Deotis Roberts, *Liberation and Reconciliation: A Black Theology* (Philadelphia: Westminster Press, 1971), 192.
44. Douglas, *The Black Christ*, 62–63.

the Christian faith."[45] But the particularism that Roberts had in mind when he contemplated how Jesus Christ is real for black people was grounded in a level of symbolic realism rather than a literal reduplication of the historical Jesus. "I do not take the figure of the black Messiah in a literal historical sense," he wrote; rather, "it [the black Messiah] is a symbol or a myth with profound meaning for black people."[46] A symbol for Roberts is simply a sign of something else, while myth is not a fairy tale but a true story about reality. Often precritical and nonlogical (as opposed to illogical), myths and symbols touch us at profoundly deep levels in our consciousness as human beings.

As an astute student of world religions, Roberts was sensitive to the tendency of all cultures to understand and conceive of the divine in culturally specific images. And insofar as Christian faith has spread across geographical and cultural boundaries, "the picture of Christ as being one of them [participants in cultures other than those in the West] does not preclude the possibility that he may relate to others also. Only in this sense may he be Christ for all men."[47] If Christ is to be the "desire of all nations," as Roberts posits as an ideal, then no one physical portrayal of Christ will be suitable: "Only in a symbolic or mythical sense, then, must we understand the black Messiah in the context of the black religious experience."[48] In a passage redolent with an appreciation of the dialectic between particularism and universalism, as well as the profound power of myth, Roberts summarizes the meaning of the black Messiah:

> The black Christ participates in the black experience. In some sense Christ makes contact with what the black Christian is aware of in his unique history and personal experience. He *encounters* Christ *in* that experience and is *confronted* by the claims of Christ also in his black experience. But at the same time, the *confrontation* of the black Christian with the black Messiah, who is also the *universal* Christ, points him beyond the mere symbolism that is rooted in his experience. In other words, the universal Christ is particularized for the black Christian in the black experience of the black Messiah, but the black Messiah is at the same time universalized in the Christ of the Gospels who meets all men in their situation. The *black* Messiah liberates the black man. The universal Christ *reconciles* the black man with the rest of mankind.[49]

---

45. J. Deotis Roberts, *Liberation and Reconciliation*, 130.
46. Ibid., 130.
47. Ibid., 136.
48. Ibid., 139.
49. Ibid., 139–40.

CRITIQUES OF BLACK CHRISTOLOGIES

Upon reflection on these Christologies, we are left with the question as to whether the views expressed offer a credible and workable view of Jesus as Christ. From the perspective of the framework and methodology that guides this present work, I would have to judge that the result is a mixed one.

There can be no questioning of the value that many black revolutionaries derived from the insights and boldness of Albert Cleage's Christology. His political consciousness led many to see an affinity between the contemporary black condition in America and the Roman occupation in first-century Palestine. Without a doubt, his Christology offered psychic support for the black revolutionary struggle. Such a Christ was a familiar figure in black religious consciousness, as we recall how slave religion presumed that Jesus was a friend, even down in "de mire" of misery and oppression. Thus in the drudgery of life, *especially* in the drudgery of mundane existence, in the day-to-day tedium of enduring oppression, a Christ that was a member of a despised minority people, a Christ that shared the physical and existential condition of the oppressed, was consistent with Cleage's vision of Jesus.

But inherent within Cleage's approach is a real problem. Cleage's Christology stakes its legitimacy on historical and anthropological claims and assertions relative to ethnic strains, blood lineages, racial profiling, and the like. Yet any Christology that stakes its claim to legitimacy on the methodology and findings of any academic discipline becomes the unwitting hostage of that discipline. This is the case in the implicit appeal to the racial and genetic history of Israel to justify Albert Cleage's assertion that Jesus is black. If his method is to work, Cleage must secure the blessings of competent historians, anthropologists, and even geneticists to proceed with confidence with his method for determining who Jesus was and is. In a very real sense, the anthropological historian becomes the arbiter of the legitimacy of the claims of this Christology.

But what if Cleage's claims are successfully challenged and proven incorrect? And even if a challenge is successfully rebuffed, if Christ is to be understood as reconciling *all* people to God, would it fundamentally matter? Albert Cleage's Christology, dependent upon a particular view of a Jesus of history, dependent still further on the investigations of historians and anthropologists, thus appears to be seriously flawed. The aspect of black Christology that stakes its claim to legitimacy based on investigations into the "real" and "actual" Jesus is bound to be ultimately disappointed. Even investigations into the ethnic history of Jesus are not likely to yield incontrovertible results. Moreover, modern fixations on color as the means of identifying persons is at variance with the much older—and more confident—means of identifying persons based on cultural affinities. Since the

"Jesus of history" is not therefore completely accessible to us, to base a Christology on investigations into that historicity is not wise at all. There is little therefore to be gained by investigations into the pigmentation of Jesus' skin or the genetic background of his heritage.

While James Cone's Christology avoids the racial and cultural reductionism of Albert Cleage's method, it cannot seem to avoid a basic duality that seems problematic at one level and contradictory at another. Basically, Cone tries to reconcile two visions of Jesus Christ. One is that of Jesus Christ viewed through the hermeneutic of black consciousness of oppression. The other is the vision of Jesus in and of himself as manifested in the reign ("kingdom" for Cone) of God. But in the final analysis, that vision grounded in the particularities of political oppression seems to win the day, and that vision is inextricably linked with the condition of oppression.

Cone's system works—and works well—as long as at least two variables hold constant: Jesus must be linked with the oppressed, and the oppressed must be linked with blackness. But the problem here is the presumption of a sociological *stasis* associated with blackness. It presumes that the black condition will never change; that is to say, it will never move from a condition of oppression. Is this nothing but the obverse of the racist assumption that the political and social inferiority of black people is unalterably genetically and culturally grounded? Thus, just as Cleage's Christology was held hostage to cultural anthropologists, Cone's is held hostage to a concept of social stasis. His method only works as long as black people occupy only one level in society, namely, that of being oppressed. Such an assumption refuses to allow for any social mobility or recognition of the economic and political ferment that is so much a part of contemporary African American life. Moreover, the method assumes that oppression, imposed from above and experienced from below, can only be of a material nature. In other words, it may presume that oppression is only of an economic or political nature. The method cannot envision oppression of a spiritual nature, such that even when political and economic power is achieved one might still be anxious, unfulfilled, and at odds with a desired destiny.

The Christology of J. Deotis Roberts is commendable in that it attempts to ground a vision of Jesus Christ with the existential reality of black existence while recognizing that if Jesus is to be the "desire of the nations," then the black experience alone cannot be considered as the exclusive normative context in which to articulate a Christology. Yet the black believer can affirm the symbolic power and the shared existential reality in which that believer and Jesus Christ participate. Such a Christology recognizes that a system that is not grounded in some cultural mooring is likely to evaporate into ethereal abstraction. The Christ of an abstract universalism is not only in danger of devolving into a vacuous and meaningless system but also is in danger of innocuous sentimentality. The pathos of Jesus' suffering, the full import of his confrontation with the civil and religious establishment of his day, and his penetrating insistence on obedience to the specific mandates of God's reign may become adumbrated in a notion of Jesus Christ that is shrouded in abstract universalism.

At some critical point, in order to preserve a credible Christology that takes note of the concerns raised throughout this chapter, it is important that we view Jesus as that aspect of God's nature that seeks to reconcile all human beings to Godself, as J. Deotis Roberts has insisted. Moreover that aspect of James Cone's Christology that affirms the primacy of the reign of God is also, I believe, consistent with the assertion that Christology and God's reconciling work must be linked. And, to be sure, the perception of this reconciliation must be viewed within the particular context of human beings' existential condition, that is, within the social and cultural parameters of their existence. Yet we will err if we presume that the divine action that we see evidenced as Christ reconciling in our particular cultural and historical contexts is viewed as normative for all people. Our context can never be presumed to be normative and absolute for all.

The framework that I have proposed in this book suggests that a Christology should offer a view of Jesus as Christ that is cognizant of the paradox that we identified when we sought to secure a viable view of God. Just as we recognized in our reflections about God, at some point in our quest for the Jesus of Nazareth who became the Christ of faith, we must admit that such a person will remain forever beyond our full intellectual and cognitive grasp. He eludes us and is forever on the other side of an epistemological veil. Yet we are compelled to affirm that insofar as he is yet alive in our consciousness, and is "more than" the extent of his physicality, he must become visible to us through the cultural lenses available to us. We must admit, however, that such lenses are only *ours,* limited in scope, fallible in our ability to offer indisputably a "true" Jesus Christ.

TOWARD A CHRISTOLOGY FOR OUR TIME AND NEEDS

Christologies have been historic attempts to explain the nature of Jesus Christ, the Son of God, and his relationship to God the Father and the perceived role of Christ in the believer's redemption. The classical christological formulations of Nicea (325), Constantinople (381), Ephesus (431), Chalcedon (431), and even the Second Council of Constantinople (680) reflected the use of intellectual constructs that may seem rather difficult for modern consciousness to grasp. These creeds played an important role in that they helped provide the church with some basis for common affirmation of the nature of Jesus Christ. Such affirmation no doubt contributed to a stronger faith for many Christians during the first centuries of the faith.

The strength of creeds, however, becomes their unwitting weakness: they harbor an unjustified presumption that they have actually explained and captured, without possibility of error, the object of the creed's affirmation. I must agree with Diogenes Allen, who in reflecting on the attempt of the Nicene Creed to explain the incarnation, says: "The Incarnation, which removes the contradiction that exists in the notion of union between beings which are on completely different levels—an infinite and whole being, and finite and sinful beings—does not enable us to understand how God became human. The picture of intersecting planes is only an analogy, not an explanation."[50] The best we can do is to recognize the poverty of our language and thought system when we confront the ineffableness of God and to repair to analogy, similes, and imagery when we seek to explain the Divine, or in the case of Christologies, the relationship between God and Jesus Christ.

Yet persist we do, and persist we must in our attempts to express the meaning of Jesus Christ in such a way that coherence is achieved, particularly a coherence within the cultural contexts in which we live. I propose that a Christology for our time, one particularly for an African American Christian ethic, may be found at the confluence of two concepts that have already been given prominence within the thinking of Cone and Roberts and within the tradition of the church in general. I propose that a Christology be based on the belief that God offers to all people freedom through reconciliation with Godself, made incarnate through Jesus' call to participation in the reign of God. Thus the critical focus of such a Christology is a recognition of the freedom God offers to all persons by virtue of reconciliation with God through Jesus Christ. It is therefore at the level of our existential condition as human beings that God effects such freedom in reconciliation. A transformation in our being is effected through this reconciliation. As a result of this transformation, we are indeed "new creatures." But insofar as we actualize our new existential condition in the world, we are invited to participate in God's reign, which Jesus announced with so much power and expectancy. We are called upon to act out our freedom within the structure, obligations, and demands of God's reign. Indeed, we may freely become "slaves to Christ" within the context of our new freedom. Let me now conclude this chapter by suggesting the outlines for this christological vision within the context of the African American moral life.

---

50. Diogenes Allen, *Christian Belief in a Postmodern World* (Louisville: Westminster/John Knox Press, 1989), 198.

Freedom through Reconciliation with God

In his second letter to the church at Corinth, Paul offers a hint as to how the christological paradox might be resolved in such a way that the methodological concerns we raised earlier with respect to a black Christology might be addressed: "In Christ God was reconciling the world to himself" (2 Cor. 5:19). Jesus as Christ becomes that One who, in reconciling the world to God, always challenges the world—and us—to move decisively and inexorably to a state of freedom. We are challenged to embrace a state of freedom from any thing or any condition that would compromise the viability of our being. God, as ground of our being, is pleased only when the freedom to live fully in our being is honored. Jesus as Christ has shown humankind the way.

Affirmation of Jesus Christ as Lord has been foundational for Christian consciousness for centuries. So central in fact has been this Christ-inspired consciousness for Christians that articulation of such faith has exuded from the cultural moorings in which believers have led their lives. We have seen this to be the case even in the travail of slavery experienced by black Americans. African Americans understood their travail, in part, through reference to the redemptive suffering experienced by the mortal Jesus. They expressed hope through the presence and power of the risen Christ.

Schubert M. Ogden has helped us understand that ultimately a credible and appropriate Christology will be based not so much on assertions about Jesus only, "but also and at the same time as a question about the meaning of ultimate reality for human existence."[51] According to Ogden, Jesus is the "decisive re-presentation of the meaning of ultimate reality for us, and thus explicitly authorizes our authentic self-understanding as human beings."[52] We have argued that an African American Christian ethic would do well to focus on God as the ground of being, rather than God viewed through the dynamics of personal-being theism. In this chapter we have suggested that Jesus as Christ always points the way toward God. Jesus as Christ incarnates the reconciling force that brings us ever closer to God and shapes our lives in conformity to the will of God. In the African American experience, at least in the slave religious consciousness, Jesus as Liberator held a prominent position. This is not surprising and indeed seems reasonable. But freedom is a condition of existence that is endemic to the fullness of all individuals; people cannot enjoy that which God intends for them to have unless they are free. To participate fully in being is to be free to participate in being, including obviously the dismantling of any shackles, especially civil or literal shackles. All human beings are meant to be free.

---

51. Schubert M. Ogden, *The Point of Christology* (San Francisco: Harper & Row, 1982), 87.
52. Ibid., 149.

How would a Christology within the context of the view of God I am proposing be formulated? Being the Son of God would have to mean something different than it did with the personal-being concept of God intact. Freed from the anthropomorphic constraints inherent in a personal-being theism, we could be free as well to ponder the implications of a Christology that was not inordinately grounded in the physical features of Jesus. Jesus has become the Christ because he has shown us the full meaning of what it means to be a human being, an *inspirited being*, radically obedient to God's will. Through such obedience comes true freedom. Jesus as Christ becomes the model of those who would risk all for the goal of self-actualizing and true freedom in God. Life is more than flesh, and fullness of life transcends our physicality. Life is essentially unbounded, and one should resist any and all attempts to impose boundaries upon it. Whenever immoral (and artificial) attempts to impose such boundaries come forth (examples being slavery, social and political oppression), then those who are in Christ are called upon to resist such attempts and move inexorably toward the full actualization of their humanity. This may, and usually will, mean taking risks, disobeying unjust laws and customs. But we are nevertheless called to follow, and to the extent we do so, we inevitably develop, and embody, the will to follow.

Freedom in the Kingdom of God

As Christians, we believe, as the Negro spirituals asserted, that we have freedom in and through Jesus Christ. But it should always be kept in mind that a clear understanding of "freedom in Christ" must always keep in clear focus a notion of who and what Jesus Christ *is* for us and what human freedom itself *is* for us. We must avoid two distortions or polarities in our thinking about Jesus Christ and human freedom. Freedom in Christ must steer between the tight confines of political machinations, as fidelity to the Jesus of history would suggest, and freedom as an abstract ideal, as fidelity to an innocuous and universal Christ of faith might suggest. The problem with associating freedom in Christ with particular political struggles is precisely the fact that they are *particular* struggles, *our* particular struggles in which we are always poised against some enemy at a particular point in history and time. Given the temporality of life, it must be acknowledged that social, economic, and political conditions are but *temporary* manifestations of the human condition. Human societies are always in flux: social classes swell, shrink, go through fluctuations based on changing circumstances and changing political interests. There is no such thing as social stasis. One must wonder then about a Christology that seems to assume that social stasis is the norm, that no change in the social and economic conditions will take place. What happens when black people change their economic and political status? Would not this then make the paradigm of such a Christ/Jesus obsolete?

We must be mindful of the exact nature of the freedom we have in Jesus Christ. Our knowledge of what we must do to achieve such freedom is not achieved merely through a mastery of the details of the life of the Jesus of history. There is a distinction between the Jesus of history and the Christ of faith. Knowledge of the Jesus of history will only take us so far. Even learning all we can about the Jesus of history still will not address the issue of whether he is and should be considered the Christ of faith. This is true because Christ is not an object of knowledge but an object of faith.[53] Yet focusing only on the Christ of faith and an eschatological vision of ultimate justice brought about by God's hand may lull Christians into a passive acceptance of injustices in the political order. The advice to spurn all political action on the presumption that "God will take care of it" results from this posture. Rather, that which Jesus as Christ calls us to *do* is perceived only in the context of the pain and pathos of human cultures and the human condition. Therein is the challenge to discern all that must be done to seek a level of freedom to be. Discerning this challenge and determining to meet it constitute the will to follow this Christ.

We are called to participate and be faithful in *God's* reign, as announced by Jesus Christ, and not to hold as absolute the transitory political agendas of our present generation. Following Christ will mean seizing political means to confront political systems, even as he confronted them. Thus, the appropriation of Jesus as a paradigm for political and economic liberation should always be considered as *penultimate* goals, not as ultimate goals. If political or economic liberation is made the sole criterion for the validity of appropriating Jesus as an exemplar, the model soon exhibits a real paucity. In the final analysis, any condition manifested within the context of our transitory mortality—whether economic oppression, spiritual poverty, spiritual anxiety, even chattel slavery—is a condition that requires the liberating power of Jesus as Christ. As long as we are clothed in mortality and finitude, there will always be some condition that cries out for liberation, some level of paucity on our part that only Jesus as Christ can assuage.

The Christ of Expanding Interfaith Dialogue

Of one thing we can be certain: the uncertainty of life and all that will unfold before us in our futures. Yet of another truth we can be equally certain: the relevance of Jesus Christ to our lives as Christians will remain intact even as we experience changes around us and in the cultural contexts in which we

---

53. Søren Kierkegaard, *Training in Christianity* (Princeton: Princeton University Press, 1941), 28; quoted in Macquarrie, *Christology Revisited*, 25.

lead our lives. In this respect, the confidence of Hebrews 13:8 continues to ring true: "Jesus Christ is the same yesterday and today and forever."

Within the exciting and sometimes bewildering changes and fluctuations within contemporary African American culture and life, a challenge is presented to the Christian theologian/ethicist to discern how Christ might in fact be relevant to these evolving contexts. For example, one of the little-appreciated facts within the religious culture of African Americans is the expanding options for spiritual enrichment that now present themselves. African Americans practice Buddhism and follow Bahai, Unity, and Islam. Should these trends continue, practicing African American Christians will have a number of options before them with respect to how they might engage these other faiths. (1) African American Christians can pretend that these other faith orientations are not viable alternatives for a spiritually enriching life, that they are only for those idiosyncratic persons on the fringe of black culture. (2) They can begin to effect strategic alliances with some of them, as has been the case with some Christian-Muslim contacts. (3) They can begin to discuss areas of common theological, ethical, and cultural concerns.

The first option would seem to be rather reactionary and seriously questionable. Narrow-minded and blind, it flies in the face of the changing demographics. The second has been attempted, although the alliances between black Christians and black Muslims have been limited to *political* concerns that have brought the two groups together, for example, voter registration campaigns and public policy issues like capital punishment or the poverty of real political power that plagues the national black community. The third option holds out the real possibility of engaging in substantive *theological and religious* dialogue between Christians and members of other faith orientations in the black community. A working question would therefore be, how does the notion of Jesus Christ inhibit or foster interfaith dialogue within the national black community? In other words, does the logic of freedom through reconciliation with God suggest that those blacks who have found self-authenticity in Bahai and Islam are at variance with Christian faith or are indeed fellow travelers in the common journey toward God?

Another area of interest might be the creative ferment that is evident in the so-called hip-hop phenomenon, which is now moving into an increasing level of maturity within the African American community. Much of the lyrics and the posturing of hip-hop artists have admittedly offended those within the mainstream of African American and the wider American culture. Yet for all of the raw and sometimes angry exertions that come from this segment of our national culture, one suspects that some profound questions about human existence and meaning are being raised. What answers can the Christ of Christian faith have for such questions?

The questions I have just raised suggest that the African American community is not a static community, that the intellectual, cultural, and spiritual ferment among America's black people is real. Without question, God must be affirmed as present in this ferment, seeking now as ever to reconcile human beings to Godself. A Christology must be affirmed that is capable of showing how God continues to reconcile black people to Godself through Jesus Christ in the midst of this ferment. A Christology must be affirmed that offers a sound vision of freedom in authentic newness of life. A Christology must be embraced as well as African Americans seek to live out their lives in freedom, submissive only to the dictates of God's reign. Such a Christology was glimpsed by the slave who knew that 'de Lawd' beckoned to freedom's land. A Christology that beckons that slave's descendants to contemporary liberation in our own time and place is required as well.

4

The Holy Spirit
as Counselor and Inspirer

The letter kills, but the Spirit gives life.
— 2 Corinthians 3:6

When he [God] speaks to me now in the Spirit,
I move and move with certainty.
— Testimony of former slave,
God Struck Me Dead

Christian faith would be severely impoverished were it not for a belief in the power and efficacy of the Holy Spirit. Just as Christian faith would not be recognizable as a faith system without the belief that through God's grace Jesus of Nazareth became the Christ of faith, so as well would that faith be something quite different were it not for a belief in the Holy Spirit. In fact a belief in Jesus Christ leads inexorably to some affirmation of the role of the Holy Spirit in the believer's life. Adolf Holl, a German Catholic scholar, has boldly declared that "without this Holy Spirit, Jesus would never have become Christ, and the religion that traces itself to Jesus Christ would have had to look for another name."[1] Thus, both in creedal formulations and in day-to-day discourse amongst each other, Christians virtually everywhere declare a belief in the Holy Spirit.

Similarly, within the unique perspective that African Americans bring to Christian faith, there has been and still is an affirmation that the Holy Spirit is operative and functional in the spiritual life. Such a belief has enormous implications for the ethical life of the African American Christian as well. The thrust of this chapter is to investigate the meaning of the Holy Spirit for the ethical integrity in the life of the African American Christian believer.

Virtually all Christian theological systems affirm that God, the Holy Spirit, and Christ as Son of God share a mystical unity in the Trinity. The notion of the Trinity asserts, not that there are three Gods that are worshiped,

---

1. Adolf Holl, *The Left Hand of God: A Biography of the Holy Spirit* (New York: Doubleday, 1998), 6.

but that in one God there are three aspects. Any notion or interpretation of the Holy Spirit must acknowledge that God is essentially *spiritual*. It is absolutely clear that if God is to be God, then God must transcend matter, not be contingent upon matter, and therefore must be beyond matter. God *must* be spiritual. If God is the ground of being, that without which being cannot be, then it would follow that being itself should have a spiritual quality. Thus the essence of God and that of being itself, of which God is ground, is the spiritual. Jesus, the One who became the Christ by virtue of his exemplary absorption into the infinitude of the Father's will and in so doing became "one with the Father," recognized as well the essential spiritual nature of God. Said Jesus, according to the Gospel recorded in John: "God is spirit, and those who worship him must worship him in spirit and truth" (John 4:24).

Christology developed as a result of attempts by early thinkers in the faith to solve the essential paradox of how Jesus could be God and man, how he could be very God and very man, as the Chalcedonian Creed affirms. Now, it may be argued, a fully developed Christology need not presume a doctrine of the Trinity. Christology affirms the oneness of God with Christ as Son and solves the nettlesome problem of explaining the divinity of Christ. Would not the introduction of yet a third person in a view of God undermine the concept of the oneness of God? Would not a doctrine of the Trinity cause more problems than it could possibly solve? And what *was* the problem that the concept of the Trinity sought to solve? These and other questions will claim our attention in this chapter.

On our way to answering these enigmas, it might be well to review the biblical witness with respect to the notion of God's spirit, the basic theological concept that would become the basis for the notion of the Holy Spirit. We must do this because, as Geoffrey Wainwright reminds us, in the Old Testament the spirit of God or the spirit of the Lord "indicates a distinction-in-identity that will eventually allow the Christian church, after the coming of Christ and the pentecostal outpouring of 'Holy Spirit,' to elaborate its doctrine in a trinitarian direction."[2] What does the Old Testament have to say about God's spirit, the harbinger of later notions of the Holy Spirit?

OLD TESTAMENT IMAGES OF THE SPIRIT OF GOD

The Old Testament views God as a spirit whose very essence is the spiritual. Moreover, God, as spirit, also has a spirit. God's very nature is to have one. While the designation "holy spirit" appears relatively few times in the Old

---

2. Geoffrey Wainwright, "The Holy Spirit," in *The Cambridge Companion to Christian Doctrine*, ed. Colin E. Gunton (New York: Cambridge University Press, 1997), 273.

Testament (Ps. 51:11; Isa. 63:10, 11), it is equivalent to the more frequently used "spirit of God" or "spirit of the Lord."

The image of God as "wind" (*ruah*) functioned as an excellent metaphor in the Hebrew mind as it sought to portray the ineffable, nonmaterial, and essentially spiritual nature of God. Indeed, during the event when God discloses Godself in a powerful way to effect the Hebrews' escape from slavery in Egypt, it is this *wind* that is so conspicuous. The slaves are able to escape their Egyptian pursuers by walking across a dry Red Sea because "the LORD drove the sea back by a strong east wind all night" (Exod. 14:21).

Centuries later when writers sought to explain the beginning of all that is, the Hebrew mind would further understand God's creative act of the cosmos as when a "wind from God swept over the face of the waters" (Gen. 1:2). In Hebrew consciousness, and later affirmed within Christian understanding, this God, as spirit, can do what it wills. God's absolute freedom in the context of creation cannot be abridged, even to the point of entertaining the paradoxical belief that God can create out of nothing. Jesus would later affirm the absolute freedom of the Spirit in his midnight conversation with Nicodemus when the latter displayed an inability to understand how God could effect a man's rebirth. Said Jesus: "What is born of the flesh is flesh, and what is born of the Spirit is spirit. Do not be astonished that I said to you, 'You must be born from above.' The wind blows where it chooses, and you hear the sound of it, but you do not know where it comes from or where it goes. So it is with everyone who is born of the Spirit" (John 3:6–8). And of course, the pinnacle manifestation of the Spirit for the early church was the day of Pentecost when again, as a mighty wind, it swept through the place where the believers were gathered. As Luke records it: "Suddenly from heaven there came a sound like the rush of a violent wind, and it filled the entire house where they were sitting.... All of them were filled with the Holy Spirit and began to speak in other languages, as the Spirit gave them ability" (Acts 2:2–4).

Not only is the notion of the spirit integrally related and identified with God; there is also a belief in the Hebrew mind that the spirit has definite effects upon human beings, particularly in preparing them for difficult tasks and assignments. Moses was given the ability to lead Israel out of bondage, as well as the ability to prophesy and judge. Others were given the gift of leadership, particularly when divine initiative conflicted with the political designs of human beings. For example, after the Exodus God commands Moses to assemble seventy elders outside the camp in order that they might be commissioned to share the leadership responsibilities with him. There, God would "come down and talk with you there; and I will take some of the spirit that is upon you and put it on them" (Num. 11:17), an indication of which would be their ability to prophesy. Meanwhile, back inside the camp, two men, Eldad and Medad, begin to prophesy, to Joshua's utter shock and dismay. Outraged, he complains to Moses about this apparent affront by the two men, not realizing that the spirit of the Lord has been put upon them as well. Moses responds to Joshua, "Are you jealous for my sake? Would that all of the LORD's people were prophets, and that the LORD would put his spirit upon them" (Num. 11:29).

The heroic in the human comes forth when the spirit of the Lord rests upon persons. During the era of the judges, it seems that the spirit of the Lord "took possession of" Gideon (Judg. 6:34), Jephthah (Judg. 11:29), and implicitly is present in the birth circumstances of the mighty Samson (Judg. 13:3–5). The influx of the spirit provides strength, particularly in crisis situations, as when as a youth Samson was confronted by a young lion. As recorded in Judges 14:5–6, "A young lion roared at him. The spirit of the LORD rushed on him, and he tore the lion apart barehanded as one might tear apart a kid." When the hated Philistines "came shouting to meet him; and the spirit of the LORD rushed on him, and the ropes that were on his arms became like flax that has caught fire, and his bonds melted off his hands. Then he found a fresh jawbone of a donkey, reached down and took it, and with it he killed a thousand men" (Judg. 15:14–15). When Samuel anointed David as king of Israel, "the spirit of the LORD came mightily upon David from that day forward" (1 Sam. 16:13).

But not only can the spirit of the Lord inspire heroic exploits among people; that same spirit is conspicuous even when they undertake less spectacular and mundane tasks. Thus in order to construct the sanctuary, Bezalel and Oholiab were filled "with divine spirit, with skill, intelligence, and knowledge in every kind of craft, to devise artistic designs, to work in gold, silver, and bronze, in cutting stones for setting, and in carving wood, in every kind of craft. And he [the spirit of God] has inspired him to teach, both him and Oholiab" (Exod. 35:30–34). The same artistic virtuosity was given as well to Bezalel (Exod. 31:1). The ability to govern Israel was given to Othniel, after a brief eight-year period of subjection to the king of Mesopotamia (Judg. 3:10). Thus, the spirit of God comes upon some persons, to their eventual personal enhancement as in the case of quickened artistic ability, or to the benefit of Israel, as that nation recoups its political fortunes or is delivered from oppression. In the spectacular and in the mundane, the spirit of God informs these transactions. This impetus for the spirit's resting selectively on certain persons cannot be explained; it is God's alone to do or not to do. With equal inexplicability, the spirit of the Lord could be withdrawn from persons as well. The hapless Saul is such an example. When divine favor is taken away from Saul and David is anointed as king, we are told that "the spirit of the LORD departed from Saul, and an evil spirit from the LORD tormented him" (1 Sam. 16:14).

Perhaps because the Old Testament Hebrew is aware of the essential inexplicability of the will of this spirit of God, it would therefore be appropriate and prudent to always entreat that spirit to remain indefinitely with a person, guiding and protecting all the time. Thus the psalmist prays,

> Create in me a clean heart, O God,
> and put a new and right spirit within me.
> Do not cast me away from your presence,
> and do not take your holy Spirit from me.
> (Ps. 51:10–11; see also Ezek. 11:19–20)

And also:

> Teach me to do your will,
> for you are my God.
> Let your good spirit lead me
> on a level path. (Ps. 143:10)

The Old Testament therefore affirms God essentially as a spirit, recognizes the powerful import of that spirit, how it can bestow prodigious powers on human beings and how it can be inexplicably withdrawn from persons. This spirit aids in mundane affairs as well as spectacular events; it is ubiquitous.

NEW TESTAMENT IMAGES OF THE SPIRIT OF GOD

In the earliest of the New Testament writings, the Pauline epistles, the apostle seems to evidence two ways of understanding the Spirit. (1) Paul continues the Old Testament penchant for understanding God and the Spirit of God as one and the same.[3] (2) At the same time, this Spirit accounts for prodigious spiritual feats believers are capable of when the Spirit comes upon them. In the letter to the Ephesians, Paul admonishes readers not to "grieve the Holy Spirit of God (*pneuma to agion tou theou*), with which you were marked with a seal for the day of redemption" (Eph. 4:30). Paul also affirms that the Spirit performs specific tasks relative to the believer. In Romans 8:14, the Spirit of God leads: "For all who are led by the Spirit of God are children of God." In Romans 9:1, Paul says, "I am speaking the truth in Christ—I am not lying; my conscience confirms it by the Holy Spirit." Further on in Romans 12:11, Paul admonishes believers, "Do not lag in zeal, be ardent in the spirit, serve the Lord." In Romans 14:17–18, he says: "For the kingdom

---

3. Generally, when the three Synoptic Gospel writers (Mark, Luke, and Matthew) and Paul refer to the Spirit of God, the Greek does not offer a definite article. This observation will have decided importance when we note a shift in the book of John.

of God is not food and drink but righteousness and peace and joy in the Holy Spirit. The one who thus serves Christ is acceptable to God and has human approval." In 1 Corinthians 6:11, the apostle reminds believers of their past sinful condition: "And this is what some of you used to be. But you were washed, you were sanctified, you were justified in the name of the Lord Jesus Christ and in the Spirit of our God."

In Paul's exposition on gifts in 1 Corinthians 12, there is every indication that by "Spirit" Paul means "the essence of God." Moreover, God as Spirit is responsible for the outpouring of gifts: "Now there are varieties of gifts, but the same Spirit; and there are varieties of service, but the same Lord; and there are varieties of activities, but it is the same God who activates all of them in everyone" (vv. 4–6). All gifts are "activated by one and the same Spirit, who allots to each one individually just as the Spirit chooses" (v. 11). The Spirit bears witness, as in Romans 8:14–16: "For all who are led by the Spirit of God are children of God. For you did not receive a spirit of slavery to fall back into fear, but you have received a spirit of adoption. When we cry, 'Abba! Father!' it is that very Spirit bearing witness with our spirit that we are children of God."

In the Gospels of the New Testament, the notion that the Spirit of God can come upon persons and endow them with divine favor continues. In Luke, an angel announces to Zechariah and Elizabeth the impending birth of their son, John. The angel assures them that he will be filled with [the] Holy Spirit (*pneumatos agiou*; Luke 1:15). In a similar fashion, in the annunciation to Mary, the angel says: "The Holy Spirit will come upon you, and the power of the Most High will overshadow you" (Luke 1:35). When Jesus is baptized by John in the Jordan, Jesus "saw the Spirit of God (*pneuma theou*) descending like a dove and alighting on him. And a voice from heaven said, 'This is my Son, the Beloved, with whom I am well pleased'" (Matt. 3:16–17). Full of the Holy Spirit (*pleres pneumatos agiou*; Luke 4:1), Jesus was then "led by the Spirit (*pneumati*) into the wilderness, where for forty days, he was tempted by the devil." When Jesus promises the Holy Spirit to those who will ask the Father, in Luke 11:13 the rendering is *pneuma agion*.

Only in the last Gospel, that of John, may we perceive a significant shift in the way Jesus, from John's perspective, himself seems to understand and articulate what he means by "the Spirit of God." In the so-called Farewell Discourses with his disciples just prior his arrest, Jesus begins to prepare them for the time when he would not be physically with them. Consequently, there is a momentous shift in the identity of the Spirit. At this point in time *pneumatos agiou* (Holy Spirit) begins to legitimately be understood as *to pneumatos agiou* (*the* Holy Spirit), so distinct that it requires yet another name altogether, that of *Paraclete*. This designation is very clear in the fourteenth chapter of the Gospel according to John:

"I will ask the Father, and he will give you another Advocate (*Parakletos*), to be with you forever. This is the Spirit of truth, whom the world cannot receive, because it neither sees him nor knows him. You know him, because he abides with you, and he will be in you." (John 14:16–17)

This *Parakletos* is the same as *to pneuma tes aletheias,* or "the Spirit of truth." At another point Jesus tells his disciples: "But the Advocate (*o de paracletos*), the Holy Spirit, whom the Father will send in my name, will teach you everything, and remind you of all that I have said to you" (John 14:26). Moreover, says Jesus, when "the Advocate comes, whom I will send to you from the Father, the Spirit of truth who comes from the Father, he will testify on my behalf" (John 15:26). Finally, Jesus says to his disciples:

"It is to your advantage that I go away, for if I do not go away, the Advocate (*Parakletos*) will not come to you; but if I go, I will send him to you. And when he comes, he will prove the world wrong about sin and righteousness and judgment: about sin, because they do not believe in me; about righteousness, because I am going to the Father and you will see me no longer; about judgment, because the ruler of this world has been condemned. "I still have many things to say to you, but you cannot bear them now. When the Spirit of truth comes, he will guide you into all the truth; for he will not speak on his own, but will speak whatever he hears, and he will declare to you the things that are to come. He will glorify me, because he will take what is mine and declare it to you. All that the Father has is mine. For this reason I said that he will take what is mine and declare it to you." (John 16:7–15)

Thus, the New Testament continues the Old Testament tradition of identifying God as spirit and appreciating how that Spirit can inspire and prepare persons for extraordinary feats. Jesus, prior to his departure from the disciples, prepares them by promising to send an Advocate, a Paraclete. Yet, while called by a different name, this Paraclete is not alien to God's Spirit. In fact, Jesus terms it "the Spirit of truth," whom the Father will send in Jesus' name. This Paraclete will teach and will be a constant companion to the disciples.

PNEUMATOLOGY AND THE TRINITY: THE PATRISTICS

In much of the Bible, Old and New Testaments, the "Spirit of God" is another way of speaking of God. But the Farewell Discourses of Jesus do raise questions: Is the Spirit of God distinct from God, as implied by the clear designation of the Paraclete? If so, why should there be a distinction, and what is the importance of the distinction? What is Jesus conveying to us by designating this Paraclete as distinct from the Father yet coextensive with the Spirit of truth, which, to be sure, is another way of talking about God? These questions point to an enigma, which is similar in many ways to the paradox that gave rise to the christological debates and formulas: If God is one, how can any aspect of God be conceived of as having a personality apart from God? On what basis can anyone, even including our Lord Jesus Christ, conceive of a special aspect of God's being in such a way that it requires an image that suggests another personality facet of God?

Surely sensing that the biblical record had set the foundation for a notion of God as Spirit, the early church forebears sought to articulate the truth regarding the Spirit with some degree of coherency. Inspired by the baptismal formula in Matthew 28:19, the Great Commission, they sought earnestly to explicate this enigma of the Spirit. Their effort was of mixed success and led to not a small degree of confusion. For example, the *Didache*, probably the earliest of the church's nonscriptural writings, uses the triune name once (7.1.3); otherwise, the Spirit is not discussed. But when some of the church forebears reflect on the Spirit, the insights are fascinating and provide an absolutely critical backdrop to our understanding of the third aspect of the Trinity.

Writing in the middle of the second century, Irenaeus affirmed the posture of the Spirit as he reflected on Christ's nature. Said Irenaeus: "For I have shown from the scriptures, that no one of the sons of Adam is as to everything, and absolutely, called God, or named Lord. But that He is Himself in His own right, beyond all men who ever lived, God and Lord and King Eternal, and Incarnate Word, proclaimed by all the prophets, the apostles, and by the Spirit Himself."[4] In his *Letter to the Ephesians*, Ignatius, bishop of Antioch, sensing his imminent martyrdom, voiced a hope to "have the good fortune to fight with wild beasts in Rome."[5] He confidently spoke of "God incarnate, genuine life in the midst of death, sprung from Mary as well as God, Jesus Christ our Lord."[6] In seeking to bolster the faith of the Ephesians, Ignatius describes the persecution they are undergoing as a means of "being hoisted up by Jesus Christ, as with a crane (that's the cross!), while the rope you use is the Holy Spirit."[7] In his *Letter to the Magnesians,* Ignatius links Christ to the Father repeatedly, "Jesus Christ, who came forth from one Father"[8] But then toward the end of the letter, in an attempt to

---

4. Irenaeus *Against Heresies* 19.2.
5. Ignatius *Letter to the Ephesians* 1.2, in *Early Christian Fathers,* ed. Cyril C. Richardson (Philadelphia: Westminster Press, 1953), 88.
6. Ignatius *Letter to the Ephesians* 7.2.
7. Ignatius *Letter to the Ephesians* 9.1.
8. Ignatius *Letter to the Magnesians* 7.2.

bolster their faith, he admonishes them to "defer to the bishop and to one another as Jesus Christ did to the Father in the days of his flesh, and as the apostles did to Christ, to the Father, and to the Spirit. In that way we shall achieve complete unity."[9] For Ignatius, the unity within the believer is complemented by the unity within the Trinity itself. In his classic formulation of this unity within the Trinity, he wrote to the Philadelphians:

> We have drunk of one Spirit. And it is manifest that all these gifts [possessed by believers] work one and the self-same Spirit. There are not then either three Fathers, or three Sons, or three Paracletes, but one Father, and one Son, and one Paraclete. Wherefore also the Lord, when he sent forth the apostles to make disciples of all nations, commanded them to "baptize in the name of the Father, and of the Son, and of the Holy Ghost," not into one [person] having three names, nor into three [persons] who became incarnate, but into three possessed of equal honor.[10]

By 140 Aristides was able to affirm that "Christians are they who, above every people of the Earth, have found the truth, for they acknowledge God, the creator and maker of all things, in the only-begotten Son and in the Holy Spirit."[11] In the same period, writing about 150, Justin Martyr could rebuff the criticism that was being heaped upon Christian thought by defending the faith in this way:

> We will prove that we worship him reasonably; for we have learned that he is the Son of the true God Himself, that he holds a second place, and the Spirit of prophecy a third. For this they accuse us of madness, saying that we attribute to a crucified man a place second to the unchangeable and eternal God, the Creator of all things; but they are ignorant of the Mystery which lies therein.[12]

Always seeking to correlate Christian faith with its own interior logic, so as to make the faith more palatable to a Hellenistic world that was fascinated with logic, Justin saw a role for the Spirit in the Godhead. Wrote Justin, "God begot before all creatures a Beginning, who was a certain rational power from himself and whom the Holy Spirit calls . . . sometimes the Son, . . . sometimes Lord and Word."[13] Toward the end of the second century, Bishop Irenaeus of Lyons could write:

---

9. Ignatius *Letter to the Magnesians* 13.2.
10. Ignatius *Letter to the Philadelphians* 2.
11. Aristides *Apology* 16.
12. Justin Martyr *First Apology* 13.5–6.
13. Justin Martyr *Dialogue with Trypho the Jew* 62.

It was not angels...who made us nor who formed us, neither had angels power to make an image of God, nor anyone else....For God did not stand in need of these in order to the accomplishing of what he had himself determined with himself beforehand should be done, as if he did not possess his own hands. For with him [the Father] were always present the Word and Wisdom, the Son and the Spirit, by whom and in whom, freely and spontaneously, he made all things, to whom he also speaks.[14]

Tertullian (ca. 150–220), while certainly not a speculative theologian, was among the earliest to address this enigma but did so in quite straightforward apologist fashion. Writing about five years before his death, he affirmed what has become the essence of Christian orthodoxy with respect to the relationship between God, the Son, and the Holy Spirit:

We believe that there is only one God, but under the following dispensation...that this one only God has also a Son, His Word, who proceeded from Himself...after He had been raised again by the Father and taken back to heaven, to be sitting at the right hand of the Father, and that He will come to judge the quick and the dead; who sent also from heaven from the Father, according to His own promise, the Holy Ghost, the Paraclete, the sanctifier of the faith of those who believe in the Father, and in the Son, and in the Holy Ghost.[15]

Fundamentally, Tertullian's attitude toward the pagan Greek world was that the latter's penchant for rational inquiry was at odds with the mystery inherent in God's relationship with humanity. Tertullian's articulation of the Godhead anticipates the Nicene Creed a century later when he declared:

All are of one, by unity of substance; while the mystery of the dispensation is still guarded which distributes the unity into a Trinity, placing in their order the three, the Father, the Son, and the Holy Spirit; three, however...not in substance but in form; not in power but in appearance, for they are of one substance and one essence and one power, inasmuch as He is one God from whom these degrees and forms and aspects are reckoned under the name of the Father, and of the Son, and of the Holy Spirit.[16]

---

14. Irenaeus *Against Heresies* 4.20.1.
15. Tertullian *Against Praxeas* 2.
16. Ibid.

To be sure, Tertullian understood "persons" not as personalities but as modes of being; God had to be one but could have different aspects of being, of which the Son and Holy Spirit were manifestations.[17]

As we struggle to deal with this paradox involving the Spirit and God, we are spared one problem that was inherent in the christological paradox: we do not have to reconcile the antithetical aspects of divinity and humanity cohering within the same being. In the case of the Holy Spirit, we may presume that both God and Holy Spirit are divine since both are spiritual. But can we really say this with certainty? Are all spirits divine? Not necessarily. Even scripture recognizes some spirits that are malevolent, evil, flawed, certainly not divine in the sense that we understand divinity, with its connotation of moral purity and uprightness. Thus we are still left with a possible rift between God and the notion of any other aspect of God known as Spirit. How can we continually affirm the oneness of God and still proclaim that a Holy Spirit, a different aspect of God, however subtly conceived or as boldly proclaimed as the Paraclete by Jesus, exists? How can we reconcile a tenacious belief in the oneness of God's substance and the proposition that inhering in that one substance are three hypostases? And how can we affirm these three hypostases inhering in the same substance without affirming a tritheism?

One of the more fascinating chapters in the early struggle of the Christian church to define for itself a coherent notion of the Trinity was the feat in theological thinking accomplished by three men, the so-called Cappadocian Fathers. These men were Basil of Caesarea in Cappadocia, Gregory of Nazianzus, and Gregory of Nyssa. They sought to bring a greater measure of sharpness to the Nicene Creed of 325 in terms of the exact understanding of the Trinity and the exact relationship between the Father, Son, and Holy Spirit. Hence they were known as the New-Nicene Party.[18]

Availing themselves of Hellenistic philosophy in support of Christian faith, the Cappadocians affirmed the consubstantiality of the Holy Spirit. While they recognized the Trinity as essentially a mystery, they hammered out a notion of the Trinity that affirmed their conviction that God revealed Godself as three hypostases, all possessing one nature. These hypostases are not three personalities but three modes of being. The Cappadocians' success in conceiving and articulating the views of the Trinity with insight and power resulted in the adoption of the revised Nicene Creed of 381, which came out of the Council of Constantinople in the same year. This Nicene-Constantinopolitan creed states that

---

17. Williston Walker, *A History of the Christian Church*, rev. ed. (New York: Scribner's, 1959), 66; Tertullian *Against Praxeas* 12.

18. Walker, *A History of the Christian Church*, 116.

> We believe in the Holy Ghost
> The Lord and Giver of life,
> Who proceeds from the Father,
> Who with the Father and the Son is worshipped and glorified,
> Who spoke through the prophets.

Thus the Spirit does divine things such as giving life, is of divine origin, reveals to us what God wills, and is worshiped as God. The idea that the Holy Spirit "is" God is stated indirectly but clearly by the fact that there is a specific section for the Spirit in the creed. Thus the early church ascribed godly authority for a Spirit who is God.

Perhaps representing the culmination of the patristic era, the thought of Augustine offers particularly helpful insights on the nature of the Holy Spirit. In his great work *On the Trinity*, which was arranged in fifteen books and written between 400 and 416, he defends the unity of the Trinity against Arianism, the ultimately heretical belief that overemphasized the utter humanity of Jesus. Basically, the heart of Augustine's method in approaching the Trinity is rooted squarely in his assessment that human beings are created and live out their existence in the image of God. If this is true, we can reason backward and infer that within the Trinity we may see some characteristics that are startling reminders of human consciousness. The Augustinian scholar Mary T. Clark appreciates this practical appeal to human consciousness in Augustine's method. She believes that Augustine took the position that "because doctrines have practical significance, faith in them entails a probing for as much understanding as possible."[19] We get a glimpse of his method in Book 13 of his *Confessions* as he probes the nature of the Trinity and how that understanding is linked to human consciousness:

> Who can understand the almighty Trinity? Yet we all speak of it, if it really is the Trinity of which we speak. Rare is the soul which in what it says of the Trinity knows what it is saying. And men struggle and contend, and no one without peace sees that vision. I would like men to consider three aspects of their own selves. These three are something very different from the Trinity—The three things I mean are existence, knowledge, will. For I am and I know and I will. I am a being that knows and wills. I know that I am, and I know that I will. I will to be and I will to know. Now he who is capable of doing so will see how there is in these three an inseparable life—one life, one mind, one essence—and how, finally, how inseparable a distinction there is between them, yet there is a distinction.[20]

---

19. Mary T. Clark, *Augustine* (London: Geoffrey Chapman, 1994), 67.
20. Augustine *Confessions* 13.2.

Clark further suggests that in *On the Trinity* Augustine made these three aspects somewhat more "psychological," as they become the mind—its knowing—its loving, followed by remembering, knowing, and loving oneself.[21] Sensing that there is a distinction in the persons of the Trinity, Augustine offers in Book 7 the image of the Trinity in the human soul as remembering, knowing, and loving God. But "remembering" here means one's awareness of the presence of God and conforming oneself to the Trinity of wisdom and love by knowing and loving them. Through love, the gift of the Spirit, one is united with the Trinity, and the more that love increases, the greater becomes the likeness to the Trinity.[22] This focus on love, the very gift of the Holy Spirit, puts one squarely within the confines of the ethical life because it is love of neighbor and love of God that are not only foundational to the fulfillment of the law as Jesus understood it but foundational to the Christian moral life as well.

Even after all of the early church's attempts to understand the Trinity, even after appreciating the theological brilliance of the Cappadocians and others whose penetrating analysis and prayerful reflections resulted in the creeds by which the faithful have expressed the work of the Holy Spirit, we must admit that God's manifestation as the Holy Spirit remains a mystery. Yet it is a mystery, made a bit more recognizable to beings within our nature, as Augustine would suggest, because of a tripartite nature of human consciousness, consciousness that must be summoned if we are ever to be in union with God in three persons.

THE HOLY SPIRIT AND HUMAN NEEDS

In all our contemplation about the nature of God, and in this case, even the Trinity, it is imperative that we make allowances for the full import of such notions on the spiritual vitality of human beings who would seek to understand and serve God. The clarity of our conceptions, the sharpness of our insights, should always serve ultimately the human agenda of serving God. Clarifying our conceptions is more than an academic exercise or an intellectual pursuit only, for the integrity of the ethical life hangs in the balance. The power to discern that which must be done to achieve an ethical life is a critical issue of vast importance for the Christian. The question then becomes to what extent the Holy Spirit within the context of the Trinity serves these ends.

In our wrestling with the paradox that involves God and the Holy Spirit, we are inexorably thrown back to the assertion that God is spirit, which

---

21. Mary T. Clark, *Augustine*, 68.
22. Augustine *On the Trinity* 7.10.14; Mary T. Clark, *Augustine*, 68.

is incontestable not only as a statement of faith but is borne out by prima facie evidence in the court of reason. God cannot be anything other than spirit. Moreover, God must be benevolent, benign, and free from evil to qualify as a divine spirit and be worthy of being called God. As human beings we participate in being in a twofold way: through the material of our bodies and through the access to infinitude that is provided through our spiritual makeup. In fact, we have access to this sphere of the infinite in God *only* through the spiritual parts of our makeup. God, as ground of our being, must always hold out the means of access for us to be absorbed into the infinitude of God. Jesus as Christ has already shown us the way to do this, fraught with suffering as it may be, surely mandating that our wills be absorbed into the will of God.

That part of God within the context of the Trinity that constantly seeks to effect our absorption into the infinite richness of God might be conceived of as the work of the Holy Spirit. If our access to the infinite is to be effected, God must do it, and we believe God does exactly that. We trust that God will always make a way to ensure that creatures, in our case, human creatures, have a means of securing access to Godself. God creates the means whereby we might be absorbed into and submitted to God's will. God creates grace, and grace emanates from God. Karl Barth affirms this assertion in his book *The Holy Spirit and the Christian Life: The Theological Basis of Ethics.*[23] It is the very nature of God to effect this. To the extent that the Holy Spirit is Reconciler, Barth is also right. It is the very nature of God to reconcile by bringing us to Godself. And to the extent that the Holy Spirit is always engaged in our redemption, Barth is again correct, for it is the very nature of God to redeem. Hence our speaking of the Holy Spirit is not a commentary on the affairs of some spirit alien to God, certainly not another being. It is simply another way of speaking about what God does. It is the very nature of God to do the very things we know the Holy Spirit to be doing. When we see the Spirit creating, reconciling, and redeeming, we are seeing exactly what God is doing.

But can we know and have access to that which accomplishes the creating, the reconciling, and the redeeming? I would affirm that we can answer that question in the affirmative. We are able to gain access to that which reconciles us, persistently creates within us, and redeems us to the extent that we can fully participate in our being as humans. Without question, this is the point where God meets us. God's Holy Spirit meets us there as well and does all the things we have attributed to the Spirit. As we seek to interact with this Holy Spirit, our context as human beings is central. Such a

---

23. Karl Barth, *The Holy Spirit and the Christian Life: The Theological Basis of Ethics,* trans. R. Birch Hoyle and foreword by Robin Lovin (Louisville: Westminster/John Knox Press, 1993).

context cannot be alien to us or our nature as human beings, for beings who participate *in* being meet God at the basic level of being, which is the level at which the Spirit accomplishes its work and meets us. That aspect of us that is spiritual and desperately craves contact with God desires as well contact with the Holy Spirit. The surest and deepest connection between God and human beings is made at the level of the spiritual; the Holy Spirit is that aspect of God that ensures such contact.

Thus, insofar as God has effects upon us as human beings, we would expect the deepest and most meaningful effects to be at the level of the spiritual. After all, surely a spiritual quickening accounted for the courageous leadership of Moses, the prodigious physical exploits of Samson, and the mental and manual dexterity of Bezalel and Oholiab as they engaged in crafts in preparing the sanctuary. All great human achievements are born at the level of the spiritual and the mind, precisely at that level where the Holy Spirit engages us. Moreover, it is at this level of the spiritual and the mind that the moral quality of acts we do is determined. The evil and the good have their genesis in the spiritual precincts of the mind.

The Old and New Testaments bear out these assertions. Almost without exception in biblical consciousness, when the "spirit" of a person is discussed, his or her "mind" is being discussed as well. In this context, "mind" is understood, not as "intellect," the tool of rational thought per se, but as the state of consciousness that determines human action. To be sure, the outcome of such action might in the long run prove to be rational, as in "having a mind" to obey a red light. But one might also "have a mind" to risk oneself in combat, in the face of overwhelming odds in order to save comrades. Such an act would not be considered rational in the conventional sense of that term, assuming that self-preservation is an indicator of rational behavior.

In the Old and New Testaments, the spirit of a person and the mind of a person are conflated to such an extent that the regeneration of one means the regeneration of the other, and conversely the degeneration of one means the degeneration of the other. For example, when confronted with the prospect of losing his slaves, Pharaoh's spirit becomes troubled (Gen. 41:8). The implication is clear that it is his mind that is troubled as well. No other aspect of the kingdom or the court is jeopardized; only his mind has been assaulted. When Moses asked the Israelites for materials with which to build the tabernacle, "they came, everyone whose heart was stirred, and everyone whose spirit was willing, and brought the LORD's offering to be used for the tent of meeting" (Exod. 35:21). The implication is clear: unless the people's spirit had been favorable to acceding to Moses' request, they would not have had a mind to follow through on it. The graphic metaphor of adultery in Hosea illustrates the link between spirit and mind on a corporate level as well: "For a spirit of whoredom has led them astray, and they have played the whore, forsaking their God" (Hos. 4:12). Jesus also presumes a link between the interior spirit of a person and the disposition of the mind. In the Beatitudes, the "poor in spirit" are blessed and become inheritors of the reign of God precisely because they have the disposition of mind required. To be sure, spirit and mind are often in a warring conflict with the flesh, as in "Keep awake and pray that you may not come into the time of trial; the spirit indeed is willing, but the flesh is weak" (Mark 14:38). Yet in the final analysis, the flesh cannot conquer the quickened spirit, for "it is the spirit that gives life; the flesh is useless" (John 6:63).

The Holy Spirit is that aspect of God that seeks to have influence over us, that seeks to forge our wills in conformity with the will of God. Therefore, the work of the Holy Spirit is uniquely suited to effect the moral regeneration of believers. It is within the purview of the Holy Spirit to meet the spirits of human beings and, where necessary, to transform spirits that are rebellious to the will of God into spirits that are submissive to the will of God. All of this has enormous implications for the ethical life. In a real sense, nothing of ethical import happens within life until the human will is involved, either negatively or positively. Negatively speaking, a perverted will, a will that is rebellious against the will of God, will cause the person to commit immoral or even evil acts. Positively speaking, a will that seeks to be in conformity with the will of God will cause the person to commit moral and good acts. The will must be harnessed in accordance with the good. But since we have already shown that the human mind and will are lodged under the purview of the spiritual, it follows that the aspect of God that most dynamically quickens the human mind and spirit is the Spirit of God, or the Holy Spirit.

At the level of the spiritual, the level of the mind and the will, the Holy Spirit makes deep and abiding contact with human beings, which seems to be exactly what Jesus is assuming when he spoke of the work of the Holy Spirit as a necessary aspect of preparation for the moral life. Again, during the Farewell Discourses, Jesus prepares his disciples for his imminent departure and teaches that which will be needed to lead the moral and ethical life: the quickening of the mind and will. John records these words of Jesus:

> "I have said these things to you while I am still with you. But the Advocate, the Holy Spirit, whom the Father will send in my name, will teach you everything, and remind you of all that I have said to you." (John 14:25–26)

The hope is that the Spirit would bring to remembrance what has been taught. In the aftermath of Jesus' departure this same Counselor will "prove the world wrong about sin and righteousness and judgment: about sin, because they do not believe in me; about righteousness, because I am going to the Father" (John 16:8–10).

THE TESTIMONY FROM SLAVERY ABOUT THE HOLY SPIRIT

It remains now for us to investigate whether there are any peculiar linkages between African American religious consciousness and the ethical quickening that is available through the work of the Holy Spirit. Almost without exception, the cultures of the enslaved Africans who would come to America were imbued with a sense of the powerful presence of the spiritual. In all aspects of life—commerce, statecraft, art, social relations—the spiritual was deeply embedded. In fact the legitimacy and integrity of these aspects of life were assured to the extent that the realm of the spiritual blessed and condoned secular activities. In a real sense, it is not even proper to speak of a "secular" in traditional African cultures. Life is whole and one, a seamless garment stitched by spirits but worn by mortals.

The West African cultures from whence the enslaved came initiated young people of both genders into the rights and responsibilities of adulthood. At this critical point in the life cycle, during adolescence, the initiated received as well a special induction into a lifelong relationship with a deity, or an *orisha* in the Yoruba faith, for example. While fellow humans were pivotal in effecting the initiated's induction into the cult of an *orisha*, the deity as well caused the person to safely undergo the rigorous tests required for him or her to become a member of that cult. The god broke through and did so through the medium of dreams. Thus all through West Africa the role of dreams in effecting conversion to religious loyalties was well in place by the time Africans came to America. And to be sure, such beliefs would factor into the dynamics by which these Africans would come to embrace the Christian faith.

Humphrey Fisher documents how in 1862 an Ijaye captive who had but a "slight contact...with Christianity" and was devoted to his *orisha* Osun told how in one of his dreams he saw himself and his *orisha* chained near a large fire in which they both were to be burned. He saw his *orisha* put into the fire, but he himself was set free. In the final dream of the series, the dreamer was commanded never to bow down to *orisha* again. The captive awoke in great torment and could not be comforted until he was converted to Christianity.[24] Many other African Americans cited their

---

24. Humphrey J. Fisher, "Dreams and Conversion in Black Africa," in *Conversion to Islam,* ed. Nehemia Levtzion (New York: Holmes & Meier, 1979), 217–35. See also Mechal Sobel, "The Revolution in Selves: Black and White Inner Aliens," in *Through a Glass Darkly: Reflections on Personal Identity in Early America,* ed. Ronald Hoffman, Mechal Sobel, and Fredrika J. Teute (Chapel Hill: University of North Carolina Press, 1997), 163–205. Other

dreams in their conversion to Christianity. As late as the early twentieth century, older African Americans, some of whom were born during the final years of bondage, could remember the role dreams played in their conversion experiences and in calls to preach the gospel.[25]

In the antebellum Sea Island communities, just off the coasts of Georgia and South Carolina, where many Africanisms survived, dreams were absolutely critical to gaining insight into one's destiny and how one should negotiate through life. In the mid-1930s, Samuel Miller Lawton, who lived on Port Royal Island for more than a year, conducted a revealing study of Sea Island beliefs and practices. Lawton interviewed fifty-five adult believers, "28 of whom were ex-slaves." Of all the adults, 86 percent were "directed by the Spirit in a dream or vision" to choose their particular guide. Of fifty-five adults, all but one had a vision during the period in which they were "seekin'" salvation.[26] In his preface to *God Struck Me Dead*, the classic work on slave conversion experiences, the theorist of religion Paul Radin observed that slave conversion experiences had three critical aspects. These experiences always began "with a sense of sin and nonrealization and terminated with one of cleanliness, certainty, and reintegration, the three things every Negro was denied in life."[27] Making no pretense at being systematic or dogmatic Christian theologians, African American slaves nevertheless articulated and evidenced a powerful understanding of the role of the Holy Spirit, or simply "the Spirit," in their lives. As recorded in *God Struck Me Dead*, the reminiscences of persons whose youth was deeply etched by slavery reveal amazing similarities with biblical testimonies about the power and capabilities of the Holy Spirit. One respondent who eventually answered the call to preach the gospel recalled how the Spirit enabled him to overcome physical ailments so that he could keep a commitment to preach to a waiting congregation:

> I felt awful bad when I first got to church and took my place on the stand, waiting for the congregation to gather. And then the spirit lifted me up. I forgot all about the pain and just lost sight of the world and

examples of dream reports by African Americans in the eighteenth and nineteenth centuries can be found in George White, *A Brief Account of the Life, Experience, Travels, and Gospel Labours of George White, an African*, in Graham Russell Hodges, ed., *Black Itinerants of the Gospel: The Narratives of John Jea and George White* Madison, Wisc.: Madison House, 1993.

25. Clifton H. Johnson and A. P. Watson, eds., *God Struck Me Dead: Religious Conversion Experiences and Autobiographies of Ex-slaves* (Philadelphia: The Pilgrim Press, 1969).

26. Samuel Miller Lawton, "The Religious Life of South Carolina Coastal and Sea Island Negroes" (Ph.D. diss., George Peabody College for Teachers, 1939), 131–50; Margaret Washington Creel, *"A Peculiar People": Slave Religion and Community-Culture among the Gullahs* (New York: New York University Press, 1988), 284–302.

27. Paul Radin, foreword to *God Struck Me Dead: Religious Conversion Experiences and Autobiographies of Ex-slaves,* ed. Clifton H. Johnson and A. P. Watson (Philadelphia: The Pilgrim Press, 1969), viii.

all the things of the world. When the spirit begins to work with one it don't have any cares for pain or anything of the world. My mind gets fixed on God and I feel a deep love, joy, and desire to be with God.[28]

This one testimony evidences all the functions that Karl Barth identified in his study of the Holy Spirit. Barth affirmed that the Holy Spirit does exactly what God does and that when we see the work of the Holy Spirit, we see the work of God. The Holy Spirit creates, redeems, and reconciles. With respect to the prior referenced testimony of the slave preacher, we can see the work of the Holy Spirit. The generative force for all the preacher's creative acts, his mind and his subsequently forged will, became fixed on God through the power of the Spirit. A felt "deep love, joy" betokened the redemption that Barth experienced as he celebrated reconciliation with God, or the "desire to be with God."

The world of the spirits, as personified by the Holy Spirit, in African American religious consciousness fulfills certain mundane and pedestrian functions as well. In *God Struck Me Dead*, a respondent recalled that after surviving the rigors of slavery and the turmoil of the Civil War, he would experience the fullness of the Holy Spirit even during his workday in a lumber mill. At some moments he would even "get happy and shout." Pressed to explain why, he responded by saying, "I don't know why, but it looked like the Spirit would begin to move on the inside, and I just couldn't hold my piece. I shouted, sang and cried. I got along well."[29] The rather laconic "I got along well" betokens a close relationship between the intensity of spiritual life and the integrity of mundane existence.

More than a few testimonies note how the Spirit ensures material wellbeing, that is, undergirds life in the work-a-day world of everyday existence. The Spirit directs one woman to secure peach-tree leaves to form a polstice to apply to an injured limb. The efficacy of such treatment was attested by the fact that "I haven't been bothered since."[30] The Spirit enabled former slaves to perform prodigious feats reminiscent of the exploits of famous biblical figures. Though illiterate, one man was able to preach by being "full of the spirit."[31] Through the aegis of the Spirit, religious conversion brought for many a sense of self-confidence and certainty of direction in life. One respondent affirmed that "ever since that day I have been falling down and getting up, always looking to God because He promised to never leave me alone or forsake me. I am always forewarned to trouble. When He speaks to

---

28. Johnson and Watson, *God Struck Me Dead*, 23.
29. Ibid., 56.
30. Ibid., 60.
31. Ibid., 68.

me now in the Spirit, I move and move with certainty."[32] This same person articulated how a belief in the work of the Holy Spirit could inform the close connection between belief in God and the integrity of life. Said he, "I have seen many visions. This is why I believe in God more strongly. Everything I have asked him to show me he has shown."

THE CONTINUING WORK OF THE HOLY SPIRIT IN AFRICAN AMERICAN ETHICAL CONSCIOUSNESS

The desire to "move, and move with certainty" impels the descendants of African American slaves to seek counsel and inspiration from the Holy Spirit in their contemporary contexts and challenges. We can observe and celebrate a contemporary appropriation of the power of the Holy Spirit as black people seek to sharpen their ethical consciousness in contemporary society. Such appropriation of the Spirit will yield a sharpened proficiency among black people in their ethical discernment and can proceed through the rekindling of past modes and methods by which the Spirit has moved within the history of black people. We have seen models of such leading in the ways by which African American slaves interacted with the world superintended by the "Spirit." Where might we look for the peculiar movement of "the Spirit" in the spiritual and ethical lives of contemporary African Americans? I propose that we can see the work of the Spirit at the confluence of liturgical vibrancy and renewed efforts at ethical integrity, in other words, at the intersection of "worship and work."

Contemporary African American life is characterized by a basic anomaly: the gradual rise in economic and social advancement of a segmented proportion of black Americans in the face of continuing overt and subtle forms of racism bent on thwarting those advances. The more obvious effects of such racism may be the continuing existence of an economic underclass whose members cannot seem to find a way out of intergenerational poverty. Thus, two classes have emerged with increasingly sharpened contours since the era of the civil rights movement: a middle class that grew because it stubbornly sought the benefits of a legally desegregated society and an underclass that met the stubborn resistance of that society to accord it entrée to those benefits. Both classes have paid a great spiritual price. The middle class either has been seduced into abandoning the spiritual moorings from which most of its members sprang before they acquired their newly found wealth or has developed a confused and inchoate posture with regard to spirituality as a result of the fatigue experienced from fighting corporate white America. The underclass either has maintained a belief in the magical aspects of spir-

---

32. Ibid., 94.

ituality or has succumbed to a functional atheism consistent with the bleak economic outlook, itself consistent with the despair experienced in so many of the nation's inner cities. In both classes, a shared spiritual malaise has become apparent; each class shares to a great extent feelings of alienation and spiritual poverty.

Within the past generation or so, a growing number of African American churches, both within traditional denominations and in many congregations transcending denominational affiliations, have experienced a liturgical revival. Within traditional denominations, congregations like Bethel African Methodist Episcopal Church in Baltimore, First African Methodist Episcopal Church in Los Angeles, or Faithful Central Missionary Baptist in the same city have experienced phenomenal growth in the past fifteen years, in large part due to new liturgical patterns and forms of worship. Other congregations that had grown restive of denominational structures include the three-thousand-member Resurrection Prayer Worship Center of Brandywine, Maryland, a congregation that recently severed ties with the United Methodist Church.[33] Another example is From the Heart Church Ministries, a twenty-four-thousand-member congregation in Prince George's County, Maryland, that left the African Methodist Episcopal Zion Church in the fall of 1999.[34] There are, as well, congregations that have bypassed denominational affiliation altogether. Examples include the Christ Universal Temple in Chicago, who under the leadership of a dynamic woman pastor, Johnnie Colemon, has grown to become a congregation of ten thousand members that meets in a sprawling $10.5 million complex on the city's South Side. Another lively exemplar of the independent charismatic movement is the ten-thousand-member Crenshaw Christian Center of Los Angeles.[35]

The music, liturgy, style of worship, and the experience derived from the worship services in these renewed congregations represent a radical departure from the ways of worship that characterized traditional mainline African American churches. The hymnody and corpus of anthems based on European sacred music have been replaced by an organic aesthetic that has sprung forth from contemporary dynamics and exigencies, which have been occasioned by the challenge of finding new ways of expressing the joy of spirituality within the context of corporate worship. The leaders of these worship settings have made a concerted effort to offer to the believer a context in which to experience a deep encounter with God, to feel the power

33. *Washington Post*, December 1, 1999.
34. *Washington Post*, October 27, 1999.
35. Joseph J. Kane, Sylvester Monroe, and Janice C. Simpson, "Strains on the Heart"*Time Magazine*, November 19, 1990, 88–90.

of the Holy Spirit, or to "enjoy God."[36] The result is a confluence of personal spiritual exuberance in the context of corporate participation. For this reason, not a few members of these congregations praise the ethos of these worship settings for the space to "be themselves" even as they participate in a larger corporate setting.

Two other very important dynamics may be observed within this phenomenon. First, there is a devaluing of formal worship characterized by predictable points in an order of worship. The congregation and the leaders of worship intuitively discern the ineffableness of the movement of the Holy Spirit; that is, the Spirit "blows where it wills." Yet the worship is not devoid of a sense of order; all facets of it are designed to facilitate an encounter with the divine. The playing of high-tech musical instruments by versatile and capable musicians and engaging visual displays combine to facilitate a deep *sensual* embrace of the dimension of the spiritual. Any sense of contrivance is mitigated by the belief that the use of these high-tech instruments, even the choreography of movements of the participants, are but facilitators for the ultimate experience of a heightened spirituality. A powerful religious experience ensues; the immediacy of the Holy Spirit is found.

Second, the all-encompassing nature of the religious experience and the epiphany of personal transformation that takes place become the harbinger for the effacing of a distinction between the secular and the sacred. Within such an experience, within the corporate environment of worship, within the confluence of personal and corporate testimony, the believer may in fact *feel* so transformed that a radical ethical alternative is presented. The believer in that moment assesses past moral failings and present moral challenges and makes an implicit vow to aspire to a greater level of fidelity. Many believers vow "to do better."[37] This vow made in the context of a powerful worship service undergirds a moral dimension of Christian worship in the African American church and becomes a powerful foundation for the renewed ethical life. For the believer, the Holy Spirit "triggers" the will to listen or discern the appropriate response in any given ethical dilemma. Moreover, in the context of the worship services, when the Spirit moves, it creates a moral dimension such that good ethical vision and behavior seem as worthy goals for the believer to achieve. The pursuit of normative ideals seems plausible and right. Thus after the worship service, the Spirit prepares the believer to risk following in subsequent encounters in the world a lifestyle that is consistent with the vision experienced during the worship service. The believer becomes determined to make the *real* consistent with the *ideal*. In other

36. A favorite expression of Rev. Dwight C. Jones, pastor of a dynamic and growing congregation in Richmond, Va., the First Baptist Church of South Richmond.

37. Conversation with Dr. Frank Madison Reid III, pastor of Bethel AME Church, Baltimore, Maryland, after morning worship on August 30, 1998.

words, to use a colloquialism of contemporary culture, one is prepared to "walk the talk."

To the extent that a revival of the Holy Spirit has been experienced in many African American churches in the last two decades of the twentieth century, we may presume that the Holy Spirit holds out resources to heal the alienation in the black middle class and the black underclass. Beverly Hall Lawrence, in a book entitled *Reviving the Spirit: A Generation of African Americans Goes Home to Church*, documents how the sense of invisibility, dehumanization, and alienation experienced by many professional African Americans in the corporate and higher education worlds has been mitigated by the secure sense of identity that these professionals have found in the black church. In the context of the economic poverty of the inner cities, when persons trapped in the underclass are drawn into the infectious energy of worship services at these churches, they begin to experience a profound sense of empowerment that in many instances results in their climb out of poverty. The Holy Spirit creates the context of reconciliation and redemption of persons caught in the alienation experienced in both classes. Liberation, manifested existentially in all aspects of life, becomes embodied through the work of the Holy Spirit.[38] The Holy Spirit acts therefore in creating a context in which these spiritual transformations may take place. According to the biblical and christological heritage, the Holy Spirit has been sent to the believing community in the aftermath of the ascension of the resurrected Christ, whose physical body was tortured/crucified/maimed. The Holy Spirit is now affirmed to be a guiding, consulting, and creative force in the life of the believing community, that is to say, the church.

The Holy Spirit, at one with God and witness to God's proclamation that Jesus was God's own Son at his baptism (Mark 1:11), holds out therefore to us the continuing promise for reconciliation, creation, and redemption. The Spirit is also very much alive to those persons who are able to make the vital connection between integrity in worship and integrity in the moral life. It is also available to persons caught in the doldrums of middle-class alienation as well as the despair of life in the underclass. In the wonderful and mysterious encounter with the Spirit during a spirited worship service, such persons make sacred vows to live lives quickened in God's Spirit. The Spirit constantly speaks to these people and seeks to be their moral tutor. The challenge now before the African American community, and all human communities that would seek renewal, is to submit to the Spirit's tutelage with joy.

---

38. For a fuller discussion of my views of the role of the Holy Spirit in the existential liberation of black Christians, see my article "Sufficiency and the Holy Spirit: Theologies for the Black Church's Future," *The Christian Ministry* (November–December 1997): 11–12, 38.

PART II: SOURCES

5

People of the Book

For the word of the LORD is upright,
and all his work is done in faithfulness.
— Psalm 33:4

Go to the third of Matthew and
Read the chapter through.
It is a guide for Christians
And tells them what to do.
— "Been a Listening"
American Negro spiritual

Christianity, like Islam and Judaism, is said to be a "religion of the book." What is meant by this assertion is the recognition that normative understandings of faith and practice have been written down and codified in what are regarded as sacred texts. Moreover, adherents presume that such texts have been sanctioned and approved by God. Indeed, many of the sayings and declarations inherent in the writing of these sacred texts are believed to have come from the very mouth of God. Muslims follow the revelation of Allah and the teaching of Muhammad as recorded in the Koran; Jews acknowledge the Torah, much of it attributed to divine utterance, as foundational for an understanding of the nature of God, covenant, and community. Christians acknowledge the Holy Bible, comprising the Hebrew Bible and later writings that were prompted by the revelation of God in the life and meaning of Jesus Christ, writings that came to be known as the New Testament. As Christians, we are a "people of the book."

The Bible is a breathtaking compilation of different and various sorts of literature, religious witness, and declarations of the way God has interacted with humanity and creation. Love stories; accounts of political intrigue, geopolitical developments, and military campaigns; meditations on the nature of God, the cosmos, reality, and human destiny; tragedies; prophecies; poetry; and wisdom sayings—all have made their way into the book we know as the Holy Bible. The Hebrew Scriptures are composed of twenty-four books that cover the period from the beginning of the Hebrew people to their

125

release from Babylonian captivity, as recorded in the second volume of the book of Chronicles. Christians generally recognize the Hebrew Scriptures plus twelve other books as constituting the Old Testament. With the closing of the Jewish canon toward the end of the first century, all of the books that Christians regard as the Old Testament were gathered into one composite whole. With the closing of the New Testament canon, generally dated in the middle of the seventh century, all of the sacred texts that Christians regard as constituent of the new dispensation were gathered together.

The Bible was written over a period of time that far antedates our own moment in history. We are able to date some of the earliest sources, particularly myths, sagas, and legends, that made their way into books of the Old Testament as early as three thousand years ago. The last of the writings that became a part of the New Testament were written over eighteen hundred years ago. Thus a gulf of time separates us from the historical periods covered in the Bible. Moreover, the writings of the Bible—both Old and New Testaments—came from cultures and traditions that are distinctly different from our own cultures that are steeped in modernism. There is a gulf as well between the worldviews inherent in biblical writings and the way of looking at the world and the perceptions of reality that undergird our own worldviews. Given these great gulfs of time and culture, we confront an enormous problem with respect to our ability to "get inside" the worlds and cultures of the Bible. How can we derive any wisdom for our own age as long as these great gulfs are ever before us? Even if we develop an appreciation for the genius of these past ages and cultures that produced the writings of the Bible, what makes us certain that we can even "get inside" those ages and cultures, given where we are in our own age and cultures? Even if we were absolute literalists, that is to say, took every word of the Bible at its face value, we still would have a problem as to how to transfer the message of the Bible to our own context. In modern society, the vast majority of us do not live in pastoral communities, nor do we have any knowledge of cubits, shekels, or whatever. Scientific discoveries have opened new ways of explaining the physical universe that were not available to the ancient world or to the world during the time of Jesus. How can we fathom the ancient mind and the social consciousness of that time?

THE INEVITABLE NECESSITY OF INTERPRETATION

We face the plethora of stories, events, and admonitions inherent in the biblical witness from the perspective of our own time and place. When we seek to make the connection between the biblical witness and our quest for guidance, we must inevitably face the task of interpreting the Bible according to the exigencies of our contexts. We are ultimately faced with the challenge of interpreting ancient texts and those produced in the first and second centuries in such a way that they are able to speak to our age and to the various cultures in which Christians find themselves. Thus, hermeneutics, or the discipline of interpretation, has come to be recognized as an absolutely vital part of biblical studies.

Since Christian ethics attempts to determine normative behavior and ethical consciousness for the Christian, it follows that Christian ethics must seek to discern the relevance the Bible has for Christian behavior and ethical consciousness. After all, the Bible contains rich illustrations of how God interacts with human beings, models for human interaction, and lessons on how human beings should treat one another. But once we begin to approach the Bible seeking illustrations and lessons for life, we soon discover that the Bible is all *too* rich with lessons and illustrations. Are we to be prudent as the ant and save all we can as the book of Proverbs suggests, or are we to give away all of our goods to the poor? Are we to invoke the death penalty on children who are disobedient to their parents as the book of Leviticus demands, or are we to offer leniency to convicted murderers? Are we to love God as the sovereign of all nations or fear God as the one who commands the utter destruction of native people as God's own people conquer a promised land? All of these—and others—are bewildering questions for which we have scant comfort when we are told, "The answer is in the Bible." If the answer is there, in what verse shall we find it? Which incident is normative? Which occurrence is worthy of emulating? We will soon find that as we search for ethical answers in the bewildering array of potential answers in the Bible, we must ally ourselves with those whose task it is to understand the hermeneutics of biblical discourse. Ethical discernment in a biblical context must confront the issue of interpretation.

Biblical Interpretation in the Early Church

As early as the third century it was apparent that the early church was in need of something like hermeneutics to enable it to get in touch with writings that were scarcely two centuries old, writings that eventually came to be recognized as the New Testament canon. By many accounts the first self-conscious effort devoted to hermeneutics within the early church was the so-called Alexandria school in northern Africa. The figures most closely associated with this school were Clement (ca. 150–215) and Origen (185–254), both of whom showed evidence that they were greatly influenced by Hellenistic thought and culture.

In his book *The Instructor (Paidogogos),* perhaps "the first book which could be described as an exposition of Christian ethics,"[1] Clement forth-

---

1. George W. Forell, ed., *Christian Social Teachings* (Minneapolis: Augsburg Publishing House, 1966, 1971), 51.

rightly declares that "everything that is contrary to right reason is sin,"[2] a notion that would hardly be consonant with the first-century sentiment of Paul or even that of Tertullian (b. ca. 160), the second-century apologist. Moreover, no doubt because of the changed upwardly mobile status of Christians by the time he wrote, Clement could display a remarkable tendency to minimize the stringent expectations inherent in Jesus' calls to discipleship. So unwilling was he to accept Jesus' dictates with respect to riches and wealth at face value that he ultimately came to espouse allegorizing the particularly uncompromising mandates of Jesus with respect to wealth. In *The Rich Man's Salvation*, Clement suggested Jesus' commandment enjoining his disciples to sell all they had and give to the poor "is not what some hastily take it to be, a command to fling away the substance that belongs to him . . . but to banish from the soul its *opinions* about riches, its *attachment* to them, its excessive *desire*, its morbid *excitement* over them."[3]

Origen was greatly influenced by Philo, the first-century Jewish commentator, who himself was under the sway of Hellenism. Origen, as well as Philo before him, introduced allegorical exegesis into his studies, primarily to reconcile apparent contradictions within biblical texts under review. He was not reluctant to admit that the Bible contained many such contradictions and unhistorical and literally false statements. Yet he was convinced that the Bible should remain the authoritative source for those in the faith. The question was how could one appropriately interpret the Bible, especially any problematic texts?

The work of these third-century writers represented the exertions of brilliant individual biblical scholars who were attempting to make advances in biblical interpretation from their own particular points of view and perspectives. However, beginning in the fourth century it soon became clear to church leaders that the interpretation of the Bible, especially that of controversial or problematic texts, could not be left to the personal hermeneutical devices of individual scholars, however enlightened or gifted they might be. Catholic theological orthodoxy therefore soon insinuated itself as the sole and legitimate arbiter of textual interpretation. At the same time Catholic orthodoxy allowed for some elasticity in interpretation by affirming that there were many levels or layers of meaning in any text. Such levels in any given text would require the application of a specific type of exegetical thrust in order to unlock the true meaning of that text for the reader or hearer. This notion was expressed in verse:

2. Clement *The Instructor* 1.13, in Forell, *Christian Social Teachings*, 52.
3. Clement *The Rich Man's Salvation*, in Forell, *Christian Social Teachings*, 54.

The letter shows us what God and our Fathers did;
The allegory shows us where our faith is hid;
The moral meaning gives us rules of daily life;
The anagogy shows us where we end our strife.[4]

Catholic theological orthodoxy and hegemony with respect to the interpretation of the Bible remained relatively unchallenged until the advent of the Renaissance and the humanistic stirrings of Erasmus. A popular expression avers that "Erasmus laid the egg that Luther hatched."[5] On the eve of the Reformation, it was beginning to be clear that the interpretation of the Bible from the perspective of questioning *individuals* apart from the authority of any *religious establishment* was in the offing. The work of Erasmus highlighted this trend and development. After Erasmus and these early stirrings, biblical interpretation was heading in one direction: no ecclesial authority would be able to pen up the desires of individuals to interpret scripture as they were directed.

Biblical Interpretation of the Reformation

With the Reformation of Martin Luther and John Calvin, the flood gates were thoroughly opened. The Reformation revived the Pauline affirmation of the primacy of grace poured out directly from God on undeserving sinners as the means for salvation. In affirming this doctrine, the Reformation rejected the Catholic belief in the salvific power of the church, the institutional body of Christ. For centuries the church had affirmed the doctrine *extra ecclesia nulla salus*; that is to say, outside of the church there is no salvation. Luther and Calvin would teach that God could deal directly with individual men and women as salvation was dispensed. The Reformation insisted also on the notion of *sola scriptura* (by scripture alone); in other words, individual men and women have access to the revelatory Scripture that assures them of the means for salvation. To be sure, Luther distinguished between the Word of God and the Scriptures. The Scriptures are not the whole Word of God; not all that is in the Scriptures *is* the Word of God. Yet within the Scriptures, individuals have access to a revealed way whereby salvation is offered to humanity.

If the Reformation rejected the salvific power of the church and presumed that God dealt directly with each individual, then it followed that each individual had the implicit responsibility to discern directly through scripture God's plan for salvation. Thus in a very real sense, while the Reformation

---

4. Robert M. Grant, *The Bible in the Church* (New York: Macmillan, 1948), 101; quoted in Jerry Wayne Brown, *The Rise of Biblical Criticism in America, 1800–1870: The New England Scholars* (Middletown, Conn.: Wesleyan University Press, 1969), 4.

5. See Erasmus-Luther, *Discourse on Free Will*, trans. Ernst F. Winter (New York: Continuum, 1990), v.

freed persons from the power of the church to determine the meaning of the Scriptures, it actually shifted the burden for such a grave task from the mighty shoulders of the church to the more modest capabilities of each individual. At least under the hegemony of the church, the individual could rely upon the richness of the tradition, the accumulated wisdom of enlightened scholars, the persuasive power of allegory. In the wake of the Reformation two broad paths emerged that would offer methods by which individuals could interpret scripture. One path was that of reason. Provided by the Enlightenment, it culminated in the rise of biblical criticism in the eighteenth century. The other path was the conservative reaction to any presumed liberalism in the thought of Luther and Calvin, who both tended to make a distinction between the Word of God and the literal text of the Bible. Later Protestants feared the dangers of subjective interpretation. "They did not think of the Holy Spirit as working through the interpreter to transform the literal words of the Bible into the Word of God," writes Jerry Wayne Brown, "but rather as inspiring the very writing of the books of the Bible. They therefore developed the doctrines of inspiration and infallibility. Instead of the Bible speaking to the Spirit-quickened heart of human beings, the Bible became the hard, infallible 'stuff' of which dogmatic systems were made."[6] Thus was born the seeds of what would come to be called biblical literalism, or biblical fundamentalism.

The Enlightenment and the Rise of Biblical Criticism

The philosophical movement known as the Enlightenment (late seventeenth through late eighteenth century) laid the foundation for what would emerge in the latter part of the eighteenth century as the rise of biblical criticism, that is, the sustained and relentless inquiry into the development of the texts that came to form the Bible. Such study would have enormous implications for the task of interpretation. Just over a century after the start of the Reformation, innovations in the interpretation of scripture were being suggested.

Recognizing that the biblical text in Hebrew and Greek had not been preserved intact, French scholars began to focus on textual studies. The English philosopher Thomas Hobbes affirmed that responsible study of the Bible should include proper dating of the various writings. He suggested that much of the Old Testament had been written after the Exile and that Moses could not have written all of Deuteronomy or all the books of the Pentateuch attributed to him. The Jewish philosopher Baruch Spinoza, who argued for free critical examination of the Scriptures, described the corpus of writings from Genesis to 2 Kings as a work composed of various con-

---

6. Jerry Wayne Brown, *The Rise of Biblical Criticism in America*, 5.

tradictory elements compiled by the scribe Ezra. The French priest Richard Simon concurred with Spinoza and in his *Histoire critique du Vieux Testament* (1678) provided the first critical introduction to the Old Testament.[7] Critical inquiries into the formation of biblical texts reached a culmination in the development of biblical criticism within the secular universities of Germany in the first half of the nineteenth century. L. F. Constantin von Tischendorf, who discovered the Codex Siniaticus, offered the JEDP thesis, the very plausible suggestion of the fourfold authorship of much of the Pentateuch. Basing his thesis on stylistic differences and other factors, he discerned at least four authors (anonymous it seems), whom he called J (Yahwist), E (Eloist), D (Deuteronomist), and P (Priestly). Moreover, biblical criticism began to suggest in ever stronger terms the fact that human beings wrote these texts and that while they might have been inspired by God, the texts themselves were products of human hands and the tenor of their times.

The ultimate goal of biblical criticism was to submit the Bible to as much scrutiny as could be imagined. Hence, it is not surprising that virtually all aspects of human inquiry were summoned for this task. Archaeological excavations supplemented historical investigation into biblical times; cross-cultural analyses helped inform textual and literary criticism (the study of the various genres of literature that ultimately became incorporated into biblical texts). Source criticism developed as a result of inquiries into the origin of biblical writings. The search led investigators to oral sayings, oracles, hymns, even extrabiblical texts such as the Code of Hammurabi, linking this secular judicial code with the formation of ancient Israel's evolving moral and legal consciousness. Source criticism in New Testament studies led early investigators to reflect on the similarities between the Gospels of Mark, Luke, and Matthew and their common divergence from the Gospel of John, which led theorists to infer that a common source for these three synoptic Gospels had to exist. The source, known as Q (from the German word for "source," *Quelle*), has been given a virtually indisputable place in New Testament biblical studies.

Other types of criticism abounded. Redaction criticism—the study of the way texts overlapped each other—is the meticulous unraveling of how various editions of the text were either lain on top of another or melded into others. This type of literary criticism draws investigators in attempts to discern if the text under review is a composite or is an integral piece of work. If the text is judged to be a composite, then the task becomes discerning the several authors and determining the principal one, the secondary one, the tertiary one, and so on and determining whether a principal editor was

---

7. See Robert H. Pfeiffer, *Introduction to the Old Testament* (New York: Harper, 1948), 46; quoted in Jerry Wayne Brown, *The Rise of Biblical Criticism in America*, 6.

at work on this text. But most prominent among all the critical methods has perhaps been the historical-critical method. This method, which has held sway for much of the twentieth century, has attempted to understand what the biblical texts meant to their original audiences. In other words, the method is an attempt to understand the historical consciousness of persons and believers in past times.

The overall scrutiny of the biblical texts mounted by biblical criticism constituted an unparalleled inquiry into the formation of sacred texts that had presumably been recorded at the behest of God. As such then, for many Christians biblical criticism was tantamount to an attack upon the authority of the Bible. Because the Bible itself was deemed inerrant by many of these same Christians, any inquiry that pointed out the blatant inconsistencies and embarrassing anomalies was bound to disturb attitudes toward these texts. This was inevitable, and for many it must have been painful. Cherished concepts and beliefs were attacked. As a product of the Enlightenment, that philosophical movement that laid the foundations for modernism, biblical criticism has assaulted ways and modes of interpreting the Bible that either implicitly or unabashedly affirm a premodern consciousness.

Along with the assault on premodern consciousness came an assault on the form of biblical authority inherent in such a consciousness. This happened for several reasons. First of all, the increased discoveries of science revealed apparent contradictions relative to the realm of nature. The cosmology of the Bible, especially the Old Testament, presumes a prescientific understanding of the universe. The earth was thought to be a relatively flat expanse, over which God had placed the gigantic crystalline vault of the firmament. There were waters above this dome, which could fall down through windows in the firmament in the form of rain and other precipitation, and there were waters beneath it, which welled up in the form of springs. However, a scientific perspective will discern problems in the sequence of events in the creation cycle. In Genesis 1:3-5, God creates light first but then creates the sun, moon, and stars on the fourth day. Before the fourth day, from what does this light come? If the writer had meant to say that such light came from God, why is not this stated forthrightly, as it would later be implied in some New Testament references to the light coming forth from the eternal Logos (John 1:4-5)?

Problems with history arise as well. Joshua's presentation of the conquest of Canaan as occurring in a relatively short time is at odds with the more accurate historical view that it took a much longer period. Then there are problems with the morality inherent in biblical texts. We intuitively feel that some of the practices condoned by the Bible cannot enjoy moral justification today: the subjugation of women, slavery, and genocide, being among them. In the fifteenth chapter of 1 Samuel the practice of genocide seems to be condoned: "Thus says the LORD. . . . 'Now go and attack Amalek, and utterly destroy all that they have; do not spare them, but kill both man and woman, child and infant, ox and sheep, camel and donkey.' . . . Saul defeated the Amalekites. . . . utterly destroyed all the people with the edge of the sword" (1 Sam. 15:2–3, 7–8).

Then too, the Bible is replete with vying "theologies," or views of the nature of God. When these theologies are seen side by side, it makes the Bible seem contradictory. An example is found in comparing 1 Chronicles 21:1 and the earlier 2 Samuel 24:1. First Chronicles 21:1 reads: "Satan stood up against Israel, and incited David to count the people of Israel." The earlier 2 Samuel 24:1 reads: "Again the anger of the LORD was kindled against Israel, and he incited David against them, saying, 'Go, count the people of Israel and Judah.'" Both of these biblical writers could not be right. Why could they not agree? The reason is that they represented "two quite different theologies, two contrasting modes of belief."[8] In the earlier passage Samuel, the author, assumed that God, when angry, might very well act as an angry human being would. Among other things, God might entrap the object of divine ire into some action so flagrantly illegitimate as to justify God's vengeance. Much later on, the author of 1 Chronicles included this story but revised its view of God. Instead, "the religion of the day attributed such entrapment to a member of God's court, a kind of celestial prosecuting attorney known as 'Satan,' the 'Adversary.'"[9]

CONTEMPORARY MODES OF BIBLICAL INTERPRETATION

Given the welter of contradictions and problems inherent in biblical texts, many Christians who come to the Bible for ethical guidance develop feelings and attitudes ranging from bewilderment, through ambiguity, to outright dismay that it ever could be a reliable guide in ethical matters. Our dilemma is that we have a book of sacred texts that is *necessary* but also problematic. The Bible must exercise authority for us as Christians, or else it must be irrelevant to us. But how does it exercise that authority?

No Christian believes that the Bible is irrelevant to the task of discerning that which should be normative in thought and practice in the Christian life. Specific events in the Bible, such as fanciful accounts of the deeds of God and heroic persons and the various miracles, may strain the credulity of many persons, yet all Christians hold the Bible as authoritative to some degree in their lives. If we ponder the matter further, we will soon discover that if we are to appropriate the Bible as an authoritative book for our actions

---

8. L. William Countryman, *Biblical Authority or Biblical Tyranny* (Valley Forge, Pa.: Trinity Press International, 1994), 10.

9. Ibid.

as Christians, and if it is to be relevant to such decisions, our own roles as *interpreters* of the Bible cannot be avoided or diminished. And if our role as interpreters is to be critical in our use of the Bible for ethical discernment, then the role of human reason cannot be ignored. We must *think* and think deeply as we confront the Bible and seek to derive guidance in the ethical morass of the modern world. As interpreters we must inevitably call upon our human judgment and reason at some basic level in order to fulfill the hermeneutical task.

Not surprisingly several options with respect to interpretive styles and hermeneutical methods have surfaced as Christians have sought ways and means of interpreting the Bible, especially as interpretations have a critical bearing on ethical decisions and thinking. We may discern at this point in the development of biblical interpretation at least five options that lie before us as we seek to derive ethical guidance from the Bible.

Biblical Literalism

A near majority of Christians employ literalism and its closely linked doctrine infallibilism to interpret the Bible. Literalists believe that the Bible is literally true, that every word can be taken on face value as inherently conforming to an objective view of reality. Biblical fundamentalists and literalists take the position that scripture is, in the words of John Jefferson Davis, "the very Word of God, the only infallible and inerrant rule of faith and practice."[10]

The strength of the fundamentalist position is its certainty, based primarily on the level of congruence it is able to discern between the actual pronouncements in the Bible and the presumed situation in the here and now. It seeks a virtual one-to-one correspondence between the biblical world and its mandates and the demand that they be enacted in the modern world. One must obey the texts without hesitation; for example, wives must be literally submissive to husbands. But what if it is not possible to make the correspondence "sit still," that is to say, to make a neat one-to-one correspondence between biblical mandates and the context of the modern world? How exactly does one do something in the modern world that the Bible never mentions?

Countless examples of moral issues in the modern world are never mentioned or alluded to in the biblical world. Nowhere in the Bible is there a protracted discussion of genetic engineering, despite Jacob's use of folk wisdom in an attempt to alter the genetic coding of Laban's lambs in his desire to extract revenge on his uncle (Gen. 30:37–43). Conversely, dilemmas of the

---

10. John Jefferson Davis, "Biblical Authority," in Paul Jersild et al., *Moral Issues and Christian Response*, 6th ed. (New York: Harcourt Brace College Publishers, 1998), 30.

biblical world may no longer be relevant or operative today. When such difficulties arise, the fundamentalist must adjust the method, which will mean relying on some degree of human judgment in order to get some meaning out of the text. Davis talks about "deducing from the text" the moral imperative that might be theoretically operative in the modern context. But does not deduction call for some level of subjective bias, personal perspective, or use of human reason? If literalism must be supplemented by reason or judgment to determine the meaning of scripture for ethical dilemmas, does this not point to an inherent flaw in literalism? The necessary tools for making the method work must be imported from the domain of human reason, a domain that many fundamentalists mistrust and some despise. In an effort to mitigate the problems of literalism, adherents embrace several "backup" positions, among these being the tendency to allegorize and another being the development of a modified infallibilist position. Those Christians who wish to affirm the authority of the Bible with a literalist mode are thus provided with at least two options by which they have been able to forge what for them is a justifiable interpretation of texts.

The first option is to continue the tradition of allegorizing that was espoused by some in the early church, notably Clement of Alexandria. But allegorists always have the problem of forcing a "fit" between the texts of scripture and the situations to which they are attempting to apply them. The fit is oftentimes unwieldy, troublesome, and sometimes downright sloppy. Moreover, it is very difficult to account for all of the images and nuances within an allegory. Forcing a "fit" between a scriptural passage and our situation may well result in our missing the entire point of the original text or the intent of the original author.

The option of adopting a modified infallibilist position rests on two basic presumptions. The first is the insistence that the Bible offers clear and unambiguous commandments that conform to a standard of rightness that is autonomous from human valuation; that is, it exists independently of us and our value systems or cultural biases. The other presumption is the sufficiency of the Bible. In other words, while the Bible might not provide specific answers to every moral question, we can deduce from scripture the answers we need. The difficulty here is justifying the inferences made. The modified infallibilist position insists on the unambiguous nature of biblical commandments and depends on human beings to infer rightly from those commandments. But what else but their perspectives can human beings bring to the Bible in their attempts to infer what the biblical commandment means? Thus even this method must defer, although it does not admit it, to the valuing systems of human beings.

Only with these presumptions in place can the Bible be regarded as a handbook. Generally such a notion finds expression in the concept of "natural law" or to a lesser degree in the concept of "conscience." Those holding the literalist position freely admit that any degree of authority that is granted to the Bible is exactly that: deference that human beings *by their volition* must grant to the Bible. Why would anyone do such a thing? Literalists do so because for them the Bible holds the best and most satisfying portrayal of how God interacts with the created order and with humanity. The extent to which we resonate with these visions in the Bible is the extent to which we will be able to grant the Bible authority to guide us in our moral dilemmas. The problem here of course is holding in adequate tension any notion of "infallibilism" and the admission that it is by virtue of human norms and consciousness that any sense of authority is conferred upon the Bible.

Liberalism

The tradition of nineteenth-century liberalism is the second classic option for biblical interpretation. This tradition has sought to effect a reconciliation between the rationality presumed in natural science and the biblical world and the dictates that emanate from it. At the inception of liberalism, the idea was to seek a dialogue with science, particularly the science of biology and the emerging notion of evolution, as well as the discoveries that were being made in astronomy and implicitly in cosmology. The liberals' goal has been to be at the same time a faithful Christian and an intelligent person in the modern world.

Liberals have had no fear of biblical criticism. In fact, they have welcomed a scientific approach to biblical studies, affirming that no inherently divine truths had any need to fear scientific scrutiny. By employing science and commonsense reasoning, liberalism has sought to explain troublesome texts in the Bible and the accounts of events that are repugnant to reason. Thus liberals have explained the miracles through recourse to natural science. The Exodus was explained through extensive treatises on meteorological anomalies that supposedly could occur periodically in the ancient Near East, involving a confluence of great winds and tidal regressions. A great irony thus characterizes liberalism. For all of its appeal to the sophistication of natural science, this type of liberalism has betrayed an inherent captivity to infallibilism. It *has had* to prove the particular text under review literally true, no matter how torturous the exercise might be.

The liberal, either of the nineteenth century or today, presumes that a universal, absolute core of truth exists in scripture and can be applicable to modern consciousness and issues. Each of us, from our different vantage points, can appropriate this core of truth of and in the gospel and have it speak to us. Thus the liberal hopes to achieve a level of congruency between the world of the Bible and our own world. For example, a liberationist theologian like James Cone can see Christ as the One who is oppressed and affirm that Jesus leads the oppressed in their quest for freedom. A feminist theologian can see in Jesus a revolutionary consciousness with respect to the liberation of women and the valuing of them. All people can see the Christ through the lenses of their own agendas and perspectives.

The liberal agenda is beset with the basic problem of trying to reconcile a presumed absolute core inherent in the gospel with the legitimate right of persons from many perspectives in appropriating that truth and acting on it. If the black liberationist affirms her right to see in Jesus the paradigm for human redemption, then to be consistent she must accord the gay liberationist the same right to see in Christ a model for his liberation. Liberalism seeks to reconcile the absolutism of the gospel with the relativism of many perspectives on that gospel. The concept that has captured this spirit in the history of biblical interpretation is known as the "canon within a canon" school of thought. In this option, one unabashedly says some texts in the Bible are morally and normatively repugnant given one's operative faith orientation or the exigencies of one's context. Actually, the notion of a "canon" (from the Greek word for "rod" or "measuring stick") dates to the period toward the end of the first century of the common era when Judaism was assuming more and more a combative posture with the burgeoning Christian faith. A way had to be devised to "measure" the level of fidelity some Jews of questionable piety had toward the Jewish writings. The method that emerged was the positing of a selected number of Jewish writings deemed as normative expositions of the faith. Thus the Jewish canon was "closed" around 90 C.E. After this point, no other writings could properly be considered among the sacred writings of this faith.

Within its first five centuries and for somewhat similar reasons, Christianity had to come to terms with the problems and issues that the establishment of a "canon" theoretically solved. For the first three centuries of the faith, bishops and leaders in the church regarded texts differentially with regard to normative value and spiritual worthiness. They wrestled with many questions: Which writings best embody the gospel and message of Jesus? Which authors are legitimate? Which are fraudulent? How are such questions answered anyway? The answers did, and continued to, determine the bases upon which various "canons" were contemplated. Even Jesus evidences an awareness of the issues surrounding the establishment of a canon.

While Jesus' message and stance were at some levels always in tension with the classic Torah, or Law, of Judaism, he always maintained that he came, not to abrogate the law, but to fulfill it (Matt. 5:17–19). Paul seems to go a step further and regard the law as only a preliminary step toward full justification. Faith has delivered us from bondage under the law and the frantic attempt to fulfill the law. As he wrote to the Romans, "The one who is righteous will live by faith" (Rom. 1:17; Gal. 3:11). The early church forebears struggled with the question of determining which available writings were most consistent with the spirit of the gospel and the message of Jesus. The earliest Christian document to cite passages from the Gospels as Holy Scripture is 2 Clement (ca. 150).[11] Marcion, Origen, Irenaeus, and others all had distinct and strongly argued views as to which writings deserved to be regarded as normative for Christians. Jerome is remembered for being the first to translate the Bible, including the twenty-seven books that eventually became known as the New Testament, into Latin; this is known as the Vulgate.

Christians settled, not entirely conclusively, the matter of establishing a canon of the New Testament in 616 C.E. Yet even close to a thousand years later there would still be disputes as to what books ought or ought not belong among sacred scriptures for Christians. Luther, following Paul's notion of the primacy of grace as opposed to the importance of law, refused to recognize the book of James as canonical; he also excluded Hebrews, Jude, and Revelation on theological grounds (see his original translation of the New Testament, September 1522). Luther said after his translation, "I will stay by the books that offer me Christ bright and clear."[12] In his judgment, these disputed books did not adequately portray for him the essence of the Word of God: that unmerited grace is poured out on a meritless humanity by a gracious God.

Thus from Marcion to Jerome, from Irenaeus to Luther, the concept of "canon within a canon" has betrayed a perennial desire to extract from scriptural texts the distilled essence of the gospel *as one understands that gospel*. Moreover, there is the tendency to declare with firm conviction one's faith orientation as one scrutinizes those texts, even if such a declaration goes against conventional wisdom. But there are problems here, despite the oftentimes bravery exhibited in the positions liberalism has inspired. Ironically, the strength of the "canon within a canon" posture, its willingness to state unapologetically its point of departure in judging the worth of texts of the Bible, may harbor a serious flaw. The relativity of our own positions may compromise the integrity of the presumed absolute. Once we start down this path, unless there are constraints imposed on our method, we are bound to encounter the infamous "hermeneutical circle" in which we shall see only that which we are predisposed to see or indeed want to see. But how are we to know that that which we desire to see is consistent with the essence of the gospel or indeed God's will?

---

11. "Canon of the New Testament," in *The Interpreter's Dictionary of the Bible* (New York: Abingdon Press, 1962), 1:525.

12. "Biblical Criticism," in *The Interpreter's Dictionary of the Bible* (New York: Abingdon Press, 1962), 1:408.

Postliberalism

Postliberalism seeks not only a vibrant dialogue between the biblical world and the modern world but recognizes the historical forces that seem to be shaping the modern world as well. Postliberalism has drawn its inspiration mainly from the method and spirit of Shailer Mathews. Mathews was deeply influenced by the social gospel and the deep optimism with regard to human progress that this movement affirmed. Yet Mathews was not so naïve as to believe that human progress always represented a straight line forward. "Christians," he advised, "must realize the darker side of social progress."[13] Actually, the message of history for Mathews was a complex one. He saw lessons to be learned in the stress and the tug and pull of human interaction. Within such history we can discern the will of God, which when made manifest in human history may involve stress and turmoil. With amazing prescience he wrote in 1935 the following words: "The message of Jesus is a call to the privileged to give justice. If they do not make the sacrifice involved, the underprivileged will seek to get justice by force."[14] Thus Mathews and the postliberals see God at work in the inexorable march of human history, even when the results are fraught with much pain. It is this spirit that Abraham Lincoln evidenced in his Second Inaugural Address as he reflected on the painful Civil War in which his second term in office was launched. Said Lincoln on the steps of the Capitol, "Yet, if God wills that it [the War] continue until all the wealth piled by the bondsman's two hundred and fifty years of unrequited toil shall be sunk, and until every drop of blood drawn with the lash shall be paid by another drawn with the sword, as was said three thousand years ago, so still it must be said, 'The judgments of the Lord are true and righteous altogether.' "[15] For postliberals, human beings may experience within human history an enlargement of moral vision, thus giving them an orientation that they then can impose upon the Bible to determine which texts are authoritative and meaningful for the pursuit of ethical living. A good example in our own day is the apparent historical progress we seem to be making in recognizing the equality of women and in making some halting signs of progress in race relations, if we compare the current situation with previous times when the inferiority of women and people of color were simply "givens" in many quarters. The postliberal sees God's truth being enacted in the often turbulent and stressful pull of human

---

13. Shailer Mathews, *Creative Christianity* (Nashville: Cokesbury Press, 1935), 90.

14. Ibid. See also Shailer Mathews, *The Church and the Changing Order* (London: Macmillan, 1908); and idem, *Christianity and Social Progress* (New York: Harper & Brothers, 1934).

15. Abraham Lincoln, "Second Inaugural Address," in Forell, *Christian Social Teachings*, 328. Although not an official member of a Christian denomination, Lincoln was fond of quoting scriptures. This quote is from Psalm 19:9 (KJV).

history, instead of being forever locked in the biblical texts. Recognizing what God seems to be doing in moving creation to a greater level of moral integrity forms for the postliberal the "Word of God," a word that is then imposed back upon the biblical texts to determine what exactly in the texts is most consistent with the "Word of God" discerned in history.

Modernism

Yet another option, and one that also is a response to liberalism, is the stance known now as modernism. According to Kenneth Cauthen, the modernist gives up on the notion of an absolute truth inherent in the gospel message and suggests that the contemporary modern interpreter must decide what is highest and most consistent with Christian reason. Modernists like Cauthen[16] believe that liberals found it necessary to identify something universal in scripture that could be distinguished from the particular worldview in which that scripture was expressed and articulated. The intent was to locate a gospel that transcended all cultures but could speak to every culture. However, every attempt to express the unique faith once delivered to the saints turns out to be particular and relative, one interpretation among many. Each version differs from and sometimes conflicts with the others. Hence, plurality and relativity seem to undercut the original project of preserving the one and true gospel.

Here enters the modernist, "who makes a bold move: the modernist is a relativist and a pragmatist who centers on the importance of the interpreter. Every interpretation of biblical religion reflects the interests, needs, intellectual outlook, and cultural particularity of the interpreter." Relativism is not total, but it cannot be totally escaped either. In this situation, the modernist urges us to "acknowledge pragmatically the priority of the interpreter and make the best of it." As Cauthen goes on to say:

> The most daring and dangerous move of the modernist is to insist that what is crucial is not the preservation of some ancient tradition but the achievement of salvation here and now. We must decide in the light of the best understanding we can come up with from any source what is most likely to save us if we act on it.[17]

At this point one could legitimately expect that this "any source" from which the modernist could derive saving truth could be both within and *outside of* the Bible. Yet Cauthen stops short of this pronouncement. For him,

---

16. Kenneth Cauthen, *Toward a New Modernism* (Lanham, Md.: University Press of America, 1997), 45–60.

17. Kenneth Cauthen, "Interpreting the Bible Today," *Encounter* (autumn 1990): 380. See also Cauthen, *Toward a New Modernism,* chap. 4.

the modernist finds saving truth in the Bible. The modernist, at least of Cauthen's variety, believes that "only what in Scripture is irresistibly convincing to our own Christian reason in the light of what we cannot otherwise deny as modern human beings can be regarded as the authoritative Word of God for us."[18] Thus while the logic and the spirit of the modernist would seem to move ineluctably to embracing texts that are beyond the Bible as holding truth, the modernist stops short of these claims. And since the modernist does so, it is difficult to see how this view differs dramatically from classic liberalism, although the modernist avers that "the theological aim, however, is not to make a futile attempt to discover some universal, absolute definition of the one and only Gospel but to find some local and presently compelling interpretation that provides us with our best hopes for now. That however, is enough. It must be, since the alternative is fruitless."[19]

Postmodernism

If the modernists were to act on one logical implication in their stance, they would soon find themselves embracing a stance that could be truly called postmodernism. Postmodernists assume that God is still speaking to us and that the Bible may not hold the exclusive corpus of texts from which God might be revealing God's will for the world. In other words, God may be speaking in texts that are clearly outside the established canons that are recognized in the Judeo-Christian heritage, that is, in extrabiblical texts or even texts that are now considered secular or blasphemous, just as the Song of Solomon was considered secular and scandalous by some Puritan Christians. (Note that the book of Esther was allowed into the Jewish canon, and embraced by Christians later, although the word "God" never appears within its pages.)

Reminding us that the closing of the canons constituted decisions made by human beings and were not at all the proven result of divine intervention or infallible revelation, postmodernists ask whether the canon can still be open. Church tradition has ruled in the negative. But if we assume that it remains open, we would need to use our own sense of judgment and human experience when asked to determine among extrabiblical sources which ones adequately show us our notion of the will of God. The use of human judgment, whether understood as the marshaling of the power of reason or other evaluative instruments, in the discernment of biblical truths for guidance in ethical matters cannot be escaped or long denied.

18. Cauthen, *Toward a New Modernism*, 52.
19. Ibid., 54.

Literalism, liberalism, postliberalism, modernism, and postmodernism represent five hermeneutical postures with respect to how human beings can understood the import of the biblical message and how that message informs the ethical life. Though the Enlightenment engendered an undermining of biblical authority for some Christians, believing Christians who recognize the value of biblical criticism need not fear that the edifice of faith has been undermined merely because someone takes a close inspection of one of the pillars of faith. There is a way of respecting the rich results of biblical criticism while at the same time affirming that the text may be able to exert normative authority upon the interpreter. To allow biblical criticism to destroy faith is a tacit confession that biblical criticism has been invested with much more authority than it deserves. A literary critic may indeed shed new light on the authorship of a text, but the literary critic can never suggest to the believer *why* she should believe the words of the text. The historical critic may be quite successful in laying bare the assumptions that were in the minds of the author and the audience to whom the text was addressed, but the same critic can never suggest to the believer *what* questions should be in his mind as he comes to the text from his own culture. There is no escaping the conclusion that the integrity of the hermeneutical task depends greatly on what questions the present-day believer brings to the hermeneutical moment. In other words, biblical criticism and biblical critics cannot establish what meaning we derive from the text or how we answer the questions we bring to the texts. We must do that ourselves.

THE FORGING OF AFRICAN AMERICAN
BIBLICAL CONSCIOUSNESS

During slavery, an African American biblical consciousness was shaped by the natural proclivity of the enslaved to focus on biblical images and ideas mediated through an oral tradition that affirmed liberation as the ultimate normative value. Slaves were of course forbidden from gaining access to the written word and gaining literacy with respect to the Bible and the words that constitute Holy Scripture. However, this did not prevent slaves from mastering the means whereby they gained access to the essence, as they understood it, of the biblical message. In fact, in a very curious way, the design of slaveholders to deprive slaves of the full array of biblical messages may have worked to enable slaves to focus *only* on those images and ideas consistent with their hope for liberation.

Much of the African American experience with respect to biblical interpretation has implicitly endorsed the spirit of "canon within a canon." One must keep in mind that the Bible is not a univocal book; that is to say, there is no total consistency throughout the Bible, reflecting as it does many points of view recorded over many centuries and reflecting many contexts. Both slavery and liberation are implicitly condoned; both the liberation and subjugation of women may be deduced. If one is to appropriate the Bible, one must make a choice as to which parts of the Bible best comport with one's notion of the norm or the ideal. Slaves intuitively knew this when they opted forcefully to emphasize those parts of the Bible that accentuated freedom and liberation and denounced and ignored those sections that seemed to seal their fate as slaves. Proof that the Bible could be used to justify their slave status was made patently clear each time they heard a white preacher expound on the virtue of slaves being "obedient to your master." Slaves, on the other hand, had to use as a touchstone for biblical integrity only those texts and occurrences that bolstered their claim for liberation and freedom.

Christian African Americans have always sought to understand the peculiar message that the Bible held for them in their peculiar journey on the American shores. Insofar as they have sought a "word" from the Bible, they have been concerned to bring the following questions to the hermeneutical task: Which particular texts, authors, genres, and periods of history covered in the Bible are of most relevance to African Americans? Why would the texts, authors, genres, and periods of history have authoritative value for African Americans?

Before addressing these questions, we must consider other issues that are foundational to the hermeneutical task. First of all, we must make the logical distinction between God and the portraits of God as presented in the Bible. Not only logical, this assertion comports with our intuitive ability to make a distinction between God-in-Godself and our designations and portraits of God. Our portraits of God, if not critically considered, may tend to reflect the biases and presumptions of our cultures and perspectives. God-in-Godself, however, may hold out for us a vision that trumps the narrow vision of our own perspective; it is "alien" to our own vision. And, this alien world may lead us to affirm another distinction: the Word of God is distinct from the particular "words" or texts in the Bible; moreover, this Word of God precedes any texts that come under our consideration. We gain a theological advantage when we keep this distinction ever before us. When we focus on the task of seeking in the texts wherein the Word of God might be, we are seeking to discern the will for our lives that God might be speaking in the texts at hand. As long as our task is to discern the Word of God, that living encounter between God and humanity, then we are spared the fruitless and ultimately dubious task of focusing on texts, many of which are fraught with internal contradictions, textual variances, and so on. It is only when we are focused on the Word of God that we are likely to discern only that which can aspire to normative value in the ethical life.

Our analysis of the way Christian thinkers have understood the challenges of hermeneutics and the meaning of the Word of God leads to our realization that any notion of the "canon" depends upon one's understanding of "the Word of God." Since the "Word of God" stands prior to, apart from, and independent of the texts of the Scriptures, which constitute only a part of the Word of God, "canon" will mean one thing for one person and another thing for another person, will mean one thing for one community and another for another community.

Not surprisingly, a distinct African American canon has emerged within black religious consciousness. That canon exists as an appropriation of texts, personages, events, and themes within the Holy Scriptures that are judged to be consistent with the Word of God. What is that Word of God? It is that all people are meant to be free, that the continued enslavement of blacks was an affront to the will of God, and that God, through Jesus Christ, always moves to assure their freedom and the freedom of all humanity.

The fierce determination of black slaves to affirm their own hermeneutic of liberation with regard to Christian faith and the Holy Scriptures of that faith was forged in the struggle against whites who sought to impose upon them a hermeneutic that would justify their oppression. The most notorious attempt to indoctrinate slaves in a mode of Christian faith that would justify the aims of slaveholders was exemplified by the efforts of Rev. Charles C. Jones, the self-styled "apostle to the slaves." The slaves rebuffed Jones's attempt to indoctrinate them and rejected his version of the gospel as well as his selective interpretation of texts within the Holy Book.

Jones recorded the slaves' reaction to one of his sermons:

> I was preaching to a large congregation on the Epistle of Philemon and when I insisted upon fidelity and obedience as Christian virtues in servants and upon the authority of Paul, condemned the practice of *running away,* one half of my audience deliberately rose up and walked off with themselves, and those that remained looked anything but satisfied, either with the preacher or his doctrine.[20]

Jones further recalled that at the end of the service, the remaining slaves had expressed anger and contempt toward him and his ideas. Several had

20. Erskine Clarke, *Wrestlin' Jacob: A Portrait of Religion in the Old South* (Atlanta: John Knox Press, 1979), 40. Other "catechisms" were devised and used with the hope in mind of accommodating slaves to their servile status. The South Carolina Episcopal bishop William Capers published *A Short Catechism for the Use of Colored Members on Trial in the Methodist Episcopal Church, South Carolina* in 1832; the Southern Baptists produced a similar manual designed by the principal of Richmond College, Robert Ryland, entitled *The Scripture Catechism for Colored People,* in 1848. See Olli Alho, *The Religion of the Slaves: A Study of the Religious Tradition and Behavior of Plantation Slaves in the United States 1830–1865* (Helsinki: Soumalainen Tiedeakatemia Academia Scientiarum Fennica, 1976), 63ff.

agreed "that there was no such an Epistle in the Bible"; others had said that such a message "was not the Gospel," while some had insisted that Jones preached only "to please the masters" and had declared that they would not come to hear him preach again. The action of these slaves was a dangerous undertaking and an amazing display of open resistance to a white man who, while not their owner, was still a powerful neighboring slaveholder. Emboldened by their hermeneutic of liberation, the slaves could challenge the theological presumptions of this "apostle" who, unlike an earlier apostle at Corinth, received no believers when he preached.

Ironically, by being deprived of full access to literacy in their servile status, African American slaves were spared an option of focusing on the various texts of the Bible, which a more prevalent literacy among them could have facilitated. Their holders and self-styled evangelists such as Charles C. Jones always could use particular texts to justify slavery, but the slaves knew that the Word of God forbade and trumped any focus on a particular text. The slaves even boldly declared, as some told Jones to his face, that any scripture that justified slavery had no place in the canon anyway. They were truly free to focus on the Word of God, which for them was always consistent with their desire to be free. Black people have always sought to understand why they were placed in the condition of slavery and how they would be delivered from such a condition. Moreover, to the extent that they trusted in God, they always sought a word from God as to how these questions could be answered. To the extent that the Bible offered answers is the extent to which scripture has played a part in African American Christian ethical consciousness.

THE TESTIMONY FROM THE SPIRITUALS OF AFRICAN AMERICAN BIBLICAL CONSCIOUSNESS

If ever we hope to discern the "canon" that African American slaves employed to fashion a normative understanding of faith and practice as derived from Christian scripture, we shall find it in the Negro spirituals, which offer a striking richness of allusion and direct reference, biblical personages, events, issues, and problems as well as seminal ideas for African American Christian theology and doctrine. Moreover, the spirituals represent a corporate commentary on the texts of the Bible that were either read by literate slaves or selectively appropriated from the teaching and preaching of black and white Christians.

The Fisk Jubilee Singers became recognized as an acclaimed chorale that could make the musical genius of the Negro spirituals available to a world audience. During their triumphant European tour in the 1870s, they sang at the personal invitation of Queen Victoria. In 1884, Theodore F. Seward and George L. White produced a compilation of the spirituals sung by the chorale entitled *Jubilee Songs: As Sung by the Jubilee Singers*.[21] These songs sung by former slaves and their sons and daughters reveal the contours and essence of a uniquely African American canon of the Christian Scriptures.[22]

Compilations of spirituals continued to be published in the twentieth century. In 1901, Emily Hallowell compiled a volume known as *Calhoun Plantation Songs*. During the flowering of literature and culture among African Americans known as the Harlem Renaissance, two lions of that movement, James Weldon Johnson and J. Rosamond Johnson, produced *The Book of American Negro Spirituals* in 1925. Five years later, Mary Ellen Grissom came forward with the volume *The Negro Sings a New Heaven*. These are but a few of the many volumes presenting the genius of the Negro spirituals that have emerged over the years.

A lack of mastery of the literate aspects of the Bible did not prevent African Americans in bondage from gaining mastery of the insights and inner core of biblical messages. Sung corporately, the spirituals offer a type of commentary on biblical themes, personages, and images of a general and specific nature. In terms of references of a general nature, the spirituals are replete with ideas in the Bible such as heaven, God, Judgment Day, and of course Jesus as Savior. The spirituals speak of the paradisiacal nature of heaven, the fiery torment of hell, the joy of redemption—all general themes of Christian religion. Also appearing in the spirituals are derivative ideas and images, such as the "ship of Zion," which drew its inspiration from scripture, though it was not specifically noted in the Bible as such. The spirituals reflect general and accepted beliefs such as the assurance of heaven for the faithful and the assurance of Jesus' companionship. In addition to these various general images, specific personages, events, and images came to have peculiar and particular relevance to the slaves' experiences. The spirituals regard Moses, rather than the slaveholder Pharaoh, as a hero. The spirituals exalt Lazarus, the beggar, more than Dives, the rich man.

While most slaves were not literate and had no ability to locate a personage or event within a biblical verse, some spirituals actually offer a recasting of particular Bible verses. For example, among the songs sung by the Fisk Jubilee Singers is the spiritual "The Rocks and the Mountains." In this spiritual is a recounting of Judgment Day, when the "rocks and the mountains

---

21. Theodore F. Seward and George L. White, comps., *Jubilee Songs: As Sung by the Jubilee Singers* (New York: Biglow and Main, 1884).

22. See as well J. B. T. Marsh, *The Story of the Jubilee Singers* (Boston: Houghton Mifflin, 1880). Marsh's book compiled the complete repertory of the Jubilee Singers and offered brief biographical sketches of the members, giving evidence that many among them were the sons and daughters of slaves or themselves former slaves, and therefore brought to their stint with the group an invaluable authenticity.

shall all flee away,"[23] which is a direct allusion to Revelation 6:15: "Then the kings of the earth and the magnates and the generals and the rich and the powerful, and every one, slave and free, hid in the caves and among the rocks of the mountains." On Judgment day,

> Oh, the rocks and the mountains shall all flee away.
> And you shall have a new hiding place that day.
> Seeker, Seeker, give up your heart to God,
> And you shall have a new hiding place that day.[24]

Another instance in which a spiritual offers a direct allusion to specific biblical texts is the second stanza of the song "Been a Listening." This spiritual admonishes the listener to "go to the third [chapter] of Matthew, and read the chapter through. It is a guide for Christians, and tells them what to do."[25] The spiritual that describes Ezekiel's "wheel in the middle of a wheel" of course alludes to Ezekiel 1:16: "As for the appearance of the wheels and their construction: their appearance was like the gleaming of beryl; and the four had the same form, their construction being something like a wheel within a wheel."

The spirituals speak eloquently of the bleakness of slave life, drawing upon the biblical image of "those who mourn." Indeed there is a special solace for those who mourn, which is surely an allusion to Jesus' Sermon on the Mount, with particular reference to the assurance inherent in the words "Blessed are those who mourn" (Matt. 5:4). The words of the spiritual "Rise, Mourners" must have had not only a poignant sound but a particular relevance to the singers, whose very existence was marked by mourning:

> Rise, mourners, rise mourners,
> O can't you rise and tell,
> What the Lord has done for you.
>
> Yes, he's taken my feet out of the miry clay
> And he's placed them on the right side of my Father.[26]

The Negro spirituals may be viewed as not only the beautiful but plaintive music of an oppressed people but also a form of biblical commentary as well. Denied full access to the literary corpus of Christian scriptures, African American slaves devised in the spirituals an oral tradition that posited what in their judgment constituted the essence of the gospel and the inner core of Christian faith. Insofar as the Bible offered images, ideas, and personages

---

23. Seward and White, *Jubilee Songs,* 28.
24. Ibid.
25. Ibid., 25.
26. Ibid., 11.

that were consistent with their beliefs, slaves corporately composed sagas and spirituals that brought those images and ideas to life. Freed from slavish and literal fidelity to *all* of the Scriptures—for some of them denied their aspirations as free men and women—they could focus on those scriptures that they knew constituted the Word of God, or God's will that they be free. Thus every slave who sang a spiritual became a biblical commentator, one who in that creative moment peered into the Scriptures and extracted the living Word of God.

A NOTION OF BIBLICAL AUTHORITY WITHIN THE AFRICAN AMERICAN EXPERIENCE

Moving toward a constructive statement about how an African American Christian ethic might regard the Bible as authoritative, we must find a way of articulating how the Bible has authority for African Americans and the best way of interpreting the Bible as African Americans seek to develop an adequate Christian ethical consciousness. African Americans might find some comfort in all five hermeneutical options we reviewed. The certainty that God has commanded and indeed authored the exact texts as they appear in the Bible has certainly resonated with many African Americans whose faith has been anchored in the belief that every word of the Bible is literally true. An absolute God must ensure that every word is absolutely true. Yet, the African American experience has perforce had to assume some of the boldness of the modernist stance. Knowing that a slaveholding culture utilized the Bible to justify their bondage, slaves rejected that agenda. They knew at some point that they would have to move beyond the liberal posture that implicitly gave legitimacy to *all* relative positions. The slave knew that the position of the slaveholder could not be right, despite the attempts of slaveholders to find justification for slavery in the Bible. The modernist spirit within slave biblical consciousness took the leap and affirmed that the salvation of the enslaved could only be envisioned through the consciousness of the enslaved themselves, and none others. They themselves became the focal point of all hermeneutical endeavors. In this regard they resembled Jesus, who in his confrontation with the traditional authorities of his day, boldly declared, "Again, you have heard that it was said to those of ancient times, ... but *I* say unto you" (Matt. 5:33–34). The postliberal spirit, the tendency to see the Word of God in the crucible of human history, certainly resonates in African American prophetic consciousness, particularly as that consciousness recognizes the movement of God in the stress of historical moments. Martin Luther King was fond of quoting Julia Ward Howe's *Battle Hymn of the Republic,* with its allusions to a God of history who "is tramping out the vintage where the grapes of wrath are stored." Finally, one could argue that inherent in all of African American literature has been the confrontation of creative genius with the historical experience of terror—remembered terror of kidnapping from Africa, terror in surviving the dark night of slavery. In such straits, there has always been a search for the "terms for order" in a moral universe.[27]

Of the five options available for an African American Christian hermeneutic, the literalist and the liberal frameworks have been the most conspicuous among African American Christians as they seek to relate the Bible to the ethical life. But we have already seen the shortcomings of both. Thus we need a way of affirming the Bible as authoritative without falling into the pitfalls of literalism or the inadequacies of the "canon within the canon" framework. Even the fallback position of literalism, that of allegorizing, holds out no surefire promise. Ultimately, the danger of liberalism was its "hermeneutical circle," that is, the tendency to see in the text what we want to see. If we are not careful, we will trivialize the biblical world and fashion it ultimately to suit our own needs. We must find a way out.

What must be done first of all is to recognize the reality of at least four elements in the interpretive process: (1) the faith community that produced the text, (2) the world represented in the text (the social, economic, and political forms of the time), (3) the contemporary faith community, and (4) its own "world."[28] Now, to be sure, we are encouraged to use analogies to make connections between the issues and meanings that confronted persons in past times and our own times. That is to say, if we can discern the critical questions that were on the minds of the past authors and past audiences, then by analogy we might be able to discern how that text might speak to us today. We might be able to fathom how that text might answer the peculiar questions we now bring to the text.

After acknowledging the world back then and the world in which we find ourselves and suggesting that we can effect a symmetry between the two worlds through the use of analogy, we must remember that fundamentally our challenge is to relate, not so much to the "world" of the Bible, but to the alien world that confronted the biblical world and confronts our world as well. Feminist critic Sandra M. Schneiders is correct in advising us that the goal of hermeneutical reflection is not primarily to grasp the world *of* the text or the world *behind* the text, namely, the horizon of the authors. Rather it seeks engagement with the world *before* the text, that is, the life it introduces us into. Hermeneutics aims at "appropriation...[of] an

27. Houston A. Baker Jr., *The Journey Back: Issues in Black Literature and Criticism* (Chicago: University of Chicago Press, 1980), 1.

28. William C. Spohn, *What Are They Saying about Scripture and Ethics?* (New York: Paulist Press, 1995), 7.

experience of conversion by participation in the world before the text."[29] This world that is *before* the text is an alien world, a "world" radically different from that of the audience to whom biblical texts were addressed, radically different from the world of the authors of those texts, and certainly different from our own world today. It is a strange world but one that demands our ultimate attention.

A sufficient African American Christian ethic affirms that before every text that appears in the Bible is an alien world in which only God's will reigns supreme. This will cannot be consistent with the value systems or cultures of this world, which reflect sins such as human greed and the desire of some humans to subjugate others. God's will, reflective of this alien world, may not even be consistent with the worlds of some biblical writers, to the extent that their writings seemed to approve of sins such as slavery or human exploitation. But wherever there are writings that in our prayerful judgment seem to be consistent with God's will that creatures of God's creation enjoy freedom, there will we find the Word of God. It is important to keep in mind, however, that the touchstone for determining the normative value of certain texts in the Bible is, not the demands of our world, even the African American world, but rather the alien world reflective of God's will, a world that seems so alien to all the worlds that humans devise. Thus we avoid having to grant every text equal normative value, as the literalist is logically forced to do. On the other hand, we avoid having to grant each cultural context equal normative value, as the liberal logically is forced to do.

The African American slave knew that her suffering was not consistent with the will of God. He knew intuitively that the God of justice, made manifest in scriptures that he could not always read, would never countenance the gratuitous violence daily visited upon his family and his person. Rather African Americans discerned within the Holy Bible the will of God that they and all people who mourn should ultimately be saved. Their descendants continue to affirm the will of this God, glimpses of which are still available within Holy Scripture. But descendants affirm as well that "the kingdoms of our God are not the kingdoms of this world." Our hope is that ultimately our realms, our histories, all of our cultural contexts, will be brought under the sway of an alien world, a world seen all too dimly through finite eyes.

29. Sandra M. Schneiders, *The Revelatory Text: Interpreting the New Testament as Sacred Scripture* (San Francisco: HarperCollins, 1991), 168.

6

The Church as
the Keeper of the Tradition

So then, brothers and sisters, stand firm and hold fast to the traditions
that you were taught by us, either by word of mouth or by our letter.
— 2 Thessalonians 2:15

There's a great camp meeting on the other side.
— American Negro spiritual

The social and cultural contexts in which we live ground all our moral sensibilities. Even our perception of the transcendent, that sphere of existence
that we intuit to be beyond our social place and time, is articulated using
the thought forms and ideas grounded in our spatial and cultural contexts.
We can never confront the world around us except insofar as we do so
within the context of our culture and the social space in which we lead our
lives. We can never deny successfully the full impact of tradition on our
ways of thinking and acting in the world. Tradition is ever with us. Tradition anchors and grounds our sense of perspective on issues and approaches
to solving the enigmas of life. Without tradition it is nearly impossible for
human societies to establish a sense of continuity with the past or the ability to meet effectively the challenges of the future. One certainly could not
have a sense of historical consciousness were it not for the power and influence of tradition. Even the ways and means whereby we entertain options
to tackle problems in the present and those that we may confront in the
future are circumscribed, all too often, by tradition. Even in our critical and
questioning posture toward the cultures of which we are members, we must
acknowledge the power and pervasiveness of tradition.

In a sense, tradition functions as a temporal extension of the social and
cultural contexts around us. Because the powerful forces that are at play
within culture span the generations and do not usually die with the passing of
one generation, we have grown accustomed to the "ongoingness" of culture
and the normative pressures that culture exerts upon us. Tradition represents
the powerful resilience of culture and social context, extended through time

with such power that the sinews that hold our cultural moorings in place stay in place well beyond the span of our own lifetimes. We are born into traditions and inherit them. And when we die, we expect that we would leave some traditions behind to be the legacy for succeeding generations. Yet we also admit that the traditions that we inherit are also changing even as we live within them. No tradition can long remain vital and relevant to the persons who live within it unless it changes to some extent. Traditions must evolve in order to accommodate our peculiar needs that come to be in the present. The resilience of traditions is proven by this ability to accommodate the needs and requirements of the present generation.

To the extent that tradition helps inform our perspective and worldviews, tradition cannot help but inform how the world *ought* to look. Thus, at a basic and minimal level, tradition informs the moral perspectives of human beings. Tradition seeks to impose upon us normative views of order, of how things should be. If we understand social institutions to be essentially regularized patterns of human behavior, then the connection between tradition and social institutions is clear. What is not so clear is the causal relationship between the two. Do traditions produce social institutions, or do human beings, conscious and intent on preserving the legitimacy of social institutions, impose traditions upon societies in order to justify those institutions?

TWO WAYS OF UNDERSTANDING "TRADITION"

Within this problematic of the causal relationship between tradition and social institutions, we may already discern two aspects of what we mean by "tradition." As Jeffrey Stout reminds us, the term "tradition" can refer either to something handed down from generation to generation (*traditum*) or to the mode of transmission itself *(traditio)*.[1] We intuit the power of *traditum* as in, for example, the tradition of the eldest son receiving half of an inheritance. Yet *traditio*, that is to say, the mechanism by which the tradition is passed down, is an equally powerful component as well, although less recognized and not always understood as such, of what we mean by "tradition." There must be some social entity or mechanism by which all traditions are safeguarded and are passed down from one generation to another. If, for example, a council of elders ensures the legitimacy of the inheritances, even adjudicating disputes among relatives, then that council would function as a kind of *traditio*.

For Christians the one institution throughout the centuries that has historically safeguarded the traditions of the faithful and believers in the area of

---

1. Jeffrey Stout, "Tradition," in *Westminster Dictionary of Christian Ethics*, ed. James F. Childress and John Macquarrie (Louisville: Westminster/John Knox Press, 1986).

moral discernment and functioned as the mechanism to safeguard that which is passed down has been the Christian church. Christian ethics has long acknowledged and affirmed the role of believing communities in not only the decision making of Christians but also in the development of their character and disposition, factors without which decisions could not be made in the first place. Christians are believers who assemble in communities of faith and who believe in the reality of God and the power of Christ. Inevitably these communities of faith will develop traditions that aid the believers in making ethical decisions and forming ethical consciousness. The burden of this chapter will be to discern if there is a relationship between ecclesiology, or a doctrine of the church, and moral discernment. If there is such a relationship, we will examine how it might be articulated. The ultimate goal of this chapter will be to account for the presence of a sense of tradition that has overtly and implicitly informed an African American Christian ethic and to examine how such an ethic has been mediated historically through the African American churches. Thus, this chapter will attempt to develop an African American ecclesiology and to show how a doctrine of the church within African American culture has informed moral discernment and Christian ethical consciousness.

TWO RIVAL ECCLESIOLOGIES

Two rival doctrines have informed a notion of the Christian church and theoretically have been available for African Americans in their historical embrace of Christian faith. One is the tradition of Roman Catholicism, seen in its classical form during the High Middle Ages during the period that roughly extended from the twelfth century through the beginning of the Renaissance in the fifteenth century. The other tradition is the one engendered by the theological revolt from Rome, the Protestant Reformation of the sixteenth century. Both traditions have affirmed radically different perspectives on the extent to which the church might function as a means of aiding the believer in moral discernment.

The eventual monopolistic control that the Catholic Church had over European societies at the height of the medieval period was of course presaged with Emperor Constantine's decision to make Christianity the religion of the empire in 313. The Edict of Milan in that same year effectively made Christianity the official religion of the Holy Roman Empire. During the so-called medieval synthesis, which is typified by the thought of Thomas Aquinas, Roman Catholicism took the position that the goodness of God's creation is so pervasive that all of creation constantly seeks the goodness of God, its source and origin. All aspects of the created order are arranged in a hierarchical order from the perfect goodness of God down to lesser degrees of goodness, but all aspects of the order are blessed by God. Although there is differentiation within the created order, unity exists to the extent that everything seeks the goodness of God. To be sure, while creation is not perfect and is thus a perpetual harbinger of sin, creation is always yearning to reach the goodness of God. A kind of continuum exists between nature and grace, between the created world and the Creator.

God has made available to the created world the means of grace, the saving work of Jesus Christ. Ernst Troeltsch brilliantly observed that the essence of the church in the High Middle Ages was its "objective institutional character." The church would come to superintend all aspects of European societies where it held sway, as well as the lives of individual members of those societies: the "individual is born into it, and through infant baptism he comes under its miraculous influence."[2] The Catholic Church of the High Middle Ages also affirmed the doctrine *extra ecclesia nulla salus*, that is, "outside of the church, there is no salvation." Troeltsch observed:

> The priesthood and the hierarchy, which hold the keys to the tradition of the Church, to sacramental grace and ecclesiastical jurisdiction, represent the objective treasury of grace; even when the individual priest may happen to be unworthy; this Divine treasure only needs to be set always upon the lampstand and made effective through the sacraments, and it will inevitably do its work by virtue of the miraculous power which the Church contains.[3]

This hierarchy, or the *magisterium,* has functioned as an embodiment of the power of authority inherent in tradition. The prominence of the living *magisterium* is evidence of the Roman Catholic focus on *traditio,* the mode of transmission of traditional beliefs and ideas, as that official hierarchy within the church has helped the believer interpret scripture relative to moral issues and problems. This official organ also has the power to rule on matters of dogma and teachings of the church as well, especially where the Bible is silent on an issue. Individual interpretations must always conform to the dictates of this *magisterium.*

Insofar as the church could presume to be an "objective treasury of grace" for every individual person in the society, it could assume a superintending power in the society as a whole. But a price was paid. In the Church's

> extension of the Incarnation, the objective organization of miraculous power, from which, by means of the Divine Providential government of the world, subjective results will appear quite naturally. From this

---

2. Ernst Troeltsch, *The Social Teachings of the Christian Churches* (1911: New York: Harper & Row Publishers, 1960), 1:338.

3. Ibid.

point of view compromise with the world, and the connection with the preparatory stages and dispositions which it contained, was possible; for in spite of all individual inadequacy the institutional remains holy and Divine, and it contains the promise of its capacity to overcome the world by means of the miraculous power which dwells within it.[4]

In other words, just as in the biblical image of the wheat and the tare growing together in a spiritually undifferentiated society, the ascetic and the libertine, the monk and the layman—all can find a haven within the objective treasury of grace that was the church. "The one vitally important thing" as Troeltsch further observed, "is that every individual should come within the range of the influence of these saving energies of grace; hence the Church is forced to dominate Society, compelling all the members of Society to come under its sphere and influence."[5]

Protestantism, on the other hand, in its pure sectarian form, made no pretensions to effect a coextensive nexus between church and society. The pure sect is that religious collectivity that rebels against the presumed spiritual laxity of other groups. With Protestantism there was a radical break, even at the level of the individual: "Compared with this institutional principle of an objective organism [the Catholic Church], the sect is a voluntary community whose members join it of their own free will."[6] Within the sect the spiritual progress of each individual depends, not upon "the objective impartation of Grace through the Sacrament, but upon individual personal effort." Thus the sect welcomes, not the spiritually undifferentiated masses, but those who wish to leave them. In this spirit, therefore, the sect does not, in Troeltsch's words, "educate nations in the mass, but it gathers a select group of the elect, and places it in sharp opposition to the world."[7]

While the Catholic *magisterium* could be relied upon to aid the believer in moral discernment, no such mechanism was available in Protestantism. In fact, Protestantism generally looked askance at the role of tradition in moral reasoning, taking a cue either from the spirit of Enlightenment thinking or from a more evangelical stance of Luther (*sola scriptura*). Modern secularism has also discounted the role of tradition, regarding it as a dispensable aid to fallible human reason and, at worst, a "repository of superstition and a threat to autonomy."[8]

One would think that Protestantism would not have evolved a focus on *traditio,* given the historic suspicion of the aims and scope of the Catholic

4. Ibid.
5. Ibid.
6. Ibid., 1:339.
7. Ibid.
8. Stout, "Tradition."

magisterium. Protestant affirmation of the doctrine of *sola scriptura*, revelation mediated to each believer through his or her reading of scripture, was always suspicious of the vaunted power of the *magisterium* to dictate to the believer exactly how scripture was to be interpreted. Each person, guided by the Holy Spirit, appeared sufficiently able to interpret scripture rightly. Yet the Protestant celebration of the role of the "community of believers" has meant that *traditio* has functioned in at least some minimal fashion in helping the believer interpret scripture and lead the moral life. After all, it is always within the context of a community of believers that Protestant consciousness acknowledges the minimal requirements for individual access to the values and standards inherent in the moral life. Jaroslav Pelikan, in a significant work written in the mid-twentieth century, could report then how "tradition, which was a term of opprobrium for the reformers, is now becoming an acceptable concept among Protestant theologians and biblical interpreters."[9] Indeed, thinkers such as James Gustafson and Stanley Hauerwas are insistent on the primacy of community for the Christian. Hauerwas considers the church to be a "community of shared memory."[10]

We have, therefore, within Christianity, particularly within Roman Catholicism and Protestantism, mechanisms by which traditions are passed down from generation to generation. In varying degrees tradition, either understood as *traditum* or *traditio*, offers resources for moral reasoning for the believer. By extension, we have as well at least two notions of the church, or underlying ecclesiologies, that is, conceptions and doctrines of the church. Two models of the church, or ecclesiologies, would theoretically have been available to African captives who would become African American Christians. One model would assert the power of a *magisterium* to aid the believer in moral decision making and the development of ethical consciousness. The other would emphasize the primacy of the "community of believers." As it turned out, however, a combination of sociological and historical forces would determine the exact contours of the ecclesiology that would emerge from the African American worshiping community and function as a source for Christian moral discernment.

AN AFRICAN AMERICAN ECCLESIOLOGY

African American Christian ethics must recognize the immense formative and normative power of tradition. All around us we feel the power of tradition to help shape and form not only images of ourselves as black people but

---

9. Jaroslav Pelikan, *The Riddle of Roman Catholicism* (New York: Abingdon Press, 1959), 193.

10. See Stanley Hauerwas, *A Community of Character* (Notre Dame: University of Notre Dame Press, 1981).

also the patterns of the normative, however subtle and indirect that power might be exerted. Within African American culture and tradition, the most conspicuous social institution that has functioned as the mode by which traditions have been passed down from generation to generation has been the black churches. Hence, by tradition I mean *ecclesial* tradition, that is to say, those values and patterns of behavior and thought within African American culture that have been germinated under the aegis of the African American churches, or "the black church."

How shall we attempt to understand the phenomenon known all too vaguely and imprecisely as "the black church" or even "the black churches"? In theory, insofar as black ecclesial bodies have Christian foundations, they owe their parentage to Catholic as well as Protestant roots. Black churches have taken root in evangelical as well as in more liturgically oriented communions. Therefore, the term "the black church" belies the immense complexity lying behind the development of the churches in which blacks eventually became adherents. An ecclesiology of the black churches shares many characteristics of the Roman Catholic *magisterium* and the Protestant "community of believers" yet is quite distinct from both. Like the *magisterium,* African American ecclesiology has been able to exert hegemony over the secular and the sacred. And yet much of the essence of African American ecclesiology has been inspired by the sectarian impulse, the desire to part from the inhospitable and oftentimes hostile mainstream. If we are to fully understand "the black churches," we must come to terms with all of the formative factors that have contributed to their development. As we will see, the spectrum of "black churches" covers the highly liturgical to the highly unstructured, the culturally integrationist to the culturally nationalistic. Thus, this chapter will essentially affirm that an *ecclesiology* of African American churches exists and that that ecclesiology has functioned as a powerful source for an African American ethic. There has been in effect as well a dual aspect of tradition within African American ecclesiology: various aspects of a *traditum* have been preserved and passed down from generation to generation within the context of a *traditio*. Most assuredly, tradition (*traditum*) has been mediated through the African American churches (or the *traditio*).

Any analysis of an African American ecclesiology must acknowledge the inescapable assertion that Christian faith was embraced by a community in bondage. Yet while in bondage, blacks could forge an ecclesiology that would not only mitigate the bondage but would provide the means for spiritual transformation and the foundation for liberation and eventual viable living. This one observation has determined the shape and contours of the ecclesiology of the African American churches. Insofar as that community embraced Christian faith, it inevitably would seek a vision of God that would sustain the community during the ordeal of slavery and ultimately deliver it from bondage. The fact that Christian faith was embraced by a community in bondage has helped shape the tone and texture of black worship, theology, and an emergent ecclesiology. It produced the classical choral musical genre known as the Negro spirituals and set the foundation for an emergent gospel music. It produced the foundation for a theology of black liberation. And finally, it produced an ecclesiology that suggested that the black church could presume to be a community center, bridging the sacred and the secular.

Thus, to secure a definition of an African American ecclesiology, we must presume a historical consciousness of bondage and oppression. Enslaved Africans and their descendants embraced faiths (primarily Christianity and Islam) that were not of their ancestors yet adapted these faiths to their spiritual needs. I would argue that the rudiments for an ecclesiology of African American churches is the following: The African American church is an "alien" community of believers who worship a God who wills their ultimate liberation. The "alien" status of African Americans is not owing to denominational affiliation or even creedal affirmations, realities that occasioned a similar pariah status among other groups in American religious history, for example, the Mormons. No, the "alien" status of blacks is due almost totally to racial identification, not denominational affiliation or allegiance to different Christian creeds. In fact, African American Christians, in slavery and in freedom, have been tormented by whites who shared the same denominational polity, as in the case of Southern Baptists, Presbyterians, and Methodists who might have imposed racist constrictions on their fellow black denominational adherents. The alien nature of race precluded a "oneness in Christ," or unity in one faith or denominational body.

In addition, all African American ecclesiologies presume the need to prepare adherents to live fruitfully either in resistance to the secular forces that seek to undermine African American integrity or in creative and collaborative tension with the secular order. Any church type is an attempt to construct for the believer a societal means whereby the people of faith are organized in such a way that access to divine favor within the context of living in a mundane context might be achieved. All church types are attempts to be faithful to the divine within the confines of historical designs and social exigencies. It is within these two oftentimes opposing realities—the social/historical on one hand and the transcendent divine on the other—that the dynamics of church life are played out. Thus there is bound to be some tension between the two. Having stated these two observations about the inherent nature of African American ecclesiologies, we may now go on to sketch a typology for such an ecclesiology of the African American churches.

Seen from the perspective of these presumptions, African American churches may emerge from a decidedly limited and superficial assessment that denominational histories have offered. One simply cannot understand the rich dynamic of the African American churches by simply treating them as "black Presbyterians" or "black Catholics." The other dynamics at play are often obscured in strictly denominational histories. Black churches are more than the labels imply, that is, Presbyterian or Methodist or Catholic. Black churches, of whatever denominational stripe, represent a common "alien" status within the American social order.

Hans Baer and Merrill Singer have provided a useful typology of an African American ecclesiology. While the typology is geared for an understanding of black sectarianism, it is nevertheless useful for an understanding of ecclesiology as we have understood it thus far.[11] Baer and Singer develop a matrix grid formed by the intersection of two axes. The horizontal axis describes the range of "strategies of social action" available to religious groups. These strategies range from the socially quietist or "expressive," that is, the tendency to focus inwardly, in which the religion provides for "release of the emotional tensions accumulated through the experience of its members in an oppressive situation," to more overt forms of social action against social injustice in the society. The vertical axis describes the range of attitudes a group might have toward the American social order, ranging from rejection to acceptance of the values of the dominant group of the larger American society. The intersection of these two axes produces four quadrants, in which may be viewed four distinct types of religious groupings or church types, according to Baer and Singer. We now move to discuss each: the established sects, the conversionist sects, the messianic-nationalist sects, and the thaumaturgical sects.

THE ESTABLISHED SECTS

The quadrant that results from a relatively high regard for the values of the wider society and a penchant to take active steps for social change is what Baer and Singer call the "established sects." Seen in historical perspective, the established sects among African Americans represented an impulse to combine Christian faith with African American religious sensibilities using the available church structure and polity of evangelical Protestantism. These religious sensibilities ranged from a penchant for expressive and often highly emotionally charged worship to a tendency to view liberation from slavery and the struggle for justice as decidedly theological undertakings. The regard for the values of the wider society is always relative; it covers a wide range. But given the opprobrium that blacks have always suffered at the hands

---

11. Hans Baer and Merrill Singer, "Toward a Typology of Black Sectarianism as a Response to Racial Stratification," *Anthropological Quarterly* 54, no. 1 (January 1981): 1–14. See also Hans A. Baer and Merrill Singer, *African-American Religion in the Twentieth Century: Varieties of Protest and Accommodation* (Knoxville: University of Tennessee Press, 1992).

of the wider society, no black established sect has ever embraced all of the values of the wider society in an uncritical fashion. The embrace of values has been selective and always to the advantage of the group. Generally, the values of the wider society that black established sects have embraced have been those ideals of democracy, which while historically denied black Americans continued to be regarded as foundational to the American experiment and the best hope for the amelioration of conditions. Thus a level of ambiguity has always plagued the black established sects with regard to the "values of the wider society." A brief review of the emergence of the African Methodists, the black Presbyterians, and the black Baptists will illustrate the emergence of the established-sect church type and the cultural ambiguity experienced by these groups.

The seeds of the established sects among African Americans corresponded with the rise of what has been called the "independent black church." Perhaps the earliest seeds of what would become the independent black church and the established sects among African Americans were planted in the First Great Awakening in the American colonies, when for the first time a great number of blacks could taste the gospel freshly preached in their hearing. This awakening began in the third decade of the 1700s with the preaching of Jonathan Edwards at Northampton Church in Massachusetts and that of George Wakefield, an Anglican cleric who arrived in the colonies in 1738. The First Great Awakening also included the preaching of the Wesley brothers, notably John, whose preaching in Georgia to black slaves in the mid-1730s proclaimed unmistakable abolitionist sentiments. Wesley had confided to his *Journal* that the slave trade was the "execrable sum of all villainies."[12]

Of all of the denominations that were caught up in the First Great Awakening, three more than any of the others drew black adherents and believers: the prorevivalists Baptists (the so-called New Light Baptists), the Methodists, and the Presbyterians. These denominations could accommodate the yearning for fervent religious expression, which seemed to be the particular desire of black people. Certainly the emphasis on the revived heart struck the blacks as being very important, and they responded in kind, being particularly attracted to the Baptists and the Methodists, groups that did not discourage elements of West African religion, examples being the "shout" in the camp-meeting revivals. The very nature of evangelical preaching, emphasizing as it did the primacy of personal religious experience and personal regeneration, opened up the possibilities for some measure of black autonomy, even within the confines of slavery. Since the New Light Baptists encouraged local autonomy and the independence of each con-

---

12. John Wesley, *The Journal of John Wesley*, ed. Nehemiah Curnock (London: Epworth Press, 1938), 445–46.

gregation, many "blacks seized this principle and created congregations of their own."[13]

The Baptists provide a good case study on how blacks were able to achieve a level of independence and autonomy, although in a limited sense, during slavery in the antebellum South. More than any other denomination they gave leeway to their black members to preach to other slaves on plantations.[14] Although these preachers were illiterate, they were effective. While, to be sure, these preachers were always subject to the close scrutiny of whites, they managed to exert leadership and serve their fellow slave congregants as spiritual and social guides. In some cities of the South the relative freedom of the black preacher was quite obvious and notable. Black ministers and laypeople were active in the biracial First Baptist Church of Richmond, Virginia, "which had a large slave membership" and "at one time included five Negro preachers and seven black exhorters,"[15] although they were assigned to inferior seating arrangements and had to endure a host of indignities. Even under these circumstances, these black preachers were crucial in the further extension of Christian faith to fellow slaves and free blacks.

Wherever they were tolerated, little congregations of black people arose. Sometimes they were obliged to meet in secrecy. In at least two towns, Petersburg, Virginia, and Savannah, Georgia, black Baptists organized churches *before* white Baptists did so. The eventual independence of some black congregations in the South came after a predictable swelling of tensions attendant to the dramatic rise of black membership, thus unsettling many whites in the congregation. With the increase in racial indignities suffered by the blacks, they would petition to form their own congregation. Relieved to be rid of their troublesome cocongregants, the whites often gave such permission gladly. For example, blacks had worshiped in the gallery of the First Baptist Church of Richmond since 1780. By 1838, the proportion of black members had swelled to some 1,600 to only 356 white members. White officials erected a new building for themselves, and in 1841 gladly sold the old church to the black members for $6,500, who by that time were voicing some separatist sentiments, desiring their own building and the desire to chart their own destiny.[16]

The entrenchment of slavery in the South meant that no truly independent black church movement could flourish with any degree of true autonomy and freedom from white oversight and scrutiny. As Albert Raboteau ob-

---

13. Edward D. Smith, *Climbing Jacob's Ladder: The Rise of Black Churches in Eastern American Cities, 1740–1877* (Washington, D.C.: Smithsonian Press, 1988), 31.

14. Albert J. Raboteau, *Slave Religion: The Invisible Institution in the Antebellum South* (New York: Oxford University Press, 1978), 135.

15. Edward D. Smith, *Climbing Jacob's Ladder*, 136.

16. Ibid., 92.

serves, "The independence of black churches and black ministers in the South was always threatened by restrictions."[17] Moreover, fear of rebellions prompted civil authorities and southern whites in general to always be wary of any tendency of blacks to organize, even along religious lines. In spite of the appearance of black congregations in some areas of the South, most whites continued to fear Christianized blacks and viewed black preachers with deep suspicion. Such fears were not unfounded. Two major slave conspiracies, the Denmark Vesey conspiracy of 1822 and the Nat Turner slave revolt of 1831, grew out of religious activities.[18]

The relative freedom for the independent black church movement to fully flourish could have only taken place on the soil of the ostensibly free North. By the end of the eighteenth century, certainly by 1805, every northern state had abolished slavery or begun a program of gradual emancipation. In New England and the middle states, the free black population was about twenty-seven thousand in 1790, the time of the first census (surprisingly, there were thirty thousand free blacks in the South at the same time). The number of free blacks in the North would double by 1800 and would increase to seventy-five thousand by 1810.[19] But at the same time, free blacks were not fully welcomed into the local societies of these states. Free states discriminated against free blacks, economically by discriminating against them in favor of whites for jobs and politically by imposing property qualifications for the right to vote or simply withholding that right merely on grounds of color. And to be sure, slave catchers from southern states could always threaten the tenuous safety of any slave who had managed to escape.

The independent black church movement and the established sects came into being in the context of this rather tenuous freedom. The same religious fervor of the Great Awakening that kindled the quest for Christian discipleship among black slaves in the South kindled as well that same quest among free blacks in the North. By the time Richard Allen, the man who is generally recognized as the founder of the African Methodist Episcopal Church, was baptized in Delaware in 1777 by a Methodist circuit rider, the stage was set for the full flowering of this movement.

The seeds of Methodism had been firmly planted in the American colonies, particularly in the southern and mid-Atlantic states, by the time of Allen's birth in 1760. The growth of Methodism would increase even more with the arrival in 1771 of Francis Asbury, who had been sent to the colonies by John Wesley. Allen had been born a slave and raised partly in Philadelphia and partly in Delaware. He underwent a tremendous religious conversion

17. Raboteau, *Slave Religion*, 143.
18. Edward D. Smith, *Climbing Jacob's Ladder*, 85.
19. Jane H. Pease and William H. Pease, *They Who Would Be Free: Blacks' Search for Freedom, 1830–1861* (1974; Urbana: University of Illinois Press, 1990), 18.

at age seventeen. By the time of his twentieth birthday in 1780, his owner was presumably so influenced by Methodist preaching and Allen's piety that he offered Allen and his brother the opportunity to purchase their freedom. This they subsequently did for the sum of $2,000 in inflated Continental currency. Taking a surname as the mark of a free man, Allen began working as a sawyer, a wagon driver, and an itinerant Methodist preacher on the circuits between Pennsylvania, New York, and the Carolinas, meeting on one of these trips Francis Asbury himself. Word of Allen's preaching prowess led to an invitation in 1786 for him to preach to blacks in Philadelphia in St. George's Methodist Church, "a poor, dirt floored structure in a German part of the city."[20]

Blacks had been a part of St. George's Methodist Church since its establishment in 1767. They had also chaffed under the practice of segregation during most of those years. After Allen's arrival his preaching ability and general piety were made evident to all, white and black. He was put in charge of holding early morning Sunday services for blacks, at the rather inconvenient hour of 5:00 A.M., so as not to interfere with the services for the whites. He also was asked to conduct prayer services, supervise classes in the Methodist manner, and generally look after the spiritual welfare of black Methodists in the congregation. Soon despairing of the humiliation of the segregated practices, Allen suggested that the blacks form their own church. Forming a Methodist church, however, would require the support of already appointed Methodist elders (all of whom were white), and no support was forthcoming. Allen himself inquired into the prospects of getting the support from the Methodist elders and was refused in language that was "very degrading and insulting."[21]

A compromise of sorts was hammered out. Blacks would remain in the church but would establish a nonsectarian and benevolent organization, named the Free African Society, aimed at meeting the social needs of the congregants. Incorporated in May 1787, the Free African Society became extremely active in the life of black Philadelphia during these years.[22] Given the economic precariousness of black existence, even among free blacks, it functioned as a virtual mutual aid society. The Articles of Association that the members adopted established the society as a benevolent organization, concerned about the welfare of its members, their children, spouses, widows, and widowers.

---

20. Gary B. Nash, *Forging Freedom: The Formation of Philadelphia's Black Community, 1720–1840* (Cambridge: Harvard University Press, 1988), 96.

21. Richard Allen, *The Life Experience and Gospel Labors of the Rt. Rev. Richard Allen* (Philadelphia: Martin and Boston, 1833), 20.

22. Carol V. R. George, *Segregated Sabbaths: Richard Allen and the Emergence of Independent Black Churches, 1760–1840* (New York: Oxford University Press, 1973), 51.

Meanwhile, the atmosphere at worship within St. George's remained offensive to the blacks and soon grew to be intolerable. It was becoming clear that no viable biracial membership could continue under these circumstances. The break finally came one Sunday when Allen and others were kneeling at the prayer rail. A trustee rudely pulled them up. Still continuing their prayer and still harassed by now more trustees, Allen and others ended their prayer and their relationship with St. George's. Proud, even in being rebuffed, they walked out of the church, and according to Allen, "they were no more plagued with us in the church."[23]

The withdrawal from St. George's occurred in November 1787, seven months after the formation of the Free African Society. After the departure from St. George's, the society became the group around which disaffected black members of the church rallied. But Allen would eventually leave the society, dismayed because of its gradual drift toward Quakerism, a move that did not square with his more evangelical posture and his fondness for enthusiastic preaching.[24] The group that stayed with Allen soon coalesced and eventually built the venerable parent church of the African Methodist Episcopal (AME) Church, Bethel, which was dedicated in August 1794. The burgeoning denomination was officially incorporated in 1816, with Allen elected as its first bishop. By 1846 the AME Church, which began with eight clergy and five churches in 1816, had grown to 176 clergy, 296 churches, and 17,375 members.

The same racial tension that spawned the Free African Society in Philadelphia and eventually the AME Church produced a painful birth as well of the African Methodist Episcopal Zion Church ninety miles to the north in New York City during this same period. The John Street Methodist Church began to show strains as the black membership increased toward the middle years of the 1790s. As their membership increased, blacks began to resent the restrictions placed on them. Thus in 1796 Peter Williams, a slave who had purchased his freedom from a fellow church member, and James Varick and others left the church after having received permission from Bishop Francis Asbury to do so. Because they could get no aid in ordination procedures from the whites and because they did not want to succumb to the overpowering force of Allen's personality, they formed their own church, with Varick elected as their first bishop in 1799.[25]

---

23. Richard Allen, *The Life Experience and Gospel Labors*, 25; George, *Segregated Sabbaths,* 55; and Charles H. Wesley, *Richard Allen: Apostle of Freedom* (Washington, D.C.: Associated Publishers, 1969), 53.

24. George, *Segregated Sabbaths,* 57.

25. See Christopher Rush, *A Short Account of the Rise and Progress of the African Methodist Episcopal Church Zion in America* (New York: published by author, 1843).

Soon after the beginning of the nineteenth century, black Presbyterians began to rally in Philadelphia and in 1807 formed the First African Presbyterian Church under the leadership of Rev. John Gloucester Sr. The formation of the first Baptist churches among blacks followed the pattern that had been set among the Methodist congregations. White and black Baptists would coexist in a biracial church, only to experience racial tension, after which blacks would petition for independence, enthusiastically given by relieved whites. By 1805, Rev. Thomas Paul had helped found the First African Baptist Church in Boston. Shortly after this founding, he was summoned to New York City to help adjudicate tensions between whites and blacks in that city's First Baptist Church on Gold Street. The blacks were unwilling to tolerate the miserable treatment they were receiving from their white fellow congregants. Paul convinced First Baptist to grant a letter of dismissal to four men and twelve women, who subsequently organized the Abyssinian Baptist Church of New York City in 1807. This congregation was destined to be the largest black church in America by the mid-twentieth century.

The Inherent Ambiguity of the Established Sects

At the very heart of their genesis, the established sects among African Americans betrayed a basic ambiguity with respect to American culture and Christian faith. The blacks who eventually made their way into these religious groups were not at all averse to associating with social institutions of the wider society. In fact it was a presumed mark of their access to the freedoms theoretically afforded by that society to seek entry into such institutions. Consequently the first generations or so of free blacks in the North were not particularly race conscious in the sense of wanting to associate only with other blacks in all-black associations. Only when they were rebuffed would they know the value of forming their own institutions. In a penetrating study of late eighteenth- and early nineteenth-century America, Donald R. Wright has pointed out that

> African Americans did not enter freedom intent on establishing their own, separate, distinct social institutions. Most welcomed the opportunity to attend Christian worship services in established congregations and to have their children benefit from existing schools. But in these white-dominated institutions, blacks were denied admission or segregated and treated as inferior. The alternative, therefore, was for African-Americans to create their own institutions.[26]

---

26. Donald R. Wright, *African Americans in the Early Republic, 1789–1831* (Arlington Heights, Ill.: Harlan Davidson, 1990), 152.

Baer and Singer assert that established sects are "committed, at least in theory, to a reformist strategy of social activism which will enable blacks to become better integrated into the political, economic and social institutions of the larger society."[27] However, the history of established sects among African Americans has been a bit more nuanced than the Baer and Singer thesis would suggest. Attitudes of the established sects about the so-called values of the wider American society have ranged from outright rejection when those values were at odds with the aspirations of black religious adherents to implicit endorsement at other times. In other words, the black established sects have appeared to be ambiguous about the values of the wider society only because some of those values were inconsistent with the aims blacks themselves posited while other values were clearly consistent with their aims. This explains the intense militancy of these churches historically while at the same time affirming some democratic values perceived in American ideals.

During the struggle against slavery in the nineteenth century, African Methodists, Baptists, and Presbyterians were caught up in the struggle for justice and liberty. The black abolitionist movement and the struggle against slavery were allied with, indeed born in, the established sects. In January 1817 Mother Bethel Church in Philadelphia was the scene of a mass meeting that drew prominent black social activists to protest the racist presumptions of the American Colonization Society. Richard Allen himself was acknowledged leader of the first national protest organization among blacks in this country, the Convention Movement, during the 1830s.[28] The eight black men who were numbered among the founders of the American and Foreign Anti-Slavery Society in May 1840 were all clergy in established sects—Jehiel C. Beman and his son, Amos G. Beman; Christopher Rush, second bishop of the AME Zion Church, and five Presbyterians, including Samuel Cornish, the editor of the *Colored American*, and Henry Highland Garnet.[29]

While there can be no doubt about the identification of established sects in the liberation struggle for black people, there nevertheless has always been an inherent ambiguity in the determination of what might be called "cultural authenticity." While it was clear that Richard Allen recognized the value of authentic black cultural and religious expressions, later bishops, notably Daniel Payne, disparaged the use of what he termed "plantation ditties" in the AME worship services. Payne viewed as normative for worship European-oriented anthems, hymns, and liturgies. In the latter part of the nineteenth century and into the twentieth, the AME churches and the

---

27. Baer and Singer, "Toward a Typology of Black Sectarianism."
28. See Pease and Pease, *They Who Would Be Free*, 120.
29. Benjamin Quarles, *Black Abolitionists* (New York: Oxford University Press, 1969), 68.

established Baptist churches have been unquestionably identified as the religious bastion of middle-class aspirations, values, and sensibilities. Having always displayed a tendency to defend the basic values inherent in American democracy, these churches have been forever caught on the horns of this dilemma. As such then, it is no wonder that they have been the spiritual homes of the great black middle class, that portion of the African American community that has perpetually striven for entry into the American mainstream, all the while having to maintain a fierce combative mood in doing so. This middle class has historically ended up defending the very values of the institutions that sought to keep them out.

The tradition that the established black sects have thus fostered has been one of genuine social activism, an activism occasioned by the fact that such activism was necessary because the values they most cherished within American society were being withheld. These sects did not repudiate the values of Americanism, only the fact that racist elements within America sought to withhold those rights from them. The established black sects would never denounce the whole of American culture, as would the messianic-nationalists, or be indifferent to that culture, as would be the conversionists, two alternatives to the established sects we will discuss presently. Thus there was a real ambiguity with respect to the established sects and their espousal of the values of the wider American society.

An ambiguity developed as well with respect to the interplay between the secular and the sacred in the African American community within the consciousness of the established sects. This ambiguity was part of the phenomenon we may call the "hegemonic" function of the established sect churches among African Americans. By "hegemonic," I am referring to the power implicitly accorded any social institution to determine the normative values for others within that society so that persons accede to those norms even in unconscious ways and levels of their being.[30] The reasons for the development of this hegemonic function of these established sects, the mainline black churches, owe to peculiar historical and sociological factors endemic to black culture. Of all the aspects of life only the religious was under the independent purview of slaves themselves. After emancipation, religion and the religious establishment among blacks continued this hegemony. Thus the culture that would emerge from slavery would be one characterized by the

---

30. The concept of "hegemony" was articulated by Antonio Gramsci, Italian socialist and theorist, in the early years of this century. Hegemony has been defined by one Gramsci scholar as "the formulation and elaboration of a conception of the world that has been transformed into the accepted and 'normal' ensemble of ideas and beliefs that interpret and define the world." See Benedetto Fontana, *Hegemony and Power: On the Relation between Gramsci and Machiavelli* (Minneapolis: University of Minnesota Press, 1993), 20. See as well T. J. Jackson Lears, "The Concept of Cultural Hegemony: Problems and Possibilities," *American Historical Review* 90, no. 3 (June 1985): 567–93.

hegemony of religion and the recognized power of those who superintended religious tradition. Not a theocracy as in the case of the attempt to form a state according to a theological vision, what emerged was a way of life organized around the primacy of religious orientation. This particular religious orientation was the conviction that a *community in bondage* had been assured eventual liberation through the grace of God. Hence all aspects of the community—its education, political dynamics, economic functions—all came under the influence of religion, which explains the close ties between economics and religious and quasi-religious organizations within the black community before and after slavery, such as the role of mutual aid societies and insurance and burial associations.

The hegemony of religion helps explain the close relationship between religion and politics, religion and education, and religion and music in the black community. After emancipation and during Reconstruction, the first elected persons from the black community were generally clergy. Rev. R. H. Cain, an AME cleric from Charleston, was elected to the South Carolina state legislature in 1867; Hiram Revels, elected as a U.S. senator from Alabama in 1870, was an AME minister as well. Churches were also the driving forces in the establishment of the first black colleges and normal schools. Religion blessed the economic sphere as well. Booker T. Washington, the epitome of African American aspirations to business acumen, and the religious establishment were in a generally mutually reinforcing relationship. The church could be as well the source of the creative energies that would eventuate in gospel music and, to the extent that African American culture became increasingly affected by the vicissitudes of modernism in the late nineteenth century, the blues as well. Each individual's lament in the face of these vicissitudes became the substance of the blues. Yet the church might still be seen as the ultimate progenitor of the blues, for as the critic Amiri Baraka observed, "The blues is formed out of the same social and musical fabric that the spirituals issued from, but with the blues the social emphasis becomes more personal."[31] Interestingly, while owing its parentage to the church, the blues would become an art form more closely associated with secular, even profane and earthy, considerations most likely because the blues would take on the sensibilities of urban ennui, riding the waves of black migrations to the cities, as blacks moved from the "cabin to the cabaret." The hegemony of religion overcame the dichotomy between the sacred and the secular in the black community, but it wasn't without cost. While the black church could absorb all the varied segments of the black community—the political, the educational, the cultural—effectively sacral-

---

31. Amiri Baraka, aka Leroi Jones, *Blues People: The Negro Experience in White America and the Music That Developed from It* (New York: William Morrow, 1963), 63.

izing them and thereby obscuring any real difference between them and the sacred, a price was to be paid, which was to deprive these other institutions of sufficient power and credibility to sustain themselves according to principles that were not derived primarily from the religious realm. While black churches produced educational institutions, a latent anti-intellectualism also emerged within black culture. Freedom of thought was tolerated only to the extent that it stayed within the safe confines and boundaries of polite middle-class sensibilities. In the area of politics, the price paid was the inability of autonomous political institutions to develop apart from church oversight. Gayraud Wilmore's trenchant characterization of the black church as "the NAACP on its knees" recognizes the close—and certainly welcomed—political activism of the black churches. Yet one wonders if Adolph Reed is not correct. In his assessment of Jesse Jackson's political campaigns, he alleges that a clergy-dominated campaign "usurped the rational democratic political process within the national black community and would ultimately hurt the development of an effective black political movement."[32] In music, there would a contempt for the blues and other so-called secular music, even though the blues and its beat and harmonic progressions drew inspiration from the hegemonic culture overseen by the church.

Revolt against the Established Sects

Despite the hegemony achieved by the established sects, there has always been inherent within them the seeds for their own disruption or their purification and reformation. While the ecclesiology of the established sects has evidenced a spirit like the *magisterium,* it has also evidenced the countervailing pressures from the "called out," or the "community of believers," in essence, a very generic Protestant impulse at work within the established black churches. This spirit, which has always sought to purify the theology and spiritual life of members of established churches, has been sectarian, volatile, disruptive, and suspicious of the fusionist tendencies of the hegemonic church. That is to say, this sectarian spirit has manifested a suspicion of the fusion of the secular and the sacred that was always so much a part of the established-sect agenda. At least three types of "communities of believers" that represent alternatives to the established-sect type in African American church types, as suggested by the Baer-Singer model, have come to the surface. They are the conversionist, the messianic-nationalist, and the thaumaturgical. We shall now discuss each of them.

---

32. Gayraud S. Wilmore, *Black Religion and Black Radicalism,* 2d ed. (Maryknoll, N.Y.: Orbis Books, 1983), 197; Adolph Reed, *The Jesse Jackson Phenomenon: The Crisis of Purpose in Afro-American Politics* (New Haven: Yale University Press, 1986), 86. See also Gary Marx, *Protest and Prejudice* (New York: Harper & Row, 1967).

THE CONVERSIONIST SECTS

While the established sects represent a confluence between a relatively high regard for the values of the wider culture and the affirmation of active strategies for social change, the conversionist sects focus on inward religious purity. So focused are the conversionist sects on inward purity that they are indifferent or even hostile to the values of the wider society. The emergence of conversionist sects within African American churches has represented a reformation of sorts within these churches.

Toward the latter years of the nineteenth century, the Holiness and Pentecostal churches emerged as an indictment against the apparent coldness of the black Methodist and Baptist churches, respectively. Their adherents placed great value on sanctification, or "holiness," in attitude and behavior that was manifested in old-time revivalist religion.[33] No longer content with the increasingly staid respectability of these communions, these early conversionists sects emphasized spiritual renewal and vitality and insisted on the necessity of yet another baptism experience, this time "in the Holy Spirit." In fact, the Pentecostals, under the former Baptist W. J. Seymour, would come to propose the doctrine of the second baptism in the Holy Spirit.

Within the Baer-Singer model, the conversionist sects represent the confluence of reluctance to engage in overt strategies for social change and a rather negative attitude toward the wider culture. Conversionist sects are typically suspicious of secularism, modernity, and any efforts that compromise full allegiance and attention to religious matters. They have no patience with efforts to bridge the secular and the sacred, ultimately the aim of established sects. Such groups typically have a rather dismal outlook on secular culture, regarding all those not "saved," those outside of the "arc of safety" of the called apart, as worthy of hell's torment. Conversionist sects therefore disdain those in the established churches because of their implicit league with secular culture in their hegemonic functions. All must be rejected and then purified according to the conversionist vision.

In broad historical terms, the Holiness movement that emerged at the end of the nineteenth century grew out of Methodism. The historical irony is that Methodism itself, under the vision of John Wesley, grew out of an attempt to purify Anglicanism in the eighteenth century. Wesley's emphasis on sanctification signaled this hoped for regeneration within Anglicanism. Then, at the end of the nineteenth century and on American soil, Wesley's movement would find itself spawning yet another reformist impulse. Just after the Civil War, American Methodism experienced an explosion of revival-type crusades across the nation. These revivals soon eventuated into the National

---

33. William E. Montgomery, *Under Their Own Vine and Fig Tree: The African-American Church in the South, 1865–1900* (Baton Rouge: Louisiana State University Press, 1992), 346.

Holiness Camp Meeting Association, which was begun at Vineland, New Jersey, in 1867.[34] Thousands of people came to these camp meetings and claimed to have received the second blessing of sanctification.

The Holiness movement enjoyed the support of many churches until around 1880, when the movement began actually to implore persons to leave their churches. The term "come-outers" was disparagingly applied to them by established church leaders at the time. Among the "come-outers" was a man named Daniel Warner, who was founder of the Evening Light Church of God in Anderson, Indiana. Warner's church, sometimes called the "Evening Light Saints," would provide a spiritual home for William J. Seymour, the black man universally acknowledged as the initial light of American Pentecostalism in his revivals at the Azusa Street Mission in Los Angeles, as well as for Charles Fox Parham, a close collaborator of Seymour's. Seymour was impressed by the seeming genuineness of the Evening Light Saints, their progressive interracial policies, and their teaching regarding the new baptism in the Spirit.

Prior to Seymour's work in Los Angeles, the Holiness movement drew to its ranks another significant African American by the name of Charles H. Mason, who would eventually found the Church of God in Christ in 1897. A former Baptist, Mason claimed in 1894 to have undergone a sanctification and withdrew from the Baptists to build a Holiness denomination. A constellation of events centering around the turn of the twentieth century eventually led to the birthing of the Pentecostal movement during the Azusa Street Mission in Los Angeles in 1906. In 1901 Charles Fox Parham, after leaving the Evening Light Church, went to Topeka, Kansas, and began revivals, accentuating the gift of glossolalia, or speaking in tongues. For Parham, this gift was necessary evidence of a baptism in the Holy Spirit. Parham left Topeka and went to Houston, Texas, where he began a Bible school. Seymour would journey to this school in 1905 to learn more about Parham's beliefs and ideas and was invited to Los Angeles by a black Holiness church in 1906 to conduct a revival, from which would emerge the historic meeting that began American Pentecostalism.

From April 1906 and continuing for the next three years, Seymour's crusade continued. In three services a day, seven days a week, thousands of seekers, black and white, received the baptism of the Holy Spirit and the ability to speak in tongues. One of these seekers was Charles Harrison Mason, who journeyed to Los Angeles in 1906 and returned to Memphis, Tennessee, to spread the pentecostal fire in the Church of God in Christ, the group he

---

34. Vinson Synan, Oral Roberts website, *www.oru.edu*, Pentecostal History, December 3, 1999, 2; see also Vinson Synan, *The Holiness-Pentecostal Movement in the United States* (Grand Rapids: Eerdmans, 1971). See as well Arthur E. Paris, *Black Pentecostalism* (Amherst: University of Massachusetts Press, 1982).

and Rev. C. P. Jones had cofounded in 1897. He and Jones would part company soon because the latter would not insist on the gift of speaking in tongues. But Mason did so insist, and his church flourished, so much so that by 1993 it would be by far the largest Pentecostal denomination in North America, claiming some 5,500,000 members in 15,300 local churches.[35] Unfortunately the interracial aspect that was so much a part of the Azusa Street phenomenon soon gave way to the popular racism of the time. An Azusa Street pilgrim, William H. Durham of Chicago soon led many white Pentecostals into a virtually all-white organization, the Assemblies of God, formed in 1914. Yet, William J. Seymour, the son of slaves, born in 1870 amidst dire poverty and racial oppression, is forever remembered as the guiding light that gave rise to a worldwide denomination.[36]

The conversionist sects remind us of the constant need for spiritual sharpening and reformation when organized religious groups become complacent, staid, and unresponsive to the spiritual questing of their adherents. All religions should aid devotees in their desire to secure and maintain a close relationship with the wholly Other, that ineffable aspect of reality theoretically understood to be the focus of all religions. A problem, however, with conversionist sects is that they make too complete a seal between the believer and the secular world and its realities. Conversionist sects, if they are not careful, may facilitate an accommodation to unjust power structures and inequitable social systems. Happily, religious bodies such as the Church of God in Christ, having now become a formidable presence on the religious scene by virtue of burgeoning membership rolls, are now becoming more politically involved in contemporary social ills and problems.

THE MESSIANIC-NATIONALIST SECTS

Another radical rejection of the established sects and their embrace, however fraught with ambiguity, of the values of the wider society led to the messianic-nationalist sects. These groups emerge at the confluence in the Baer-Singer model of a strong vision for social change but a high rejection of the values of the wider society. African American messianic-nationalist sects constitute an attempt to sharpen and recast the cultural identity of American blacks by shifting the focal point of that identity from the American context, with the history of degradation and slavery, to a pre-American past in Africa and even further back to a glorious age in an ancient East. As such, it was, in the case of the Nation of Islam or black Judaism, a re-

---

35. Synan, Oral Roberts website, *www.oru.edu*, Pentecostal History, 5.

36. See Iain MacRobert, *The Blacks Roots and White Racism of Early Pentecostalism in the USA* (New York: St. Martin's Press, 1988), 37–59.

pudiation of the African American embrace of Christian faith. The Black Muslims would come to term Christian faith that "old slave religion."

But a black Christian messianic-nationalism emerged as well, as exemplified by the movement led by Marcus Garvey. This movement would constitute a reshaping of Christian faith in such a way that Christianity could speak to the nationalist aspirations of black people. Garvey was born in 1887 in Jamaica and came to head the Universal Negro Improvement Association (UNIA), which he founded in Jamaica in 1914. While Garvey would eventually affirm black Christian nationalism, there were early attempts within his movement to steer the group toward black Judaism. That attempt was mounted by Rabbi Arnold Ford, another West Indian Garvey follower and eventually director of the UNIA band and choirmaster. Garvey opposed this suggestion, opting for Christian faith, but he wanted a religion that offered an unabashedly nationalist orientation, one that would give theological embodiment to one of his favorite biblical pronouncements, "Princes shall come out of Egypt; Ethiopia shall soon stretch out her hands unto God" (Ps. 68:31 KJV).

Garvey's UNIA functioned in a way reminiscent of the mutual aid societies that had worked so effectively in black communities in the United States. The UNIA had many facets: economic, acting as a job development and job referral agency; recreational and cultural, providing public lectures, parades, and concerts emphasizing black heritage and pride. The UNIA had a religious component as well. An analysis of some of Garvey's speeches reveals that he himself viewed the movement he founded in religious terms. In a speech delivered in February 1921 in the movement's Liberty Hall in Harlem, he stated:

> I wish I could *convert* the world of Negroes overnight to the tremendous possibilities of the Universal Improvement Association. It pains me every moment of the day when I see Negroes losing the grasp they should have on their own. You of Liberty Hall I must ask you to *go out as missionaries* and *preach this doctrine* of the Universal Negro Improvement Association. Let all the world know that *this is the hour;* this is the time *for our salvation.* Prayer alone will not save us; sentiment alone will not save us. We have to work and work and work *if we are to be saved*... the time is now to *preach the beatitude of bread and butter.* I have contributed my bit to *preaching of this doctrine.*[37]

---

37. Marcus Garvey, speech in the *New World,* February 19, 1921, 4, emphasis added; quoted in Randall Burkett, "Religious Ethos of the UNIA," in *African American Religious Studies: An Interdisciplinary Anthology,* ed. Gayraud S. Wilmore (Durham, N.C.: Duke University Press, 1989), 67.

Garvey's ultimate vision for a Christian nationalism embodied in the work of the UNIA was brought to fruition by an Episcopal priest and follower, Rev. George Alexander McGuire. McGuire would become the chaplain-general of the UNIA. Having grown disaffected in the Episcopal Church, he gathered a group of dissident black Episcopalians to form the Independent Episcopal Church but was unable to receive authorization from either the Episcopal Church or the Roman Catholic Church. With Garvey's support and ecclesiastical affirmation from the American Catholic Church, he was able to found the African Orthodox Church in 1921. By 1942, the church reported membership of thirty thousand in the United States and overseas, 239 priests, five bishops, and two seminaries.

Another religious offshoot of Garveyism was the Rastafari movement, which saw in the emperor of Ethiopia, Haile Selassie, or Ras Tafari, the fulfillment of a prophecy attributed to Garvey: "Look to Africa, when a black king shall be crowned, for the day of deliverance is near."[38] Rastafari followers regarded Selassie's ascension to the throne in 1930 as a portentous event. Believed to be a descendant of Solomon and the queen of Sheba, and crowned His Imperial Majesty Haile Selassie I, Conquering Lion of Judah, Selassie was regarded as an embodiment of the Second Coming of the Messiah.

Other messianic-nationalist groups took inspiration from Judaism. William S. Crowdy's black Jewish group, rather incongruously named the Church of God and Saints of Christ, could not help but mix Christian messianism with the allure of counter-Christian heritage. His church was established in 1896 in Lawrence, Kansas, but it moved its national headquarters to Philadelphia in 1900. Following Crowdy's death, the leadership passed to his handpicked successor, Bishop H. Z. Plummer. Under Plummer, the group emphasized communalism and economic self-sufficiency.

Other black Jewish groups formed around the turn of the twentieth century, including the Moorish Zionist Temple, which was founded in 1899 by Rabbi Leon Richlieu in Brooklyn, New York. Another black Jewish group was led by Rabbi Wentworth Arthur Matthew, who was born in Lagos, Nigeria, in 1892 but came to the United States and established his version of Orthodox Judaism for blacks in 1919. These followers were called the Commandment Keepers, Holy Church of the Living God, Pillar and Ground of the Truth. Many of his followers were former Garveyites. Matthew instructed his followers in Yiddish and admonished them to keep dietary laws as outlined in the Hebrew Scriptures. He also preached to his followers that they were connected with the Falasha Jews of Ethiopia.[39]

---

38. See ibid., 67, 75.
39. Milton C. Sernett, ed., *Afro-American Religious History: A Documentary Witness* (Durham, N.C.: Duke University Press, 1985), 399. See also Howard Brotz, *The Black Jews*

Among all the messianic-nationalist groups, black Islam captured the popular imagination in terms of serving as a focal point for a counter-Christian messianic-nationalism. Historically, perhaps the first group that appeared on the scene was the Moorish Science Temple, founded in 1914 by Timothy Drew, who came to be known as Noble Drew Ali. Born in North Carolina, Noble Drew Ali moved to Newark, New Jersey, in his late twenties in 1913 and began to preach a homespun version of Islam to his fellow migrants from the South. According to Moorish Science legend, Drew claimed that he visited North Africa, where he received a commission from the king of either Egypt or Morocco to teach Islam to African Americans. Ali taught his followers that they were not "Negroes" or any name given them by slaveholders. He claimed that African Americans were the descendants ultimately of the Moors or Asiatics.[40] A review of the literature issued by the group, *The Holy Koran of the Moorish Science Temple of America,* reveals the messianic aspirations of Noble Drew Ali. He is identified as "the prophet . . . sent to redeem the people from their sinful ways."[41]

Of the messianic-nationalist movements inspired by Islam, the Nation of Islam has probably received the most attention from the American public. Begun in the depths of the depression in Detroit by a mysterious preacher of Islam, remembered as W. D. Fard, the movement came to national prominence by midcentury through Fard's successor, Elijah Muhammad, and Muhammad's disciple, the charismatic Malcolm X. Both Fard and Elijah propagated a theology that portrayed blacks as the "original man" and whites as devils who were grafted from blacks by a mad scientist named Yakub, who wanted to produce an evil race that would rule the world. This theology envisioned a racial Armageddon in America, given all the violence that white devils have inflicted upon blacks. But other theological themes of the Nation emphasized self-help, clean living, self-discipline, and economic self-help.[42]

The messianic-nationalist sects have provided a rich source for a transformed and renewed sense of identity for many African Americans whose self-images have been marred and defaced by the value system of the wider American culture. For persons whose outlook on life and whose sense of self-worth have been shaped by the hopelessness and despair of ghetto life, the message of salvation in the here-and-now, of redemption for black Amer-

---

of Harlem (New York: Schocken Books, 1970); Albert Ehrman, "The Commandment Keepers: A Negro 'Jewish' Cult in America Today," *Judaism* 8 (1959): 266–72; Israel J. Gerber, *The Heritage Seekers: Black Jews in Search of Identity* (Middle Village, N.Y.: Jonathan David Publishers, 1977).

40. Baer and Singer, "Toward a Typology of Black Sectarianism," 118.

41. *The Holy Koran of the Moorish Science Temple of America,* 1.

42. The classic and authoritative treatment of the Nation of Islam remains C. Eric Lincoln, *The Black Muslims in America* (Boston: Beacon Press, 1961).

ica and Africa, resonates with peculiar force and persuasion. To be sure, the mythic structures that have been marshaled to ground such a vision of redemption have often strained credulity, yet we must acknowledge that in the enterprise of "world-making," to which religion contributes, a myth is not necessarily a fairy tale. Myths can be a powerful means of organizing a person's outlook on the way the "real" world around us will take shape. Moreover, the level of economic development inherent in some messianic-nationalist sects and the powerful testimonies of personal lives that were redeemed by these sects offer ample evidence of their positive value for many persons in the African American community.

THE THAUMATURGICAL SECTS

Thaumaturgical sects represent an attempt among some African Americans to combine a search for general well-being, particularly economic prosperity, with religious grounding and theological reference. This type of sect emerges at the confluence of an indifferent attitude toward active social change and a high regard for the values of the wider society, particularly economic well-being. The name derives from the Greek word *thaumatos* for "miracle." Thaumaturgically oriented sects seek to reorder the intellectual and moral universe of the believer to such an extent that through access to a special knowledge or by virtue of new insights, a radical reversal of fortune might ensue. This orientation to the sacred is instrumental and pragmatic; in fact, there is a tendency to reduce the mysterious to an empirically organized way of knowledge, hence the nomenclature of "life science" in the names of many groups oriented to this philosophy.

In a sense, a strand of West African traditional religion has inspired the thaumaturgically oriented faiths. A rather pragmatic aspect of West African faiths asserted that the world of mystery was available for the benefit of the believer or the devotee to the cult. Thaumaturgical sects also emphasize the role of a practitioner in performing practical tasks for either cultic devotees or private clients. Moreover, religions in the African diaspora such as Santeria in Cuba, Condomble in Brazil or Vodou in Haiti are in this tradition.

In the United States, the so-called spiritualist churches have a vibrant, if unacknowledged, history, beginning with the increased urbanization of African Americans in the first two decades of this century.[43] That tradition has been tapped into by the movement known as the Church of Mind

---

43. See Claude F. Jacobs and Andrew J. Kaslow, *The Spiritual Churches of New Orleans: Origins, Beliefs, and Rituals of an African-American Religion* (Knoxville: University of Tennessee Press, 1991).

Science, based in New York and Boston, which was headed by Rev. Ike (formally known as Rev. Frederick Eichenkrotter). The former pop singer O. C. Smith pastors a church in Los Angeles known as the City of Angels Religious Science. The latent "gospel of prosperity" inherent in the messages of Rev. Creflo Dollar and the early Fred Price of the Crenshaw Christian Center of Los Angeles is also reminiscent of the thaumaturgical spirit.

These various movements and churches harness faith for very practical results, not the least of which is economic well-being. The message even in some established churches of the practical benefits of tithing may have a subliminal thaumaturgical message. Even the mantra "Prayer changes things," if viewed only as a magical incantation, may have the unintended result of being associated with the thaumaturgical impulse.

While the thaumaturgical sects may surely be criticized for their tendency to reduce the spiritual realm to a transaction between clients and servers, these sects do respond to an impulse deeply embedded within religious consciousness. That impulse is the need to correlate a vision of the spiritual with an assurance of mental and physical well-being. While that impulse all too often eventuates in a self-serving quest merely for more financial gain, one must accord some validity to the desire to seek human fulfillment and well-being, a desire that the thaumaturgical sects believe they fulfill.

CRITICAL THEORY AND AN AFRICAN AMERICAN ECCLESIOLOGY

As noted, at least four church types have emerged within the African American social context, each with strengths, weaknesses, and corresponding ethical dilemmas. We have been obliged to look carefully at each of these types in order to avoid a simplistic analysis of "the black church," as has been the tendency of many observers of this complex phenomenon. There is no such thing as *the* black church. And yet, even given the complexity of the phenomenon of all of these religious collectivities in the African American community, we are still obliged to seek an ecclesiology that suits the purposes of this book.

What would constitute the core of African American ecclesial tradition as a source for a Christian ethic? Where might we find it among the many traditions that are historically available within the African American community? Insofar as the various traditions come together, representing all the ways in which religious expressions have emerged from black culture, we might expect that somewhere in the interstices between all four we might find the basic outlines of an ecclesiology. But more work is needed before we can settle on this assertion as the answer to our quest.

In a book on Roman Catholic ecclesiology, Paul Lakeland employs Jürgen Habermas's notion of *critical theory* as a means of formulating an ecclesiology that would have sufficient power to serve as a viable foundation for the church's work in the world.[44] We might adapt this effort and discern the extent to which a notion of critical theory might provide sufficient power for an African American ecclesiology that would provide a foundation and source for moral consciousness and discernment.

What is critical theory? In terms of historical progression, critical theory is a result of modern consciousness's ability to assume a posture of "disenchantment" with the world and the attendant social structures in the world. The natural outgrowth of Enlightenment thinking, critical theory is the tendency to critique radically all human institutions and thought systems. Critical theory is, as Paul Lakeland says,

> an intellectual tool whose claim to usefulness rests in the final analysis on its avoidance of ideology. It seeks to unmask illusion and false consciousness, themselves the legitimate children of ideologies. To the extent that it succeeds in stripping them bare, it must lead to the dissolution of those same phenomena. Thus it opens up space for a purified praxis, a praxis of human emancipation.[45]

Ideologies are essentially faith systems. In a penetrating study of these historical phenomena, Patrick Corbett defines ideologies as "any intellectual structure consisting of a set of beliefs about the conduct of life and the organization of society."[46] Ideologies are essentially uncritical visions of social organization and action that purport to need no other warrant outside of their own existence for legitimization. Ideologies are therefore the very essence of *uncritical* social theory and action. Neither reason nor critical reflection is necessary to justify the legitimacy of the ideology in the minds of its adherents; in fact for the ideologue, reason and critical reflection are considered anathema. Only the "true believer" or the zealot is at home in an ideology, which is why in Lakeland's view they are poised to become the victims of critical theory: they cannot withstand the relentless scrutiny that critical theory brings to bear on them. In terms of our task, critical theory becomes a powerful tool for a relentless reflection on the incipient ideologies inherent in each of the church types we have discussed. Our ultimate goal is to lay bare these possible ideologies with such clarity that any tendency toward ideology in each of them will be discovered and finally avoided.

---

44. Paul Lakeland, *Theology and Critical Theory: The Discourse of the Church* (Nashville: Abingdon Press, 1990); for Jürgen Habermas's work on critical theory, see his *Legitimation Crisis* (Boston: Beacon Press, 1975); and *Knowledge and Human Interests* (Boston: Beacon Press, 1971).
45. Lakeland, *Theology and Critical Theory*, 37.
46. Patrick Corbett, *Ideologies* (New York: Harcourt, Brace & World, 1965), 12.

Critical Theory and the Established Sects

In the case of the established sects, the tendency toward a posture of ideology is revealed in a facile assumption in the minds of many of the members of those groups, especially their leaders, that the hegemony of the churches over secular interests is a "natural right." A posture nurtured by critical theory would always be aware that any provenance religion has over secular interests in African American culture is a product of history, not of ontological necessity. In retrospect, we rejoice that in the ordeal of slavery there was at least one institution that slaves could control with some relative power, that of their religion. Thus it should not be too surprising that even after emancipation, religion would continue to play a dominant role in the total context of African American life. But the early hegemonic role of religion in black life was the result of historical necessity, owing to a particular time and circumstance, a time and circumstance that cannot be necessarily grafted onto subsequent times and contexts. Thus critical theory suggests that while the established sects have played a necessary role in ensuring, as best they could, the full integrity of all institutions in black life, including secular interests, the full autonomy of these secular interests must inevitably be accorded.

A case in point is in the realm of black religion and politics. In 1903, when W. E. B. Du Bois wrote his classic set of essays entitled *The Souls of Black Folk*, he observed that less than forty years after slavery an enlarged professional class was able to challenge the near monopoly that preachers exerted in the political affairs of black people.[47] That broad historical movement identified by Du Bois has continued. For example, in 1982 three of the thirteen black congressional representatives were clerics. But by 1995 only one in thirty-nine was a cleric, and that preacher, Rep. Floyd Flake (Democrat of New York), chose not to run for reelection, deciding instead to focus all of his energies on the thriving ministry at his church.

The fact that Du Bois's observation has continued to evidence credence should not be construed as an indictment against black preachers who have led black people with so much courage and resourcefulness. Rather it should be hailed as an indication of the full flowering of leadership within the black community, leadership that can be enhanced by gifts from all quarters of that community. Moreover, freed from the implicit obligation to run for office that established-sect hegemony suggested, black preachers can be free to assume a true prophetic and critical stance toward the political structure, rather than succumbing to all the pressures inherent in seeking elective office. Thus, the black church has no need to assume this air of hegemony over the political realm; rather, the black churches may be called upon to be in

---

47. W. E. B. Du Bois, *The Souls of Black Folk* (New York: Blue Heron Press, 1953), 80.

creative dialogue with the political realm and with other aspects of black culture. The established sects, once forced to assume a hegemonic posture because of historical exigencies, can now acknowledge the fact that God alone rules society, not the flawed human institutions that are the churches.

Critical Theory and the Conversionist Sects

The conversionist sects need to guard against the implicit ideology that insulates spirituality from everyday life. The genius of the conversionist sects is that they constantly hold out for the believer the ever receding goal of spiritual purity and fulfillment. This focus and attention on spiritual matters ought to be the envy of less committed adherents to religion. The problem occurs when attention to this ever receding goal diverts the believer from pressing social problems and concerns and is further compounded when the world "out there" is viewed as being so irredeemable that neither its ills nor its benefits are of interest to the believer.

Fortunately, there appear to be some historical forces at work within black Pentecostalism such that a rapprochement with the secular world is coming into maturity. Black Pentecostals are becoming much more active in the political arena. When Bill Clinton campaigned in Memphis, Tennessee, during his quest for the presidency, he was hosted on the same platform by Bishop Ithiel Clemons, one of the high-ranking officers in the Church of God in Christ. Bishop Charles Blake's West Angeles Church of God in Christ is a recognized political force in the city of Los Angeles. In terms of per capita income and percentage of their young people who go on to college, one cannot assume that black Pentecostals are forever locked out of upward mobility or fear exposure to higher education.

Critical Theory and the Messianic-Nationalist Sects

Inherent in messianic-nationalist sects are powerful mythical constructs that justify the antipathy of the adherents to the wider society and insulation in the counterworld that the individual sect constructs. Without doubt, such myths have functional value: they concretize the enemies of the faithful, they anchor the convictions of followers, and they protect believers from internal doubts. Ultimately these sects build a disciplined cadre of leaders and followers and redeem lives that would otherwise be wasted by the dissolution of ghetto life. Yet in the course of achieving such laudatory results, the messianic-nationalist sects seem to be insulated from a critical assessment of the very myths and normative values that give the group success in some quarters. However, notable breakthroughs are appearing on the scene.

Diverted by its demonization of Louis Farrakhan, much of the American public is not aware that a significant minority within the Nation of Islam believes that Farrakhan abandoned the original teachings of Elijah Muhammad when he engaged in concerted political efforts with black leaders outside the Nation. Farrakhan's opponent in the Nation, one Silas Muhammad, head of the Atlanta-based Lost-Found Nation of Islam, criticized Farrakhan during the planning stages of the Million Man March of October 16, 1995. In a letter to Farrakhan stating the reasons for his refusal to participate in the march, Silas wrote: "I cannot, in good consciousness [sic] seek partnership with America, nor can I encourage my people to vote in its national political elections."[48] Thus, there are indications that the Nation of Islam seems to be in process of moving out of its insulated confines, at least in terms of political exertions. References to the "Yakub" myth are rarely heard anymore; even referring to whites as "blue-eyed devils" has been tempered. A hard-nosed assessment of political and economic options available to the Nation and to black America in general seems now to be the prevailing sentiment.

Critical Theory and the Thaumaturgical Sects

The thaumaturgical sects betray an implicit ideology that I would term an "enchantment of the economic order." Through a presumed use of the magical power of religion and faith, the thaumaturgical sects hope to create wealth and well-being for their adherents. While there are certain intangibles that are absolutely essential for economic success, such as determination, a focused mind, daring, and courage, a rational plan is necessary as well. Thaumaturgical sects eschew the rational aspect of economic planning. Ironically, a critical-theory posture would temper the tendency within thaumaturgical sects to reduce faith to material pursuits and would suggest that a mature faith is one that can adequately handle ambiguity and uncertainty in life. A critical-theory posture would echo the biblical assertion that faith is the "conviction of things not seen" (Heb. 11:1).

A VISION FOR THE AFRICAN AMERICAN CHURCH

An adequate ecclesiology of the African American churches will have to take the best of all the ecclesial traditions that have grown organically within the soil of the African American experience. Such an ecclesiology must come to recognize the heritage of bondage and the human resources that have been divinely ordained to secure and maintain the full liberation of black people's liberation. Thus it must recognize the rightful role of the church in that liberation but would allow for the full flowering of, and critical interface with, other secular institutions. Such an ecclesiology should be ever vigilant to maintain spiritual alertness but would never advocate retreating

---

48. "One Nation?" *Vibe Magazine*, February 1996, 72–73.

from the world. This ecclesiology must search deeply within the heritage of the people for images that inspire pride and self-worth without resorting to myths that strain credulity. Finally, an ecclesiology that will support a vigorous African American Christian ethic must fashion church contexts in which faith can be nurtured in such a way that the ambiguity of modern life can be confronted squarely rather than by retreating from the challenges of modern life. Moreover, such an ecclesiology must, in the context of the demands of economic integrity, prove to be every bit as functional as other intangibles, such as courage, tenacity, and vision.

The Christian churches have always been at their best when they gathered believers into a nurturing environment that facilitated praise of God, faithful living in the world, and reassuring care of each believer. African American churches, particularly the historically established sects and the messianic-nationalist sects, have always sought to effect real structures for social change in society that would ensure justice for black people. The established churches have assumed a hegemonic posture, while the messianic-nationalist sects withdrew from the wider society. The conversionist sects have always sought a level of purer spirituality and faithfulness, while the thaumaturgical sects sought to fashion faith in such a way that material well-being might ensue.

Black churches have done what they had to do, given the constraints placed upon them and the enormous challenges racism presented to them. Despairing of a society that accorded them no rights, black preachers led their people with the Bible in one hand and a political tract in the other. Despairing of the possibility for genuine salvation in a sinful world led some black churches to assume a conversionist posture. Despairing of any hope of full inclusion in American culture led still others to seek identity in the mystical Orient or a mythology of an ancient past. And to be sure, those whose economic precariousness was so acute that they sought an instrumental value of faith were led into the waiting arms of the thaumaturgical priests of mammon. Yet, through it all, these black religious collectivities have in their own peculiar ways sought to move their people from perceived fetters of bondage to a promised land. Within such a land could be seen the dim outlines of the "the old camp meeting on the other side," the slaves' eschatological vision of an ecclesial body. All black church traditions have been attempts to secure this vision, seen however dimly from afar.

7

Human Nature and Freedom

"Why are you concerned for us weaklings?"
You have made us a little lower than you yourself.
— Psalm 8:4–5 CEV

I am a poor wayfaring pilgrim.
— American Negro spiritual

We should never lose sight of the fact that an ethical system can only have coherence, meaning, and integrity insofar as it enables us to solve moral dilemmas and encounter issues and problems as *human beings.* As beings in nature, we seek to construct moral systems not as angels, elves, or any other imaginary creatures, nor do we contemplate that which we are morally compelled to do as other creatures we encounter in nature, such as lions that stalk the savannah or pike that roam in rivers. We seek to be moral as *humans.* We can be nothing else.

Of course, our nature as human beings constitutes in good measure the reasons for our dilemma when it comes to deciding what is right amongst us. All living creatures will inevitably generate action determined in large measure by their nature as creatures. The kind of beings creatures are will determine the kind of acts they are capable of doing. For other animals in nature the *right* secures grounding in the *natural,* or that which is grounded in nature. Lions do not debate the moral implications of seizing and devouring gazelles; they simply do naturally that which has been encoded in their natural dispositions. They kill violently to eat. The right is the natural. But as human beings, what exactly is the relationship between our presumed nature and the determination of the morality of the acts we do? As human beings, can we infer as easily that the right is determined by that which is simply natural? And what is *natural* to human beings?

Compared to other creatures in nature, we have precious little instinctual apparatus within us, except for drives relative to sex and food, to tell us what we *must* do in order to negotiate through the life cycle. We are not programmed as intricately as other creatures seem to be. For example, while we share the instinct of satisfying sexual desire as a means of propagating

183

our species, as humans we have no built-in code about *how* our sexuality is to be manifested or lived out. Mating rituals, nesting patterns, and the way dens are designed are virtually encoded in the instinctual apparatus of other animals in nature. In contrast, humans have at their disposal varied ways in which to declare affection for an intended mate, to mate, and to construct households. Now, it could be argued that we do not actually have choices with respect to practices like mating and household preparation because societies dictate to their members the prescribed ways of carrying on these activities. But that is precisely the point: the fact that these patterns are in place and vary from culture to culture means that human beings have made choices as to how a basic human drive is to be manifested.

Perhaps we are alone among the creatures in nature that are compelled to construct a moral order, although recent work by primatologists suggests the moral underpinnings of our nearest relatives on the evolutionary scale.[1] To be sure, lower primates vent anger, show compassion, and punish those who violate clan and community norms. Yet, it would be difficult to suggest that these primates, as sensitive as they are, are motivated by a *value system* in the meting out of punishment or in the showing of compassion. The mere presence of community norms, say in a primate clan, does not necessarily prove that the discernment of values within that community was at work. The discernment and positing of values implies the ability to make choices, to reject options, and to decide. We are not really certain that primates, even higher order primates, have these capabilities. But humans do.

Is there something unique to humans that allows us to ask questions and entertain ideas and concepts that eventuate in ethical systems? Why would pondering the question of what it means to be human be a necessary exercise in the course of asking questions about human ethics? What does it mean to talk of human nature and the attendant issues of human experience? Why is human experience an important factor in the genesis of ethics? These are age-old questions because it has been the very nature of human beings to pose questions, chief among which are those that go to the very question of human identity. What is the fundamental nature of human beings? From our nature, are there fundamental ways humans have of answering basic questions, such as, Why are we here? How should we behave amongst ourselves? What is our purpose? What is our destiny?

For many persons, even the drift of the questions just raised will betray an unacceptably reductionist bent. The charge will be leveled that if the ethical systems that humans devise are a result of the questions that humans bring to such systems, then the resulting systems will be as flawed

---

1. Frans B. M. de Waal, *Good Natured: The Origins of Right and Wrong in Humans and Other Animals* (Cambridge: Harvard University Press, 1996).

or blameworthy as the humans who devise the systems. The antidote to such a problem is to suggest that for an ethical system to have ultimate integrity, it must be imposed by a divine being upon humanity. But the moment we accept the wisdom of this proposition, we are immediately confronted with questions: How can we humans, in our contemplation, consider that which a divine being wishes to impose upon us in ways other than *as human beings?* By what else than the cognitive and apparatus available to us *as humans* are we even able to understand the revelation of this divine being? We are then thrown back to the assertions that prompted the charge of reductionism, and the argument goes back and forth, apparently without resolution.

Various theories attempting to explain human nature have prevailed. One notion is typified by the thought of Thomas Hobbes, the seventeenth-century English philosopher, who held that human beings are essentially selfish and deeply flawed. In their natural state, human beings are ineluctably drawn into conflict with one another. Hobbes had a rather bleak view of human society, viewing it essentially as a conflict of "all against all," an insight that served as the foundation for Hobbes's theory of the origin of the state and civil society. Since human beings must acknowledge that left to their own devices they would be in perpetual conflict, Hobbes believed they must covenant among themselves to acknowledge one among them as sovereign, who would have the right to exert authority over all of them. Thus is born the legitimacy of absolutism, notably monarchy, the theory of which he proposed in his classic work on political theory, *Leviathan.*[2]

The counternotion is that of Jean Jacques Rousseau, who held that human beings are born and continue to be essentially innocent and are only corrupted by forces and situations outside of themselves. It is civil society, particularly the dubious advances of science and notions of progress, that has corrupted human beings. "Everything is good as it comes from the hand of the Author of Nature," Rousseau declared in the opening lines of *Emile,* "but everything degenerates in the hands of man."[3] Rousseau's notion of original human goodness was of course not original. Its roots lay in that part of classical Greek culture that affirmed the unity of the soul and the body and the beauty of both, as well as in the humanism that was a culmination of the Renaissance, which itself was a harkening back to Greek classicism. But what is important to remember here is the affirmation that people are born good. This, in essence, is the counternotion to the Christian orthodoxy of the patristic era that all humans are born in original sin, which was reechoed in

---

2. Thomas Hobbes, *Leviathan* (1651).

3. Jean Jacques Rousseau, *Emile, or Treatise on Education* (New York: D. Appleton, 1926), 1.

the Reformation. The assumption of the natural goodness of human beings has come to be a hallmark of modern humanism and rationalism. Ironically, Rousseau's notion of goodness was initially understood as a rejection of the rationalism of Hobbes and others who determined from their rationalism a justification for the inherent flawed nature of human beings.

As strikingly different as these two views are, that we are inherently flawed or inherently good, they both suffer from some degree of conceptual poverty for the simple reason that each begs a very important question: human beings are inherently flawed or good *as compared to what?* If we presume that human beings are unique among all the creatures in nature for the simple reason that there is no other creature *exactly* like the human, then it follows that there is no other creature by which we can legitimately compare the human. On the one hand, to do an *interspecies* comparison of creatures might be an interesting exercise, but it fundamentally would be fruitless and yield little vital information about the essential nature of the creatures under scrutiny. On the other hand, if we confine our search for the essential nature of the human only to the realm of the human, with only the human as the standard, we are bound to return to the original problem that confronted us. If the human is the only standard for comparison, then on what basis can we judge the human inherently selfish or good?

If, however, we did proceed in an *interspecies* comparison between ourselves and other creatures in nature, we could assert that all creatures must be endowed with some degree, however minimal, of consciousness. Merely being alive, being sentient, means to have some level of consciousness of the external world. Consciousness of the external world is the first step in securing adequate knowledge about that world and performing critical strategic moves in interacting with that world and negotiating the steps to survive in that world. The organism must experience and know the world in order to survive in it. In a very real sense, some knowledge of the world must be prior to all purposeful activity of all living creatures. To what else but a perceived end available through consciousness (or telos in an Aristotelian sense) would any action be directed? All actions of any creatures in nature, all modes of acting and living in the world, are the result of knowledge about the world. But there are various ways available by which all creatures might acquire knowledge of that world in which they live and go through life. Basically, three modes are available: instinct, intuition, or rational thought. We believe that of the three modes available to living creatures something akin to instinct of genetic encoding is the characteristic of nonhuman creatures, while intuition and rational thought are the chief modes of knowledge for human beings.

THE DISTINGUISHING FEATURE OF HUMAN NATURE

There may perhaps be another way of discerning the absolutely irreducible contours of human nature. If we seek to discern the one irreducible aspect of humanity, that which distinguishes us from other creatures in nature, it would have to be the possession of consciousness of ourselves as thinking creatures. Now, insofar as human beings have consciousness of themselves as thinking creatures, they have the unique ability to *be* in nature and to *transcend* nature. Other creatures, however, to the extent that they have no self-consciousness are consigned only to exist in nature; they can never enjoy the possibility of transcending nature. For their benefit, creatures within nature are blessed with instinctual apparatus by which they can navigate and negotiate the various perils inherent in nature. In fact, their survival within nature is assured through such instinctual apparatus. Moreover, their instinctual apparatus may in fact be stronger than it is for human beings. Obviating the need to consider and weigh options as to how the creature is to live and survive in nature, instinct points to the drives to satisfy the need for nourishment, sex, and survival. No evaluative process is called for, for example, in nesting or ways in which to construct a den. For creatures within nature, instinct dictates how such things are to be accomplished.

Human beings, however, are endowed with only a limited instinctual apparatus by which purposeful actions in the world might be effected. With humans, instinct cannot in any way stipulate the exact ways *how* such needs are to be addressed, as is the case with other animals in nature. For humans, there are a myriad of ways in which, for example, sexuality is recognized and culturally sanctioned; the types and forms of marriages among the world's cultures are a testimony to this fact. Instinct can only carry us part of the distance on the way toward fulfilling our agenda for survival and flourishing. Intuition and rational thought, reinforced and affirmed by cultural norms, to be sure, carry us the rest of the way. Such is basically how we are able to survive within nature.

Human beings exist in nature but are able to transcend nature. Thus all questions pertaining to human identity and destiny, the purpose and meaning of life, should properly be deduced from this assertion. Within the human being, pure instinctual apparatus is of limited value with respect to the ways we negotiate our ways through life and indeed the ways by which we seek to identify ourselves as living creatures. In terms of charting our moral order and discerning our ultimate destiny, instinct will not help us, although this is of small consequence since we have limited instinctual apparatus anyway! In the realm of the transcendent, that which goes beyond nature, humans have relied upon intuition and rational thought. In the next chapter we shall use this insight to launch a fuller discussion of the role of human reason in ethical discernment. But for now, the observation that humans exist in nature but are able to transcend it becomes for us the foundation for our analysis of human nature as a factor in Christian ethical consciousness.

Several traditions have offered notions of fundamental visions of human nature, insights into the every essence of what it means to be human. Spanning the world in terms of religious traditions and cultural options, these traditions of the notions of human nature offer us a rich variety of views. They are as rich in texture and nuances as the creature they attempt to describe—the human being.

THE ANCIENT LIGHT OF INDIA AND AFRICA

One traditional perspective that purports to give insight into human nature is the ancient belief, coming from India and Africa, that there is no radical distinction between the essence of humanity and the nature of reality in general, that all is in flux. One of the ancient religions of the Indian subcontinent and indeed all of Asia is Hinduism. Inspired by the Upanishads, the earliest of which were composed in northern India in the seventh or eighth century B.C.E., Hinduism affirms that there is a single unifying principle undergirding the entire universe and that all living creatures participate in this reality. In fact, there is no separate essence for all beings that participate in being, for to assert such would deny the absolute unity of the essence that pervades the universe. Since an interconnected unity exists throughout the universe, the essential self, in terms of human nature, is actually the connection with all other selves within the universe. According to the *Brihad Aranyaka Upanishad*, "The self within all is this self of yours."[4] The ultimate self, or the *atman*, is neither autonomous nor separate from all other selves; all humans, and all selves of all creatures, are part of it as well: "This very self (*atman*) is the lord and king of all beings. As all the spokes are fastened to the hub and the rim of a wheel, so to one's self are fastened all beings, all the gods, all the world, all the breaths, and all these bodies"[5]

African religious consciousness, particularly embodied in West African religious traditions, affirms as well a spiritual substance that permeates the entire universe and in which all creatures participate in their being. The Ashanti word *nyama* recognizes a force that animates the entire universe and everything that is within the universe, even seemingly nonsentient beings. In African religious consciousness, it only appears that some entities have no sentience, for all entities that exist have within them this substance, emanating from *nyama,* that gives integrity to their being.

---

4. *Brihad Aranyaka Upanishad* 3.5.1.
5. *Brihad Aranyaka Upanishad* 2.5.15.

One can discern just from an etymological standpoint the close relationship between the highest deity in the Ashanti pantheon, Nyame, and this pervasive power within the universe, *nyama*. An Ashanti proverb captures this vision of the highest god: "Wope aka asem akyere onyankopan a, ka kyere mframa," which means, "If you wish to tell anything to the Supreme Being, tell it to the winds."[6] In traditional African faiths, human beings have been created and placed in a world in which there is no substantial difference between the sacred and the profane; all is woven together in a seamless web. Humans live out life in the interstice between the spiritual and the mundane. All of life is ritualized, for one is ever aware of the awesome implications of all actions taken. An action taken in the world of daily activities might have profound—and tragic—consequences as viewed from the world of gods and ancestors that superintends the mundane world.

This African concept of the person strikes a balance between collective identity and individual identity as a member of society. The person lives out life at the interstice between the spiritual and the mundane and also between the personal and the communal. African philosophy in general tends to define persons in terms of the social groups to which they belong. A person is thought of first of all as a constituent of a particular community, for it is the community that defines who the person is and who they can become. As John Mbiti has aptly put it, "The individual is conscious of himself in terms of 'I am because we are, and since we are, therefore I am.' "[7] But African thought also recognizes that each individual is a unique person endowed by the Creator with one's own personality and talents and motivated by one's own particular needs and ambitions. To this extent, African thought acknowledges the transcendence of individuals over their own sociocultural conditions. However, the emphasis upon a person's individuality and freedom is always balanced against the total social and historical context. Freedom and individuality are always balanced by destiny and community, and these in turn are balanced by natural and supernatural powers. Every person is a nexus of interacting elements of the self and of the world, which shape and are shaped by one's behavior.[8]

Thus Hinduism's vision of human nature posits the human being securely within the substance of all that is within the universe. The individual self and the universal *atman* participate in each other. West African notions of the nature of the human being affirm as well the inextricable link between the spiritual world and the mundane world, although some allowance is

---

6. R. S. Rattray, *Ashanti* (Oxford: Clarendon Press, 1923), 142.

7. John Mbiti, *African Religions and Philosophies* (New York: Praeger, 1970), 282.

8. Benjamin C. Ray, *African Religions: Symbol, Ritual, and Community* (Englewood Cliffs, N.J.: Prentice-Hall, 1976), 132.

made for individual manifestation of each individual life, held in tension, to be sure, with other factors such as community and destiny.

HUMAN NATURE AS AUTONOMOUS

In a real sense, the emergence of Hebraic, and later Christian, thought represents the notion that the human self, while created by a Creator, is nevertheless separate from that Creator. The creation story in the book of Genesis affirms that human beings are created by God and moreover are created to enjoy a special relationship with God and to have a special place in the physical universe. Genesis 1:26 suggests that human beings are created in the image of God; as rational creatures they are to have dominion over the rest of creation. But at the same time human beings are in nature. They are made from the "dust from the ground" (Gen. 2:7), that is to say, the same physical matter that is endemic to all other living creatures. It is absolutely critical to remember that in the Hebrew mind there is no dualism implied here, as would be the case with Greek thought, no antipathy between an immaterial spirit and a material body within the human being. Rather, for the Hebrew mind, the person does not *have* a spirit but *is* a spirit. The "breath of life" (Gen. 2:7) that God is described as breathing into Adam's nostrils is not a soul but the gift of life itself.[9]

As a created living soul, created in the image of God and thereby having rationality and imagination, the human being is thereby granted freedom. The freedom is essentially the possession of choice whether to obey God or not. Disobedience is essentially the germ of sin. Rectifying such sin will not be simply a matter of knowing the good, as would be the prescription of Platonic thought. Rather for the Hebrew mind, the aim is achieving human goodness by submitting to God's will and law. When in the New Testament the flesh is juxtaposed to the spirit, no dualism is implied. In the case of Paul, what is being contrasted is unregenerate and regenerate humanity.[10] Thus in Christian thought, the human being is a created inspirited being, who by virtue of disobedient living is not in a righteous relationship with God. By being uniquely present in the life, death, and resurrection of Jesus Christ, God has moved to restore humanity to a right relationship with Godself.

Although the Greek rationalistic impulse differs radically from the Hebraic and Christian notions of human nature, Greek thought shares a commonality with these two traditions because it asserts as well that the human being is radically autonomous from the universe. The crucial difference, however, is that Platonic rationalism affirms that the human mind has

---

9. Leslie Stevenson and David L. Haberman, *Ten Theories of Human Nature* (New York: Oxford University Press, 1998), 75.
10. Ibid., 78.

the power to intellectually grasp the meaning and essence of the universe. For Plato, the only *real* aspect of reality is the world of enduring and immutable forms that give structure to the very universe we live in. The sense organs, limited as they are, are not fully able to understand the world of the forms; only the intellect has the power to grasp them. Therefore, Plato looks to no mystical union with this world, as would be the desire in Hinduism or existentially lived out in African thought. Only one aspect of the person, the intellect, seeks, not so much to be in mystical union with the universe, but rather calmly and assuredly to understand it.

HUMAN NATURE AS A CONDITIONED ENTITY

A third broad tradition holds that if there is any such thing as human nature, it appears to us as an entity conditioned by material condition (Marx), complex unconscious psychological dynamics (Freud), or biological evolution (Lorenz). Karl Marx (1818–83) is recognized with Friedrich Engels as one of the fathers of the doctrine of dialectical materialism. This explanation of human progress was indebted to the thought of the German philosopher Georg Wilhelm Hegel, under whose spell Marx fell during his studies at the Faculty of Law of the University of Berlin in the late 1830s. Hegel believed that human progress could be explained by the driving force of *Geist,* or spirit. Through successive stages in human history, each stage fraught with conflicting tendencies, human progress lurches forward. Marx was convinced that Hegel was essentially right in terms of the dialectical nature of human progress but wrong in terms of the causal factors in such progress. Marx argued that it was material condition, not any spiritual entity as such, that was the real driving force in historical change. This notion became the ideological foundation for the working classes' revolutions of the mid-nineteenth century and ultimately for the Bolshevik Revolution in Russia in 1917.[11]

In Marxist thought, human consciousness, the essence of what it means to be human, is a direct product of one's material condition, not the appropriation of or infusion of some spiritual reality. Moreover, the exact contours of human consciousness are the results of the social relations that develop within the specific material conditions at hand. Nothing is fixed; the nature of the human becomes shaped by the social relations around us within the context of our material environment.

---

11. For the essence of Marx and Engels's social thought, see their *The German Ideology* (New York: International Publishers, 1947). See as well *Marx and Engels: Basic Writings on Politics and Philosophy,* ed. L. S. Feuer (New York: Anchor Books, 1959). For a classic criticism of Marxism, see Karl Popper, *The Open Society and Its Enemies,* vol. 1, 5th ed. (London: Routledge, 1966).

Sigmund Freud, the father of psychoanalysis, believed that the key to human nature lay deep within the recesses of the unconscious mind, the probing of which could only be facilitated through the trained expertise of a psychoanalyst. A materialism of sorts lurks behind Freud's work in the sense that he was convinced of a physiological basis for all emotional states. Freud also believed that prior psychological trauma could cause subsequent psychological illnesses. All psychological states were therefore determined by these trauma, although the experience of these trauma was not always available to the *conscious* mind of the patient, so deeply embedded in the *unconscious* were they. According to Freud, also deeply embedded within all of us are certain instincts and drives. He identified the sexual drive, or the libido, along with the drive for self-preservation, as being particularly critical in the developmental account of individual human character.[12]

In a sense, the "obverse" of Freudian psychology is the behaviorism of B. F. Skinner. While Freud believed that the key to human nature lies in internal mental states, Skinner believed that the key lies in external environmental factors and that human nature eventuates as a result of *reinforcement* experienced by human beings in the context of their environments. He sought throughout his life to isolate these patterns of reinforcement, patterns that he was convinced acted within human life as physical laws acted within mechanical science.[13]

Finally, the notion that human nature has been conditioned by the complex factors of evolutionary biology has been suggested by the work of Konrad Lorenz (1903–89). Evolutionary biology arose in part as a criticism of behaviorism, which sought explanations for human behavior in factors that were external to the person. Evolutionary biology was convinced that the factors were innate and could be traced back to the dawn of human history. Of course Charles Darwin's publication of the *Origin of Species* in 1859 set the stage for the subsequent theorizing of Lorenz. True to the evolutionist spirit that Darwin engendered, Lorenz explained the existence of any particular organ or behavior pattern by referencing its survival value for the species.[14] Certain patterns of behavior have survived within the human species precisely because they have contributed to the survival of the species. These patterns are innate rather than learned, as was the argument of behaviorism. Lorenz argued that these innate patterns were often at the disposal

12. Freud's approach was signaled in his "Five Lectures on Psycho-Analysis," reprinted in *Two Short Accounts of Psycho-Analysis* (London: Penguin, 1962). See also *A General Selection from the Works of Sigmund Freud*, ed. J. Rickman (New York: Doubleday Anchor, 1957).

13. See B. F. Skinner, *Science and Human Behavior* (New York: Macmillan, 1953). Skinner's utopian novel *Walden Two* (New York: Macmillan, 1953) and his *Beyond Freedom and Dignity* (New York: Bantam Books, 1972; London: Penguin, 1973).

14. Stevenson and Haberman, *Ten Theories of Human Nature*, 212.

of one or more of the "four big drives"—feeding, reproduction, flight, and fighting or aggression.[15]

EXISTENTIAL NIHILISM AND HUMAN NATURE

If a fourth broad category of visions of human nature exists, it is the belief that there is no essence at all in a presumed entity called "human nature." There is simply nothing there at all. Any methodological nihilism with respect to a theory about human nature in existentialism is a result of some basic convictions of existentialist thought. First, existentialism resists any broad generalizing about human nature. Each individual exists in a unique and irreplaceable fashion. Second, existentialism is intent on discovering and commenting on the *meaning* of each individual life. Third, there is a strong emphasis on the *freedom* of human beings, "on each individual's ability to choose his or her attitudes, purposes, values and actions."[16] Significant thinkers have been categorized as existentialist, among them Søren Kierkegaard (1813–55), Friedrich Nietzsche (1844–1900), and the twentieth-century thinker Martin Heidegger (1889–1976). The most famous French existentialist is Jean-Paul Sartre (1905–80), whose philosophy forged during the dark days of French resistance to German occupation during World War II became the crucible for a compelling notion of existentialist thought. In various plays, essays, and the work *Being and Nothingness,* Sartre articulated, and embodied, another option for a view of human nature.

Denying the existence of God and a self-evident "human nature," Sartre expressed his basic view through the general formula "Man's existence precedes his essence."[17] By this he means that we have no "essential" nature. We simply exist *before* anything of moral or epistemological consequence occurs. There are no universal moral prescriptions. However, there is perhaps only one moral prescription: human beings must act within the freedom that is theirs. We are, as he says, "condemned to be free; there is no limit to our freedom, except that we cannot cease being free."[18] Formative to his notion

---

15. Konrad Lorenz, *On Aggression*, trans. Marjorie Latzke (London: Methuen, 1966; New York: Bantam Books, 1974), chap. 2. For criticism of Lorenz, see Erich Fromm, *The Anatomy of Human Destructiveness* (Greenwich, Conn.: Fawcett Publications, 1973); *Man and Aggression*, 2d ed., ed. M. F. Ashley Montagu (New York: Oxford University Press, 1973); and Steven Rose, R. C. Lewontin, and Leon J. Kamin, *Not in Our Genes: Biology, Ideology, and Human Nature* (Harmondsworth, U.K.: Penguin, 1984). For a helpful assessment of the evolutionary psychology discipline, see as well George Mandler, *Human Nature Explored* (New York: Oxford University Press, 1997).

16. Stevenson and Haberman, *Ten Theories of Human Nature*, 169.

17. Jean-Paul Sartre, *Being and Nothingness*, trans. Hazel E. Barnes (New York: Philosophical Library, 1956; London: Methuen, 1957), 438–39.

18. Ibid., 439.

of freedom is a concept we noted at the beginning of this chapter: human consciousness.

In Sartre's case human consciousness is always consciousness of *something,* the world around us. And moreover, as subjects who have consciousness of the world, we are conscious of ourselves having consciousness of the world. As thinking creatures, we can, with equal ease, think of *what is not.* This is really the heart of his concept of *nothingness* in the title of the book. Now, the crucial role of nothingness in Sartre seems to make a conceptual connection between consciousness and freedom because "the ability to conceive of what is not the case involves the freedom to imagine other possibilities and the freedom to try to bring them about."[19] Thus humans are forever consigned to be free and must act on that freedom in whatever state they are in, for in whatever state they are in, a counterstate, a "nothingness," can be contemplated. This is the perpetual burden of freedom we have as humans in Jean-Paul Sartre's vision of human nature. The burden of freedom is also the harbinger for true liberation for humans, for having seen a counterstate, in their freedom, they are obliged to act on this vision and bring it into being. The revolutionary import of this sense of freedom is enormous and accounts for the explosive power of existentialism despite the dreariness of its nihilism.

VIEWS OF HUMAN NATURE IN THE AFRICAN AMERICAN SPIRITUALS

As the repository of the African American "canon," the Negro spirituals offer us profound and amazingly subtle insights into human nature. Forged within the crucible of suffering and extreme hardship, these insights come from the minds and hearts of the enslaved and the oppressed, yet their universality commends them to the embrace of all the world's cultures and peoples.

Within the spirituals and within African American slave consciousness is a definite assertion of the fragility of human existence and limitations of human power over circumstances, which is not surprising given the perspective of the oppressed, always constricted in their efforts to change their lot. The spirituals also always bespeak the awareness of a profound tension between the present and the "not yet," the power over which the human being has not full measure. The singers of the spirituals were forever cognizant that the present condition is tenuous; one can be up one moment and down the next. The slaves' knowledge that social bonds could be shattered at any

---

19. Stevenson and Haberman, *Ten Theories of Human Nature,* 176; Sartre, *Being and Nothingness,* 433ff.

moment by the possibility of being sold away reinforced their certainty of the fragility of existence. Beyond these exigencies is an awareness of the very fragility of *being* itself, a condition that goes to the very heart of being a human being. The spiritual "Keep Me from Sinking Down" that the Fisk Jubilee Singers sang embodies this belief:[20] The words are:

> Oh, Lord, Oh, my Lord Oh, my Lord!
> Keep me from sinking down.
> I tell you what I mean to do;
> Keep me from sinking down;
> I mean to go to heaven too;
> Keep me from sinking down.
> I look up yonder, and what do I see;
> Keep me from sinking down:
> I see the angels beckoning to me;
> Keep me from sinking down.

This spiritual very poignantly juxtaposes the desire that one might have at one moment and the very real possibility that that desire might not come to pass, in other words, that one has not the necessary ability to make good on a desire. I may tell you what I "mean to do," that is to say, express some hope about a desire, but the cry for help, "Keep me from sinking!" must be uttered nevertheless. No boat sails with certainty on the sea of life; all paths are followed in a tenuous manner; each step is taken haltingly, with the possibility of "sinking down" ever before one.

Life itself seems to be a perpetual task of trying to stay afloat, as it were, on a tenuous body of water. Perhaps in the face of death the slave feels the impotence of mortality most. In the spirituals, the imminence of death is pervasive, a constant reminder of the impermanence of life. For this reason, many spirituals articulate the desire on the part of the person to "be ready" to die. The spiritual "Prepare Me" invokes God to

> Prepare me, Prepare me, Prepare me,
> When death shall shake this frame.
> As I go down the stream of time,
> When death shall shake this frame,
> I'll leave this sinful world behind,
> When death shall shake this frame.[21]

---

20. Theodore F. Seward and George L. White, comps., *Jubilee Songs as Sung by the Jubilee Singers* (New York: Biglow and Main, 1884), 107.
21. Ibid., 49.

Within the hard rigors of the material life and the impermanence of life lived out in such direful circumstances, the full contours of the notion of human nature within the spirituals take full shape. The slaves' ability to survive and even achieve a level of internal integrity and coherence is facilitated by the fact that the slave, as a human being, is both body and spirit. In fact, the human being is an inspirited being. The spiritual "Shine, Shine" makes this assertion:

> I don't care where you bury my body,
> Don't care where you bury my body,
> Don't care where you bury my body,
> O my little soul's going to shine, shine,
> O my little soul's going to shine, shine,
> All around the heaven going to shine, shine,
> All around the heaven going to shine, shine.[22]

Another spiritual, "Now We Take This Feeble Body," articulates the same theme. Sung as a funeral dirge, this spiritual recognizes the reality of death:

> Now we take this feeble body,
> And we carry it to the grave,
> And we all leave it there.

But this is not the end of the spiritual. Immediately after acknowledging the reality of physical death, the spiritual goes on to triumphantly exult, "Hallelujah, Hallelujah, Hallelujah."[23] There would be no reason to sing these words of joy were it not for the assurance in the mind of the singer that the person mourned is more than merely a now inert corpse.

The spirituals thus affirm the integration of soul and body; that is, the spiritual and the physical form the composite human being. It is precisely within the context of such integration of body and spirit that the slave could become resolute, courageous, and ironically able to live a measure of freedom even in bondage. Since life is uncertain and since human powers are inadequate to meet all of life's exigencies, then one must be ever diligent and watchful in order to remain ethically upright and spiritually worthy. But as an inspirited being, the person has been provided the requisite spiritual resources to assume this alert and upright posture. One must, however, ever be watchful, especially for Satan and his minions: "Satan is like a snake in the grass. If you don't mind he'll get you at las.' "[24]

---

22. Ibid., 107.
23. Ibid., 110.
24. Olli Alho, *The Religion of the Slaves: A Study of the Religious Tradition and Behavior of Plantation Slaves in the United States 1830–1865* (Helsinki: Soumalainen Tiedeakatemia Academia Scientiarum Fennica, 1976), 111.

Spiritual alertness became therefore a watchword for the slave. Two spirituals are worth noting in this regard: "Keep Your Lamps Trimmed" and "We Are Almost Home." The former alludes to the New Testament parable concerning the five foolish maidens and the five wise ones. While the foolish ones had no oil in their lamps, the lamps of the wise ones were ready, enabling them to greet the coming bridegroom. The spiritual admonishes the believer to

> Keep your lamps trim'd and a burning,
> Keep your lamps trim'd and a burning,
> Keep your lamps trim'd and a burning.
> For this work's almost done.
> Brother (Sisters, Preachers), don't grow weary,
> Brothers, don't grow weary,
> For this work's almost done.[25]

In the spiritual "We Are Almost Home," the theme of struggling to reach the prize of heaven, which is within sight but not yet attained, is sounded:

> We are almost home,
> We are almost home,
> We are almost home,
> To ring those charming bells.[26]

Perhaps no character in the spirituals is in more need of diligence and personal vigilance than the unfortunate "sinner man." He typifies flawed human nature and an unwillingness to get ready in the face of certain death and subsequent judgment at the hands of God Almighty. The Fisk Jubilee Singers sang of the "sinner man" in this way:

> Oh! Sinner, Oh! Sinner man, Oh! Sinner,
> Oh! Which way are you going?
> Oh come back, sinner, and don't go there,
> Which way are you going?
> For hell is deep and dark despair,
> Oh which way are you going?
>
> Though days be dark and nights be long,
> Which way are you going?
> We'll shout and sing till we get home,
> Which way are you going?

---

25. Ibid., 88.
26. Ibid., 89.

> 'Twas just about the break of day,
> Which way are you going?
> My sins forgiven and soul set free,
> Which way are you going?

This spiritual might just show the essential fragility of the moral life and the spiritual makeup of any person, particularly the slave believer, and especially for the hapless "sinner man." If, therefore, life is fragile and people may not believe that they have the requisite strength to always meet the challenges of life, this might explain why many spirituals are intent on positing a condition of alertness as a model for human behavior. For instance, the young maidens are admonished to keep their lamps "trim'd and a burning."

One conspicuous image throughout the spirituals is that of the soldier. In the spiritual "In the Army of the Lord," the singer declares proudly, "I'm a soljuh in the Army of thuh Lawd." Other verses continue the story by declaring: "I've had a hahd time in the Army of thuh Lawd"; "I've come a long way in the Army of thuh Lawd"; and even painfully, "My mother died in the Army of thuh Lawd." But each adversity is resolved with the full expectation that "I'll live again in the Army of thuh Lawd." If "I've had a hahd time in the Army of the thuh Lawd," then I will be vindicated, for "I'm fightin' faw mah rights in the Army of thuh Lawd." Or if "my mother died in the Army of thuh Lawd," she'll "live again in the Army of thuh Lawd."[27] In another spiritual, the singer can exult in the fact that "I got mah swoad [sword] in mah han'."[28] Another spiritual, recognizing the hardship of life, can actually say, "Thank God I'm in de Field":

> Lord I neber knowed de battle was so hard
> Lord I neber knowed de battle was so hard
> Lord I neber knowed de battle was so hard
> Thank God I'm in de field.[29]

In the final analysis, any notion of human nature within Negro spirituals recognizes the slaves' dire straits, the reality of their suffering, yet resolves to resist such circumstances with courage. The spirituals posit a counterworld to the world that is thrust upon the slaves. In this way, the slaves embody exactly the existentialist notion of Jean-Paul Sartre. That notion recognizes the power of the human being to posit an alternative to the world around oneself; it is the option to entertain a vision of that which is not but that which can be. Sartre's term "nothingness," an unwieldy term to be sure, is

---

27. Mary Ellen Grissom, ed., *The Negro Sings a New Heaven: A Collection of Songs* (1930; New York: Dover Publications, 1969), 61.

28. Ibid., 65.

29. *Calhoun Plantation Songs*, ed. Emily Hallowell (Boston: C. W. Thompson, 1907), 15.

amazingly precise in describing the power of even the oppressed to negate the world that the oppressor wishes to thrust upon them. The action on the part of the slave to be a soldier, to keep the lamps lit and trimmed, is nothing short of the resolve to stay vigilant and to act decisively when the time comes. In acting decisively, the slave, and all similarly situated human beings, can personify the freedom inherent in human nature and human existence. Affirming a counterworld and subsequently acting on the presumption of the negation of the oppressor's world become the inspiration to struggle against slavery. Of such was the African American slaves' vision, and of such is always the human yearning for the free life.

8

Knowledge and Reason in Relationship with Faith

> ...but by knowledge the righteous are delivered.
> —Proverbs 11:9

> Oh, the rocks and the mountains shall flee away,
> And you shall have a new hiding place that day.
> Doubter, doubter, give up your heart to God.
> —American Negro spiritual

Our unrelenting effort as human beings is always to know and understand that which fascinates us, intrigues us; we seek to know even that which transcends us. We desire to know as well the world around us. Moreover, as we seek to know the world around us, we seek greater and greater levels of clarity with respect to warrants for our actions as moral beings. We need to know if we have made mistakes with respect to relations with neighbor, friend, community, or nation. Was our judgment impaired as decisions were made? What if we had only *known?* And to be sure, in back of this question, as any philosopher can assert, is the age-old query, What *can* we ever know?

If there is a necessary link between the consciousness of the world possessed by any living creature and the nature of action that that creature is capable of doing, it follows that there is a link as well between knowledge and action. Surely knowledge is grounded in consciousness. In the preceding chapter on human nature, the launching point for that discussion was the assertion that human beings are in nature but are able to transcend nature, which became the foundation for our exploration of the shadings and contours of that entity we call "human nature." This assertion will help us launch the discussion of the role of human knowledge in ethical discernment. We now proceed with that task.

Other creatures in nature are relatively more endowed than humans are with instinctual apparatus that allows them to negotiate through the perils of life. We, on the other hand, must construct our moral orders using intuition, reason, or divine revelation. Instinct will carry us only so far. We must *know*

200

that which we must do. But the problem is this: because of our limited nature, our finitude, how can we ever be sure that complete and certain knowledge is possible for us? Our very nature—being able to transcend nature but very much in nature—seems to preclude this hope. Yet we need to know that of which we cannot have full knowledge. This is our condition and our fate. Perhaps an indubitable indication of our nature as beings is our need to know with a level of certainty all that we profess to know. After all, to know something at all should mean that we know it well. What would be the point of knowing it partially or feeling only half confidently that that which we profess to know is in fact the case?

So important is this search for certainty in knowledge that philosophy has a subbranch discipline devoted to it; it is called "epistemology." More than just the study of knowledge; this subbranch is the study of the theories of how *certainty* in knowledge might be achieved. But at every turn, it is quite possible that epistemology is a doomed enterprise. The human quest for knowledge is marked by the fact that it, like the human beings that seek knowledge, is by its very nature limited and finite. Thus we have our view of human nature, fraught with difficulty though it may be. Human beings are essentially seekers of knowledge, knowledge about that with which they seek to be in harmony with the will of God, or the very nature of reality itself. Moreover, complete and satisfactory knowledge of that which we seek is not possible, yet we must continue in the search for knowledge in order to remain as we are, humans who seek knowledge.

The human condition is, to be sure, circular and paradoxical. Humans must search but will never fully find. If we were to hazard an assertion that would reflect how human nature informs the quest for knowledge, it would be this: humans are by their very nature seekers of that which is forever elusive, complete knowledge of that which they seek. As finite creatures, forever separated from the object of their epistemological inquiry, humans are subject to error and flaws. Thus as we face the problem of human knowledge in ethical discernment, we face as well a considerable paradox: we must know that of which we may never have complete knowledge because of our very nature as human beings. Yet we persist, for we sense a need to proceed in our ethical lives with some measure of confidence. In the recognition of this need, we therefore acknowledge the role of *knowing* in Christian ethical reflection.

As creatures that live in nature but are able to transcend nature, human beings have available two ways of knowing the world: intuitive, or experiential, knowledge and rational thought. Both ways of knowing presume some general competency about gaining knowledge of the subjects to which each mode is directed as well as a level of certainty about the knowledge gained. These two modes of *knowing* have been foundational to at least three broad epistemological traditions that have sought to discern that which humans *must know* in order to achieve ultimate happiness and a moral order *as humans.*

The intuitive, or experiential, route to certain knowledge was cogently explicated by Henri Bergson in his work *An Introduction to Metaphysics.* Bergson boldly proclaims that there "is a reality that is external and yet given immediately to the mind."[1] For Bergson, this reality is always in motion, fluid: "This reality is mobility. Not *things* made, but things in the making, not self-sustaining *states*, but only changing states, exist."[2] Thus the mistake the mind makes in its attempt to understand reality is to perceive it in fixed states: "Our intellect, when it follows its natural bent, proceeds, on the one hand, by solid perceptions, and, on the other, by stable conceptions."[3] Thus in our attempt to understand reality, we render it rather like a photo album, comprised of individual snapshots, but reality is in fact much like a moving picture, or a stream of consciousness. We can, Bergson was convinced, put our intelligence "within the mobile reality, and adopt its ceaselessly changing direction; in short, can grasp it by means of that intellectual sympathy which we call intuition."[4]

Presumably for Bergson, we will never know with certainty the nature of this "mobile reality" unless we immerse ourselves within it, swim in the stream, so to speak. We must *experience* it. If we do this, we can, at long last, move away from a dubious generalization about facts, to an *integral experience.*[5] Thus experience is so critical for true and reliable intuitive knowledge. For this reason, religious experience, that experience purported to move human beings to the deepest and most profound experience of intimacy with the Ultimate, has been so closely associated with intuitive and experiential knowledge.

Of the three traditions I have chosen to discuss, two have been religious in nature, while the third looks to rational thought as a means toward human fulfillment and happiness. The first tradition, in terms of its longevity within human cultural history, is the one that affirms that only when humans secure a sufficient level of *harmony with the transcendent* will they secure knowledge of that world and, indeed, knowledge about the moral order such that fruitful living can ensue. Religious cultures that embody this hope include the traditions of the Indian subcontinent, such as Hinduism and Buddhism, and the cultures and traditions of Africa. The second tradition presumes

---

1. Henri Bergson, *An Introduction to Metaphysics*, trans. T. E. Hulme (New York: Liberal Arts Press, 1949), 49.
2. Ibid.
3. Ibid.
4. Ibid.
5. Ibid., 62, Bergson's emphasis.

that reliable experiential knowledge about what one must do in the world is gained through submission to the will of the transcendent God. Religions representative of this impulse are Judaism, Islam, and Christianity. Finally, a third tradition presumes the ability of the human mind to know with certainty the nature of reality and the highest good in reality, in such a way that having intellectually grasped the good, one is then potentially able to do it. The Platonic school of thought is representative of this tradition.

KNOWLEDGE THROUGH HARMONY WITH THE TRANSCENDENT

One of the earliest metaphysical preoccupations of the peoples of the Indus Valley in antiquity was the nature of the human condition, with special reference to the problem of human suffering and human destiny, particularly the destiny of the human soul. Why is life fraught with pain, disappointment, and suffering? Is there a part of us that survives the mortal body? If so, what becomes of it? If there is a soul, what is its destiny? The answer that came from Hinduism was the notion of the transmigration (from the Sanskrit *samsara*) of the soul; that is, the soul is forever reincarnated in a succession of reappearances until at long last it achieves ultimate bliss, or *nirvana* (literally "extinction" in Sanskrit). Later on, an enduring insight came from Gautama Buddha, the founder of Buddhism, who affirmed that human suffering proceeds from the unfortunate *desire* that is in the heart of human beings. If persons could divest themselves of the desire for things that they craved, then the cause for suffering would be eliminated. He explicated this insight in his initial sermon on the Four Noble Truths.[6]

Ultimately, one's assurance of achieving enlightenment and bliss would depend upon the quality of one's *karma*, a Sanskrit word meaning literally "work," "deeds," or "action." In practice it has come to mean "excellence of action according to one's place in life," somewhat analogous to the Western notion of virtue, which connotes excellence of character. Within Hinduism, Buddhism, and Jainism, this notion of karma has suggested that good karma brings a good afterlife, while evil karma a bad one. However, karma is not the same as the Greco-Roman tradition's concept of fate, against which human beings struggle in vain. Within Hinduism and Buddhism, there is ostensibly some degree of freedom accorded persons in the charting of their destiny. Theoretically, they have it within their power to do good deeds, thereby building good karma and assuring a better destiny for the soul.

---

6. The first truth is the reality of Suffering or Pain (*dukkha* in Pali). The second is the Cause of Suffering (*samudaya*). The third is the Cessation of Suffering, or *nirodha*. Finally, the fourth is the truth of the Way (*magga*), which leads to cessation of suffering, i.e., the Noble Eightfold Path.

That is, it is within one's power to determine the disposition of one's condition within the next reincarnation. Present inequalities in life are thought to represent the inevitable working out of previous lives in which good or bad karma was exhibited.

The peoples of Africa are to be counted among the world's most inventive in religious customs and ideas. Among the rich cultures of West Africa is a pervasive preoccupation with understanding the human being's place within the cosmic order and how best to maintain that sense of place. The African mind understands that all of reality is permeated with a supernatural force called variously by the cognate *nya* in many West African cultures. In the Ashanti religion of Ghana and Nigeria, it is called *nyama*. A close relationship exists between this pervasive force in the universe and the High God, known as Nyame in the Ashanti culture. But since the High God is generally neither consulted nor appealed to except in extremely dire circumstances, the vast majority of interactions between humanity and that ineffable force in the universe that transcends humanity is carried on with *nyama*.

The problem is how interactions are best effected between individuals and this force. In other words, how can the distance between the power in the universe and human beings be overcome? The Yoruba faith recognizes three modes of access to this power or force. One is through the ancestors, which is effected either through ritual, such as oblations poured out for them, or faithful maintenance of their gravesites. It is extremely important for people to maintain the good favor of their ancestors because as the *ara orun,* or "people of heaven," they have the power to intercede or punish the living for good done or for misdeeds. The mode of access to *nyama* through the ancestors involves the faithful following of the manifestations of each person's *ori,* or "soul," throughout life. The Yoruba believe that each person is a composite of visible and invisible properties integrated by a spiritual force called the *ori*. All of a person's physical characteristics and mental dispositions have been "chosen" by the High God, Olorun (in Yoruba faith), before the person's birth. This destiny is personified as *iwa,* or "character," and it is the development of *iwa pele,* or "good character," that is the moral responsibility of every Yoruba believer.[7]

Another mode of access to the power of the cosmos is through divinities, or *orisha*. However, like the ancestors, the divinities must be placated and appeased through proper ritual and offerings at their shrines. Also, their behavior, like that of the ancestors, can be quixotic and unpredictable, thus forever posing the question of whether the believers' offerings and rituals

---

7. Benjamin C. Ray, *African Religions: Symbol, Ritual, and Community* (Englewood Cliffs, N.J.: Prentice-Hall, 1976), 135–36; see as well Joseph M. Murphy, *Working the Spirit: Ceremonies of the African Diaspora* (Boston: Beacon Press, 1994), 90–91.

will be efficacious. The final mode is through divination, or *ifa*. After years of exacting training, a *babalawo*, or "diviner," is able to discern orderly patterns within the seeming chaos of reality and share such discernment with other believers.

The religious traditions of the Indian subcontinent and to a large degree that of Africa posit an ontological reality for the human soul that is superintended by a divine reality. One's karma or one's *ori* must be in conformity with a transcendent reality. A mystical union, in effect, must be in place for the soul to have integrity and for the subsequent ethical life to have coherence. In the case of the Indian religions, one seeks to live a life in accordance with good karma. In the case of Africa, particularly Yoruba faith, one seeks to live a life according to a divinely prescribed principle of good conduct and behavior.

KNOWLEDGE THROUGH SUBMISSION TO THE TRANSCENDENT

The second tradition affirms that humans must secure a knowledge of the will of God, who transcends nature, the God of the Judeo-Christian tradition and, to some extent, of Islam. The very word *Islam* means "submission to God." All three of these traditions—Judaism, Christianity, and Islam—emphasize submission to the will of the transcendent God as a means of securing righteousness. The goal here is, not to be in harmony with some principle inherent in the moral order, but to obey the will of God after discerning that will. But how is God's will to be discerned? Discernment comes through intuitive powers of the faithful, facilitated by God's revelatory will and power. Failure to discern and obey the will of God will eventuate in estrangement from God, or sin, which engenders divine punishment.

The long and oftentimes tumultuous relationship between the Hebrew people and the God of their faith began with the recognition by Abraham that there was a power in the universe that far transcended the idols worshiped by his father and ancestors in Ur of the Chaldees. Abraham was met by this God, who demanded that Abraham begin a pilgrimage of faith through life, worshiping only Godself, in exchange for which God would make Abraham's descendants a special people as numerous as the sands upon the seashore. The entire history of the Hebrew people and their relationship with their God involves the commandment that they do the divine will, as codified in Torah, and Israel's intermittent apostasy and tragic failure to live completely according to God's will. Beginning with the tradition of the judges and culminating with the prophets, Israel is constantly reminded of what "thus says the Lord." And likewise, beginning with the apostasy of the golden calf and continuing to the powerful metaphor of adultery in

Hosea's prophecy and beyond, Israel did not always live up to expectations as the chosen people of God.

KNOWLEDGE THROUGH RATIONAL THOUGHT

The rationalism of Platonism typifies the third tradition. This tradition affirms that humans, as composite beings of body and soul, may properly inquire into the nature of reality and the highest good through the use of rational thought. Plato taught that the only intelligible things in reality were those that the intellect, or the mind/soul, could grasp and understand. Alfred Lord Whitehead has rightly said that all Western philosophy is a footnote to the thought of Plato, and he is right for good reason. While Plato might not have solved completely and satisfactorily all the issues he raised, all of them have been regarded as necessary aspects of philosophical discourse ever since his time. And to be sure, one of the issues he raised was the assertion that human beings have the ability to know the world and reality around them through the use of reason. Thus, rationalism, the belief in the ability of the human mind to employ rational thought to understand reality, has enjoyed a conspicuous place in Western philosophical thought ever since.[8]

If the supposition that human beings can know reality with complete intuitive and experiential knowledge in such a way as to avoid an incipient solipsism (the belief that only individual minds exist), then a way must be found to establish a means for clear and coherent dialogue with other thinkers. And if rationalism is to serve human beings and not become captured by a view of reality that is so independent of human experience that it becomes foreign to human experience, then it must take heed of the importance of the experiences of actual human beings. As it turns out, the rapprochement between experiential knowledge and rational knowledge corresponds very closely to the agenda of the historic quest of Augustine of Hippo: "faith seeking understanding." Such a rationalism continues to hold out the vision that through the use of human reason we may truly come to understand what reality is, who and what God is for us, and what we must do if we would presume to be moral.

To be sure, the relationship between faith and reason has been a bit more complicated, and even torturous, than our discussion would suggest so far. A review of philosophy of religion and the relationship between religion and philosophy that has existed over the centuries reveals at least three discernible patterns of interaction. (1) Early on, faith exhibited antipathy

---

8. Particularly lucid accounts of Platonic thought and the general development of Western philosophy are T. Z. Lavine, *From Socrates to Sartre: The Philosophic Quest* (New York: Bantam Books, 1984); and Robert C. Solomon and Kathleen M. Higgins, *A Passion for Wisdom* (New York: Oxford University Press, 1997).

for reason. (2) In the Middle Ages, a synthesis between faith and reason developed; that is, faith and reason were viewed as allies. (3) The humanist rejection of religion and faith in the Renaissance culminated with the nineteenth-century existentialist rejoinder that faith was in no need of reason. Let me make a few comments about each of these interactions before we attempt to fathom an African American posture with regard to the relationship between faith and reason and its import for Christian ethical discernment.

By the time of the fourth century, due to the amazing theological enterprise begun by the African bishop Augustine, the old antipathy between faith and reason had been softened, if not totally eclipsed. Unlike Tertullian, who considered faith and reason to be polar opposites, Augustine regarded reason as a tool to explain faith. Before his conversion to Christianity, Augustine was a lover of philosophy, finding in Cicero a guide to the life of the mind and the quest for truth.[9] After Augustine's conversion, his love of truth was not abated, except that he now saw God as the ultimate repository of all truth. Human reason was no less a tool for getting at the truth in God for the converted Augustine than it had been for Augustine, the follower of the pagan Cicero; however, for Augustine, the Christian, the ability to reach the truth depends upon God's grace since human reason had become tainted and corrupted because of sin. Augustine also believed that because we are made in God's image, we are capable of knowing truth; thus, his whole theological enterprise was a case of "faith seeking understanding."

Some seven hundred years later, Thomas Aquinas sought to fashion a synthesis between Aristotelian thought and the inheritance from Augustine within the context of monastic life. The medieval synthesis held that God, as the Creator of all creation, would not endow humans with reason if it were not an acceptable means toward God. In other words, since human reason is a created aspect of humanity, then God uses reason as a medium through which revelation can be mediated.[10] In a sense, Thomas reversed Augustine's understanding of the relationship between faith and reason. While Augustine understood faith to be in quest of understanding, Thomas asserted, "I understand in order to believe." Unlike Augustine, Thomas did not believe that sin had unalterably corrupted human intellect and therefore held that we can come to a basic knowledge of God without special revelation; that is, the nature of God is available to all who faithfully put the intellect to work.

Though the medieval synthesis was a marvel, it could not hold together indefinitely. For one thing, it presumed that reason could never strike out on

---

9. For an excellent recent biography of Augustine, see Garry Wills, *Saint Augustine* (New York: Lipper/Viking, 1999); see as well Peter Brown, *Augustine of Hippo* (Berkeley: University of California Press, 1967).

10. Thomas Aquinas *Summa Theologiae* (London: Eyre and Spottiswoode, 1964), 1:75–88.

its own path, apart from the superintending power of the church, through which presumably God made divine will known to human beings. Apparently Thomas could not imagine a time in which reason would revolt from the church or from the commonly held dictates that were presumably blessed by God and mediated through the church. But revolt would come sooner or later. It first began with Erasmus's poking fun at the monastic orders and the dubious piety of the church in his treatise *In Praise of Folly*, which he wrote in 1511. A rift between the church and the scientific world began with Galileo's discoveries and his support of the Copernican view of the universe that the earth orbited around the sun.[11] In 1633 Galileo was brought before the Inquisition and forced to recant, but the conflict between reason and faith was too great to be squelched. Reason could never really be free as long as the church was considered its patron and sponsor.

Eventually, humanism and scientific positivism totally rejected the role of faith in human affairs and envisioned an organization of human knowledge and society based purely on scientific orientation. Erasmus was partially an inspiration for this movement, as was Francis Bacon in the early 1600s, culminating with Auguste Comte in France in the nineteenth century. According to the movement's vision, society had to be made over, not based on outworn visions that had been couched in ecclesiastical establishments or creedal formulations or on worldviews inspired by faith, but on positive law—manmade laws and visions of the good undergirded by scientific objectivism. Of course, the dark side of this legacy is the horrors of the planned totalitarian visions of twentieth century Germany, Stalinist Russia, and perhaps China and Cambodia. Positivism ignores that aspect of the human spirit that cannot be quantified, planned, and measured.

Existentialism, particularly the vision of Søren Kierkegaard, posited the relationship between faith and reason in a radically different way. The existentialists affirmed that faith does not need reason, that indeed faith, as a way toward God and human authenticity, moves on tracks that are so different from reason that it must be forever divorced from and independent of reason. Faith is content to leap into the unknown, to make a leap into the abyss, considering doubts and fears as naught. For the existentialists, human inauthenticity is essentially inaction brought about by fear in the face of the unknown. The atheist Jean-Paul Sartre would later echo this impulse in the middle of the twentieth century when he pronounced "bad faith" as doing nothing, making no decision, when the burden of freedom required human beings to act.

Human history reveals wrangling between faith and reason. But perhaps reason and faith are interlocked in this intense struggle, each struggling

---

11. Galileo *Sidereus Muncius* (1610).

against the other, because our focus is precisely on the two ways of knowing the world around us and, of course, the world that transcends us. Both seek the same aim and have sought out each other's company at some historical moments, while at other moments they have affirmed mutual detestation. In a sense, this should not be surprising since reason and faith, while seeking the same aim, view that aim through radically different eyes.

AN ANTHROPOCENTRIC PERSPECTIVE ON
THE FAITH-REASON NEXUS

What if the analysis changed slightly and we focused on the *human beings* who are doing the seeking, those who seek to know, rather than the nature of that which they seek to know? If we do that, we will soon discover that if the focus of the inquiry is on those who are seeking, on the context of their existence, then speculation as to the relationship between faith and reason takes an interesting and different turn altogether. If we keep in mind that human beings are involved in this process, we will be forced to focus on their context and their perspective. We must bear in mind the realization that as human beings seek that which they presume is knowledge, a knowledge so certain that it is independent of human value judgment and particular experiences, they pursue this quest in the context of human communities and historical contexts.

Philip Windsor reminds us that "it is impossible to consider the idea of Reason without reference to the understanding of what human beings have *made* of themselves (not just 'become') in the course of their history."[12] I would agree and argue that the exact relationship between faith and reason cannot be adequately answered until one has adequately dealt with the question of how human life is understood as the vantage point of considering this relationship in the first place. The quality of life becomes the fulcrum for the consideration of the matter. This would seem to be especially pertinent in the realm of ethics, where the questions of what a person is obliged to do with regard to other persons or how one is expected to act within the context of a social system are considered. Only until the question of the *quality of existence* is adequately addressed can one determine one's attitude toward reason and its relationship to faith as well as the exact way in which reason relates to ethics.

The medieval synthesis depended on, and presumed, a stable social order, which in fact mirrored the levels of reality as theologians envisioned it. The "great chain of being" held that God was the apex of reality and that lesser

---

12. Philip Windsor, ed., *Reason and History or Only a History of Reason?* (Ann Arbor: University of Michigan Press, 1990), 2, Windsor's emphasis and parenthesis.

beings such as angels were just below God, then sentient creatures such as humans, then animals, then nonsentient matter, all appearing at descending levels until inanimate matter was reached. Social strata mirrored this divinely ordered chain of being, with the expected consequences of powerful elites at the top and common people at the bottom.[13] Revolution and discontent within this system was out of the question. It was an orderly arrangement, meant to mirror the immutable way things had been put in place by a divine mind. Faith was therefore bolstered by reason, as appropriated by persons who were secure in their knowledge of their place within such an order. While the Middle Ages, superintended by the church, has left us a legacy of scholastic theology and notable human achievements, it has also left us a lamentable legacy of intolerance, as exemplified by the Inquisition.

The humanist and later positivist rejection of faith was couched in the societal upheavals of the post-Reformation period and the Enlightenment. The presumption was that the unfettered human mind could march bravely into a new world, a world devoid of the superstitions and outmoded faith systems of the past, which were embedded in ignorance, reaction, and intolerance. The new vision was one in which science would be sovereign and reason alone would rule.

But if faith and all the affirmations that faith supports are banished from this world, then all that is left is a world in which quantification of all aspects of human life and the eventual commodification of human life become prevailing modes of thought. The Industrial Revolution and its eventual justification of the exploitation of human labor became in a real sense a working out of this vision of the world. The exploitation of humans in slavery and the colonization of a portion of the world for the commercial aggrandizement of another portion also eventuated from this worldview. In short, if faith is either absent or subsumed under reason when reason alone rules, then the dehumanization of human beings may be in the offing. History seems to suggest that the intolerance that is possible when faith alone rules, especially through the flawed institutions of organized religion, is matched rather tragically when reason alone presumes to rule as well. With reason alone on the throne of human valuative systems, humans themselves become the prominent victims.

The existentialist rejoinder to the facile combination of faith and reason was initially couched in Søren Kierkegaard's impatience with the banal conventionality of the state church of Denmark in particular and European Christianity in general. By his time, Christianity had lost much of its ability

---

13. See Arthur Lovejoy's classic account of the great chain of being in medieval thought, *The Great Chain of Being: A Study of the History of an Idea* (1936; New York: Harper & Row, 1960).

to excite intellectuals of Kierkegaard's stripe. Others who would follow felt the same way. By the twentieth century, existentialism would devolve into the Sartrean posture in which one looks with difficulty to discern any real warrants for the ethical act. In Sartre's quest for the authentic act, the act done in good faith, the French philosopher seemed to have overlooked any real consideration of *a reason* for such an act, let alone an underlying sense of rationality about it. The important thing is to decide, to act; that seems to redeem the morality of any human act for Jean-Paul Sartre.

So far we have discerned a critical link between the faith-reason nexus and different visions of the quality of human existence. In each of the models in which faith and reason have been in critical relationship, we have seen issues of the quality of human existence surface as real problems. The medieval synthesis produced and was undergirded by a stratified society in which freedom of rational inquiry was constricted. Within the medieval synthesis, the church regimented and controlled human life. There was no room for social mobility; freedom was not possible. The humanist-positivist rejection of faith produced a legacy of totalitarian visions in which human life was severely regimented and the quality of human worth severely diminished. Under the positivist revolution, science initially freed the human spirit from the constrictions of the regimented life imposed by the church, but its legacy has been the tragic routinization and brutalization of human life in totalitarian regimes. While existentialism's response has been a brave rejoinder to the absurdity of life, it still risks cutting itself off from any spiritual and moral moorings. The existentialist fracture with reason produced an ethic, seen notably in the work of Jean-Paul Sartre, in which human loyalties are ultimately rendered tenuous. "Only to act" seems to be the answer to the moral dilemma posed of what one should do.

FAITH AND REASON IN AFRICAN AMERICAN RELIGIOUS CONSCIOUSNESS

African American religious consciousness has posited a vision about the relationship between faith and reason that can be articulated from the context of the quality of human existence within African American history and consciousness. What is this vision? What has been the quality of existence within the African American experience? Exactly how has the quality of that existence shaped the way faith and reason within the African American experience have been articulated? These questions now demand our attention.

All African American attempts at theologizing have been people's endeavors, within the context of the legacy of bondage, to make sense of the African American experience by reference to the presumed existence and goodness of God. Captured Africans who became African American slaves at some point had to ask themselves what logic could explain the awful condition in which they existed as slaves. Persons who endured a lifetime of slavery, without ever knowing the joy of freedom, must have asked as they took their last breaths, "What has it all meant?"

Of the available historical models, the one analogous to the medieval synthesis, that attempt of American Christianity to justify slavery through biblical and theological rationales and the positing of a regimented society with slaves at the bottom, was rejected out of hand by slaves. For instance, slaves in Liberty County, Georgia, rejected the crude catechisms of Rev. Charles C. Jones that sought to ground their servile status in Christian theology. Black slaves knew no concept of reason could substantiate such a theology. As long as God was understood in Jones's terms, black slaves would reject such a God and the *rationale,* or the underlying rational structure used to justify that theological system.

Later something akin to a "humanist revolt" against the presumptions of a confident assurance in God's presence occurred even within black religious culture. Benjamin Mays, in his classic work *The Negro's God,* acknowledged the attitude exemplified by the generation of writers after the turn of the twentieth century who were impatient with their elders' confident theism. In Mays's view, the poetry of Countee Cullen, the social criticism of W. E. B. Du Bois, and the novels of Jessie Redmon Fauset represented this turn of thought. To be sure, Mays had no sympathy for such thinking but could understand why it would emerge among oppressed people, "since doubt, frustration and denial of God's existence arise also from social crises."[14]

A case can also be made that the African American experience in America has essentially been an "absurd" experience, defying all manner of logic and earnest attempts to put that experience into some coherent thought system. Consistent with a Kierkegaardan existentialist posture, such an analysis would advocate mounting a constant challenge to the conventional patterns of how faith is lived out within the context of polite respectability. Another alternative is the daring will of a Sartrean determination to decide and act at every moment, with no compunction about violating existing norms and expectations.

None of these historical models, however, seems to embody the exact vision of the relationship between faith and reason within African American theological consciousness. The nature of the faith-reason nexus within African American religious consciousness has been characterized by a profound trust that God's grace is sufficient through the survival of any ordeal,

---

14. Benjamin E. Mays, *The Negro's God as Reflected in His Literature* (1938; New York: Atheneum, 1968), 242.

even though the actual experience of African Americans has sorely tested that trust. Given the tortured existence that has constituted the African American experience, how reasonable is it to believe in God? Among the many spirituals the gifted coloratura Marian Anderson made famous was the one that asked, "O Lord, how come we here?" Without question, the existential realities of the black experience within the scope of a painful American history have affected the quality and nature of black theologizing.

African American life has always been marginalized. Such existence has thus always required and indeed necessitated the plaintive questioning and testing of God's presence, which is always affirmed but never without much testing and asking. To some extent, all African American life will always be marginal to American society. This dreaded realization springs from the inherent inequities existing in American life and the failure of American society to accommodate African Americans. But this marginalization, this alienation, may constitute a thing to be sought after, lest African Americans lose the essence of a quality of existence that has brought forth a rich vision of God and God's relationship with them.

All persons, no matter their ethnic or racial history, must always be cautious of absorption into the mainstream of any culture other than one that can completely nourish their souls. Such caution in no way advocates that African Americans not participate in the civil structures of American society: the economic sphere or the political sphere. But African American Christian ethical reflection has available to it a unique consciousness that can only be nurtured by reference to the particular perspective that has engendered African American culture. This culture cannot and should not be effaced even if access to all the benefits of the wider American society are accorded. A rich store of creativity and spiritual quickening resides on the boundary of the wider culture, not in its core.

The contemporary legatees of the African American religious consciousness that was forged in bondage but always affirmed God as the God of their ultimate liberation have a rich cultural framework in which to forge Christian ethical reflection. An undeniable heritage of bondage is part of that consciousness, but an unshakable faith in a God of human liberation is part as well. Given these aspects of the African American religious heritage, it appears that a prominent element in any African American Christian ethic would have to be personal defiance in the face of overwhelming odds. The heritage evidences a willingness to dare to defy the forces that are always seemingly arrayed against the underdog and weaker elements. This foundational element surfaces in the wit, cunning, and stealth of Brer Rabbit, the improvisation of jazz, the tendency to always take things at a different tack, away and apart from the conventional mainstream.

If we were to isolate a dialectic within the African American experience that would exemplify this foundational posture, it would surely be that of the interplay between victimization and vindication. Having been set apart by the majority culture through the folly of race and color, blacks have been victimized yet have always marshaled strength to overcome the victimization and secure vindication. Yet by virtue of continued marginalization in the majority culture, the vindication does not necessarily mean that the victimization ceases. The dialectic continues; the struggle does not abate.

The last stanza of the Negro national anthem, "Lift Every Voice and Sing," petitions the God who, it was believed, would always vindicate the oppressed in this way:

> Thou who hast by thy might, led us into the light,
> Keep us forever in the path, we pray
> Lest our feet stray from the places, our God, where we met thee
> Lest our hearts, drunk with the wine of the world, we forget thee.[15]

True to that original vision, glimpsed in suffering and bondage to be sure, a contemporary African American Christian ethic seeks within the will of that God a clear vision of how to walk in a path determined by God, a path leading inexorably to freedom.

---

15. "Lift Every Voice and Sing," in *Lift Every Voice and Sing: An African American Hymnal* (New York: Church Hymnal Corporation, 1993), 1.

PART III: CONTEXTS

9

Sexuality, Commitment, and Family Life

"Arise, my love, my fair one,
  and come away;
for now the winter is past,
. . . .
and the voice of the turtledove
  is heard in our land."
—Song of Solomon 2:10–12

There's a love feast in the heaven by and by, children
There's a love feast in the heaven by and by
Yes, a love feast in the heaven by and by, children
There's a love feast in the heaven by and by.
— "Rise, Shine for Thy Light Is Coming"
American Negro spiritual

The continuation of human life, as we presently know it, would be impossible without human sexuality. Through the natural urges of sex, we are conceived, and through the mystery of sex, we know a sublime joy inherent in our being as sexual creatures. As creatures, we know that we are the loving result of a Creator's will that we would be brought into existence. And through sexual reproduction, our progeny as well come to know and enjoy life. Without sex, there is no life, and deeply embedded in life is our natural disposition to function as sexual beings.

A topic fraught with much anxiety and tension within the African American community today, human sexuality looms large as a topic of discussion, whether it be lyrics of pop and hip-hop records, the issue of unwed pregnancy, gender wars between men and women, calls for responsible sexuality, or advocacy of the rights of homosexuals. At the national level and in countless panel discussions held in hundreds of secondary schools, community social centers, sometimes even churches, the quest for a responsible sexual ethic is being explored and pondered. This chapter will consider the

217

import of human sexuality within contemporary African American social consciousness.

Our goal is to fashion a Christian sexual ethic for African Americans. First and foremost, we seek a Christian ethic that engages African Americans in their condition as *human beings* and speaks to their sense of human personhood. This sexual ethic will also have to be squared with a perception of God as ground of our being, since our sense of sexuality is linked closely with our sense of being. We also need to shape the ethic in such a way that our sexuality is shaped according to the model we have in Christ as radical obedience to God's will. Finally, our sexuality will be viewed as a medium whereby the communicative power of the Holy Spirit is enjoyed at the deepest levels of our being. This emerging sexual ethic will take into consideration the counsel of scripture, the wisdom of tradition, and the voice of human reason, all appropriated within the context of human experience.

THE NECESSITY OF SEX

At some basic level of existence, human sexuality can be viewed within the context of sexuality that exists in all of nature. Except for organisms that procreate by the process of parthenogenesis (reproduction requiring no fertilization), creatures within nature depend upon the union of male and female sex organs in order to produce offspring for the next generation. In this respect our species is not alone. We join countless other species of living creatures in participating in sexual union in order to perpetuate ourselves. Since we share so much with other living creatures in nature, it is not surprising that many similarities between ourselves and other creatures are apparent. In fact, if we look deep enough inside our genetic makeup, the similarities between us and other creatures of nature are rather startling. For example, we share fully 98.1 percent of our genetic makeup with our nearest relatives on the evolutionary ladder—chimpanzees—and share almost as much with gorillas. We certainly follow and yield to sexual and biological urges and hormonal shifts in our physiology much as other mammals in the animal kingdom do.

Yet for all our similarities with other species of creatures, we are distinctly different from them, especially in some areas of sexuality. One critical feature, one that will factor in the theoretical framework for our ethical approach, is the relatively temporal expansiveness of human sexuality. Human females, and presumably willing males, may be desirous of sexual relations at any time, including during the menstrual period, although such behavior is generally proscribed in most cultures. The acting out of female sexual urges is not limited by the estrous cycle, that built-in immutable determinant of the time to become active sexually that is so prevalent in many other mammals.

Not constrained by the limitations of the estrous cycle, we are, relatively speaking, less shackled by our genetic encoding as determinants of exactly when we may enact our basic sexuality. Our fellow creatures in nature seem to be unalterably guided, and constrained, by such instinctual apparatus.

Another critical feature of human sexuality is that human females, unlike females in most other species, are able to hide the time at which they are most fertile from male partners. The theories for the evolution of this sexual phenomenon aside,[1] this ability to obscure the time when impregnation is most likely has proven to be a powerful determinant in the way in which humans have developed the types and the quality of pair bonding between the sexes. The ability to obscure female ovulation has had the attendant effect of diminishing the certainty of paternity on the part of males.

At the heart, therefore, of male and female relations over the evolutionary period is a basic ambiguity. Thus the terms on which any eventual pair bonding proceeds have to be negotiated between male and female within the context of this ambiguity. In fact, the very essence of gender relations may have been determined by the resolution of this ambiguity. Perhaps the ability of the female to obscure her moment of fertility has factored into the uniquely human way in which humans have developed practices and notions of commitment. Male attentiveness to domestic duties may have, in the long process of evolution, facilitated the mitigation of this ambiguity, resulting in the basic structure of commitment between the sexes.

FREEDOM AND THE NECESSITY OF CHOICE

The broadened temporal context in which human sexuality may be enacted and the ambiguous fertility of the female constitute the moral context in which male and female must create an ethical norm as to how they will engage each other. Human males and females are in a very real sense freer than other animals to determine the exact nature of the relationship with one another. Other animals are not burdened by the demands of such freedom. These other animals have the benefit of instinct to guide them in establishing the relations between the sexes. Humans have the raw stuff of sexual urges

---

1. One theory holds that concealed ovulation confuses male partners who may be constantly on the watch for other sexual partners. A male who is certain of the time of his mate's fertility knows when she can conceive and when she cannot. Since he is most concerned that all of her offspring bear his genetic marking, the male would find it advantageous when she cannot conceive, thus giving him the window of opportunity to visit potential sexual partners. Concealing ovulation thus ensures his fidelity. The other theory recognizes the practice, prevalent in much of the primate world, of infanticide, especially by male adults. A male will kill a litter in order to bring on estrous, thus making that female available to bear his own offspring. Should the female desire to engage in promiscuity, concealing her fertility would mean that none of her offspring would be endangered; none of her partners would run the risk of killing his own offspring.

and little else—except the creativity inherent in their freedom. All of this means that human beings must create the norms and procedures that will determine *how* the time for enacting sexuality is used and *how* the relations between the genders are established in the face of the ambiguity of fertility.

So inevitably some very critical ethical questions emerge: How shall the norms for enacting sexuality be established? On what basis are we to proceed in filling out the blank canvas on which gender relations and ethical engagement between male and female are to be forged? How ought we to use the freedom with which we can enact our sexuality? What can humans use to make the right choices with respect to acting out their inherent sexuality? What is at our disposal to determine that which we ought to do in sexual matters? Bereft of the instinctual framework that helps other animals determine how they will act out their sexuality and having relatively more time available in which to act out sexuality, human beings are faced with these ethical questions, questions that do not plague other animals in nature.

Nature, which has been so generous to other animals in giving them instinctual tools by which sexuality can be ordered, appears to have been rather stingy with humans. Endowed with freedom and confronted with ambiguity, humans must make decisions and forge an ethical posture. We are able and must decide how to enact our sexuality. What human beings lack in instinctual apparatus relative to acting out the impulses of sexuality is made up in the ability to make decisions and choices with respect to establishing sexual norms. As such then, the choices we make as a species become inevitably embedded in social institutions, or regularized patterns of human behavior. Such an institution is marriage and family life, of which are various forms in the various human cultures.

All of this background leads to one inevitable question: How shall we decide how to enact our sexuality? That is, according to what code shall we interact with each other as sexual beings? What inevitably will Christian ethics have to say to African Americans as they work through the difficulties of finding personal and communal integrity in sexual relationships? Since we seek a Christian ethic for African Americans, we would expect that ultimately whatever ethic we embrace will be one in which God is presumed to be a transcendent reality whose being serves as a reference point for determining the validity of that ethic. In addition, that ethic must accord with our nature as human beings, in other words, must be compatible with our condition in existence.

While there may be genetic links between our species and other creatures in nature, Homo sapiens appears to be rather different from all the others. For instance, human beings are created in nature but are able to transcend nature. Humans seem to be the only animals capable of evidencing self-consciousness, or awareness of themselves as conscious thinking beings. Lower-order animals do not appear to have this capability. Moreover, just as humans are aware of themselves as conscious beings, they are also aware of that which transcends them in their place in nature. Humans are aware that some aspect of their being, their spiritual nature, can transcend nature. The human ability to imagine, dream, and make distinctions between what *is* and what *ought* to be is an indication of this transcendent aspect of human nature. Other animals, even those closest to humans in the evolutionary scale, do not appear to have this ability. Thus humans are self-conscious, thinking beings capable of participating in a realm of existence that transcends nature, while at the same time living out their lives within nature. Humans are beings in which spirit and matter coexist; humans are the embodiment of consciousness. In other words, humans are *inspirited beings*.

Two absolutely certain affirmations are foundational to our search for a sexual ethic. The first is the absolute necessity of sexuality for the procreation of our species. The second is the characterization of the human species as inspirited beings. From these two fundamental assertions, all else will follow. We know the first assertion is true through our observation of how life indeed emerges among humans; we know the second assertion is true through the certainty of our faith. We believe that we are inspirited beings and that God has created us as such. As we hold these two affirmations together under the rubric of one reality, their analytical power becomes apparent.

FALSE DUALISM AND A FALSE DICHOTOMY

When we affirm the necessity of sex for the propagation of the species and the nature of the human species as inspirited beings, we must wonder how the early church could have ever been seduced into the conviction of a radical dualism that deprecated the sexual aspects of the human body and lauded the contemplative aspects of the mind. Old Testament attitudes toward human sexuality seem to know no such dualism. The Hebrew Scriptures casually recognize the sexual potency of the patriarchs, who in advanced age could still sire children. The love story of Ruth and Boaz is redolent with loving sexuality. No more frank evocation of sexual love between man and woman can be found than that preserved in the Song of Solomon.

Yet by the patristic era and the time of Augustine, the church exhibits a decided aversion to physical sex and human sexuality. We must attribute much of this aversion to the influence of Hellenistic thought and culture on the early church. The Stoics posited the ideal of inner tranquility based on self-discipline and freedom from passion, an ideal accomplished in part by withdrawing from the material world and its physical preoccupations in deference to ascetic, spiritual concerns. Epicureans aspired to a peace of mind forged in part by suppressing raging physical desires.[2] As the early church sought converts among the Gentiles, its Jewish heritage tended to diminish while Greek influences increased. With the rise of the Gnostics, virginity became an important virtue. Marriage was an allowance for the spiritually weak. Paul himself seems to make celibacy an ideal: "It is well for a man not to touch a woman" (1 Cor. 7:1). He also regards marriage as a concession for those who cannot live up to this ideal: "But if they are not practicing self-control, they should marry. For it is better to marry than to be aflame with passion" (1 Cor. 7:9). After a sexually indulgent youth spent with a mistress, Augustine renounced his past and "exhorted humans to abrogate bodily pleasures for the higher ideal of contemplation."[3]

But if we must be sexual in order for us to perpetuate ourselves and if God has made us, body and spirit, as inspirited beings, then a dualism juxtaposing depraved sex against exalted mind is unwarranted. If in fact we must have sex to continue to be who and what we are, there are no grounds for diminishing any aspect of our being, particularly the sexual aspect of who we are.

Another issue that confronts us as we ponder the ethical implications of our sexuality is whether the human body and our sexuality are designed primarily for procreation or pleasure. Much depends on how we resolve this issue, but unfortunately the issue is all too often framed in the context of a dichotomy. Some proponents of the pleasure thesis base their stand on the presence of organs in the human body, such as the female clitoris, the only purpose for which seems to be the sensation of pleasure.[4] While such a view affirms the obvious truth that sex is pleasurable, it presumes too much. The view presumes that one aspect of sex—in this case, plea-sure—has the power to determine the ontic value of sex itself, but it ignores that fact that while sex does indeed yield pleasure, sex itself is more than pleasure.

The pleasure sensed through an organ such as the clitoris is a function of an effect of sex; it is caused *by* sex and therefore could never be presumed to be a necessary cause *for* sex. The pleasure sensed by the clitoris, closely linked to the experience of orgasm experienced by both male and female, is a consequence of sex, not a cause for sex or even a reason for sex. In fact, pleasure for pleasure's sake, via clitoral stimulation or male masturbation, can be accomplished relatively simply *without* sexual contact with another

---

2. Raymond A. Belliotti, "Sex," in *A Companion to Ethics,* ed. Peter Singer (Oxford: Blackwell Publishers, 1991), 316.

3. Ibid., 317.

4. See Christine Gudorf, *Body, Sex, and Pleasure: Reconstructing Christian Sexual Ethics* (Cleveland: The Pilgrim Press, 1994).

human being. Thus if sexual organs can in and of themselves be instrumental in the delivery of pleasure without the sexual union, then the case has not been made establishing the necessary coextensiveness of pleasure and sexual union.

However, a case can be made for the coextensiveness of the desire for procreation and sexual union. Unless there are artificial or natural barriers to the union of sperm and egg in sex or artificial contexts for insemination, such as laboratories, then it is without question a certainty that sexual union will eventuate in procreation. This is undeniable. In terms of the overall evolution of the human species, the only logical reason for the evolution of sex was to perpetuate the species. Now, it is also a fact that pleasure is obviously derived from sex. But that is precisely the point: such pleasure is *derivative from* sexual union rather than *contributive to* the ontic value of the sex act. In other words, the necessary connection between sex and procreation enjoys more validity than does that between sex and pleasure. Sex and pleasure do not share necessary ontic coextensiveness, whereas sex and procreation do.

The necessary link between sex and procreation and the resultant connection with pleasure means that inherent in the gift of our sexual functioning—the means of perpetuating our species—is a basis for joy. Such joy is, however, a joy moderated and tempered by a constant consideration of the teleological orientation of sex itself. Sex is always oriented beyond itself, and insofar as it achieves that which it seeks beyond itself, it will always bring joy and pleasure. This recognition of the derivative nature of the joy of sex can temper any undisciplined libertarian tendencies that are associated with the conspicuous hedonism with respect to sex in much of contemporary American culture. Moreover, such tempering of this tendency can help preserve a proper perspective on sex: that sex itself should be regarded, not in an idolatrous fashion, but only as a gift from God *for* a purpose quite beyond itself. That purpose is life—life ever renewed through procreation and life renewed through divine reference and redemptive power.

SEXUALITY AND COMMITMENT: UNITY IN DIVINE GROUNDING

We are without a doubt sexual inspirited beings and can presume that the inherent integrity of our being must at some critical level assume the legitimacy of our sexuality. So far, however, this assertion involves only the "isness" of sexuality. Another issue is the "oughtness" of our sexuality. How ought we to interact with others as we live out our sexuality? How *ought* we to behave sexually?

Central to any Christian sexual ethic must be the issue of commitment. Must sex involve commitment for the Christian? In order to answer this question, we must again consider our basic nature as human beings. Unless we are able to understand who we are as creatures and how our sexuality is fundamental to who we are as creatures, then we will never be in a position to understand adequately the issue of commitment. In other words, we will never recognize the relationship between sex and commitment until we have some clarity about the nature of our sexuality as that sexuality is informed by who we are as humans.

If we make the presumption that we are never able to fundamentally understand ourselves apart from the concept of community, apart from others with whom we are always in deep relationship, then it would appear that individual radical egoism cannot presume to function as a philosophical basis for a Christian notion of sexuality, let alone, a notion of commitment. This is why, for example, masturbation can never be considered a fully legitimate and adequate means of expressing our sexuality. Several problems are inherent in autosexualism, which is to be distinguished from autoeroticism, in which one may in fact discern much beauty and derive pleasure in one's own body, insofar as that body is regarded as a gift from God. Autosexualism inevitably must cave back in upon itself as it seeks an other for whom the self yearns. For the self to love the self and desire only the self deprives that self of any other that can complement it. Therefore, insofar as we are social beings and understand our nature as necessarily linked to our sense of community, the full working out of our sexuality must per force include other human beings. But what do we owe other human beings with whom we are sexually involved? Must commitment to another be linked with active sexuality?

At the level of natural ethics, that is, ethics without the benefit of a faith orientation, the answer to this question might in fact be rather equivocal. A libertarian ethic might suggest that the primacy of personal pleasure need not necessarily imply that commitment with another person is necessary. But we have already discounted the notion that the ontic value of sex is to be found necessarily in its pleasure-producing possibilities. Yet another natural ethic, a utilitarian-oriented ethic, might actually suggest the wisdom of commitment and monogamy in a sexual relationship but would do so from a purely utilitarian point of view. Evolutionary psychologists give credence to one theory for the development of human monogamy. This theory posits a presumed utilitarian cost-benefit analysis that paleolithic human males carried out as they struggled with the ambiguity of when females were most fertile. If, for example, a male were to spend more time in "mate guarding" rather than pursuing every available female, "he might be better off, reproductively speaking, both because the odds of impregnating the woman would increase and because he'd be monopolizing her energy and keeping her from the advances of other sperm bearers."[5] A commitment, of sorts, becomes the result of such an analysis for our prehistoric ancestor.

Christian ethics must presume a set of suppositions different from those presumptive in natural ethics. Christian faith presumes that human sexuality is a gift from God and is meant to be shared by two persons in a committed relationship. Christian faith, as well as the logic of the correspondence between the nature of sex and the nature of love, teaches that the deepest levels of sexuality can only be expressed in a context of love. In other words, authentic sex must be necessarily linked with love, and love is best embodied in contexts that aspire to ontological depth and temporal continuity consistent with our notions of commitment. It can be shown that sex and love are necessarily bound together if we are able to agree on the nature of ourselves as humans, the meaning of love, and the capabilities of sex between two humans.

THE NECESSARY LINK BETWEEN AUTHENTIC SEX AND LOVE

Human beings are spiritual as well as physical. In a very real sense, we are beings in which the vitality of spirit exists; we are *inspirited beings*. As we consider the sexuality of human beings within the context of community, autosexualism and radical egoism have no viable foundation for human sexuality. Thus, in whatever way we will eventually conceive of commitment, we must view sex in an interpersonal context, never within the limited context of personal gratification alone. And we must also assume that the persons in any such sexual relationship must be inspirited beings as well.

In order to understand the relationship between sex, love, and commitment, we must define love. If we are to understand love in its deepest meaning and essence, we must discount the notion that love is exclusively connected to the feelings we have since it is self-evident that feelings are transitory and in many instances short-lived. Love may, in fact, produce feelings of warmth for another person, even ardor, but we could not say that such feelings are themselves necessarily constant. These feelings are fleeting, transitory, deeply felt to be sure, but transitory nevertheless. If we can presume with Paul Tillich that "love in all its forms is the drive towards the reunion of the separated,"[6] then we can appreciate how love goes to a deeper ontological level than the mere feelings we have when we acknowledge the

---

5. Natalie Angier, "Men, Women, Sex, and Darwin," *New York Times Magazine*, February 21, 1999.

6. Paul Tillich, *Love, Power, and Justice: Ontological Analysis and Ethical Applications* (New York: Oxford University Press, 1960), 28.

power of love. Love can unite like nothing else that which has been separated. Love brings two human beings together in a way that no other human emotion can. In fact if we really listen to Tillich, we will soon be persuaded that love is more than an emotion; it is a state of being. If we can define sex as the desire for union with another person, a union that is the very embodiment of love, and if we can further presume that nothing that two humans can do together so fuses in one physical act the ultimate union of flesh and spirit as does sexual union, then it follows that love must be joined with sex between two inspirited beings, two human beings. Both sex and love seek union with that which is separated. Sex desires what love seeks in union. There is, therefore, a necessary link between sex and love.[7]

The necessary link between sex and love helps explain the spiritual and psychological confusion that promiscuity engenders. First of all, promiscuity tends to confuse the identity of persons engaging in either anonymous or casual sex. With each sexual encounter with each different person, insofar as *inspirited beings* are involved in sexual encounters, they are potentially drawn into identity-shaping dynamics that reach to the depths of their being. Sex opens the human to such an experience. Thus each encounter, shared with different persons, ushers us to this depth of our personhood and the powerful factors that can moderate, even change, aspects of our personhood, our persona, which becomes precisely the problem for the sexual libertine.

At a purely practical level, the sexual libertine must constantly ask himself, "What persona shall I wear in my encounter with this sexual partner, as opposed to that one? What mask shall I wear in this encounter?" This becomes an issue of no small importance for such a person, if for no other reason than remembering the name of the person with whom one is during the height of passion! The sheer variety of sexual partners prevents the libertine from being able to focus on her sexual identity. Unable to establish a persona that issues forth from one substantial sexual experience, the libertine ultimately becomes alone and alienated. Such is the picture of the legendary Don Juan at the end of his escapades; he is a pitiful and essentially *lonely* man. Another question for the libertine is discerning the point at which the variety of ways in which the depth of one's being is accessed through sex shifts from pleasant variety to manic confusion.

The form of sexual promiscuity that focuses only on the physical side of sex obscures and violates our true nature as inspirited beings. Focusing unduly on the physical tends to trivialize sex, for the sexual life is reduced

---

7. See as well the lively discussion of this presumed necessary link between sex and love in Mike W. Martin, *Everyday Morality: An Introduction to Applied Ethics* 2d ed. (Belmont, Calif.: Wadsworth, 1995), 217–27.

to a fixation on physical acts, physical stimulation, and physical release. Forsaking any sensitivity to a spiritual aspect of sexuality, the sexual libertine ultimately becomes a glutton, never able to make any distinctions between persons, encounters, and experiences. The sexual life becomes a series of repetitive encounters, indiscriminately initiated, casually undergone, and indifferently concluded.

Another form of promiscuity issues forth from a distortion of the human self by inflating and idealizing the spiritual aspect of our selves, our personality. The desire to find the perfect, idealized person gives birth to promiscuity, for such a person never exists, while the frantic search for this elusive person never ceases. Such persons are constantly "looking for Mr. Right" or the perfect woman. The qualifications, couched as they are in idealized expectations, can never square with the persons who are encountered in the flesh, the live human beings who form the passing parade of sexual encounters.

If love is uniting that which was separated and if sex is the desire for the one united by love, it follows that there is a necessary link between sex and love. With love, however, comes vulnerability. Such vulnerability, in the context of sexual love, is strikingly portrayed in the creation story in the book of Genesis. After the writer notes how man and woman "become one flesh," the two are said to be "both naked, and were not ashamed" (Gen. 2:24–25). Vulnerability presumes the will to live without masks. Masks are needed when we are convinced that other persons seek to challenge our authentic existence; we therefore become defensive and use the mask to mitigate our vulnerability. In this regard, it may be a concession to our human nature to acknowledge that vulnerability is so threatening to human beings and potentially so painful that it is almost natural for us to devise means to mitigate the consequences of our vulnerability. What can mitigate the natural vulnerability when unconditional love is offered? The answer is commitment from both persons involved in a sexual love relationship.

Lest we fall into the identity confusion and all the other problems we saw plaguing the libertine, *exclusive* mutual commitment is required to mitigate the natural vulnerability that results when love is offered unconditionally. Why should vulnerability need shoring up or anything at all to mitigate it? Acknowledging our flawed human nature, we can never presume that we will use our freedom responsibly. We do require mitigating structures and procedures to "help" the ideals we put in place. The vulnerability attendant to love requires a mitigating condition, lest the vulnerability that we avow when we love be abused. Commitment is crucial in order that the trust and security needed to sustain vulnerability might be developed.

MARRIAGE AND FAMILY LIFE

Commitment thus becomes the necessary mitigating factor to sustain and support the unconditional love that persons pledge implicitly when they are in sexual love relationships. At this point, it could suffice for many persons to simply acknowledge that the commitment between them requires no institutional mooring, no legal sanction or ecclesiastical blessing. In other words, for some persons a formal marriage may not be necessary to show empirical verification of the commitment. Many, in fact, may become outraged if it is suggested that the quality of the commitment is somehow contingent upon institutional and legal trappings such as marriage ties and the contractual arrangements that are inherent in marriage as a social institution.

Yet, the logical conclusion of our analysis seems to suggest that some existential referent of commitment must go beyond the two persons involved. That is, if the two people themselves are communal beings, then there must be some communal referent to their commitment. Remember our earlier assertion that human beings have a social nature and that their sense of being is always linked to a communal referent. We cannot be or become who we wish to become without the necessary guidance and support of our communal contexts. We can never be absolutely alone, nor do we desire to ever be so.

To the extent that we live in community, the great commitments we make in life, the great milestones we reach in life, must at some level be grounded in the reality of the context of community. Within the Christian community, marriage suggests that the two persons affirm mutual trust and commitment and also are in covenant with the believing community of which they are a part. For the Christian, personal identity for the Christian must necessarily include some reference to the believing community. A critical aspect of the community's life together is the ritual life they share. Ritual encapsulates a vision of the world, a way of ordering reality. The marriage vows, freely affirmed in the company of believers, decidedly anchor the identity of the lovers within the community, for the ritual in which they participate has meaning only within the context of that community.

And yet at this point we recognize that most Christian churches comply with the state requirement that all marriages be recorded by the state. Why would not the marriage in the religious community suffice? Why must the state be involved? One answer is that the secular community of which we are a part, that in which we are full citizens, extends far beyond the boundaries of the believing community. Another answer is found in our vision of the good, in this case the validity of vulnerability and commitment and the attendant institutionalization of commitment that marriage symbolizes. We should affirm this as a good for the entire society; thus, we have no problem with having our marriages recognized by the secular society. We further have no problem with our marriages being recorded in the courthouse by the elected clerk. We know, however, that any marriage celebrated in the believing community is confirmed initially in the presence of the believing community and does not need the state to ensure its viability and integrity.

THE AFRICAN AMERICAN APPROPRIATION OF SEXUAL COMMITMENT AND INTEGRITY

Any discussion of sexuality and commitment within the African American social context must take into consideration the historical dynamics that inform such consciousness. African Americans have had to overcome tremendous historical forces and sociological impediments in order to maintain an acceptable degree of integrity and internal viability. One of the realities of slavery was the sexual as well as economic exploitation of black men and women. Since human bodies were owned, the owners felt no compunction about exploiting those bodies for their sexual gratification and did so with impunity. Thus black women were routinely subjected to sexual abuse, and black men were regarded as progenitors of new slaves through siring. Another effect of the abuse suffered in slavery was the proliferation of stereotypical myths about black sexuality that were calculated to demean both male and female integrity. Despite valiant attempts of black families to maintain close ties and integrity in gender relations, the realities of slavery, including the constant threat of being separated or the psychological terror caused by sexual abuse suffered at the hands of owners, proved to be constant irritants that undermined the black family.

While historically somewhat remote, the effects of slavery have been alleged to still play a role in levels of dysfunctionality seen in some quarters of the African American community. More recently, the massive shifts of large portions of the black community from the rural South to the urbanized North caused fractures in the family that have not totally healed. Since the 1950s the out-of-wedlock birthrate has skyrocketed in the national black community, as well as among whites. The current rate of unwed pregnancies in the black community is still over 60 percent of live births. The traditional nuclear family is undergoing tremendous shifts and changes. The black family is under extraordinary stress. Forty-two percent of black families are headed by a single female. The divorce rate hovers at 50 percent, thereby further endangering small children whose destiny might be living in an economically challenged house headed by a working mother trying to make ends meet.

The relations between black men and women continue to be fraught with much tension and ambiguity. The absence of so many men from the marriage pool either through imprisonment or early death through inner-city violence further frustrates the ability of young women to find eligible partners and thus form eventual stable family lives. The ratio of eligible women to men, estimated by Harvard sociologist Orlando Patterson to be 1,000 to 672, obviously favors black men. These demographics could exasperate the already tenuous relations between black men and black women. Sensing the advantage inherent in these demographics could lead many black men to form abusive relationships with black women, women who see themselves disadvantaged in their quest for eligible partners. Thus an ethic of commitment in the spirit of the one we have outlined in this chapter is absolutely necessary to mitigate and counter any such development along these lines. Moreover, the growing differential between college-educated black women and black men threatens to undermine the ability of a stable black middle class to perpetuate itself.[8] All of these issues factor prominently in the consideration of a Christian sexual ethic for African Americans. Such an ethic is needed to prevent abuse, exploitation, and the tragic alienation between the genders.

One issue at the heart of the sexual anxiety now besieging the national black community is precisely at the level of commitment. The relationship between love and sex and therefore commitment suggests that commitment is a necessary correlate to the sexuality of African Americans. Aside from the practical and medical reasons to practice commitment, there are ethically grounded reasons to practice commitment as well. An ethic of commitment, grounded in community, could help us understand and be prepared for the inevitable social pressures that continue to challenge the black family. An ethic of commitment could also help ensure the economic integrity of the black family, presuming the self-evident economic gain when two breadwinners support the family or, should a spouse (usually a wife) choose not to work, a mutually supportive marriage that could still mitigate any economic shortcomings.

HOMOSEXUALITY AND CHRISTIAN ETHICS: STILL AN ETHICAL FRONTIER?

No discussion about sexuality within the contemporary African American community would be complete if the issue of homosexuality were not addressed forthrightly and honestly. No issue in recent memory, except for that

---

8. The historic national trend in which males outnumbered females in the nation's colleges is now being reversed, mirroring the predominance of females in black colleges that began sometime in the 1960s. The female enrollment in the nation's colleges is now at 55 percent. See the *Washington Post*, May 16, 2000.

of racial integration, has pitted one portion of the church of Christ or members of American society against one another quite they way that the issue of homosexuality has. Mainline denominations are experiencing potentially divisive fissures as they struggle to define their corporate attitudes and positions with respect to homosexuality. The African American community, as diverse as is the church, has experienced as well internal tension on this matter. We must attempt now to provide an ethical analysis of the issue in the hopes of offering guidance.

The Kinsey Report of 1947 reported that 6 to 10 percent of twelve thousand male volunteers interviewed between 1938 and 1947 had been predominantly homosexual for at least three years. From this universe of interviewees, Kinsey extrapolated that similar percentages obtained in the general population of American men.[9] Current estimates vary as to the actual number of practicing male and female homosexuals in contemporary American society, but the estimate that 4 percent of women and 6 percent of men consider themselves to be active and practicing homosexuals, advanced by Robert T. Michael and others, seems to capture the consensus.[10] Thus homosexuality appears to be a distinguishable aspect within the American population and, by extension, within the world's general population. Homosexuality appears to be a form of sexual behavior that is not confined to any one culture or society; it appears throughout the world. It has also appeared in the historic record of many of the world's cultures.

When Christians seek guidance on the issue of homosexuality, many will immediately seek counsel and help from biblical texts. References to homosexuality are in the Bible, but the full array of commentary inherent in the biblical record may not be as conclusive and univocal as many would suggest. We should not be surprised that a traditional, patriarchal culture such as ancient Israel would have taken some clear stands against homosexuality; the surprise would be if a small nation, always in need of men to defend its borders, had openly approved of a sexual practice that yielded no offspring.

While Leviticus 20:13 is rather clear in its unambiguous denunciation of homosexuality, other texts that have been used to prohibit homosexuality are more ambiguous. Take for example the story of Sodom and Gomorrah in Genesis 19:1–28. Many opponents of homosexuality use this text as a surefire biblical denunciation of the sexual practice. In this text, two angels visit Lot in his home in Sodom, whereupon he invites them to spend the night, a typical gesture of ancient hospitality. Quite unexpectedly, the men

---

9. A. C. Kinsey, W. B. Pomeroy, C. E. Martin, *Sexual Behavior in the Human Male* (Philadelphia: Saunders, 1948). See also A. C. Kinsey et al., *Sexual Behavior in the Human Female* (Philadelphia: Saunders, 1953).

10. Robert T. Michael, John H. Gagmon, Edward O. Lausmann, and Gina Kolata, *Sex in America: A Definitive Survey* (Boston: Little, Brown, 1994), 174–75.

of the town begin to clamor for these guests, wishing to have sex with them. Lot intervenes, hoping that the crowd will be appeased as he offers the men his daughters for their pleasure. The crowd refuses, still wishing to have the two guests. Lot, sensing divine displeasure at hand because of the dastardly designs of the crowd, urges his family to get out of town, after which the Lord "rained on Sodom and Gomorrah sulphur and fire" (Gen. 19:24).

At first glance, this text seems to represent an unequivocal denunciation of homosexuality. But looking further into the dynamics in the text suggests something else. The issue is really not homosexuality per se but *homosexual rape*. Even more specific, the issue is a denunciation of what could have conceivably been the vilest way of abusing a man that Middle Eastern culture could have conceived. In a patriarchal culture, the most abusive way one can treat a man is to treat him as a woman, to penetrate and violate him as one would a woman. The issue was not even about sex, proof of which is the crowd's refusing Lot's base offer to provide his daughters for their amusement. Therefore, the real issue in the story of Sodom and Gomorrah is a denunciation of the vilest form of abuse and inhospitality that could be imagined. Proof that this is the issue, and not homosexuality per se, is Jesus' reference to the Sodom and Gomorrah incident as he sent his disciples to preach to the Gentiles. If they encountered resistance or inhospitality, it would be reminiscent of these infamous twin cities: "If anyone will not welcome you or listen to your words, shake off the dust from your feet as you leave that house or town. Truly I tell you, it will be more tolerable for the land of Sodom and Gomorrah on the day of judgment than for that town" (Matt. 10:14–15).

If the many current studies that put homosexuality in a broad historical and cultural perspective are to be believed, then it would appear that there has been some ambiguity with respect to acceptance of homosexuality as a lifestyle over the long course of human history.[11] Homosexuals, while not lauded as exemplars of a sexual lifestyle for all persons, seem to have enjoyed some measure of tolerance and even acceptance, depending on the time and place. The current status of medical and scientific evidence suggests as well some measure of ambiguity with respect to homosexual orientation. Much of the new evidence seems to suggest that homosexuality is not a matter of choice. If indeed homosexuality is not a matter of choice, then we must conclude that the condition is part and parcel of one's very being. And if homosexuality is a part of one's being, a matter ostensibly controlled and ordained by God, then we are forced to admit that in rejecting homosexuality, we are rejecting something that had to have had its origin in the

---

11. See, for example, John Boswell, *Christianity, Social Tolerance, and Homosexuality* (Chicago: University of Chicago Press, 1980).

mystery of God's creative purpose. If we further persist in rejecting or denouncing someone based on what God had done, then we risk putting God in a rather untenable position. Does God make mistakes in the creation of human beings?

SACRED UNIONS FOR HOMOSEXUALS?

Assuming that there are grounds for accepting homosexuals based on the ambiguity of the biblical record and the ambiguity of the cultural and historical record, does it follow that we must accord homosexuals the right to endorse unions ceremonially in our communities or give them legal sanction in the context of our civil laws? As homosexuals press their claims to rights and legal protection under the law, there appears to be a gradual increase in the perceived legitimacy of those rights within the American citizenry. In recent years, four states have begun allowing gay couples to adopt children jointly, and half a dozen have overturned sodomy laws that targeted homosexual acts. Meanwhile, scores of states, cities, and private employers have extended health insurance and other spousal benefits to "domestic partners."[12] The Supreme Court's 1996 ruling in *Romer v. Evans*, finding that government bias against homosexuals was unconstitutional, set a dramatic precedent, galvanizing a host of changes in how the courts treat gay people. Yet, as dramatic as *Romer v. Evans* was, the effects of its legal reasoning were quite limited. Twenty-nine states have adopted laws against the legality of same-sex unions, and Congress cleared the Defense of Marriage Act, intending to let states ignore same-sex marriages from other locales.

The overall national sentiment appears to be one of tolerance toward sexual variation but opposition to anything that could be viewed as promoting homosexuality. A *Washington Post* article cited a *Post*/Kaiser Family Foundation/Harvard University poll taken during 1998; the poll found that while 57 percent of the people said homosexuality was unacceptable, 87 percent of those surveyed said homosexuals should have equal rights in terms of job opportunities.[13] Although a New Jersey ruling that allows gay couples to adopt children has been hailed by many gay advocates as a harbinger of opportunity for gays to function as parents, the level of community support with respect to gays and family life is rather limited. Most gay people become parents by adopting the child of a partner who happens to be a biological parent. But many judges across the country have been increasingly willing to approve adoptions with two mothers or fathers, giving

---

12. "For Gays, Tolerance Translates to Rights," *Washington Post*, November 5, 1999.
13. Ibid.

full parental rights to the nonbiological parent, as they have long done for heterosexual stepparents. Such adoptions are no longer rare for gay couples in the District of Columbia and about twenty other states. In March 2000, the Vermont House of Representatives approved landmark legislation that will give gays and lesbians the right to seek legal recognition of their partnerships. While the legislation does not allow same-sex marriage, it will permit gay and lesbian couples to form unions that carry nearly all the benefits and responsibilities of civil marriage.

The tolerance and acceptance of gay people within the African American community are not only of great ethical import but also have implications in the shoring up of our efforts to combat the dreaded disease of AIDS. The Associated Press reported on January 14, 2000, that for the first time since the outbreak of the AIDS epidemic in the United States in the 1980s, more black and Hispanic gay men were diagnosed with the disease in 1998 than white homosexuals. The Centers for Disease Control and Prevention (CDC) suggested that one reason is that homosexuality carries a greater stigma among minorities, meaning that blacks and Hispanics are less likely than whites to identify themselves as gay or seek AIDS prevention and treatment services. The CDC reported that minorities represented 52 percent of the 18,153 gay and bisexual men who were diagnosed with AIDS in 1998. By contrast, minorities represented 31 percent in 1989. Black gay men made up one-third of the new cases in 1998, while Hispanic homosexuals made up 18 percent. Asians and Pacific Islanders accounted for 1 percent of the cases. Minorities account for about one-quarter of the overall U.S. population.

Researchers recognized this trend years ago and had projected that new cases among gay minorities would eventually overtake new cases among gay whites. Overall, among heterosexuals and homosexuals alike, the cumulative number of AIDS cases among minorities has already surpassed the number among whites. Whites represent 44 percent of all AIDS cases reported since 1981; blacks make up 37 percent; Hispanics make up 18 percent; and Asian, American Indian, and Pacific Islanders are less than 1 percent.[14] Because of the desire to hide one's homosexuality from public scrutiny, minority gays fail to be receptive to the message of practicing safe sex and to avail themselves of AIDS treatment in the early stages of the disease. Thus it would appear that in the long run, it would most assuredly be in the black community's interest to lessen the stigma of homosexuality insofar as attempts on the part of black gays to hide their sexual orientation eventuates in contracting the fatal disease of AIDS.

---

14. *Washington Post*, January 14, 2000.

As to the issue of whether Christian communions can tolerate and openly endorse homosexual unions being performed in the church, much can be said. Such unions are already taking place within one section of the church, namely, among the United Fellowship of Metropolitan Community Churches. At the same time, the United Presbyterian Church (U.S.A.) and the United Methodist Church have reaffirmed their historic stand against uniting homosexuals in marriage ceremonies recognized by the church. One United Methodist pastor who has married homosexual couples was tried in an ecclesiastical church court but not deprived of ordination status. One notable event that occurred in January 2000 was the issuance of a declaration signed by 850 mostly liberal members of the clergy and other religious figures urging all faiths to bless same-sex couples and allow openly gay ministers. Among the endorsers of the statement was the retired leader of the Episcopal Church, the presidents of the United Church of Christ and Unitarian Universalist Association, presidents or deans of fifteen Protestant seminaries, and numerous theology professors.[15] At the same time, well-respected Christian ethicists and theologians are urging churches not to revise their teachings to bless same-sex unions.

We must acknowledge a lack of unanimity within Christian churches with respect to endorsing the marriage of homosexuals. I personally recognize the immense struggle that many churches and Christians are undergoing as they seek to discern God's will on this matter, and I join them in declaring my own lack of clarity on this issue. But we should not presume to declare that the church always reflects the will of God. There have been historic discrepancies between what we may now intuit was probably the will of God and what the churches historically affirmed. Good examples are the historic stances the church took with regard to slavery and the integration of the races in worship services and how long it took the Catholic Church to recognize its historic error with regard to Galileo's assertion that the earth did indeed revolve around the sun—more than four hundred years.

Perhaps the emphasis should be not so much on what *we* might or would like to do but rather on what *God* is already doing. God just might be bringing a new thing to pass around us and in our very midst. Perhaps the vision of building a truly just society according to the Christian vision may have to declare the futility of human efforts to bring this about and rather affirm that only God, through much social and historical pain within humanity, can bring about the just society. Such may be the case with the emergence of a truly just society with regard to the issue of homosexuality. God may have to bring about that which we have neither the courage nor the ability to bring to pass. That which God might be doing might be clearly at

---

15. *New York Times*, January 18, 2000.

variance with the civil authorities and the state—or even the church. Those churches that have already caught a glimpse of the justice of welcoming homosexuals into union and into celebrating rites are clearly at variance with the state and indeed with many other churches. But then the church has been at its best when it was at variance with the state on many moral issues. It may be that in the final analysis an eschatological view of the community of Christian believers will be of such radical enormity that it will trump our current biases and prejudices with respect to what we may judge to be normative sexual orientation. Just as all of us have been convinced that in Christ there is neither male nor female, Jew nor Greek, so it may be one day a reality that sexual orientation will not foreclose the hope that we all might be one.

10

Medicine and Bioethics

When he went ashore, he saw a great crowd; and he had compassion
for them and cured their sick.   —Matthew 14:14

> Give ease to the sick, give sight to the blind
> Enable the cripple to walk;
> He'll raise the dead from under the earth,
> And give them permission to fly.
>   —Spiritual sung by Fisk Jubilee Singers, 1870

The care and nurturing of the human body have been of critical concern for
human beings as long as our species has sought a sense of well-being in the
world. Most probably the earliest inclinations toward religion were couched
in concerns about health, longevity, and physical well-being. All cultures in
all times have had to develop ways and means of treating the sick, tending to
the infirm, and curing those with maladies. Yet, matters of health have not
always been fully understandable to human beings; the causes of diseases
and physical maladies have not always been clear to us.

In prehistoric times and even in the age of the ancients, the enigmas of
health and wholeness were viewed as being particularly within the province
of deities; only gods or spirits from the transcendent realm could heal. And
to be sure, closely associated with the belief in the curative powers of deities
were the beliefs in the skills of allied practitioners such as *shamans* or priests.
E. G. Parrinder, in his studies of African traditional religions, recognized the
medicinal prowess of religiously inspired herbalists, or in his words, these
"men of the trees."[1] But even in those instances that recognized the skill of a
human medical practitioner, it was always acknowledged that the ultimate
power to heal came from a power quite beyond the mortal sphere.

Ancient and traditional Africa was no exception to this observation that
all cultures have developed ways of treating illnesses. Ancient and even contemporary practitioners of ancient rites of medicine have been known to

---

1. E. G. Parrinder, *African Traditional Religion* (Westport, Conn.: Greenhaven Press, 1970),
105.

heal sick persons of illnesses and to restore lost health. One of the great social and cultural fissures that occurred with the transatlantic slave trade was the disruption and devaluing among slaveholders of traditional African means of healing. With the devaluing of African culture and the implicit devaluing of African means of healing came as well the basic ambiguity with which the slaveholding class of white southerners attended to the health of their slaves. Slaveholders had a clear pecuniary interest in the health of their bondspeople. Since slaves were investments, only an economically irresponsible slaveholder would ignore the basic health needs of his property. But the administration of medicinal care and the assumptions behind such care always manifested white assumptions about black innate inferiority. Defenders of slavery justified the institution on the grounds that blacks were physically more suitable for either arduous work or work in rice, indigo, or cane fields where susceptibility to certain diseases might pose more of a problem for whites.

Casual observation led many slaveholders to conclude that blacks were so physically different from whites that there must be innate medical differences between the races as well. Even trained medical practitioners were convinced of these innate medical differences. The editor of a prominent Virginian medical journal confidently wrote in 1856, "Scarcely any observant medical man, having charge of negro estates, fails to discover, by experience, important modifications in the diseases and appropriate treatment of the white and black race respectively."[2] The confluence of assumptions about race and the commercial interest in slaves as property emerged quite clearly in the debate among slaveholders over blacks and malaria, the dreaded tropical disease that affected the low country of South Carolina and parts of Virginia and Louisiana. Malaria is a parasitic disease caused by the colonizing within red blood cells of a one-celled animal, plasmodium. The attention slaveholders paid to malaria was due to the cash-crop value of rice and sugar in these areas. The question was never whether blacks contracted the disease or not. Planters' journals throughout the period of slavery recorded numerous cases of households where persons, black and white, came down with the "fevers" or ague, as it was called. The point of the debate was the relative *susceptibility* of blacks to the disease and the factors that might contribute to such susceptibility.

One prominent theory that emerged even as early as the mid-nineteenth century was the presence of the sickle-cell trait in blacks that would account for a relatively high level of immunity from the disease. As a form of anemia,

---

2. Editorial, *The Monthly Stethoscope and Medical Reporter* 1 (1856): 162–63; quoted in Todd L. Savitt, *Medicine and Slavery: The Diseases and Health Care of Blacks in Antebellum Virginia* (Urbana: University of Illinois Press, 1978), 7.

inherited genetically, sickle cell did give some protection to blacks, but only against the milder form of malaria that appeared in sections of the South. But this was something of a mixed blessing, for as Todd Savitt points out, "Many of those who had sickle cell disease died from its consequences before or during adolescence."[3] We have, therefore, just in this reference to malaria a constellation of the many themes that confront us as we attempt to address the issue of medical ethics from an African American perspective. We have the issue of white racism, the economic import of the black presence within American society, as well as the neglect of elements within the black community that could be marshaled for the health benefit of that entire community.

Even after Emancipation, given the fact that medical schools in the nation refused to admit black would-be doctors, the national black community was medically underserved. The legacy of slavery in the form of economic tenuousness of black life translated into the pervasive inability of black families to pay for medical care, generally available through unsympathetic or paternalistic white doctors. With the establishment of Meharry Medical College in 1876, the number of black doctors trained to serve in their communities gradually increased. They joined the handful of black doctors who were practicing, almost without exception in African American communities, in Reconstruction America, attempting to meet the health needs of a woefully underserved population. Even today, black Americans, especially those in inner cities across the nation, are not likely to receive the same level of medical care as the general American population or be assured of access to such care. To the extent that our nation has still not been able to develop a system of universal health insurance and to the extent that poorer persons, a significant proportion of whom are black, are still medically underserved, is the extent to which the health of African Americans is at risk.

While the ethics of equitable health care is an issue of critical concern, the focus of this chapter will be on the ethics of at least two biomedical problems as they affect African Americans. The first issue is the phenomenon of reproductive technology and our ability to now screen for sickle-cell disease, a disease that disproportionately affects persons of African ancestry in America. The second is the issue of organ donation and transplantation, thus ensuring the possibility that even in the face of imminent death, life might proceed for some around us. Thus we have before us two issues, one occasioned at the moment of birth and the other occasioned when the end of life is imminent.

---

3. Savitt, *Medicine and Slavery*, 26–27.

IS THERE AN AFRICAN AMERICAN BIOETHIC?

Before addressing these issues, we must acknowledge that there has been a dearth of serious research and commentary on the ethical aspects of the health of African Americans. However, within the past twenty years a heightened awareness has emerged among many African American medical doctors, researchers, and public-health officials about the ethical importance of black health issues. In 1987, the first ever "Think Tank on Black Perspectives on Death and Dying" was held in Washington, D.C., under the leadership of Dr. Harley Flack, the dean of the College of Allied Health Sciences at Howard University, and Dr. Edmund D. Pellegrino, the director of the Georgetown University Kennedy Institute of Ethics. As a consequence of the 1987 Think Tank, another conference was held in 1989 that brought together African American perspectives on bioethics from the philosophical, historical, theological, social, anthropological, and public-policy points of view. A follow-up conference the next year produced a volume of essays that covered the genesis of the African-American Perspectives on Biomedical Ethics Project as well as attendant and various viewpoints on critical issues.[4]

Another promising development is the new Tuskegee University National Center for Bioethics in Research and Health Care, which opened on May 15, 1999. As one anticipates the decided benefits of this center in Tuskegee, there is palpable discernment of historical redemption inasmuch as Tuskegee was the place of the infamous government study begun in the 1940s in which many black men with syphilis were allowed to go untreated for forty years.[5] In 1997 President Bill Clinton went to Tuskegee and apologized on behalf of the government and the American people and pledged a $200,000 grant to help the center become a reality. Said President Benjamin Payton, the university president, at the dedication of the new center, "We expect for the first time to be training and educating significant numbers of African-Americans as bioethicists—something we don't have now."[6] The African American Perspectives on Biomedical Ethics Project and the Tuskegee Center signal that the African American medical community, public-health policy analysts, and persons from other academic disciplines are prepared to do serious reflection on the importance of biomedical issues within African American society.

Inherent in our discussion is the presumption that an African American medical ethic or bioethic exists. The African American community debates

---

4. Harley E. Flack and Edmund D. Pellegrino, eds., *African-American Perspectives on Biomedical Ethics* (Washington, D.C.: Georgetown University Press, 1992).

5. See James N. Jones, *Bad Blood: The Tuskegee Syphilis Experiment* (New York: Free Press, 1981).

6. Associated Press, May 12, 1999.

within itself whether a unique and specific African American bioethic exists. Even some of those who were present at the conferences in the 1980s do not affirm the existence of an African American bioethic. For such persons, making such an assertion runs the risk of committing the *error of redundancy*, which was first postulated by Aristotle in his thoughts on establishing categories of observation of species. This redundancy involves "treating as discrete and isolated matters that fall under the same notion," and in this case, according to William Banner, professor emeritus of philosophy at Howard University, African American and western European perspectives fall under the same notion: both are elements of a *humane* perspective. Banner takes the position that "the conduct of the science of medicine or the conduct of the science of ethics is incompatible with anything called 'ethnic perspective.' "[7] In fact, to do so would set the foundation for racial and ethnic ideologies that have been unfortunately so much a part of the thought and action of the nineteenth and twentieth centuries. Even when it is pointed out that certain illnesses are associated with certain ethnic groups, such an observation is, for Banner, simply a medical observation, not an observation determined by a perspective, ethnic or otherwise.

In contrast are those who do indeed affirm belief in an African American perspective on bioethics. Annette Dula, a participant in the conference that formed the basis for the volume *African-American Perspectives on Biomedical Ethics*, bases her argument on the rather commonsense observation that "African-Americans have a distinctive world view."[8] She goes on to assert that the more dire health status of African Americans as well as "philosophy of life" also factor into the formation of this distinct perspective on bioethics. Others believe that the combination of slavery, segregation, and racism has informed certain bioethical concepts among African Americans, notably, concepts such as personhood and bodily integrity, that differ significantly from the concepts of other ethnic groups.[9]

An assessment of the debate between these two points of view soon makes clear that a determination of the viability of each argument with respect to the other cannot be fully accomplished since there appears to be no

---

7. William A. Banner, "Is There an African-American Perspective on Biomedical Ethics? The View from Philosophy," in *African-American Perspectives on Biomedical Ethics*, ed. Flack and Pellegrino, 189.

8. Annette Dula, "Yes, There Are African-American Perspectives on Bioethics," in *African-American Perspectives on Biomedical Ethics*, ed. Flack and Pellegrino, 193.

9. Leonard Harris, *"Autonomy under Duress,"* in *African-American Perspectives on Biomedical Ethics*, ed. Flack and Pellegrino, 134. Other works that seem sensitive to the critical importance of cultural realities in the context of medical treatment are Cecil Helman, *Culture, Health, and Illness* (Boston: Butterworth-Heinemann, 1994);

Marjorie Kagawa-Singer, "Diverse Cultural Beliefs and Practices about Death and Dying in the Elderly," in *Cultural Diversity and Geriatric Care: Challenges to the Health Professions,* ed. Darryl Wieland et al. (Newbury Park, Calif.: Sage Publications, 1993).

agreement about the definition of terms. At the start, there is no implicit agreement about what *bioethics* means. For Banner, bioethics seems to be limited to the purely physiological. Since he rightly wishes to eschew a perspective that would lead to ethnic exclusivism and racism, he must affirm a universal basis for bioethical reflection. And since Dula rightly acknowledges the perspectival nature of all cultural moorings, she must insist that bioethical thinking must be formed by one's cultural and sociological location. Neither, it seems to me, fully understands the nature of bioethical reflection. I would argue that bioethics, properly understood, brings to bear on any medical assessment a normative vision of humanity as one ponders the ability of humans to ameliorate their genetic and biological condition. Such a view transcends and goes beyond the reductionist tendencies inherent in both Banner's and Dula's arguments. Bioethics is more than mere reflection about diseases or about the interplay between health status and social status. Bioethics, to be sure, will consider these factors but only in the context of judgments that someone has made about human worth, human dignity, and a vision of that which humans ought to become.

TOWARD A CHRISTIAN AFRICAN AMERICAN BIOETHIC

In Flack and Pellegrino's volume *African-American Perspectives on Biomedical Ethics*, Cheryl Sanders offers a very helpful assessment on the existence of an African-American perspective on bioethics. On one hand, she says, "We must be careful not to fall into the trap of discussing uniqueness rather than universals, so that the African-American perspective becomes strictly valued on the grounds of its uniqueness and not fully appreciated for its universal significance."[10] Yet, on the other hand, she asserts that the African American ethos is to be distinguished from European American culture in that the former is holistic rather than dualistic; inclusive rather than exclusive; communalistic rather than individualistic; spiritual rather than secular; theistic rather than agnostic or atheistic; improvisational rather than forced into fixed forms; and finally, humanistic rather than materialistic.[11] Having asserted these characteristics as inherent in the African American ethos, Sanders goes on to comment on the black theology project and its inevitable reaction to white racism. Fully aware of the limitations inherent in any particularistic notions, even the justifiable black theology that sprang from the black struggle for human dignity in the face of white racism, she

---

10. Cheryl J. Sanders, "Problems and Limitations of an African-American Perspective in Biomedical Ethics: A Theological View," in *African-American Perspectives on Biomedical Ethics*, ed. Flack and Pellegrino, 166.

11. Ibid., 167.

says: "Any theology that exclusively addresses the perspectives of one group without giving attention to the interests and concerns of others is suspect."[12] Thus, for her, if an African American perspective is to be viable, it must be "a human perspective: a concrete, particular witness to universal truth"; therefore, "the ethical question is not that of an African-American perspective but of African-American participation and inclusion."[13]

So does an African American bioethic exist? The arguments relative to this question indicate that such a bioethic does exist, as long as the enterprise seeks to assert universal values about human worth and dignity. Thus African American bioethics is a reflection on a vision of what human beings ought to be and become, a vision, to be sure, couched in the medical realities of African American life. It points to universal claims made within the context of particular social realities. Bioethics affirms a normative vision of human worth and what humans ought to do with the vast ability now at our disposal with respect to the power to intervene in nature. Insofar as African Americans participate in this enterprise, ever with an eye toward a universal human good, they are legitimate participants in the bioethical conversation, even as they ponder the health and medical realities in African American society.

Moreover, insofar as there may be an African American *Christian* ethic, we would expect to affirm some basic principles inherent in the Christian faith. We proceed by making two assertions about what we know humans to be within the framework of Christian faith. First, each human being is an embodied consciousness created by God. As such then, we are spirit and body, able to be open to a transcendent reality that goes quite far beyond the limitations of our bodies. At the same time, our physical bodies (in other words, our sheer physicality) suggest that real limits are placed upon our existence. That is, we exist within finitude and are therefore prone to all of the limitations of finitude. Since each of us represents the confluence of body and spirit, that which transcends body and that which takes form and shape in the physical, each of us is irreplaceable. We are unique, each of us. Not only is our sense of ourselves uniquely ours, but even from an objective point of view, who we are represents the manifestation of a unique person. Our personhood cannot be replicated by anyone else. Christian faith acknowledges that in God's creative act of bringing human beings into life, each person is the recipient of the breath of life. Created as such, each person is formed to be in relation to God, to be answerable to God and accountable to God. This establishes the moral foundation for personhood, inasmuch as

---

12. Ibid., 169.
13. Ibid., 171.

inherent in morality is an obligation to respond in a prescribed fashion or way and to be regarded ultimately as *responsible*.[14]

Besides being created by God, our personhood emerges in another context—that of community. If we can never fully be human unless we are in community, it follows that we can never secure personhood unless we are in community. As inspirited beings, we interact with other inspirited beings in the context of community. Such a context and such interaction manifest particular challenges regarding how we respond to each other. The determination of how we should respond, to whom we should respond, and with what is ours to respond forms in good measure the moral foundation of personhood within the context of community. Thus, the primary concept that grounds a bioethic in the Christian faith is the personhood of every human being. Inherent in this concept are the notions of moral worth and human freedom. After all, by virtue of having been created in a unique fashion by God, all human beings are accorded moral worth. Moreover, having been created by God and therefore being in relationship with God confer the option of remaining in relationship with God through obedience or risking alienation from God by disobedience, as the Genesis accounts make clear. The moral worth we accord others and the human freedom we evidence are also manifested in the context of community because in community we actively make choices as to how we shall respond to other human beings.

Also implied in my analysis is the concept of autonomy. Though the term appears quite frequently in discussions of bioethics, I have purposely refrained from using it because I cannot fully square it with the realities I presume are in place if we take the concept of community seriously. What can autonomy possibly mean if in fact the very notion of personhood is unintelligible apart from some sense of community? Generally in medical matters, especially in cases where the informed consent of patients is required, medical personnel and some ethicists refer to the "autonomy" of the patient. If the word conveys one's ability to make and enforce decisions without outside interference, then autonomy is not problematic for me. But if the word means being cut off from the normative value of community, the term is very problematic and virtually useless to me as an ethical concept. Our having been created as inspirited beings is key for my construction of the bare outlines of a Christian bioethic. We live in nature, move in our bodies, but are able to participate in spirit and transcend our bodies. We continually exist on the boundary of infinitude and finitude. We are inspirited beings created by God, thereby affording us personhood, the moral foundation that

---

14. See H. Richard Niebuhr's classic formulation of the notion of responsibility as endemic to the moral life in his *The Responsible Self: An Essay in Christian Moral Philosophy* (New York: Harper & Row, 1963).

is grounded in our relationship to God and to others in community. While we believe that we have been granted freedom and moral worth as persons, all the freedom we have is always exerted within the context of finitude, partly manifested by the constraints imposed on us by community. We are always in community, or at least should be. Being in community helps define and preserve our humanity and indeed the integrity of personhood at very critical points. With these assertions as background, we can now proceed to discuss two medical issues that have critical ethical importance for African Americans.

SICKLE-CELL ANEMIA, MEDICAL BREAKTHROUGHS, AND ETHICS

Perhaps no other disease among African Americans joins so dramatically the issues of genetic research, cultural particularity, and ethical reflection as does sickle-cell anemia. This disease is an inherited blood disorder that is particularly common among persons of African ancestry and also those whose ancestors come from South and Central American, Cuba, Saudi Arabia, India, Turkey, Greece, and Italy, but in the United States, sickle-cell anemia is most common among African Americans. Every year, about 1 in 400 African American infants is born with the disease after inheriting the genetic mutation from both parents. People who have only one copy of the mutation are said to have the sickle-cell trait. It is estimated that 1 in 12 African Americans has the trait. People with the sickle-cell trait can enjoy a moderately healthy life, although they can pass the mutation on to their children. A child conceived by two people with the sickle-cell trait has one chance in two of also having sickle-cell trait, one chance in four of having sickle-cell anemia, and one chance in four of inheriting neither the trait nor the disease, according to Dr. Lilia Talarico, who is director of the Division of Gastrointestinal and Hematologic Drug Products at the Center for Drug Evaluation and Research of the Federal Drug Administration (FDA).[15] About 8 percent of American blacks carry the gene that can cause sickle-cell anemia, but a much smaller percentage suffers the chronic pain and other health problems that it causes. One estimate puts the national number of those who actually suffer with the disease at seventy thousand.

As a blood disorder, sickle-cell anemia causes a shortage of red blood cells. In people with sickle-cell anemia, not all of their hemoglobin (the component of red blood cells that carries oxygen from the lungs to other parts of the body) works properly. Some of the hemoglobin forms long rodlike structures that cause the red blood cells to be sickle-shaped and stiff. These

---

15. Federal Drug Administration's Center for Drug Evaluation and Research and National Association for Sickle Cell Disease, pamphlet.

cells can clog small blood vessels, preventing some organs or tissues from receiving enough oxygen and resulting in severe pain or damage to organs and tissues, such as kidney failure, and perhaps leading to other serious medical problems, such as strokes. In February 1998, the FDA approved the drug Droxia (hydroxyurea) for reducing the painful episodes in adults with a severe form of sickle-cell anemia. The drug does not cure the disease, however. Prior to the discovery of the uses of hydroxyurea, penicillin was proven in 1986 to be effective in treating the disease, but again not in curing it.

Breakthroughs in Sickle-Cell Research

With startling and dazzling speed, medical sciences are making new discoveries about the human body and the means and extent of therapy and repair of physical deficiencies we might have or develop. We are no longer the prisoner of nature; we can bend nature to our will as human beings, correcting that which nature gave us either at birth or that which misfortune delivers to us in life. Recent advances in medical technology have ushered in an age in which human suffering can be relieved in ways that would have been unthinkable to our ancestors, or even to more recent generations. Moreover, we are no longer restricted to the narrow confines of what nature offers us in terms of the circumstances surrounding our birth, our journey through life, or the end of our days. We have, in a real sense, reached a point in our medical advances where we effectively can determine a good part of our physical destiny. We can determine when and how our young will come into the world, how we shall continue in life, even to the point of which organs we shall replace in the event they become worn out. It has always been within our power to *end* our lives; now we increasingly have the power to *extend* our lives until such time when some of us may decide to seek the repose of death.

This increasing ability to change what life offers us has been the case with sickle-cell anemia. In 1998 the medical field offered us two breathtaking breakthroughs in our quest for a cure for the disease. In December of that year, Keone Penn, a twelve-year-old sufferer of sickle-cell anemia in Atlanta, Georgia, became the first person to undergo treatment that led to what might be called a "cure" for the disease. The boy had had recurrent strokes since he was five years old and had been required to receive blood transfusions on a regular basis ever since. Keone's "cure" was achieved through bone-marrow transplants with genetically different marrow through stem-cell transplants.

The other breakthrough involves the treatment of human embryos. Medical personnel are now able to identify embryos with the gene for sickle-cell anemia and take corrective measures that will eventuate with the birth of a healthy child free of the sickle-cell trait. The May 12, 1999, issue of the *Journal of the American Medical Association* reported the case of a thirty-four-year-old woman who was helped to deliver two girls without the painful disease. The procedure called for in vitro fertilization, by which seven embryos were produced. Employing a genetic diagnostic technique, the researchers found that four embryos were normal, and two carried the disease, while the status of the last could not be determined. Three of the normal embryos were implanted in the woman's uterus, and she gave birth to twins without the disease after thirty-nine weeks. Thus medical science has given us tests and procedures that can assure parents that any embryo that they conceive will be sickle-cell free.

Emerging Ethical Questions

With our ability to intervene in the development of the human cell and even our ability to cure persons with a dreaded disease, inevitable ethical questions arise. At what cost can we legitimately pursue these means to achieve our aims? What *ought* we to do with the available biotechnology at our disposal? Even in regard to the procedures just cited, ones that hold out so much promise for the eventual cure of sickle-cell anemia, grave ethical questions emerge.

In the bone-marrow transplants, the stem cells in the injected marrow constitute an issue of critical importance. The source of these stem cells might constitute, for many persons, an unjustifiable use of human tissue. In the case of Keone Penn, the source of the stem cells was a newborn's umbilical cord. In this respect, the operation was a first of its kind. Doctors hope that this, the world's first cord blood transplant from an unrelated donor, will help Keone's body produce healthy blood. In the past, doctors have treated sickle-cell anemia with bone-marrow transplants from related donors, but often not even siblings provide a close enough match. With cord blood transplants, a perfect match is not necessary. However, despite much optimism about this procedure, there can be complications such as infections. Aside from the medical problems due to possible infections, the ethical concerns are troubling: How justified are we in appropriating the body parts of other human beings for our benefit? Even if consent is granted for the use of body parts or organs, are parents justified in allowing the use of their newborns' umbilical cords for the benefit of other persons? What would "informed consent" for a newborn mean? Is the transaction rendered any less problematic because the umbilical cord of a newborn is a relatively "useless" body part? Can any part of the body be termed "useless"? Under what circumstances and in what senses of the term "useless" could it be justifiably used? In the case of the use of the remaindered umbilical cord of a newborn, such tissue will not be of critical value to the life of the newborn. The newborn now has achieved the ultimate in "viability" in the process toward life; a human being now enjoys life without benefit of the umbilical cord, an organ that was vitally necessary prior to birth. Still, does this mean that we are justified in using the umbilical cord for the benefit of another?

Our notion of personhood, with the constituent concepts of moral worth of every person and human freedom within the limits of community, may give us some guidance. We must presume that the newborn infant and the child needing the precious resource from the infant's now remaindered umbilical cord enjoy equal moral worth. We may further presume that while the infant has no ability to make decisions, and therefore no ability to give informed consent for the use of the cord, the infant's parents will be bound by a sense of moral responsibility to their child as they exercise their freedom with respect to the question of the ultimate disposal of the umbilical cord. Recognizing the human need occasioned by the sickle-cell-ridden child, the parents will be asked to weigh the relative good that will be obtained by granting use of the cord as opposed to the good the cord will provide for their infant. They recognize a duty to respond to the sickle-cell-ridden child by virtue of the participation of all parties in the context of community. They must respond in some fashion; the question is how. It appears that a decision to use the cord would find reasonable justification.

The second procedure, in which several embryos are conceived through in vitro fertilization, raises a serious ethical question regarding the possible "redundancy" of some of the embryos, a redundancy ensured by the simple fact that all the embryos cannot safely be implanted in the woman. In this case, we have more than merely one remaindered body part, a body part that, as it turned out, was not vitally necessary to the sustained life of the newborn infant. Can a fully potential human being be considered in the same light as a remaindered and functionally unnecessary mass of tissue? The difference between the two is self-evident. In this case, the full meaning of the moral worth of the human person has no meaning unless it pertains to potential human life as well. The zygote, the embryo, the fetus, is potentially nothing other than a human being. It is potentially *nothing else*.

If this is the case, then no medical strategy that intentionally initiates a process for the sole purpose of creating "redundant" embryos can be justified. Human life must enjoy moral worth, even if it comes forth from a reaction in a petri dish in a laboratory. Human life is sacred, even if it is the result of medical initiatives. Has the primacy of life been invalidated just because a scientist oversaw the union of sperm and egg? If we affirm the primacy of life, whatever the conditions under which life begins, then we can never presume that any form of life, especially in this case human life, is redundant. Thus to use this method to achieve a cure for sickle-cell anemia is fraught with much ethical turmoil and, on the face of things, could not enjoy moral justification in my judgment.

ORGAN DONATION AND TRANSPLANTATION

Like all human beings, African Americans are caught between the two great poles of mortal existence, birth and death. In our analysis of stem-cell transplants from the umbilical cords of newborns, we were forced to consider the primacy of life, against which the redundancy of many embryos constituted an undermining threat. This analysis, in part, dealt with issues at the beginning of life. We move now to consider the ethical ramifications of organ transplantation, the medical phenomenon by which we may, even in the face of or the context of our own death, be the harbinger for the continued life of others.

The era of organ transplants, beginning in the decade of the 1950s, betokened our ability to extend the lives of persons who otherwise would have met death because of the irreparability of vital organs. The first successful organ transplant in the modern era was a kidney transplant performed on June 17, 1950, at a hospital in Chicago. Four years later doctors performed another kidney transplant involving twin brothers in Boston. In the case of the first operation, involving a middle-aged woman, the transplanted kidney worked for only six months. It had been implanted to take the place of a completely diseased kidney. The other kidney, functioning at about 80 percent normal ability, had not been removed. After the transplanted kidney failed, it was removed. The woman was kept alive for another five years on the partially functioning kidney. The first successful heart transplant was performed by Dr. Christiaan Barnard at Grote Schuur Hospital in Capetown, South Africa, on December 3, 1967. The first liver transplant was performed on March 1, 1963, on a three-year-old boy at the University of Colorado Medical Center in Denver. The child died on the operating table. Doctors performed the first lung transplant at the University of Mississippi Medical School on June 11, 1963, on a male who died eighteen days later. Other "firsts" during these early years in the era of organ transplants include the spleen, February 19, 1963; the pancreas, December 31, 1966; and the thymus, July 6, 1957.

The medical field has come a long way in terms of the number of medical centers around the country that are able to perform organ transplants routinely and in the number of successful transplants. In 1982, only 3 medical centers in the United States were competent enough to perform liver transplants; by 1986, the number had risen to 34. In 1982, only 5 centers could perform heart transplants; by 1986, there were 58. In 1986, more than 180 centers in the United States were performing some kind of transplant surgery.

The early complications of organ transplant procedures stemmed from the inability of host bodies to retain the grafted organs. In these early years, immunosuppressant drugs such as imuran and prednisone were able to mute the rejection response, but they also crippled the body's ability to ward off bacterial and viral invaders. In 1979, the introduction of cyclosporine improved the survival rate for donated organs to 75 percent for a three-year period after the operation. Cyclosporine has the ability to suppress that part of the immune system that is responsible for tissue rejection, while leaving intact the part that combats infection. With increasing improvement in techniques for transplantation, the success rate has soared in the last few years. Three-year patient survival rates are estimated at 95 percent for kidney transplants, 92 percent for pancreas, 91 percent for heart, 90 percent for liver, 81 percent for heart/lung, and 76 percent for lung. In 1996, 20,260 organs were transplanted in the United States.[16] Medical science is also expanding the numbers and types of organs that can now be transplanted. These organs and body areas include knees, larynx, trachea, femur, nerves, and muscles. However, the recipients must take antirejection drugs for extended periods, often for the rest of their lives, and these drugs have side effects, such as the risk of infection, diabetes, cancer, and other conditions.

Challenging Ethical Questions

Despite advances in our ability to perform a greater array of organ transplant procedures with increasing levels of success, many ethical questions abound. For example, with respect to the expanded number and types of organs that can now be transplanted, who decides if the risk is worth the reward? Who should pay for the procedure? But perhaps the most fundamental ethical question in the whole area of organ transplantation involves reconciling the relative scarcity of donors with the preponderance of patients needing organs. By what criteria should patients receive organs? Should the decision be based on the age of the potential recipients? On the severity of the disease they have? Or should we be unabashedly utilitarian in our approach and base the decision on the potential and future benefit to society the recipient might render? Yet another consideration would be whether the ability to pay for the operation ought to be a determining factor governing access to needed organs.

All ethical questions with respect to organ transplantation must in some way be squared with the concept of personhood, the very same concept that we referenced in our previous analysis of stem-cell therapy and sickle-cell anemia. Moreover, the implied notions of human freedom and the moral worth of each individual inherent in our concept of personhood must be

---

16. *Biomedical Ethics: Opposing Viewpoints* (San Diego: Greenhaven Press, College Division, 1998), 51.

addressed if we are to achieve some level of coherence in our assessment of the moral dimensions of organ transplantation. With respect to the specifics of organ donation and transplantation, the issue of human freedom is made evident in the matter of informed consent of any potential donor of a vital organ. The issue of the moral worth of every person and the sanctity of life is made evident in establishing criteria for death. We must arrive at some level of coherence with respect to these two issues if our analysis is to bear good ethical fruit and if the interests of donors and recipients are to be respected.

Informed Consent

The notion of informed consent recognizes the moral truth that human beings can never exercise their freedom unless they have complete knowledge of options available to them and, in the case of medical treatment, the full implications of any such treatment. Generally, in anticipation of death, a person may sign a consent form willingly expressing the desire to donate his or her body, or certain parts as may be needed for organ transplantation. Another aspect of informed consent is the granting of power to act on behalf of the person to an immediate next of kin.

Since such directions may figure into estate planning, the legal ramifications of informed consent became obvious. But what was not so obvious was the presence of uniform and consistent regulations across the nation governing organ donation. Thus the Uniform Anatomical Gift Act was passed by Congress in 1968. Prior to the passage of this legislation, there were no federal laws addressing organ and tissue donation, and the laws then on the books in the various states did not address the relevant issues relating to organ and tissue donation in anywhere near a complete manner.

Establishing Criteria for Death

Organ donors may be either alive or dead at the time of the transplant. However, in the case of critical organ transplantation, generally the donor has in fact expired. The problem, of course, is making certain that the conditions are medically and legally sound under which a transplantation procedure might proceed.

With our increased ability to sustain life has come the problem of determining when "death" actually occurs. Transplants of critical body organs such as the heart and liver clearly presuppose that life has ceased for the donor and furthermore that the donor has been declared dead in a legitimate way. The need for donors has kindled fear in some persons that doctors and transplantation personnel will declare death prematurely or impose dubious standards for determining death. We have therefore had to make a distinction between two conceptions of death. One conception is the "commonsense" understanding of death as clinical death, that is, when the vital body functions, such as unassisted breathing and heartbeat, cease. Such functions can at times be resuscitated, as say, in the case of a drowning victim. The other conception of death has come to be known as "brain death." In most instances potential donors are victims of violent accidents who end up brain dead. The concept of brain death became useful when the traditional method of determining death through heart and lung cardiopulmonary functions was rendered obsolete by the use of life-support machines in the 1960s. This definition of death dovetailed quite conveniently with the need to find suitable organ donors. By the time the circulatory function ceases, the organs begin to degenerate and become unusable. Thus the older commonsense definition of death, as the time when the body's vital functions, respiration and heartbeat, ceased, precludes organ donation.

In 1968, the Ad Hoc Committee at Harvard Medical School to Examine the Definition of Brain Death issued a report that ultimately became the standard in determining exactly how "brain death" was to be understood. The report stated that (1) unreceptivity and unresponsivity, (2) no movements or breathing, and (3) no reflexes are the characteristic signs of a permanently nonfunctioning brain. Further, a flat or isoelectric electroencephalograph (EEG, which is a brain-wave recording machine) confirms the diagnosis of brain death. As a precautionary measure, the report advised that all these tests should be repeated at least twenty-four hours later. If there is then no change in the data and if two further conditions (hypothermia and evidence of drug intoxication) are excluded, the patient may then be reasonably regarded as hopelessly and irreversibly brain damaged, and all those involved in major decisions affecting the patient should be so informed. Thereafter death is declared, and supportive measures are withdrawn.[17]

Another method of defining death is the integrative method, in which the crucial factor is the tension between heart, brain, and lung functioning rather than the independent functioning of any one or two parts. The method seeks to see if there is any potential for life by calculating a "dying score" based on five physiological functions: cerebral, reflexive, respiratory, circulatory, and cardiac. Each function is given a score. For example, if there is brain activity, a score of 2 is awarded; if there is potential for brain activity, the score is 1. If absent, the score is 0. Each function is scored in this way. Death is conclusive if each function scores 0. When a score of 5 or more is reached, there is life potential in the patient. Moreover, two physicians must determine that

---

17. Henry K. Beecher et al., "A Definition of Irreversible Coma," report of the Ad Hoc Committee at Harvard Medical School to Examine the Definition of Brain Death, *Journal of the American Medical Association* 205 (1968): 337–40.

death has occurred, neither of whom is on the transplantation team. Thus at least two factors should govern the possibility of a person being in a position to donate organs: (1) having given prior informed consent to do so and (2) suffering brain death of such severity that one's cardiopulmonary respiratory system cannot continue without life-support systems.

Access of African Americans to Organ Transplantation

At the present time approximately sixty thousand Americans are waiting to receive lifesaving organ transplants. The pool of potential donors is limited, perhaps only some twenty thousand per year. Moreover, careful restrictions must be placed upon any eligible donor. Generally donors should be under fifty-five years of age, and their death due to brain death, not through the loss of the integrity of vital organs. Not every dead person can be deemed a suitable donor because the lack of circulatory sensations may render some organs unusable. Thus at the very outset, some medical conditions contribute to a shortage of donors.

The scarcity of donors has a particularly acute effect on African Americans who are in need of organ transplants. African Americans are seventeen times more likely than whites to develop hypertension, a disorder that can lead to eventual kidney failure. African Americans wait almost twice as long as European Americans for their first transplant: 13.9 and 7.6 months, respectively. Although European Americans represent only 61 percent of the dialysis population, they receive 74 percent of all kidney transplants. In 1988, African Americans represented 33.5 percent of dialysis patients, but only 22.3 percent of kidney transplants went to black patients. In fact, in any given year, European American dialysis patients have approximately a 78 percent higher chance of receiving a transplant than African American dialysis patients.[18]

Because of many factors, not the least of which may be cultural bias and racism, African Americans die ten to fifteen years earlier for want of needed transplanted organs than would otherwise be the case. According to Dr. Clive O. Callender, the founder of the National Minority Organ/Tissue Transplantation Program (MOTTEP), African Americans continue to wait twice as long as other Americans for kidney transplants while constituting more than 50 percent of those waiting for kidney transplants. He reported this finding in a testimony before a joint congressional hearing on the Department of Health and Human Services Final Rule for Organ Allocation on June 18, 1998. In 1991, the Office of the Inspector General had presaged

18. Vernellia R. Randall, "Slavery, Segregation, and Racism: Trusting the Health Care System Ain't Always Easy! An African-American Perspective on Bioethics," *St. Louis University Law Review* 191 (1996): 206.

this startling statistic by noting that African Americans constituted 35 percent of the waiting lists for both liver and kidney transplants while making up only 12 percent of the national population. How then can we account for the donor shortage among African Americans? What issues are involved in the furtherance of a more equitable donor allocation?

Part of the problem has to do with genetically based aspects of organ transplantation. Successful kidney transplantation is enhanced by matching organs between members of the same ethnic or racial group. Thus, the problem of the scarcity of organs for African Americans can be mitigated in some measure through African Americans making available those needed organs. Yet, there are certain cultural and historical reasons why blacks have not been enthusiastic organ donors or have not made known their willingness to be donors through prior-consent measures.

African Americans have a historic fear and justifiable mistrust of the medical establishment in this country. The collective memory attests to mutilations and castrations from the barbaric days of slavery. Some medical experiments conducted on slaves border on the fiendish, as was the case of the test Dr. Thomas Hamilton conducted upon his slave John Brown in a makeshift open-pit oven in rural Georgia to discover the best remedies for sunstroke.[19] Dr. Walter F. Jones used a group of slaves to test a remedy for typhoid pneumonia that involved pouring five gallons of boiling water on the spinal column.[20] Abuses in antebellum medical schools as well as the illegal disinterment of slave corpses for experiments fill the sorry saga of the early American medical establishment in its treatment of black people. We have mentioned earlier in this chapter the infamous Tuskegee Syphilis Experiment that began in 1932 and extended to 1972; it is not the only example of recent medical abuse. In 1963, the United States Public Health Service, the American Cancer Society, and the Jewish Chronic Disease Hospital of Brooklyn, New York, participated in an experiment in which three physicians injected live cancer cells into twenty-two chronically ill and debilitated African American patients. The patients did not consent, nor were they aware that they were being injected with these cells.[21] All of these events become lodged in the popular mind of African Americans and confirm the suspicion that the medical establishment does not hold the interests of black patients dear or important and that blacks are expendable subjects of medical experimentation.

Encountering the medical establishment, perceived to be overwhelmingly white and controlled by seemingly impersonal doctors who presumably are

---

19. Savitt, *Medicine and Slavery*, 293.
20. Ibid., 299.
21. *Baltimore Sun,* March 19, 1995.

interested in blacks only as a means and not an end, becomes a foreboding prospect. The case of Bruce Tucker of Richmond, Virginia, illustrates the fear that many blacks have toward the medical establishment and reluctance to participate in organ donation programs. On May 24, 1968, Mr. Tucker, a fifty-six-year-old African American laborer in Richmond, fell and seriously injured his brain. He was taken to the Medical College of Virginia Hospital. Efforts were made to care for him, but by the next day his attending physician decided that Tucker would not recover and that death was imminent. In the same hospital was a patient in need of a heart transplant. After Tucker was examined by an EEG, his doctor determined that he showed no evidence of brain activity. The respirator to which he was attached was stopped for five minutes. Since he did not breathe spontaneously, he was pronounced dead. The respirator was restarted, and his heart was removed with the permission of the medical examiner. His brother, William Tucker, was not notified of these procedures.[22] He subsequently sued the transplant team on the grounds that his brother had been wrongfully killed. The jury decided in favor of the transplant team.

The case of Bruce Tucker lingers in the memory of black Richmonders, especially as they muse upon the viability of participating in organ donation programs. Related to the general and basic fear of the medical establishment is a fear of vulnerability, particularly in the case of kidney donation. While it has been generally accepted and proven that one can lead a normal life with one kidney, the prospect of vulnerability or the suspicion that something could go wrong with the remaining organ gives pause to many black people.

Certain cultural reasons also help explain why blacks have not been active organ donors. There is a traditional taboo against posthumous mutilation. Some people believe that in order to participate in the glorious event of a physical resurrection of the body in the afterlife, mortal bodies must be intact. Yet there are perfectly reasonable and justifiable ethical reasons for blacks to participate in organ donation and eventual transplantation. One reason is the joy of giving life to someone, especially if that person needs the organ for the sustained viability of life. Another reason is that it is in African Americans' own interest to be donors, given the disparity in the waiting time, the availability of organs, and the likelihood of success if transplants are made between persons of the same ethnic group.

African Americans have come a long way from the time when they were regarded in no higher esteem than other chattel owned by plantation owners. The barbaric and dehumanizing days of slavery are over. Yet, African Americans in the contemporary era still face serious challenges in the area

---

22. *Richmond Times Dispatch,* May 28, 1968.

of bioethics. Our ability to intervene in the world as infinitesimally small as the cell now has implications for the fate of sufferers of sickle-cell anemia. Our ability to extend life in the face of death is available through the procedures of organ transplantation. Our only hope is that through thorough and responsible ethical reflection we can secure health responsibly and enjoy life with the fullest of integrity. As people who enjoy God's gift of personhood and the attendant benefits of freedom and moral worth, we can do no less.

11

The Pursuit of Justice
in the Courts, Markets,
and Electoral Precincts

But let justice roll down like waters,
and righteousness like an ever-flowing stream.
— Amos 5:24

No more auction block for me,
No more auction block for me,
Many thousand gone.
— American Negro spiritual

Among the myths that govern the American political order, none is perhaps
more powerful than the one that affirms America as the world's most successful experiment in modern democracy. To some extent, to be sure, much
of the myth is based on some semblance of historical fact. For instance, until
the American revolt from the British Crown, the firm rule of monarchies had
never been successfully challenged in Europe or elsewhere in the world. And
the young United States did hold out a promise for truly representative democracy, as opposed to the absolutist regimes of eighteenth-century Europe.
Certainly the French Revolution of 1789, the same year the United States
was beginning to form its Constitution as a representative democracy, drew
inspiration from the American struggle. And over the years, refugees from
political oppression the world over have sought within the United States a
haven from oppression. Yet aspects of the myth of American democracy still
ring hollow, especially when we consider the systemic inequities that are so
much a part of the American civil society after two hundred years of this
"experiment." The presence of enslaved Africans during the time when the
experiment was conceived, even as the young nation celebrated the aspira-
tion to freedom and democracy, constituted the most glaring inconsistency,
a defect that this country must ultimately expunge before the "experiment"
can be judged a success.

This chapter will seek to discuss the challenge of securing acceptable levels of justice for African Americans within the American societal order. As we search for the discrete contexts in which the quest for justice is played out, three societal institutions come to mind. The first is what has been called the criminal justice system. Within this system are the legal, sociological, and cultural realities that inform the adjudication of cases of persons involved in this system. To the extent that racial prejudice continues to play a conspicuous role in this system is the extent to which our concern about the ethical considerations of the justice system and its import on the lives of African Americans is raised. A focus of concern will be an assessment of the ethical import of differential sentencing guidelines with respect to controlled substances.

The second context in which the quest for American justice is played out is the area of economics. To the extent that racial prejudice inhibits full access of African Americans to the American economic system is the extent to which an ethical consideration of the economic destiny of African Americans can be assessed. A focus of concern for us in this chapter will be an assessment of the ethical cogency of the practice of affirmative action as a means to rectify presumed past racial injustices.

The third context for the pursuit of justice is the area of electoral politics. To the extent that racial prejudice continues to frustrate the full inclusion of African Americans in the American polity is the extent to which we must assess the integrity of the normative order that presumes to undergird American democracy. Thus a focus of concern in this area will be an ethical analysis of the practice of cumulative voting as a mechanism to rectify inequitable voting practices in parts of the country. The burden of this chapter, therefore, is to assess the means whereby the American civil order can be so ordered, from a Christian ethical point of view, to ensure the full measure of juridical, economic, and political justice for African Americans and, by implication, for all Americans.

Society can be viewed as the network of mutual expectations between individuals that ensures the self-actualization of each individual and at the same time the maintenance of the society at large. Societies work best when they can ensure that all persons will be provided the means whereby they might seek their full share of self-actualization. But societies can only do this if they themselves are maintained. A society is maintained to the extent that individuals recognize the normative value of that society and defer to its norms, values, and expectations. It is a natural tendency for human beings to do all manner of things to maximize their self-actualization, their interests and their desires. But such tendencies, such efforts to maximize each person's liberty, if you will, must always be restrained to some extent in deference to the expectations of the society at large. There must eventually be a balance between the freedom *for* each individual and responsibility *to* the society. Thus no society could long endure if individuals did not recognize some constraints upon their aspirations for freedom and self-actualization and defer to others and the norms of the society at large. At the same time, no society can aspire to what we would call a just society unless it provides the means whereby individuals within that society might achieve their own self-actualization, unfettered by artificial constraints imposed upon them by that society. If there are artificial constraints imposed on them, then clearly self-actualization has not and cannot take place.

The hope of the United States of truly becoming a civil society is an ongoing hope; the "experiment" in democracy continues. The success of the experiment will depend upon whether the citizens of the American society can reasonably feel a vested interest in deferring to the common good in the full knowledge that our society values and establishes the means to ensure the full self-actualization of each citizen. As far as African Americans are concerned, the United States will never become a truly just society until matters of the economic order, the legal normative order, and the political order are attended to and equitably resolved. In practical terms, these three great issues are epitomized in the continuing debate over the problems African Americans face in the judicial system, the issue of affirmative action, and finally efforts to minimize the deleterious effects of racism in order to achieve political power. Each issue, in its own fashion, bespeaks the peculiar efforts of African Americans to forge the embodiment of a Christian ethic within the context of American society.

ENSURING JUSTICE IN THE JUDICIAL SYSTEM

Just societies function as a network of mutual expectations between individuals such that the self-actualization of individuals can proceed while at the same time ensuring the maintenance of the society as a whole. Individual liberty must be restrained at some level in order that the maintenance of the whole might be assured. To the extent that all individuals of the society affirm this network of mutual expectations, there is a formal normative basis for all just societies. An overarching standard of behavioral expectation imposed upon each person assures individual liberty within certain boundaries, boundaries that are circumscribed by the expectations that individuals acknowledge rules and standards of human behavior.

And yet not all individuals who live in societies are perfect. Human weakness, coupled with finitude and peculiar circumstances, will inevitably eventuate in some persons committing infractions against the web of mutual expectations that constitute the core of society. Whenever such infractions occur, there is a breach in the subtle contract that constitutes the substance of the network of mutual expectations. We even say that offenders are "in our debt" and that convicted criminals must "pay their debt to society." In back of such sentiments is the notion that the offender has disregarded this implicit agreement between individuals and the society to which they belong. The balance between individual liberty and deference to societal norms has been shattered; the contract has been compromised.

What can remedy such a problem? Compensation in monetary forms such as fines may suffice, but more often we demand symbolic compensation by requiring that the offender be punished. Intuitively we reckon that a measure of just punishment would be a period of time deprived of the freedom to enjoy participation in the mutual web of responsibilities and rights we call society. So violators of laws are imprisoned. We demand a portion of the offender's life as a measure of compensation for the "debt" incurred to us as a society. This seems to us just compensation as a means of eventually restoring the contract.

During this year, thousands of Americans will be arrested, tried, convicted, and sent to penal institutions to begin the process of "paying their debts" to our society. By the early months of the year 2000, there were fully two million Americans behind bars, according to the Justice Policy Institute.[1] How might Christian ethics, particularly from an African American perspective, inform an analysis of our judicial system? What principles from Christian faith and Christian ethical consciousness might mitigate some of the inequities that have unfortunately been the lot of African Americans? How might such inequities be addressed in such a fashion that justice for all Americans might become a reality?

The judicial system theoretically exists to punish the guilty among us of infractions against the legal rules that form the basis for our normative order and thus our civil society. But this presumes that we are absolutely certain as to what constitutes "guilt." What really does it mean to say that someone is "guilty"? Even accounting for the various levels of guilt inherent in our judicial system, for example, second-degree murder, manslaughter, and the like, a question of some philosophical import remains before us as we determine who among us owes us a "debt." Who is guilty? On what basis has guilt been determined?

THE PROBLEM OF FREEDOM VS. DETERMINISM

The problem of ascertaining guilt among us, even those who have been duly convicted of crimes, will inevitably raise the old philosophical problem of free will versus determinism. Are we really free as human beings, or is

---

1. William Raspberry, "2 Million and Counting," *Washington Post*, December 13, 1999.

everything we do determined by some antecedent condition? According to the theory of universal determinism, everything is governed by prior causal factors. All effects come about through prior causes. In the world of mechanics and science, we intuit this to be a commonsense truism. A cue ball will strike the eight ball and sink it in the corner pocket. And even in the world of societal and historical movement, we acknowledge that events are always caused by prior events, which in turn came about because of some prior, antecedent cause.

But surely, the opponent of universal determinism would say that we are able to change to some extent. While it is clear that we have no control over our environments, where we were born, even the abuse we suffered as children, we can press back against all of these vicissitudes and will ourselves not to commit crimes against society. We need not feel compelled to commit infractions against the normative order. Could we not therefore moderate the universal determinism to some degree and assert a "soft determinism"? We can make a distinction between voluntary and involuntary actions as cause for human acts; a distinction can be made between acts done out of coercion and acts done presumably out of free will. As long as we are capable of making voluntary acts, then the "soft" determinist will be justified in moderating the hard position of the universal determinist. Of course, the problem with this position is ascertaining whether any presumed voluntary acts are in fact acts involuntarily done by the doer unawares of the conditions existing even within oneself. In making the distinction between coercion and free will, the soft determinist merely presumes that acts are done out of freedom. Thus the argument presumes as fact only a supposition. Still the proponents of free will state that if determinism were really true, then there would be no possibility of our changing our minds and, consequently, of a different set of actions as a result of our changed minds. But do we not change our minds all the time? Can we not change our behaviors? Of course, the determinist counters and replies that any presumed change of mind is only illusory, that our feeling of control over our decisions is not real. We are hopelessly ignorant of all the forces, embedded deep within ourselves and our past, that impinge upon us at any given moment in our lives. If, in the real world of keeping laws and breaking laws, we choose to obey laws, the fact that we make this choice could very well be the result of the type of environment in which we were nurtured, the type of parents who trained us. We have absolutely no control over these prior events. Thus, the determinist replies that *whatever* we do has already been determined by previous events, even the laudatory actions we take as upstanding citizens of the civil society.

Proponents of free will, or libertarians, counter by asserting that given the same previous conditions, we could have acted otherwise. Rejecting universal causality, the libertarian affirms the notion of agent causality, namely, that each individual or agent is responsible for all actions that ensue from that individual. The inner states of the individual are not caused by any prior condition or effect. Thus, only the inner states of the individual cause the acts coming from that individual; thus, the individual is free. The libertarians admit that while the determinists seem to be on rather solid ground in asserting that much of human behavior is the result of conditions over which we have little control, the determinists seem to be unable to prove that *all* human behavior is caused by predetermined conditions. This position, however, forces the libertarian to claim all impulsive, unconditioned acts of the individual as indicators of human freedom. Thus while libertarianism rejects the image of humans as being puppetlike under determinism, their image of humans seems to fare no better. The image of the person advanced by libertarianism is a quirky, jerky, erratic person who behaves without any seeming rhyme or reason. Neither the libertarian nor the determined person is a flattering portrait of human nature. Both are *very* problematic.

Regardless of how we eventually solve the problem of free will versus determinism, it is doubtlessly true that all human beings have limited control over the conditions that lead inexorably to the actions that they commit. But a problem arises as soon as we assert that there is a definable, discrete person, a "he" or a "she" who has committed a crime or infraction. If we are all connected in the intricate web of relations that constitutes societies, and if all of us have only limited control over the conditions that lead to our actions, to what extent can the full and certain culpability be put on one discrete person, on a *him* or a *her?* This in no way exculpates or excuses any one person who either by admission or trial appears to be guilty; it only shows us the difficulty at arriving at this absolute clarity with respect to "guilt" and culpability. Moreover, since Christian faith affirms that we are all social beings and are connected at some vital points in existence, the effort of assigning clear and unambiguous guilt to any one person, to this *him* or this *her,* is made all the more challenging.

THE PHILOSOPHICAL NECESSITY OF PUNISHMENT, FORGIVENESS, AND MERCY

When we fully recognize our limited scope of power over the conditions that give rise to our eventual actions, Christian notions of forgiveness and mercy make so much sense and seem so appropriate as we deal with those among us who commit infractions against our laws. Being aware of the limited scope of power over our social destinies should force us minimally always to search for the mitigating circumstances in criminal charges and even in cases where there is proven guilt. It is such recognition that gives rise to the confession "There but for the grace of God go I." In any case, we are called upon to show mercy, not necessarily absolution or exculpation of crimes committed, but mercy. Why are we so called? Because the very circumstances that gave rise to the crime that we now judge could very well have been the ones in our own situation, our own environment, our own upbringing. We cannot control the prior events that precipitate the actions that come from our own hands.

And since this is the case and since, surely, we would want to be granted the same allowance for the impact of prior events in miscreant acts, it logically follows that we should grant forbearance to others. We are called upon to forgive. And it is only others who can forgive us; we cannot forgive ourselves. How can this be? Forgiveness presumes a break or fissure between the offender and the community against which an offense has been committed. The intricate network of mutual expectations has been put out of balance; it is not right. Insofar as all participate in good faith in this network, when someone violates the mutual expectations, the others are "owed a debt." A debt has been incurred for which someone is to be forgiven. This concept of "debt" is rendered in very graphic dimensions in the Bible, especially in the Jubilee texts and the Lord's Prayer. In the Jubilee instructions of Leviticus 25 and in the Lord's Prayer, the context points to the forgiveness of economic debt. Morally speaking, in the area of criminal justice, the criminals are in our debt because they have violated the implicit reciprocal balance inherent in civil society. All of us are enjoined to follow the law in order that all of us might live civilly with one another. We exchange keeping the law for full inclusion in the civil bond we know as society. The criminal has theoretically broken this agreement and therefore is in our debt.

Now, even after pointing out the legitimacy of a concept of moral "debt," we must recognize as well the fact that all of us are prone to miss the mark in maintaining the reciprocal agreement inherent in civil society, or avoiding being in "debt" to our fellows. We will sin, but we cannot forgive ourselves. Only God and others can do that. Since we know that God forgives and since we presume that we are created in the image of God, then it follows that we must forgive. Thus we are all connected in this web of sin and forgiveness and ought to forgive.

Are there some offenses that are unforgivable? We all recognize and affirm that there are particularly heinous and repulsive crimes. Rape and genocide are but two; all crimes against persons are repulsive. If we keep in place our theoretical framework that recognizes the regressive causation of all acts and the interconnectedness of humanity, then we must admit that there are no unforgivable crimes. And if, as Christians, we believe that nothing we do can keep us permanently alienated from God, an indication of the measure of God's grace by which we receive forgiveness, then we must forgive, even as God forgives heinous crimes.

Forgiveness, however, need not mean exculpation of deeds done or forgetting the crimes that have been committed. There can be no legitimate forgiveness if crimes are forgotten. Indeed, what is forgiven if all is forgotten? We must remember in order to forgive. We do not forgive suppositions or hallucinations; we forgive *real offenses* committed, and we must remember them if we are to forgive them. We do not harbor them or continue to hold them such that no reconciliation between us and the offender can come to pass. As we work toward reconciliation, recompense is still required, whether in some form of compensation or some form of punishment. The issue of recompense inevitably leads to questions: If forgiveness has been offered to the offender, then why should punishment be meted out? Does not forgiveness obviate the need for punishment or cancel the requirement for punishment? It would seem so except for the fact that if community is to be maintained, then the fragile web of reciprocity that we mentioned earlier must be maintained as well. One must remember that the original meaning of *mispat*, or "justice" in the Old Testament, probably referred to a restitution of a prior condition that promoted equity and harmony, a state of *shalom*, in a community. And what is this prior state but the reciprocity that we described, without which no society can long be maintained? Thus punishment recognizes the debt incurred; punishment seeks to pay that debt back, to reconcile offended and offender. But forgiveness, inevitably, is required to ultimately maintain the web of society.

It is at the punishment phase that, ethically speaking, the concept of mercy becomes so important. Mercy helps to guide us in devising and imposing ethical contexts for punishment. Mercy helps to remind us of our prior act of forgiveness that we gave out of a recognition of the limitations of human righteousness and the affirmation of our connectedness with contexts that give rise to oftentimes dysfunctional and aberrant behavior. What we do with this sense of mercy becomes the Christian's basis for interaction with the criminal justice system. How might mercy be shown during the punishment phase, if indeed punishment is justifiable and required, becomes now an operative and viable question. I want to move now to consider two significant aspects of the judicial system as it affects African Americans. The first issue is sentencing guidelines with respect to controlled substances; the second is the death penalty.

THE WAR AGAINST DRUGS

American culture has not been unique in the presence and use of mood-altering substances as conspicuous features of life. Wine in France, beer in Germany, coca leaves chewed among Central American peoples, and *khat* chewed by Middle Eastern peoples—all have functioned as culturally approved ways of alleviating the tedium of life. In a very real sense, America has always been involved in a "drug war." In 1791, the farmers of western Pennsylvania resisted attempts by the federal government to impose an excise tax on whiskey that the farmers had made. By 1794, an insurrection had flared into the open, requiring President Washington to call up a militia of nearly thirteen thousand men, one nearly as large as the Continental Army that had fought for American independence, to quell it. The thirst that Americans showed for spirituous liquors in the colonial period by no means slacked as the nation moved into the nineteenth century. In the 1830s, the average American aged fifteen or older consumed over thirty-seven gallons of absolute alcohol (resulting from an average of nine and a half gallons of spirits, a half gallon of wine, and twenty-seven gallons of beer per year), a quantity about three times the current rate.[2]

The temperance movement had its roots in the shock that many Americans had at the sight of a seeming epidemic of public drunkenness in the 1830s and 1840s. After the Civil War, further efforts to curtail the use of liquor resulted in the founding of the Women's Christian Temperance Union in 1873, followed by the Anti-Saloon League in 1893. The latter worked tirelessly for a national campaign against liquor, even if it meant amending the nation's Constitution. Their efforts resulted in the passage of the Volstead Act, the Eighteenth Amendment to the Constitution, which went into effect in January 1919, prohibiting the manufacture, sale, or transportation of intoxicating liquors in the United States. With the passage of the Volstead Act, there followed over a decade of much national hypocrisy as many otherwise law-abiding Americans danced their way through the Roaring Twenties, drinking illegally manufactured liquor in clandestine clubs whose whereabouts were an open secret to everyone. Finally, Franklin D. Roosevelt, running for president with the open support of "wets" (persons opposed to Prohibition), called for a repeal of the Eighteenth Amendment. The repeal succeeded in 1933, a few months after Roosevelt assumed office. America could thus legally indulge its fondness for alcohol again. Moreover, even in the throes of the Great Depression, a good portion of the country was enthralled in the rapture of "reefer madness" (marijuana); cocaine was actually prescribed as a therapeutic ingredient, while heroin was touted for its marvelous properties, thus the name denoted its "heroic" capabilities.

Without a doubt, however, the most recent "drug war" in which this nation has been involved makes all previous encounters seem as minor skirmishes. The level of violence between drug gangs seems to have rivaled and

---

2. N. H. Clark, *Deliver Us from Evil: An Interpretation of American Prohibition* (New York: Norton, 1976), 20; Herbert Asbury, *The Great Illusion: An Informal History of Prohibition* (New York: Greenwood Press, 1968).

surpassed even the organized crime killings of the 1920s and 1930s. At the heart of the issue seems to be the ability of international suppliers to penetrate U.S. markets and satisfy a desire for cocaine in two varieties: powder and crystalline (crack). Since cocaine, in all of its forms and varieties, is an illegal and controlled substance, those persons who have become habitual users and those who profit from its sale and use run afoul of the law and thus end up in the criminal justice system.

FEDERAL SENTENCING GUIDELINES: DISPARITIES AND NEGATIVE EFFECTS

With American prisons beginning to bulge at the seams in the wake of vigorous enforcement of drug violations in the latter years of the 1970s, Congress passed the Sentencing Reform Act in 1984. In response to complaints from the federal bench, the criminal defense bar, family members of convicted crack defendants, and civil rights groups, Congress directed the Sentencing Commission in the 1994 Crime Bill to examine the obvious disparity in sentences for crack and powder offenses. As a result of continued dissatisfaction expressed in many quarters about the inequity of longer sentences for crack cocaine as opposed to powder cocaine, the U.S. Sentencing Commission submitted to Congress on May 1, 1995, twenty-seven proposed amendments, one of which would have reduced penalties for crack cocaine. While the commission's report stated that "there is no evidence that Congress acted with any discriminatory intent in setting different statutory guideline penalties for different forms of cocaine," the great disparities according to race that did in fact eventuate meant that something had to be done. Under the Sentencing Reform Act of 1984, the commission's amendments to the sentencing guidelines would take effect November 1, 1995, unless Congress intervened.

But in this case, Congress did intervene. On June 29, 1995, the Judiciary Committee's Crime Subcommittee held a hearing to examine the Sentencing Commission's recommended changes to the sentencing guidelines that would equalize penalties for similar quantities of crack and powder cocaine. Many of the witnesses at the hearing, including members of the Sentencing Commission, acknowledged important differences between crack and powder cocaine: crack is presumed to be more addictive than powder cocaine; it accounts for more emergency-room visits; it is most popular among juveniles; it has a greater likelihood of being associated with violence; and crack dealers have more extensive criminal records than other drug dealers and tend to use young people to distribute the drug at a greater rate. And the testimony of some of the Sentencing Commission members revealed clear differences of opinion on the wisdom of reducing the sentences for crack.

After all, the Sentencing Commission's report to Congress on May 1, 1995, was not a univocal one; the report was sent with a 4–3 vote.

The minority of the members of the Sentencing Commission hammered away at the more negatives effects of crack. The most common routes of administration of the two drugs cause crack to be the more psychologically addictive of the substances, particularly because smoking crack produces quicker, more intense, and shorter-lasting effects than snorting cocaine powder. Crack can also be broken down and packaged into very small and inexpensive quantities for distribution and is thereby marketed to the most vulnerable members of society, including youth and those of lower socioeconomic status. Additionally, the open-air street markets and crack houses used for the distribution of crack contribute heavily to the deterioration of neighborhoods and communities. Finally, the present crack market is associated with violent crime to a greater extent than that of cocaine powder.

The above description of the relatively more harmful personal and social effects of crack cocaine would seem to argue against an equalization of sentencing guidelines. But the Sentencing Commission's recommendations to the 1994 Crime Bill *unanimously* disapproved of the 100-to-1 sentencing disparity for crack trafficking versus power trafficking, believing obviously that the disparity was much too harsh and could not be justified.

While the evidence clearly indicates that significant distinctions between crack and powder cocaine warrant longer sentences for crack-related offenses, it should be noted that the current 100-to-1 quantity ratio may not be the appropriate one. The goal must ultimately be to ensure that the uniquely harmful nature of crack is reflected in sentencing policy but at the same time to uphold basic principles of equity in the U.S. Code. Proponents of equalization of sentences note that just as beer and wine are two forms of the same drug (alcohol), crack cocaine and powder cocaine are two forms of the same drug. Based largely on media perceptions (and misperceptions) surrounding the death of University of Maryland basketball star Len Bias, as well as other unsupported anecdotal evidence, Congress singled out crack cocaine for much harsher penalties than powder cocaine in 1986 when it enacted the first set of federal laws for cocaine offenses. Because of its relative low cost, crack cocaine is the drug of choice for poor Americans, many of whom are African Americans living in our inner cities. Conversely, powder cocaine is much more expensive and tends to be used by more affluent white Americans. Thus, punishing crack cocaine offenses more harshly than powder cocaine offenses unjustly and disproportionately penalizes African Americans. Under current law, defendants convicted of trafficking 50 grams of crack cocaine receive the same ten-year mandatory minimum penalty as defendants convicted of trafficking 5,000 grams of powder cocaine. Conviction for trafficking a mere 5 grams of crack cocaine carries the same five-year mandatory minimum sentence as a conviction for trafficking 500 grams of powder cocaine. Another comparison is instructive: 500 grams of powder cocaine produces 2,500 to 5,000 doses with a street value in October 1999 of between $32,500 and $50,000. In contrast, 5 grams of crack cocaine produces 10 to 50 doses and has a street value of between $225 and $750. Thus, at the high end of the scale, a defendant convicted of trafficking $750 worth of crack cocaine would receive the same mandatory minimum five-year sentence as a defendant who trafficked $50,000 worth of powder cocaine.[3]

Prisons are literally filled with young African American men and women serving mandatory minimums for crack cocaine trafficking and possession offenses. Currently, 61 percent of federal inmates are serving sentences for drug offenses. That figure is expected to reach 70 percent by the year 2000.[4] The average prison stay for drug offenders has increased from 23.1 months in 1985 to 68.7 months in 1993. Twenty-one per cent of the drug law violators are classified as "low-level" security risks (e.g., no record of current or prior violence, no involvement in sophisticated criminal activity, and no prior conviction).[5] Elimination of these types of offenders alone could dramatically reduce the federal prison population. Similarly, studies have shown that $3.5 billion could be saved if the terms of already sentenced inmates were reduced to those that would have applied for powder cocaine offenses.

The image of the crack addict wildly and randomly shooting whoever crosses his or her path is often presented to justify heightened penalties for crack offenses. However, this type of drug-induced violence rarely occurs. Indeed, the drug that fits this image most appropriately is alcohol. Alcohol has been associated with more violent behavior than any other drug.[6] The image of the desperate crack cocaine addict committing series of violent crimes to support his or her drug habit is similarly misplaced. Most of the habit-supporting crime associated with crack is petty property theft, prostitution, and crack cocaine dealing itself. Drug marketplace violence accounts for the majority of crime associated with crack cocaine. Crack cocaine has created an underground economy in the inner city, and in these economies,

---

3. United States Sentencing Commission, *Cocaine and Federal Sentencing Policy*, 173 (table 19), citing United States Drug Enforcement Administration, *Illegal Price and Purity Report, United States: January 1990–December 1993* (1994); United States Drug Enforcement Administration, *U.S. Drug Threat Assessment: 1993* (1993).

4. Statement of Kathleen M. Hawk, Director of Bureau of Prisons, *Oversight Hearing on Matters Relating to Federal Prisons* (June 8, 1995).

5. Ibid.

6. Mario de la Rosa, Elizabeth Y. Lambert, and Bernard Gropper, eds., *Drugs and Violence: Causes, Correlates, and Consequences* (Rockville, Md.: U.S. Department of Health and Human Services, Public Health Service, Alcohol, Drug Abuse, and Mental Health Administration, National Institute on Drug Abuse, 1990), 31.

violence is used to achieve economic regulation and control. Such systemic marketplace violence is present in the marketplace for all illicit drugs.

Even assuming that nothing in the truncated legislative history of the federal cocaine laws would suggest the existence of a racially discriminatory intent in differentiating between sentences for crack and powder cocaine, the discriminatory impact of these laws cannot be ignored. African Americans accounted for 88.3 percent of federal crack cocaine trafficking convictions in 1993; Hispanics 7.1 percent, whites 4.1 percent, and others 0.5 percent.[7] Not only does this sentencing differential relative to crack and powder cocaine undermine the federal judicial system and its implicit aim of ensuring equity for all American citizens, it has a definite undermining effect on the national African American community. Family stability, the career paths of young offenders, and even the ability of African Americans to participate fully in the political process are negatively affected as well.

In October 1998, the *Washington Post* carried a story lamenting that a total of 1.4 million African American males nationwide—13 percent of all black men—were essentially disenfranchised, inasmuch as they were convicted felons and such persons lose their right to vote. The article went on to report that in at least ten states in the nation, more than 20 percent of the black males have lost the right to vote because of their status as convicted felons. As to whether the states offer anything analogous to "legal redemption" to felons once sentences are served, the picture is mixed. The District of Columbia and forty-six states deprive felons of the right to vote while they are in prison. In addition, thirty-two states bar offenders from voting while they are on probation, and twenty-nine bar voting while people are on parole. In fourteen of these states felons are barred for life from voting.[8] One must always remember that the right of black people to vote in this country has at various historical moments been either tenuous or nonexistent. When one further considers the incalculable costs in terms of human anguish and bloodshed required to achieve the right to vote, the prospect of that right being withheld from persons convicted in our courts under guidelines that appear arbitrary seems not only unfair but fundamentally tragic.

THE APPLICATION OF MERCY AND THE HOPE FOR REDEMPTION

The decision at the federal level to treat conviction of crack cocaine trafficking much more harshly than powder cocaine trafficking is based on spurious reasoning and faulty social data. Were sentencing guidelines more equitable,

---

7. United States Sentencing Commission, *Cocaine and Federal Sentencing Policy* (1995).
8. *Washington Post,* October 23, 1998.

the number of African Americans in the prison system would correspondingly plummet. The attendant family and community disruption would be lessened as well. Moreover, the political integrity of the African American community would not be undermined. Consistent with the spirit of the argument that would eliminate the judicial disparities by which so many of these persons end up in prison for longer sentences is the movement currently gaining ground that would give them a second chance if convicted under the existing guidelines.

William Raspberry, the Pulitzer Prize–winning columnist for the *Washington Post,* celebrates that more voices are crying out for a reversal of sentencing guidelines and the offering of what is called a "Second Chance." This amounts to *redemption,* a concept very much at home in Christian ethical consciousness. A "Second Chance" is advocated by persons as disparate in background and temperament as Charles Ogletree, the Harvard Law School professor; Ed Koch, the former mayor of New York; and the Rev. Al Sharpton, the social activist whose arrest Koch once ordered. The idea is simple: nonviolent drug offenders who have completed their sentences would be eligible to enroll in a program of drug treatment, education, and job training, which, if they complete and stay trouble-free for five years, would make them eligible to have their criminal records sealed.[9]

The problem of differential sentencing for trafficking in crack cocaine as opposed to powder cocaine is an example of one aspect of our judicial system that cries out for a greater measure of equity. Our analysis in no way should construe an exculpation of those who traffick in crack cocaine; it is a nefarious trade, exploiting the psychological and spiritual misery of addicts. Yet given the bleak prospects for life in many parts of our urban ghettos, it is a wonder that even more persons have not succumbed to the fatal lure of drugs. The fact that there has been an actual *decrease* in the use of crack among young African Americans is a bright spot in any otherwise somber social landscape.

Before the bar of justice may ultimately come at one time or another all Americans, flawed and imperfect as we are. Those whose guilt is in doubt as well as those caught "red-handed" will come before us all as we judge them. But in judging them, we judge ourselves, and we also judge the ethical integrity of our judicial system. If our system of justice is to have any semblance of equity with respect to punishment for drug trafficking, then the great disparity in sentencing must be closed.

---

9. William Raspberry, "Modest Proposal for a Second Chance," *Washington Post,* November 15, 1999.

THE DEATH PENALTY AND AFRICAN AMERICANS

Another issue in the justice system that has had peculiar significance for African Americans is the death penalty. In the history of American jurisprudence, there has been perhaps no more egregious violation of ethical principles than in the historic disparities displayed in the administration of the death penalty. The death penalty has been a recognized form of punishment—ultimate punishment as it turns out—in the American judicial system since colonial days. In the early days of the nation, the death penalty was meted out in a rather draconian way; Americans were put to death for such crimes as horse thievery and even petty burglary. Over the years many states have abolished the death penalty within their jurisdictions. But as of today, thirty-six states still prescribe capital punishment for various kinds of homicide. The death penalty is available in a few jurisdictions for other crimes as well. Presently, the seven capital crimes for which the death sentence is carried out are murder, rape, armed robbery, kidnapping, espionage, burglary, and assault by a life-term prisoner.

One of the indelible blots on American jurisprudence has been the inequitable sentencing of prisoners in capital cases based on race. Over the years the racial prejudice of juries and judges has consigned a disproportionate number of blacks to their death. In many instances in the South, black men were given the death penalty for the alleged crime of rape against white women. Posttrial evidence revealed that in many cases the sex was consensual or an attack nonexistent. Blacks charged with murder of a white person were many more times likely to face the death penalty than whites charged with murdering blacks, even if such charges were brought to trial.[10]

In an effort to bring a degree of consistency to the adjudication of capital murder cases, the landmark Supreme Court ruling in *Furman v. Georgia* in 1972 sought to impose some measure of consistency in the application of the death penalty. Prosecutors and judges were enjoined to minimize the importance of race in the way capital murder trials took their course. On another front, and in response to the charge of opponents of the death penalty that it constituted "cruel and unusual punishment," in 1976 the Supreme Court ruled in *Gregg v. Georgia* that the practice does not violate the Eighth Amendment's prohibition against cruel and unusual punishment.

Even after these decisions, there is still not evidence of the absence of racial bias in determining which convicted prisoners are to receive the death penalty. A review of the data seems to suggest that the quality of white life

---

10. Michael L. Radelet, Hugo Adam Bedau, and Constance Putnam, *In Spite of Innocence: Erroneous Convictions in Capital Cases* (Boston: Northeastern University Press, 1992); Hugo Adam Bedau and Michael L. Radelet, "Miscarriages of Justice in Potentially Capital Cases," *Stanford Law Review* 40 (1987):21–179.

is still regarded as more valuable than that of black life in many criminal trials. In a 1973 study, one year after *Furman v. Georgia*, of 1,265 cases from the states of Florida, Georgia, Louisiana, South Carolina, and Tennessee in which the race of the defendant and the sentence are known, nearly seven times as many blacks were sentenced to death as were whites. Of 882 blacks convicted of rape, 110 were sentenced to die. Among 442 whites convicted of the same crime, only 9 received a death sentence. A study of sentencing patterns in Texas in the 1970s showed that where a black or Chicano killed a white, 65 percent of the defendants were given the death penalty, while only 25 percent of whites who killed blacks or Chicanos faced the same fate.[11] In a 1983 study of Georgia sentencing, capital defendants who killed white victims were eleven times more likely to receive the death sentence than those who killed black victims. Among those indicted for killing whites, black defendants received death sentences three times as often as white defendants.[12]

Indeed, as the data indicate, even as late as 1999 the race of the victim and the race of the perpetrator still seem to play an altogether too conspicuous role in determining who receives the death sentence and who does not. According to the Death Penalty Information Center,[13] as of October 1999 the race of defendants executed since 1976 is as follows:

Race	Number Executed	Percentage of Total Executed
Black	202	35
Hispanic	39	7
White	329	56
Native American and Asian	11	2

White Defendant/Black Victim: 10
Black Defendant/White Victim: 137

Despite all the best hopes of the Supreme Court as expressed in *Furman v. Georgia*, our society still has not expunged racial bias from the administration of the death penalty.

Even assuming that we can achieve levels of parity in the administration of the death penalty, the question still remains whether this practice can enjoy ethical approval for the Christian, particularly the African American Christian. After careful consideration, and in recognition of the philosophi-

---

11. NAACP Legal Defense and Educational Fund, Inc., *Race and the Death Penalty: The Pattern of Uneven Justice* (Washington, D.C.: NAACP Legal Defense and Educational Fund, Inc., 1991).

12. Ibid.

13. Death Penalty Information Center website, *www.dpic.org*, October 23, 1999.

cal problem we discussed earlier concerning human freedom, I assert that the death penalty cannot enjoy ethical approval from a Christian perspective.

At one level, there is simply the sheer practical problem of determining the certainty of guilt and the administration of the penalty. Given the proven disparities within the administration of the death penalty, the practice will always be prone to error in imposing the death sentence on innocent persons. The death penalty—the ultimate sentence—provides no subsequent opportunity to redress any judicial errors committed during the trial process. According to a study published by the *Stanford Law Review*[14] at least 350 innocent people have been convicted since 1900 of potentially capital crimes. Judicial review of capital cases has discovered at least 27 innocent persons sentenced to death since 1972. This represents 1 innocent person discovered and released for every 4 executions carried out during that time. We may never know the exact number of persons whose innocence was not discovered but who were put to death by the states.

The administrative problems inherent in meting out the death penalty are so enormous and apparently so intractable that at its February 1997 midyear meeting, the House of Delegates of the American Bar Association (ABA) passed a resolution calling for a halt on executions until courts across the country can ensure that such cases are "administered fairly and impartially, in accordance with due process" and with minimum risk of executing innocent people. This resolution was adopted by a margin of 280 to 119 votes. It cited some of the ABA's existing policies urging jurisdictions across the country to assure that people charged with capital crimes receive due-process protections. For example, the report reaffirmed the need for competent counsel in capital punishment cases, the elimination of race discrimination in capital sentencing, and the prevention of the execution of mentally retarded persons and persons who committed crimes as minors. Particularly startling was the action of the Republican governor of Illinois, George Ryan, who in January 2000 declared a moratorium on executions in his state due to a disturbing number of cases in which the guilt of persons sentenced to die was not absolutely certain. Expanding on Governor Ryan's action, Senator Russell Feingold, Democrat of Wisconsin, has entered a bill in the United States Senate that would impose a moratorium on both state and federal executions while a national commission examines the many troubling questions in our judicial system—not least of which are the glaringly inadequate safeguards to prevent conviction and execution of the innocent.[15]

---

14. "Miscarriages of Justice in Potentially Capital Cases," *Stanford Law Review* 40 (1987): 21–179.

15. *New York Times*, May 8, 2000.

It also does not appear that the death penalty is necessarily a deterrent to crime. Persons who commit capital murder clearly fall into two categories: those who commit murder under premeditation and those who do not. In the first category, including those who commit gangland or drug-turf murders or even terrorism, there are certain logical inhibitors to assuming that the death penalty would prevent such murders. In the case of gang- or drug-related murders, the perpetrators are already betting their lives on the odds of staying alive to ply their nefarious trade. In the case of terrorism, the perpetrators believe in either some religious ideology that rewards martyrs who die for a cause or some political cause that does the same. In either case, it is not likely that persons will be deterred from committing murder. In the case of murders that are not premeditated, the category in which the vast majority of murders fall, these crimes are committed by persons in the heat of passion or under the influence of drugs or alcohol. By definition, they are committed by people in an irrational state of mind. What is to make anyone think that such persons would rationally factor in the threat of the death penalty when the murder is being committed under these circumstances?

Other evidence also suggests that the death penalty does not have deterrent value. As a group, death-penalty states do not have lower rates of criminal homicide than non-death-penalty states. During the 1980s, death-penalty states averaged an annual rate of 7.5 criminal homicides per 100,000 of population; abolition states averaged a rate of 7.4.[16] While it is extremely difficult to hold constant all variables in an analysis of the interplay between the imposition of the death penalty and crime levels, it is important to note that in neighboring states—one with the death penalty and the others without it—the one with the death penalty does not show a consistently lower rate of criminal homicide. For example, between 1972 and 1990, the homicide rate in Michigan (which has no death penalty) was generally as low as or lower than the neighboring state of Indiana, which restored the death penalty in 1973 and since then has sentenced seventy persons to death and carried out two executions.[17] About the only deterrent value that the death penalty has is deterring the further criminal activity of the person executed; however, the condemned, while awaiting executing, may perversely reason that another murder will have no consequence since there would be absolutely nothing else to lose.

Finally, the death penalty precludes the restoration of the condemned to community. The death penalty constitutes the ultimate denial of the worthiness of persons to live with us in community. It presumes that no

16. Federal Bureau of Investigation, *Uniform Crime Reports* (1980–89).
17. Federal Bureau of Investigation, *Uniform Crime Reports* (1972–1990); NAACP Legal Defense and Educational Fund, *Death Row, USA* (spring 1992).

reconciliation is possible, no restoration feasible, no reunion allowable. By its very nature, the death penalty precludes all future hope for redemption of human life and the restoration of that life to community with other persons. It violates the spirit of Christian hope and undermines a hope that human beings, though flawed, may find redemption.

AFFIRMATIVE ACTION AND THE HOPE FOR ECONOMIC JUSTICE

The second critical area in our assessment of the ethical dynamics of African American participation in American society is in the area of access to full economic activity. This area is a critical and necessary aspect of the civil society inasmuch as economic survival is necessary in modern complex society. For African Americans in this country, even when they were desirous of preparing themselves to compete in either the labor market or the marketplace to sell their goods, artificially imposed barriers to such desires were placed in their way. Either because of historic barriers couched in racism, in many instances enjoying state approval and sanction, or informal barriers owing to the racial prejudice of individuals in the economy, African Americans have suffered. We must now ponder the Christian ethical requirements for a just economic order. Without such an assessment we will be unable to propose just remedies to historic inequities in the American economic structure, especially as that order has repulsed African American attempts to participate fully in it.

A Theory of Work as Self-Actualization

We may reasonably presume that all persons in any society desire full access to the material goods that make life enjoyable and meaningful. All persons desire a sense of economic well-being, that is, the acquisition of material goods such as shelter, food, and clothing and even an intangible good such as the freedom from the fear of want. But how shall such economic well-being be attained? Historically, the principal means has been through human labor. All production of all economic goods throughout human history, whether agricultural crops, precious metals, or natural resources, has depended upon human labor to harvest or process materials for ultimate human consumption and enjoyment—or economic well-being.

Inherent in human labor is a spiritual component. Affirming again our presumption that as humans we are *inspirited beings,* we would be justified in searching for some spiritual entity that is quickened whenever we work. When we are engaged in purposeful work, we cannot help but involve an aspect of our being that is spiritual. I would suggest that the spiritual aspect of our being that is nurtured when we work is our desire for self-actualization, or our desire to forge and shape in some definite fashion the persons we seek to become. Work allows us to let ourselves fully shine forth, to come through. We even speak colloquially of "pouring yourself into your work." When we speak of such a person, we presume that we have observed in such a person a necessary link between a sense of *self* and work, and we infer that such a person must be essentially happy, or have a sense of well-being.

So far our thesis assumes that in exchange for receiving the material goods by which we may enjoy economic well-being, we are actively involved in work, an exertion of efforts on our part that has a spiritual component as well, that is to say, a means for self-actualization. But our thesis must account for situations in which there are "disjuncts" between personal aspirations with regard to work and systemic accommodations to persons with respect to their work. For example, there are situations in which persons clearly desire to work, but owing to inherent inequities in an employment context, they are underemployed since their skills and background would suggest that employment at a more substantial level would be warranted. For discussion purposes, we might call such a situation "system advantaged." At the other extreme are people who do not need to work and who have skills that far exceed a job requirement but who would be willing to work without compensation, the love for the work being just that intense. This latter situation we might call "person advantaged." In either situation—"system advantaged" or "person advantaged"—there is a theoretical disjunct between the desires of the person and the required accommodation from that economic system. In the first, the system is not willing to compensate at a just level, and in the latter, the person places no demands for a just level of compensation.

The force of the thesis we are proposing aims at a level of congruence between persons and economic systems such that personal desires with regard to compensation and systemic accommodations to those personal aims can be ethically adjudicated. Our thesis presumes that persons wish to be compensated at a level commensurate with their skills, interests, and level of preparation. When any economic order constructs artificial barriers to the full congruence between work and self-actualization, a fundamental ethical crisis is the result.

The fact can never be overstated or obscured that the occasion for the first presence of enslaved Africans in the American environment was to produce wealth and economic well-being for others, not for themselves, as any normative economic order would ensure. In the context of the analysis we just offered, slavery constituted the most heinous and demonic form of a system-advantaged economic order. The personal desire of a slave is never an issue or a factor to be considered in a slave regime. American slavery, based as it was on the need for gang labor, was oriented toward routine tasks filled with much repetitive drudgery. The tragedy here is that the transatlantic slave trade caught in its net persons from Africa from all walks of life: tradespeople, weavers, potters, skilled artisans, scholars, priests, and priestesses. Slavery reduced all of them to an artificially depressed level of personal attainment; self-actualization became a theoretical impossibility. But then again, this is not surprising since the ideology of slavery presumed that African captives were in fact not inspirited beings, capable of any self-actualization beyond the level of mere brutes meant only for mean labor. Slavery was thus inherently evil in the sense that it violated all that we have presumed human beings to be in the context of the economic order: inspirited beings who have desires and expectations with respect to self-actualization and who, in return, might expect just compensation.

Economic Exploitation and the Need for Affirmative Action

The economic history of African Americans has been a chronicle of constant struggle against artificial barriers to their self-actualization as full participants in the American economic order. We have already noted the inherent inequity in slavery in this regard. But even should slaves escape from slavery and move into a nominally "free" state, there were no guarantees that the economic order would accommodate them fully as accepted participants in the local economy. Throughout the late eighteenth century and into the nineteenth, many northern states passed legislation that curtailed the economic activity of black persons. They were barred from certain occupations and trades and did not have access to wholesalers if they wished to engage in retail trading. They were by and large consigned to menial jobs such as domestic servants and common laborers.

The presumption of the need for affirmative action rests on this foundation: the historic inequities that have artificially prevented African Americans from enjoying full participation in the economic system have produced effects that are evident even in the modern era. The evidence for such lingering effects from past discrimination was seen in bold relief at the height of the civil rights era in our nation. The federal government mandated affirmative action programs to redress racial inequality and injustice in a series of steps beginning with Executive Order 10925 issued by President John F. Kennedy in 1961; this order prohibited discrimination in federal government hiring on the basis of race, religion, or national origin. The Civil Rights Act of 1964 made discrimination illegal and established equal employment opportunity for all Americans regardless of race, cultural background, color, or religion. Subsequent executive orders, in particular Executive Order 11246 issued by President Johnson in September 1965, mandated affirmative action goals for all federally funded programs out of the White House and out of the Labor Department. The department's Office of Federal Contract

Compliance Programs (OFCCP) promulgated regulations that required all those with government contracts worth more than $10,000 to agree to a set of nondiscrimination provisions that mandated

> The contractor will take affirmative action to ensure that applicants are employed, and that employees are treated during employment, without regard to their race, color, religion, sex or national origin. Such action shall include, but not be limited to the following: employment, upgrading, demotion, or transfer; recruitment or recruitment advertising; layoff or termination; rates of pay or other forms of compensation; and selection for training, including apprenticeship.[18]

To accomplish this goal, the OFCCP required contractors to submit affirmative action plans that analyzed the demographics of their existing work force and indicated proactive measures the employer would take to move toward greater equality. Such measures might be as modest as advertising available positions in minority publications or training hiring managers in discrimination law.

Initially, affirmative action was a policy primarily aimed at correcting institutional discrimination where decisions, policies, and procedures had produced a negative impact on people of color. Affirmative action policies have come to address and redress systematic economic and political discrimination against any group of people that are underrepresented or have a history of being discriminated against in particular institutions. Beneficiaries of these programs have included white men and women, people with disabilities, and poor and working-class people, but their primary emphasis has been on addressing racial discrimination.[19] And to be sure, as long as racism is so pervasive in our society that it puts up artificial barriers that prevent *any* persons from realizing their potential, then such affirmative action measures will be needed and justified.

Proponents of Christian ethics and affirmative action share a common vision for social justice in our American society. These proponents also share a realistic assessment of the ability of human beings to construct social systems that are self-correcting. Were we not flawed and imperfect creatures, there would be no need for any intervention in the social systems we set

---

18. House Committee on Economic and Educational Opportunities, Subcommittee on Employer-Employee Relations, Executive Order 11246 and its implementing regulations, as administered by the Office of Federal Contract Compliance Programs (OFCCP); *Hearing before the Subcommittee on Employer-Employee Relations of the Committee on Economic and Educational Opportunities,* 104th Cong., 1st sess., June 21, 1995, 106.

19. Paul Kivel, "Affirmative Action Works!" *Motion Magazine,* on-line version, October 1, 1999. See also Paul Kivel, *Uprooting Racism: How White People Can Work for Racial Justice* (Philadelphia: New Society Publishers, 1996).

up; were we completely free of racism in our culture, there would be no need for affirmative action. Racism, as Paul Kivel dourly concludes, "rather than being self-correcting, is self-perpetuating."[20] In 1996, more than thirty years after President Kennedy's Executive Order 10925 prohibiting discrimination in federal government hiring, the percentage of black families below the poverty level was more than double that of white families, 28.4 percent as compared to 11.2.[21] Black and Hispanic families generally earn much less than white families. In 1996, the median annual income for white families was $37,161; for black families, it was $23,482; for Hispanic families, it was $24,906.[22] It may be reasonably inferred from this data that workers of color are more likely than white workers to have hourly earnings at or below the minimum wage. Workers of color still are concentrated in the less well-paying, unskilled sector. Thus, the disadvantages to people of color and the benefits to white people are passed on to each succeeding generation unless remedial action is taken. As long as the socially constructed benefit of "whiteness" protects and insulates some Americans from discrimination and rebuffs and exposes others, then affirmative action will be necessary to help us in our efforts to ensure a just society.

We may see the subtle effects of such insulation or exposure to discrimination in the informal networks in which all of us lead our lives. Apart from the civil networks of modern life—participation in the political order as voting citizens or in the economy as workers and consumers—much of our daily lives is spent in the rather mundane contexts of face-to-face encounters with friends and family. And it is precisely within these informal networks that many persons fail to realize the enormous role race plays in their lives, especially persons whose "whiteness" insulates them from the discrimination that persons of color must confront. "Whiteness" to white persons is as water is to fish; they are completely unaware of its vital role in their lives and the support it gives to the ease with which they may go through their daily rounds. Affirmative action is relevant here because

> most job opportunities are heard about through informal networks of friends, family and neighbors. Since the results of racism are segregated communities, schools and workplaces, this pattern leaves people of color out of the loop for many jobs, advancement opportunities, scholarships and training programs. Federal law now requires widespread and public advertisement of such opportunities so that not only people

---

20. Ibid.
21. U.S. Bureau of the Census, *Statistical Abstract of the United States: 1998,* 118th ed. (Washington, D.C., 1998), 480.
22. Ibid., 468.

of color, but white men and women who are outside the circles of information, have an equal opportunity to apply for these positions.[23]

Critics of affirmative action have contended that it has helped only middle-class black people, and not the poor or working class. This argument ignores the access to job training programs, vocational schools, semiskilled and skilled blue- and pink-collar craft jobs, and police and firefighter jobs that have increased because of affirmative action.[24] But as far as the black middle class is concerned, the informal networks by which white people have depended upon for advancement may still not be available.

But the contentious debate that affirmative action has caused has not erupted so much from granting access to black people for jobs and opportunities previously denied them because of discrimination. Rather, what has caused so much ire on the part of white people is the idea that some of their own are being denied jobs and opportunities because such are now being granted to people of color. However, affirmative action never requires the hiring of *unqualified* persons. Within any given potential hiring pool, *all* applicants are qualified for the job. Would a white person lament not having received a job if all of the applicants were white and qualified? Why then should the same person lament not having received the job when now placed among other applicants, some of whom are qualified black persons? One soon suspects that behind the white anger is the belief that *no* black person could be as qualified as whites are. Moreover, why should the lament of white persons be any more dire than the lament of black persons with respect to lost job opportunities?

Affirmative action seeks to bring to bear a societal redressing of historic patterns of discrimination suffered by African Americans and their descendants who seek access to jobs for which they are prepared and access to education that all Americans deserve. It seeks to "level the playing field" in such pursuits since historically the field has been skewed against blacks because of the pervasiveness of American racism. To the extent that documentable racism continues will be the extent to which affirmative action will continue to be needed in our society. Affirmative action is a moral and historical response to the immorality of racial discrimination lodged deeply in the American past. Redressing such wrongs and reversing the effects of such discrimination are necessarily painful to any generation that has the courage to seek such a moral ideal. Such is our predicament now at this point in American history. There is no turning back to a time when dis-

---

23. Ibid.
24. Gertrude Ezorsky, *Racism Justice: The Case for Affirmative Action* (Ithaca, N.Y.: Cornell University Press, 1991), 64.

crimination enjoyed legal sanction, and there is no turning away from the challenge to do the right thing.

Attempting to do the right thing grows out of the imperatives we presume to be operative in a Christian ethic. As we have attempted to discern such imperatives within the context of the African American experience, we have seen how notions of God, Christ, and the Holy Spirit have been absolutely necessary as foundational concepts. The assertion that affirmative action is a viable social instrument to rectify past injustices is grounded in the presumption that God, as ground of our being, must necessarily be consistent with the good. Such good as we are able to discern within our social order would necessarily preclude gratuitous discrimination, the kind clearly visible when race is used to justify discrimination. Christ as the liberating spirit of this God always seeks for ways whereby victims of discrimination might find ultimate wholeness and integrity.

To the extent that this process is accomplished is the extent to which reconciliation might be achieved for the whole society. And yet such reconciliation is not always smooth and free of conflict. To be sure, the full recognition of the need for affirmative action has been rather painful in our society; passionate debate has been generated over whether the present generation is responsible for the past injustices and exactly how, if injustices are admitted, these are to be rectified in some quantifiable way. It may be that ultimately a reliance on the discerning power available in the Holy Spirit will have to guide our thinking as we determine the exact levels of contemporary victimization from past injustices. And it may be that the same Holy Spirit will have to guide our discernment of what quantifiable means are available to rectify such victimization.

We know that scripture attests to the moral imperatives of repayment inherent in past injustice. We have only to hear Zacchaeus, the tax collector. In responding to what appeared to be to some people Jesus' improbable suggestion that they dine together, Zacchaeus said, "If I have defrauded anyone of anything, I will pay back four times as much" (Luke 19:8). Even if we were reluctant to justify affirmative action by pointing out discrete biblical injunctions that seemed to support it, one could make a case, as Abraham Lincoln appeared to do, that God's action in history required some restitution from human beings for injustices inflicted in earlier generation, however painful that restitution might be. We referred to Lincoln as an example of postliberal biblical hermeneutics in chapter 5. As in the time of Lincoln, the call to do justice on the part of the present generation will require much discernment and much guidance as it seeks to rectify the sins of earlier generations, even if that restitution be fraught with much pain.

TOWARD POLITICAL JUSTICE

As with the case for affirmative action, an economically informed ethical construct designed to mitigate past and present injustices, various political constructs have been required within the American political system to mitigate past and present political injustices. This section of the chapter will conclude with a discussion of the political construct known as cumulative voting and its ethical importance.

Slaves never have rights that are enjoyed by their holders unless the latter deign to grant them to the former. Such was the case with the African American experience during the period of slavery. When Thomas Jefferson penned the immortal words of the Declaration of Independence, "We hold these truths to be self-evident, that all men are created equal, that they are endowed by their Creator with certain unalienable Rights, that among these are Life, Liberty and the pursuit of Happiness," the African slaves in America were not in his mind. When the Constitution of the fledgling nation was ratified in 1789, neither the equality of slaves nor their voting privileges were assumed. Slaves remained political persona non grata even in the years just before the Civil War, when during the Dred Scott decision of 1857, the Supreme Court of the United States ruled that blacks, "whether slave or free, are not citizens of the United States by the Constitution."[25]

The "irrepressible conflict" that was the Civil War finally decided that the American nation could not endure, in Lincoln's words at Gettysburg, "half slave and half free." With the conclusion of the war in 1865, slavery came to an end as well. The Thirteenth Amendment, ratified on December 6, 1865—six months after the Civil War ended, permanently abolished slavery. However, the former Confederate states were stubborn in their denial of the political rights of their former chattel. One by one, they instituted "Black Codes" to replace the "Slave Codes" that governed the lives of blacks under the detested slave regime. Only the majority in Congress of Radical Republicans could push through legislation that would ensure the political viability of freed slaves. One of the major pieces of Reconstruction legislation was the Civil Rights Act of 1866. This act stated in part that "All persons within the jurisdiction of the United States shall have the same right in every State and Territory, to make and enforce contracts, to sue, be parties, give evidence, and to the full and equal benefit of all laws and proceedings for the security of persons and property as is enjoyed by white citizens." Later in that year, Congress passed the Fourteenth Amendment to the Constitution and sent it to the states for ratification. Intended to place the full weight of the Constitution behind the Civil Rights Act of 1866, the Fourteenth Amendment

---

25. *Harper's Weekly*, March 14, 1857; see also Charles Morrow Wilson, *The Scott Decision* (Philadelphia: Auerbach Publishers, 1973), 57.

also applied the Bill of Rights to the actions of state and local government. Moreover, it conferred citizenship on all persons born in the United States and required states to provide all persons with "equal protection" of the laws and "due process" of law before taking away life, liberty, or property. It was ratified on July 9, 1868. In 1869, Congress passed the last of the Civil War amendments, the Fifteenth Amendment, which guaranteed voting rights to freed male slaves. It was ratified the following year.

Beyond these measures, the Republican-controlled Congress passed other "affirmative" steps to enforce Reconstruction policies. Massive voter registration drives enrolled large numbers of freed slaves in states throughout the Old South. The Freedmen's Bureau provided emergency assistance to displaced southern blacks; special tribunals settled racial disputes, and a large Union army contingent remained to enforce these reforms. As a result of all these measures, the political landscape of the South was radically changed. In 1867, due to the refusal of many former Confederates to swear loyalty oaths to the United States, thereby relinquishing their political rights, more blacks than whites were registered to vote in the ten states of the Old Confederacy. Blacks and Radical Republicans controlled many state legislatures, and forward-thinking laws such as public education and public improvements were passed.

Yet, from the time of the granting of political rights to freed blacks and Reconstruction policies designed to enforce them, there existed all manner of means used to abrogate these rights and prevent the full exercise of the right to vote among black people. In the 1870s, the Ku Klux Klan joined with Confederate army veterans and so-called "white leagues" to use violence and intimidation against blacks and Radical Republicans. Mob violence and intimidation in the state and local elections of 1874 throughout the South caused black participation in politics to plummet, thus allowing the old-line southern Democrats to fill the vacuum.

By the time Congress passed the last piece of Reconstruction legislation, the Civil Rights Act of 1875, the tide of reform had already turned. In 1876, the Republican Party abandoned the civil rights of blacks, nominating Rutherford B. Hayes for president. In a closely contested national vote against James B. Tilden, the Democratic candidate, the "Compromise of 1877" was struck. In exchange for southern Democrat support in a hotly contested vote in the electoral college, Hayes agreed to end Reconstruction policies. Therefore, soon after he was elected, Hayes withdrew the remaining federal troops from the South. In 1883, the judicial branch added insult to injury already inflicted by the executive branch of government. The Supreme Court struck down the Civil Rights Act of 1875, which barred discrimination by nongovernmental entities. Emboldened, conservative southern legislatures passed a whole new round of segregationist statutes. By the end of Reconstruction, virtually all of the states in the Confederate South had systematically depleted the voting rolls of its black citizens. Using stratagems such as poll taxes, by which the right to vote was accompanied by a tax, or imposing the ludicrous requirement to explain obscure passages of state constitutions or the federal Constitution or outright intimidation, the numbers of blacks able to cast votes were effectively neutralized. Thus the infamous era of "Jim Crow" was born, replete with all of the inequities inherent in racially segregated life, a way of life that would not be challenged forcefully and successfully until the advent of the modern civil rights movement of the middle of the twentieth century.[26]

One of the aims of the civil rights movement was the recovery of the full right of African Americans everywhere in the United States to exercise the right to vote, free from fear and reprisals. In 1964, influenced by Southern Christian Leadership Conference–led mass protest movements, Congress finally passed the Civil Rights Act of 1964, under the prodding of President Lyndon B. Johnson. Moreover, in that same year the Twenty-fourth Amendment to the Constitution was ratified, outlawing the poll tax in federal elections. The violence of Selma, Alabama, including killings, which occurred during the Selma to Montgomery march in March 1965 moved President Johnson to urge passage of the Voting Rights Act of 1965, which in essence mustered enormous enforcement powers inherent in the Fifteenth Amendment to the Constitution. The act gave the U.S. Department of Justice broad authority to take affirmative steps to eliminate exclusionary practices, particularly in the Deep South.

On June 4, 1965, in a speech to the graduating class of Howard University, President Johnson articulated the moral reasoning behind these new "affirmative" measures. Legislation such as the Voting Rights Bill that was about to pass Congress, Johnson said, gave access to freedom—to vote, to hold a job, to go to school:

> But freedom is not enough. You do not wipe away the scars of centuries by saying: Now, you are free to go where you want, do as you desire, and choose the leaders you please. You do not take a man who for years has been hobbled by chains, liberate him, bring him to the starting line of a race, saying, "you are free to compete with all the others," and still justly believe you have been completely fair. Thus it is not enough to open the gates of opportunity. All our citizens must have the ability to walk through those gates. This is the next and more profound stage of

---

26. Helpful accounts of the Reconstruction era include Eric Foner, *Reconstruction: America's Unfinished Revolution, 1863–1877* (New York: Harper & Row, 1988); John Hope Franklin, *Reconstruction after the Civil War* (Chicago: University of Chicago Press, 1961); Kenneth M. Stampp, *The Era of Reconstruction, 1865–1877* (New York: Knopf, 1965).

the battle for civil rights. We seek not just freedom but opportunity—not just legal equity but human ability—not just equality as a right and a theory, but equality as a fact and as a result.[27]

THE PROBLEM OF MINORITY VOTING STRENGTH

As a result of the Voting Rights Act of 1965 and attendant reforms that were put in place to assure its full implementation, the political power of African Americans escalated to unprecedented levels. The Southern Christian Leadership Conference quickly registered eighty-five thousand new voters within four months.[28] Slowly but surely, black candidates for public office nationwide ran for office, and in districts and cities where there were clear black majorities, they were elected. By 1980, there were fully three thousand black mayors of municipalities and cities across the nation. Yet in many parts of the country it was soon becoming painfully clear that owing to residual prejudice and outright racism, black people were not able to mount successful candidates for at-large offices if they were in a distinct minority. Voting districts, municipalities, cities, and congressional districts in which there were clear black majorities did not constitute a problem for the exercise of black political power. It was in districts where blacks were a distinct minority or in which their voting strength could be diluted by whites that constituted a theoretical and practical issue that goes to the heart of the ethical issue that now claims our attention.

The election of President Bill Clinton in 1992 held out great hope for American blacks that the hostile stances that Republican administrations had fostered against affirmative action would come to an end. His first cabinet included four blacks, three women, and two Hispanics. Yet Clinton's less-than-vigorous defense of his nomination of University of Pennsylvania Law School professor Lani Guinier to head the Justice Department's Civil Rights Division and his withdrawal of the nomination, which appeared to be a capitulation to conservative sentiment, convinced many blacks that Clinton's embrace of affirmative action was not genuine.

At the heart of the Guinier controversy were her views on the role of "cumulative voting" to ensure political equity for blacks when they were distinct minorities, particularly in federal congressional districts. But behind this concept is an older one that is not only implicit in Guinier's thought but also inherent in representational democracy itself, that is, the political rights of a minority in a democracy. Such ideas are as old in American political theory as the debates in the Federalist Papers and James Madison's attempt

---

27. Lyndon B. Johnson, speech given at Howard University, Washington, D.C., June 4, 1966.

28. Charles D. Lowery and John F. Marszalek, eds., *Encyclopedia of African-American Civil Rights* (New York: Greenwood Press, 1992), 363.

to ensure a measure of political viability for political minorities. Such ideas were inherent as well in the Nullification Controversy of 1837, which was fomented by John C. Calhoun. Calhoun, a South Carolinian and proponent of slavery, was intent, from his point of view, on not allowing a tyranny of the majority to simply replace a tyranny of a monarch.

It is the height of irony and some hypocrisy that when Guinier's nomination was being considered, two conservative columnists, George Will and Lally Weymouth, both wrote separate columns on the same day in the *Washington Post* (July 15, 1993) praising ideas remarkably similar to hers—but in the context of South Africa, not the United States. Weymouth wrote, "There can't be democracy in South Africa without a measure of formal protection for minorities." George Will wrote, "The Framers also understood that stable, tyrannical majorities can best be prevented by the multiplication of minority interests, so the majority at any moment will be just a transitory coalition of minorities." The crucial difference, of course, in all the comments made by Weymouth, Will, and Guinier is that unlike Weymouth, who was addressing her comments to the South African political situation, and Will, who was addressing his barbs at wealthy landlords in New York City, Guinier's theories had been pointed at the plight of black people who were effectively excluded from full participation in local, county, and municipal governing bodies in America.

At the heart of Guinier's critique of the single-member system is her view "that election procedures should be made more sensitive to the preferences of minority voters—not just racial minorities but minorities of all sorts."[29] She contends that winner-take-all systems give too much power to the prevailing majority, condemning to virtual irrelevance the votes of all others. She does not object to the majority wielding the most power. She objects to the majority wielding a degree of power disproportionate to its share of the electorate, particularly insofar as this accentuates the dominance of racial minorities by the white American majority.

Guinier argues for two reforms:

One involves changing the rules governing the selection of representatives; the second involves changes in the rules governing decision making by representatives. With respect to the first, Guinier recommends the creation of multi-member districts where representatives

29. Lani Guinier, "Keeping the Faith: Black Voters in the Post-Reagan Era," Harvard Law School, *Harvard Civil Rights-Civil Liberties Law Review* no. 2 (spring 1989): 96. Guinier's views on adjudicating the role of race in electoral politics are also in "The Triumph of Tokenism: The Voting Rights Act and the Theory of Black Electoral Success," *Michigan Law Review* (1991); "No Two Seats: The Elusive Quest for Political Equality," *Virginia Law Review* (1991); "The Representation of Minority Interests: The Question of Single-Member Districts," *Cardozo Law Review* (1993).

are chosen by cumulative voting. Under such an arrangement, people can cast multiple votes up to the number of open seats and express the intensity of their preferences by aggregating their votes. A voter could, for instance, cast all of her votes for a single candidate.[30]

Thus if minority voters voted strategically, they would virtually always be assured of electing someone accountable directly to them. The other set of reforms Guinier suggests are "changes in the rules governing decision making by representatives." She proposes "supermajoritarian decision-making rule" that would "give minority groups an effective veto, thus forcing the majority to bargain with them and include them in any 'winning' coalition." Thus the majority could not ignore the minorities in their midst.[31]

What was wrong with Guinier and her ideas? Randall Kennedy, an eminent member of the Harvard Law faculty and whom Guinier subsequently joined as a fellow member of that faculty in the wake of the debacle surrounding her nomination, provided a thoughtful critique and appraisal of her ideas in *The American Prospect* in the fall of 1993.[32] Kennedy notes that foundational to the conflict that inevitably arose between her and those who criticized her nomination, even fellow members of the Democratic party, was a differential assessment of the way race continued to impact the political process. While Guinier asserted that blacks are still a pariah class within American society, thus laying the foundation for race-based remedies to ensure political equity in America, other Democrats, especially those of the center, minimized the negative effects of race in that process. They were much more sanguine about the prospects of conducting politics free from the debilitating effects of race. Thus Guinier saw the continued value of race-based affirmative action programs, whereas even some other Democrats were calling for either a scaling back of such programs or abandonment altogether.

But Lani Guinier's concern was not the race-based electoral instruments that had already been given sanction by the highest court in the land.[33] The issue for her was how we can move beyond the problems inherent in such a system to ensure more racially integrated and more participatory forms

---

30. Guinier, "Keeping the Faith," 115.

31. Ibid., 126–27.

32. Randall Kennedy, "Lani Guinier's Constitution," *The American Prospect* no. 15 (fall 1993): 36–47.

33. Such a tool is the court-approved district formed to ensure minority race representation. The Supreme Court upheld a decision in 1976 of *United Jewish Organizations v. Carey*, in which the Court upheld New York State's action of creating a predominantly black district over the objections of the UJO, which claimed that creating such a district amounted to creating an unconstitutional "racial quota" in electoral results. In 1992, for instance, thirteen of the sixteen blacks elected to Congress (nearly doubling the ranks of the Congressional Black Caucus) represented districts that were created to contain a majority of black voters.

of government. Her concern was ensuring equitable power for minorities, particularly minorities in which there *was not* an artificially created majority. Such circumstances more normally simulated the real world in which African Americans lived, except in those areas where they were congregated together, as say in urban city centers.

The need for cumulative voting as a means to mitigate the problems any minority faces in at-large elections goes to the very heart of the African American experience in America, which has always evidenced a reluctance of the general American populace to embrace fully African Americans within the political system of governance. The issues of race and racial identification have for much of our history been divisive issues that have clouded political judgments of persons and groups as politics have been played out in the American drama.

Even when economic interests coincided, the matter of race has tended to divide persons and make coalitions based ostensibly on shared economic interests a tenuous one indeed. For example, during the Reconstruction period, political judgments based purely on economic interest would have suggested that poor whites and blacks ought to have found a common cause. The injection of race into the political agenda of late-nineteenth-century southern politics, typified by the career of Senator Benjamin "Pitchfork" Tillman, foreclosed any such coalition.[34]

To the extent that contemporary white voters still are reluctant to cast votes for a black candidate, even when shared economic and political interest would suggest the wisdom of doing so, blacks will continue to represent a political minority. And to the extent that this minority status continues for the reasons just outlined, cumulative voting will remain a viable and necessary means to achieve political justice. What we seek within the political order is a measure of justice such that the full inclusion of African American political interests can receive a hearing within the context of the realities of the American political order, an order all too often marred by the presence of racism. Clearly, the liberating and reconciling work of Christ would justify our attempts to build a political order such that no group's minority status should preclude their full representative power within the political order.

Like all other Christians, African Americans must live out their lives within the contexts and claims of the society in which they are constituent parts. Recognizing the intricate web of responsibilities and privileges that constitutes society, African American Christians, as all others, must come to terms with the challenges inherent in participation in society. Claims for jus-

---

34. Stephen Kantrowitz, *Ben Tillman and the Reconstruction of White Supremacy* (Chapel Hill: University of North Carolina Press, 2000).

tice must accompany assumed burdens of responsibility. And yet the claims for justice and the burdens of responsibility that accompany such claims are adjudicated in the context of the political arena. It was in such an arena that ancient Greeks met to determine how justice could be effected in the *polis;* it is where African elders sought to discern the will of the ancestors as they held forth in village common areas; it is where the people of God seek, even now, a greater vision of the truly just society.

Epilogue

When Christians feel compelled to act responsibly in the world in ways consistent with their faith orientation, they are drawn inexorably to the domain of Christian ethics. In order to discern models for their behavior and action, Christians have always grounded these models in what they discerned to be the will of God. The will of God has been embodied most powerfully in the obedient life of Jesus Christ, affirmed as the Son of the living God. Christians have sought to follow Jesus as the model of radical obedience to the will of God, thereby ensuring the ethical integrity of their actions. Recognizing a third person inherent in the notion of the Trinity, Christians have also sought counsel in the person of the Holy Spirit, that aspect of God's being that I believe seems to always penetrate to the minds and wills of believers.

In addition to a theological, christological, and pneumatological grounding of Christian ethics, Christians have discerned the value that may be derived from a guided reading of Holy Scripture. Such reading is always "guided" in the sense that all reading of the Bible takes place within the context of an interpretive framework, or in technical terms, a hermeneutical context. Moreover, such reading is usually superintended by the norms and expectations inherent in an ecclesial tradition, a tradition that forms and shapes the character of the very Christians who go about interpreting the Bible for the purposes of moral action. But at no point in the quest to be moral is the Christian more or less than that unique creature known as a human being, that paradoxical creature marvelously made by a loving and creative God, prone to error yet capable of much good. Since we believe that human beings are created by a loving God, a God that is ground of being and all that exists in being, they possess characteristics such that they are *in* nature but are able to *transcend* nature. As such then, human beings are able to make a distinction between things as they are in nature and things as they *ought* to be in created moral and social orders. There is always a need to know with some level of certainty that which the person must do in order to be moral. Thus we have argued that there are four sources for a Christian ethic: Holy Scripture, ecclesial tradition, human nature, and the knowledge that humans can acquire relative to truth claims about moral actions.

Clearly no Christian appropriates the foundations for an ethic in a cultural or social vacuum. Nor, for that matter, does the Christian discern moral imperatives apart from the benefits—and the burdens—of historical consciousness. Throughout this book we have seen how an African American Christian ethic has emerged out of the African American experience in America. That experience has been on one level a lamentable narrative of many African peoples caught up in the nefarious slave trade that was a result of European expansionism beginning in the fifteenth century. Those enslaved Africans, displaced persons from rich heritages in ancient homelands, eventually became African Americans.

These African peoples also brought with them to the New World a religious consciousness that became transfigured into an Afro-Christianity, a faith that for the enslaved became a bulwark against the psychological terror that slavery imposed. Thus on another level the African American experience has also been a narrative of triumph over slavery, of liberation from bondage. In their attempt to forge a moral order within the context of their enslavement, they could not help but posit their liberation as God's will for their lives and for their progeny. Thus the role of Jesus Christ was understood as Liberator, and the role of the Holy Spirit was envisioned as that aspect of God that sought to connect with the will of the believer so that full liberation might be lived out in the real world. Since all but literate slaves were deprived of full access to the written words of Christian faith as recorded in Holy Scripture, African American slaves were ironically free to discern within those texts what for them was the true Word of God. That Word dictated that they should be free, as distinct from specific words of texts that their holders held up as justification for their continued bondage. African American slaves and their descendants have lived out their faith in various ecclesial traditions. Whether an established sect, a conversionist sect, a thaumaturgical sect, or a messianic-nationalist sect—all traditions provide valuable havens for many, their limitations notwithstanding. Yet even within these traditions, one may see harbingers of various aspects of the liberated life, lived out in the complexity of modern society.

The last three chapters of this book sought to discern how an African American Christian ethic might have pragmatic consequences in the actual social context in which African Americans lead their lives. Three contexts were identified. The first context was that of human sexuality, the second that of medical ethics, and finally a third area covered the various issues encountered in the quest for economic, judicial, and political justice. In each we have discerned unique challenges that must be addressed if a credible Christian ethic among African Americans is to be forged.

TOWARD A NEW PIETY AND AN ENLIVENED PRAXIS

As one now reflects on all that has been attempted in this book, several questions and implications come to mind. The first question has to do with the issue of discerning the contours of a life in which Christian thought and living come together to form a harmonious whole. This essentially is the concept conveyed by the term "piety," although that term seems hopelessly old-fashioned and even archaic. Piety is a way of living in the world with the sure and certain knowledge that God is present. Viewed in this way, piety can never ever be out of date, passé or old-fashioned; it is perennial even as God's presence is ever constant. Now the issue for African Americans is fashioning a notion of piety that takes seriously the interface between thought and meditation, reflection and spiritual repose, critical dialogue and the mutual assurance of brothers and sisters who commune in the faith. All too often thoughtful reflection and faithful living have been viewed in an unfortunate opposition, as if one precluded the other. A way must be found to meld the hard work of thinking through issues of faith and feeling the vibrancy and intensity of faith. Our notion that we are *inspirited beings* would seem to suggest that no such dichotomy between reflection and spiritual, between thinking and faithful living, is justified.

The full working out of a new sense of piety can take place on two levels: on the institutional and the personal. At the institutional level a fruitful interface can be established between speculative theological and ethical reflection within the context of the real-life concerns of the African American worshiping communities. Adventurous—but disciplined—theological thinking can flourish within such communities, and the churches that are flourishing with an energized vision of God can enrich theological thinking. Both need each other, and both can benefit from each other. What would happen if churches found ways to accommodate theological exploration for believers whose hunger for theological reflection is not satisfied by the thin gruel that passes for all too many Sunday School classes? What would happen if churches found a way to systematically allow for sabbatical leaves for their pastors? When the pastor returned, she would be so refreshed that the energies of the congregation would be even more enhanced and ready for releasing. After such a sabbatical, he would be even more disposed to craft his sense of leadership as one who is ready to serve.

The second level is at the purely personal, within the prayer and meditation life of every believer. This challenge was brought home to me in a class session while this book was being written. One day I was droning on and on about Paul Tillich's notion of God as ground of being and my insistence that we distort the nature of God when we ask God for "things 'n stuff." Finally, one student had had enough. He asked me plaintively, "But Doc, how does a Tillichean *pray?*" Attempting to compose myself as I congratulated him on the piquancy of his question with "That's a very good question" (one of my favorite stalling tactics), I issued forth a response. I attempted to answer this brilliant question by suggesting that prayer ought rightly be considered, not so much a means to an end, but an end in itself, that end being a meditation on a condition of life. In the pious life, one is always in prayer because one is always musing upon the meaning of what it means *to be* within this marvelous condition of being itself. God, as ground and giver of all that is, is praised and acknowledged as such. Thus praying is oriented, not toward asking for "things 'n stuff," but toward preparing ourselves for the self-actualizing that will eventually occur once we are in conformity with God's will. Seen in this light, Jesus' words of assurance to his disciples, themselves given to fits of anxiety about what will happen in this life, begin to make so much sense for the Christian. In their concerns about what they would drink or wear, about "things 'n stuff," Jesus' words were direct and clear: "But strive first for the kingdom of God and his righteousness, and all these things will be given to you as well" (Matt. 6:33).

A new piety that bridges the gap between thinking and faithful existence will lead inexorably to an enlivened praxis, the interplay between critical reflection and informed action. We have a model of this nexus in the life and work of Martin Luther King Jr. King *had* to act because of the ineluctable logic of the moral arguments he marshaled as he confronted the immoral and institutionalized racism of the United States during his lifetime. And the moral arguments that came from his reflection were true *because* they emerged from the tears and suffering of black people who declared that they would no longer suffer in silence. True praxis is always reflective; action calls for reflection, and reflection should eventuate in informed action. Every challenge that confronts the African American communities—attaining true political power, economic integrity, justice in the judicial system—all can be confronted from the vantage point of the type of praxis envisioned here. Since all three of these issues point to moral issues and moral flaws inherent in the American social order, it is incumbent upon African American worshiping communities to engage in sustained praxis in order to mitigate these problems.

TOWARD A NOTION OF PARTNERSHIP OF PRINCIPALS

Another implication of this book has to do with the development of a creative dialogue among African American theologians, ethicists, and principal agents from other significant spheres of African American life. I speak of leaders and ordinary practitioners in the fields of commerce, medicine, law and government, entertainment, education—all areas where the problems and promise of African American life can be seen. In the chapter on ecclesial traditions, I called for the autonomy of economic and political spheres of black life. We noted the critical role that the church played in the early transition from bondage to freedom and the indisputable role the church played in the civil rights struggle in the middle of the twentieth century. Yet, as W. E. B. Du Bois prophesied, the maturation of other leaders has come to pass in black America. The eclipse of the monopolistic power of the preachers is, not an occasion for exulting, but a cause for rejoicing that the leadership circle in black America has been widened and that its hope for constant replenishment all the more ensured. Since that maturation has come about, it makes perfectly good sense to effect critical dialogues among clerics, theologians, ethicists, and the other principal agents in these areas of African American life.

TOWARD A NEW INTERRACIAL POSTURE

Finally, we may rejoice that the critical reflection on African American theological and ethical consciousness has reached a level of maturity and self-assurance that we may move beyond the implicit reactionary mode that was inherent in the first stirrings of this movement. While we must always acknowledge the corrosive effects of racism, racism need not, even inadvertently, determine the tone and substance of our theological methodologies. I believe I have shown that while all theological pronouncements must come forth from the context of one's culture, all theological systems are doomed if they presume that the cultural imperatives of that particular culture must be presumed as normative for all human cultures. While a particular culture may give us insights into the mystery of the entire human condition, that culture is *exemplary* in the sense that it provides compelling examples, rather than exemplary in the sense of aspiring to normative exclusivity. This has been precisely the methodology of this book. At every turn I have sought to correlate a general discussion of theological issues with African American historical expressions of those issues. In the chapters on God, Christ, and the Holy Spirit, as well as the chapters on the four sources for a Christian ethic, this was the aim of my attempt. This was done, not because African American culture and history should be normative for all people, but rather because African American culture and history could be exemplary, in the sense that I am using that term. Moreover, if a people who has suffered as much and overcome as much as African Americans can still affirm Christian faith with the exuberance that they embody, then the power and vibrancy of Christian faith are affirmed all the more.

Now, having said all the above, the following concluding observations may be made. First, black theological reflection does not need the aid of white guilt to give credence to the claims of the former. Black theological reflection is too important an enterprise to be dependent, even inadvertently, on the dubious merit of guilt. If black theological and ethical reflection can proceed along a path that is guided by the inexorable tug of logic and is grounded in the organic soil of the black condition, it will continue to enjoy viability. No truly authentic interracial dialogue along theological and ethical lines can proceed as long as one group seeks to exploit another's perceived weaknesses. Both will inevitably be forced into a mutually reactive mode. This can lead to no good but will only perpetuate inauthentic dialogue and frustrate genuine communication. Moreover, no true ecumenism, whether intraracially or interracially, can proceed as long as there is inauthentic dialogue and communication.

Second, the enterprise of black theological and ethical reflection is too important and vast to be limited to a sole orthodoxy that would pretend to normative status among African American thinkers. A truly mature black theological and ethical reflective enterprise will encourage a plethora of viewpoints and perspectives; it will be truly liberal in the literal sense that it will encourage the full liberation of the human mind and spirit. For those who themselves, as well as whose ancestors, have known the bitter sting of oppression, yet who were given the vision of human liberation, couched in a God who was the Rock of their salvation, this is as it should be.

Index

Book Notes

In the Path of Virtue:
The African American Moral Tradition
Samuel K. Roberts

The cardinal virtues (prudence, justice, fortitude, and temperance) have long been a part of Western moral thought. In this engaging historical survey of the African American concept of virtue in the eighteenth and nineteenth centuries, Samuel K. Roberts explores how virtue became "a vision of a divinely ordered life that impelled its adherents to struggle against the injustice of slavery and to forge communities and structures that could ensure the development of the furthest mental and material possibilities of African Americans."

0-8298-1327-6, 176 pages, cloth $22.95

Ten Principles of Black Self-Esteem:
Letters of Heritage, Lessons of Hope
E. Hammond Oglesby

Writing with passion born of personal experience, E. Hammond Oglesby offers a means to build self-esteem among black people, both children and adults. The author offers six letters of heritage that provide examples of positive direct expression from father to son, father to daughter, brotha to brotha, brotha to sister, brotha to God—with an open letter to the "man on the mall." Between the letters, he illustrates his ten principles with stories and reflections for building self-esteem.

0-8298-1321-7, 208 pages, paper, $14.95

A Loving Home:
Caring for African American Marriage and Families
Lee Butler Jr.

What is it that creates and maintains a mutually fulfilling marriage? How is the relationship built and strengthened? Through stories and examples from personal experience and counseling couples, Lee Butler helps black men and women uncover their feelings, identify obstacles to honest relating, and build stronger relationships.

0-8298-1395-0, 128 pages, paper, $13.95

God Struck Me Dead: Voices of Ex-Slaves
Clifton H. Johnson, ed.

An invaluable collection of vivid conversation narratives and autobiographies by unlettered but powerfully articulate ex-slaves, *God Struck Me Dead* is a window into the soul of America and a source of inspiration from those whose faith was tested by the cruelest of human degradation.

0-8298-0945-7, 208 pages, paper, $15.95

To order call 800-537-3394. Fax 216-736-2206
or visit our Web site at www.pilgrimpress.com

Prices do not include shipping and handling.
Prices subject to change without notice.